Creating Capitalism

for
Jef and Tusie

Creating Capitalism

Transitions and Growth in Post-Soviet Europe

Patricia Dillon

Scripps College, Claremont, California, USA

Frank C. Wykoff

Pomona College, Claremont, California, USA

Edward Elgar

Cheltenham, UK • Northampton, MA, USA

Published by
Edward Elgar Publishing Limited
Glensanda House
Montpellier Parade
Cheltenham
Glos GL50 1UA
UK

Edward Elgar Publishing, Inc.
136 West Street
Suite 202
Northampton
Massachusetts 01060
USA

A catalogue record for this book is available from the British Library

Library of Congress Cataloguing in Publication Data

Dillon, Patricia, 1937–
Creating capitalism : transitions and growth in post Soviet Europe / Patricia Dillon, Frank C. Wykoff.
p. cm.–
Includes bibliographical references and index.
1. Europe, Eastern–Economic conditions–1989. 2. Former Soviet republics–Economic conditions. 3. Capitalism–Europe, Eastern. 4. Capitalism–Former Soviet republics. I. Wykoff, Frank C., 1942–, 1965– II. Title.

HC244.D5 2002
338.947–dc21 2002021256

ISBN 1 84064 733 7

Typeset by Manton Typesetters, Louth, Lincolnshire, UK.
Printed and bound in Great Britain by MPG Books Ltd, Bodmin, Cornwall.

Europe at the beginning of the twenty-first century

Source: U.S. Central Intelligence Agency (2001), *Europe*, Washington Government Printing Office.

Contents

List of figures

List of tables

Preface

The economic and political progress of newly independent Central and Eastern European states has been a popular subject for research since the early 1990s, generating a steady flow of articles and new magazines, journals and books. Why should you, the reader, be interested in another book on transition from planning to markets?

We think that some key issues are underrepresented in the literature and have been virtually inaccessible to the general interest reader. Ultimately it is economic growth that indicates whether transitions are working. Yet little has been done to apply growth analysis, a powerful implement in the economist's toolbox, to evaluate economic performance. Furthermore, we have ten years of evidence telling us that efforts to transplant Western economic reform measures without careful political analysis does not work well. Political and social structures in post-Soviet states have not adapted easily to economic reform programs. Some countries continue to vacillate between liberalization toward markets and reversion to various forms of socialism.

This book integrates growth theory with a public choice approach to explain why each potential reform is necessary and why reforms nevertheless encounter so much resistance. Our framework can assist those interested in the transformation of poor economies anywhere. Many nations, not only former Eastern bloc countries, want to enjoy the fruits of both decentralized market systems and democratic political systems.

ORGANIZATION OF THE BOOK

This book has three parts: the first six chapters make up the theoretical foundations; the next seven chapters are case studies of individual countries (Bulgaria, Czech Republic, Estonia, Hungary, Russia and Slovakia) and a concluding chapter; the book ends with two technical appendices.

Part I: Technical Foundations

The conceptual analysis may be read on one of three levels. For those with only a passing interest in the material in any of the first six chapters, there is a brief overview on the first page of each chapter. One can move on from these without loss of continuity.

Chapters 1 to 3 are readable by everyone and they contain no esoteric economics language that is not defined and explained. Chapters 4 and 5 will be more challenging for many readers, as they contain heuristic descriptions of how we integrate reforms into an economic growth model. We have tried to write this material for a general audience, for readers without formal training in economics. For those who want to study our growth theory analysis in greater detail, we provide Appendix A. It requires some formal economics training. Chapter 6 integrates economics into a political model. One can read only the brief chapter overview, the chapter itself, or Appendix B, depending on the desired level of study.

Part II: Country Chapters

Chapters 7 to 12 each deal with one of our sample countries. The earlier theory chapters inform our analysis of each country, which reflects forces common to all of them. The format of each chapter is roughly the same: it includes a compact history of two periods that set the stage for prospects of success in transition – the period before the Soviets and the period under their rule. The sections that follow include analysis of the political transition, progress in adopting reforms, economic performance and political developments, and recommendations and prognosis for success.

Part III: Appendices

Appendix A consists of detailed analysis of growth modeling, including evaluation of exogenous and endogenous models. While the models are standard in the growth field, we link each reform to specific parameters of a growth model. Based on these linkages, we assume that economic agents are able to assess the implication for their own self-interest of any reform. This sets the stage for the econometric work in Appendix B.

Appendix B contains a formal model, developed in Chapter 6, wherein economics and politics interact. Pooled data covering ten years in the six countries are used in an econometric analysis that tests the connections between reforms, economic performance and elections. The results tell us something about the pace and patterns of reform.

ACKNOWLEDGMENTS

We wish to acknowledge the financial support of the William and Flora Hewlett Foundation that allowed us to undertake this project. Patricia thanks Gabrielle Jungels-Winkler for research support that enabled us to finish the book. The work would still not be done were it not for Mrs Nancy Burson. A cheering section is always useful, so thanks to Janie, Kerry and Mo.

Patricia Dillon
Frank C. Wykoff
Claremont, California
June 2002

PART I

Theoretical Foundations

Introduction to Part I

Liberalization toward market economies could not get under way in communist countries until they were free of Soviet domination. Chapter 1 begins with an economic explanation for the self-destruction of the USSR based on the inability of a centrally planned system to adapt to the political, social and economic implications of the industrial revolution.

Chapters 2 to 6 continue to build the theoretical underpinnings of this book. Our central argument connects economic reforms to potential growth and then forges links between prospective reforms and a democratic election process. The theoretical models developed in these chapters provide the conceptual framework for six country case studies in Part II.

Chapter 2, applying economic reasoning, explains why certain policymakers and certain groups of individuals will resist reforms even though those same reforms will improve standards of living for the vast majority of people.

Chapter 3 introduces five specific economic reforms that characterize virtually all successful market economies in the world. Each of these reforms is shown to play an essential role in a well-designed decentralized market system.

Chapter 4 introduces and develops growth models that allow us to demonstrate in Chapter 5 exactly how each reform raises national income. A technical version of these models is available in Appendix A.

Chapter 5 integrates the five reforms into the growth models and shows how each reform contributes to greater well-being through growth in output per worker.

Chapter 6 introduces a new model that exploits growth models to connect economic reforms, through their effects on voters' growth prospects, to the political process.

The country studies in Part II of the book provide evidence that supports the predictions of this dynamic election model: economics affects politics and politics affects economics.

1. The withering away of communism[1]

Why did the USSR self-destruct? We offer an economic analysis that implies that the collapse was inevitable. The collapse of the Soviet system is treated here as an aftershock of the economic quake of the industrial revolution. The USSR failed because it was unable to deal with the social, economic and political consequences of that revolution. Its disintegration demonstrated the failure of central planning to meet the needs of a modern state. It signaled the terminal weakness of a highly centralized economic system that despite extreme efforts could not resist the pressures of modern industrial society. Standard economic models based on incremental analysis can explain the process that built up to the collapse. But standard neoclassical analysis does not address serious discontinuities that result in radical sociopolitical changes. We differentiate between incremental economic analysis and analysis of major historical discontinuities which we call economic quakes.

Adam Smith appreciated the social benefits of capitalism; Karl Marx did not. Marx was unable to foresee the staying power of capitalism and the ability of democracy to ameliorate its worst weaknesses. Lenin was a reactionary who perverted Marx by installing communism in feudal Russia. He and his followers removed everything that made capitalism work and built a system that would inevitably fail to adapt to the inherent demand for flexibility of modern industrial and commercial society. Instead of capitalism withering away, communism inevitably collapsed.

THE END OF AN IDEA

The Soviet Union, once powerful and feared, by 1989 had decayed socially, politically and economically. It was on the brink of collapse. While its military still could boast of massive strategic intercontinental missiles and numerous divisions encamped along western Soviet borders, many of its people were impoverished and disenchanted, and its political leadership had become corrupt and demoralized.[2]

At the beginning of the last decade of the twentieth century, the USSR imploded. Its Central European satellite states were spinning off and some Soviet republics were splitting into factions reflecting old ethnic and religious divisions. All that remained of empire was a disorganized federation of states led by a divided Russia. The collapse of the Soviet empire signaled the failure of an ideology, of a philosophy of social and economic organization revealed to have been as ineffectual as its severest critics had argued. From the point of view of social science, this cataclysmic event provides an extraordinarily rare natural experiment. In analyzing the economics of this event and its aftermath, our principal interest is with growth, that is, improvement in material living standards over time. What does this event have to teach us about growth and how new regimes will develop from the rubble of the collapse?

The Soviet Union was widely perceived to be one of two major models of social and economic organization, competing with the US for dominance in the Third World. The USSR and its satellites represented central planning, egalitarian distribution and socialism. Karl Marx created the underlying economic philosophy: "From each according to his ability, and to each according to his need." The US, Western Europe and Japan offered democracy and capitalism, emphasizing decentralized decision-making and individual rights and responsibilities. The underlying economic philosophy was Adam Smith's idea that "each man may reap the fruits of his labor."

Before 1991, Third World countries were the social battlegrounds for these two competing visions of socioeconomic organization. Each side developed prototypes on the frontiers of their worlds – Eastern Germany versus Western Germany, North Korea versus South Korea, North Vietnam versus South Vietnam, China versus Taiwan. Cold war flared into hot war from time to time. Although such conflicts have continued, the historical ideological conflict has not. Only a few fragments of the old empire – Cuba and North Korea – hang on. Even China's communist leadership, while clinging to power, has effectively repudiated communism as a viable form of economic organization. Are there lessons to be learned from this change? Or is this "the end of history"?[3] There is, in fact, much to be learned, both by students of social development and by practical men and women in positions of power.

How one thinks about events of such historic importance depends upon one's paradigm – one's outlook, or pattern of thinking. Ours is economic. Normally economics, with its mathematical rhetoric and parsimonious style, interests primarily other economists. We intend this book to appeal to a broader audience, because we are convinced that the implications of the end of the Soviet empire are profound, and that economic insight can enrich the understanding of human progress for any interested reader. We as economists are interested in analyzing events so that their lessons can be applied when and where appropriate and useful.

ECONOMIC ANALYSIS OF INSTITUTIONAL CHANGE

We begin by laying out a framework for understanding how economists think about events like the collapse of one regime and the transition to another. Economists organize their thoughts by building models that simplify the world by abstracting, or removing nonessential elements of a situation. Studying manageable models focuses attention on the key forces that generate change. By analogy, suppose we were to ask a scientist how an internal combustion engine powers an automobile. The scientist might sketch a model of an engine, showing its key features. This model would be far simpler than any real operational engine, but it would be general enough to explain every such engine. This abstraction from reality expresses the nature of scientific and economic modeling; it is an art that removes clutter without removing key explanatory factors.

We intend to explain two very different types of events – collapse of the old and transition to the new. We believe that one modeling approach alone cannot serve us adequately. Most important to us is the question of how political and economic decision-makers proceed after the failure of central planning. How will new leaders build and sustain successful market economies and what can they do to raise the probability of success? Before considering this issue, we want to explain why the old regime collapsed. We are convinced that there are, in this unique event, important lessons for developing economies elsewhere. Furthermore, we believe that the historical nature of communism is quite different from what its founders, advocates and practitioners imagined. We begin our analysis by partitioning economic events into two major types, helpful in understanding the growth process. One is a rare event, a massive shift in economic regime brought by a comparatively sudden shock to the entire society that unravels the existing social order and requires a complete redefinition of values, institutions and social relations. We call such a shock an economic quake. The other more common occurrence reflects incremental change within the confines of an established order. Because social stability is typical, economists begin their analysis by taking institutional, social and political environments as given. Economists commonly study incremental events, both because most events are incremental and because they are consequently amenable to marginal analysis, a tool commonly used by every mainstream modern economist.[4]

Economic Quakes

Economic quakes involve profound changes that alter the entire sociopolitical structure, uprooting the hierarchy, unhinging traditions and social norms, and tearing apart the fabric of society. Such radical occurrences are rare but quite important. Economic quakes are events like humankind learning to control fire; turning from nomadic hunting and gathering to agrarian life with the introduction of agriculture; and, more recently, the process of industrialization and urbanization. (Some people think we are on the brink of yet another major shock from industrialization to the "information age," but it is too early to tell.)[5]

Perhaps experiments with controlling fire took place over time, perhaps pockets of farming arose in small scattered regions, perhaps a few producers relied very early on the division of labor; but no one could have expected the entire social transformation brought on by each of these shocks. Both in terms of causes and consequences these were not incremental events, but instead massive shocks that altered the environment of humankind. However, each shock was probably preceded by and surely spawned numerous incremental changes – new political regimes, new social relationships, new norms of behavior, new values and new technologies.

Each event, by its nature, was probably resisted by major segments of the social, political and economic power structure of the day. It seems unlikely that the relative losers in each case gave up without a fight, generating long periods, perhaps centuries, of conflict. And of course it undoubtedly took some time to devise a new social system better equipped to deal with the new reality brought about by the shock. Nonetheless, the outcome was inevitable – domination by the system best able to accommodate to new realities created by the shock. The domination of society by monarchs, the priesthood and noblemen is a thing of the past, the landed aristocracy has lost its social and economic significance and craftsmen of all sorts have become scarce in wealthy modern countries. Economic quakes have erased power structures that must have seemed immutable in their day.

Consider, for instance, the advent of agriculture. Humankind abandoned nomadic ways that depended upon tracking and subduing prey and upon detecting and then exploiting natural cycles of plant life. Agriculture enabled peoples to form settlements, establish property rights, store supplies, accumulate wealth and enjoy greater leisure time. But it also created losers – the craftiest and strongest hunters and the most knowledgeable and able gatherers. Much expertise, passed down through generations, had gone into hunting and gathering, since both were complex and subtle arts.[6] Vernon Smith (1992) suggests that Genesis 2 to Genesis 3, wherein Adam and Eve are evicted from the Garden of Eden, can be seen as an analysis of the agricultural revolution from the perspective of a leading hunter-gatherer whose position had been eroded by the productive power of farming. Whereas Genesis 1 paints a glorious picture of the beginning (of the pastoral life), the next tale bemoans the loss of innocence and the ability to survive by gathering fruits. In this tale, God punishes Adam and Eve by requiring them and all their offspring to work the soil in order to live: 'cursed is the ground for thy sake; in sorrow shalt thou eat *of* it all the days of thy life' (Genesis 3: 17).

The industrial revolution, another quake, has been traumatic for agrarian life styles. Its effects are still being felt, hundreds of years after its accession in the eighteenth century. In the US at the beginning of the twentieth century farmers made up about 40 percent of the workforce. By the century's end they comprised less than 3 per cent, and continued winnowing of labor on farms is to be expected. Farmers have fought their decline as fiercely as did the hunters, but the outcome is inevitable. The social, political and economic power of the agricultural sector will continue to diminish in importance relative to industrial power. Are we now at the brink of another shock? It seems clear that as modern societies move from the industrial to the information age, the proportion of the labor force employed in the service sector will continue to grow relative to that in industry. Wealthy societies now employ more of their workers in service industries than in manufacturing. Agricultural employment continues to shrink nearly everywhere in the developed world.

The collapse of the Soviet Union, while not an economic quake of the magnitude of the agricultural or industrial revolution, was certainly a major tremor. Like an earthquake, the collapse was surprising, abrupt and, for those near its epicenter, profound. Can economists explain it? Or more accurately, can we explain it *ex post*? We make no claim to any special prescience on this issue. Few of us in the West anticipated the sudden and relatively peaceful implosion of an empire that had been a superpower in the post-Second World War period. Most economists thought the Soviet system was inefficient, but most also thought it was viable, that is, it appeared to be delivering the goods.

Sudden events of this sort are not typically subjects for economic analysis. Most economists believe in the concept of path dependence – that human institutions and societies tend to continue in the direction they are going, and abrupt changes are rare. Economic models, including growth models, take the sociopolitical and institutional environment as given, and concentrate instead on incremental changes to variables within that fixed framework. Major changes – what we call economic quakes – are serious historical discontinuities that are not accounted for in marginal economic analysis. Standard analytical economic models cannot characterize, predict or explain these changes.

This is not to say that economists have had nothing to say about sociopolitical and institutional change. Douglass North's Nobel Prize reflects the importance of economic history as a tool for evaluating institutional change, which restructures incentives and therefore economic behavior. Yeager (1999) provides an accessible introduction to North's argument that appropriate institutions, both informal and formal, are essential for sustainable economic growth. Mancur Olson's work on institutional change has also been seminal in this area. Friedrich Hayek foretold inherent weakness in social planning regimes well before the collapse.[7]

There has been, nevertheless, a kind of intellectual disconnect between those who employ contemporary quantitative economic methods and those who employ political and historical economic reasoning to understand institutional change. We employ both approaches in this book to provide a unified analysis of the collapse and transition. We intend to characterize the collapse of the Soviet Union as a major discontinuity, an economic quake, in order to explain its inevitability. Economic analysis of these cataclysmic changes is in its scholarly infancy, far from mature but nevertheless growing. In our view the Soviet system had to end because it could not meet the demands of a changing world. While the implosion from 1989 to 1991 was abrupt, disintegration had begun long before 1989 when the Berlin Wall fell, or 1991 when the USSR was declared to be no more.

Incremental Changes

Most of humankind's experiences involve much less radical changes than economic quakes. Some ancient societies like Egypt went for thousands of years without noticeable differences in the way of life for most people; artifacts found from periods millennia apart are very similar. In comparison, change in the twentieth-century US occurred at blinding speed. Nevertheless, even these rapid changes took place within the context of a stable social system with a constitution, a democratic form of government, a legal system including protection of property rights and private ownership of productive capital. Within this structure, economic growth is typically the result of many relatively small ongoing changes: growth in inputs, changes in the mix of public and private spending, modest changes in technology.

Such changes can be explained by applying marginal analysis, "the economic way of thinking," so called because economic theory assumes that people make decisions by weighing additional benefits against additional costs. Will a manufacturer choose to buy an incremental piece of equipment? Is a college education worth the extra expenditure? Is the student willing to take on an additional class? Economists apply models that emphasize the gains and losses of some change starting from a given position. The voter rejects a ballot measure to enlarge the local high school not because she is against education, but because as a taxpayer she is unwilling to pay the additional costs required in order to get the community benefits of the extra space for the school. Economists look at human behavior as typically involving incremental decisions, that is, decisions at the margin. This analytical approach usually assumes an unchanging institutional environment: an economic system, a political system, social customs and legal systems.

Within marginal economic analysis there are many different approaches and models, because the problems being studied differ greatly and because sometimes economists disagree about the appropriate model to apply to a given situation. Our examination of the post-USSR collapse focuses on the dynamic evolution of market economies, and for this purpose we consider two distinct (incremental) analytic approaches, one cyclical and one secular.

To examine the growth path of a Western economy over the last 150 years, one would construct some measure of aggregate performance like Gross Domestic Product (GDP); produce a time series by recording it, say annually, over the period; and use statistical techniques to analyze its movements. One could extend this model to other aggregates as well. When this is done, it becomes obvious that the paths of these aggregate variables are not smooth trajectories. They are sporadic and uneven. Research of these paths, called business cycles, indicates that they fluctuate persistently around a long-range path. Business cycles are characterized by periods of expansion reaching a peak and periods of contraction reaching a trough. The length and depth of these cycles vary considerably, but they do contain enough inertia to be systematic rather than purely random (though they may be chaotic).[8] By averaging out these fluctuations, one can observe the long-range (secular) path that tells us how the economy is growing over time. Are people becoming better off? If their lot is improving, then how rapidly? Or is the economy spiraling downward, with falling living standards?

Economic Models

When economists study macroeconomic processes within the confines of given political, legal and social institutions, they use one of two approaches. These approaches are based on the two features identified above; that is, observations over time can be decomposed into two parts, a long-range secular path and shorter-term cyclical fluctuations around the path. Economists have developed certain models for analyzing the cyclical fluctuations and different models for studying the long-range paths.

Economists who deal with fluctuations around the long-range paths, or business cycles, usually (but not always) focus on shocks to demand. A good deal of the emphasis is on government policies that may ameliorate or (inadvertently) exacerbate the cycles. The two important types of government policies typically studied are fiscal and monetary. Some of the schools of modern economic thought that deal with these issues are Keynesian, monetarist, supply-side and new classical macroeconomics, such as rational expectations approaches.

Models designed to analyze long-range paths, called growth models, are applied to the long-range trend without focusing on the short-term cycles. These models still view the non-economic world as essentially given, in the sense that they are not designed to deal with economic quakes; they are incremental in scope, taking the basic political, social and even economic institutional environment as fixed. We shall use this type of modeling to study the nature of Soviet industrialization and post-collapse transition efforts.

The Analysis of Transition

Economists have been busy for a decade analyzing the fiscal and monetary aspects of transition economies. A substantial literature exists on budget policies and on monetary and financial issues. Economists have also studied specific industry reforms, especially in finance and banking privatization. A considerable literature on sequencing, the order and pace of economic reforms introduced in the liberalization process, appeared in the early years of post-Soviet independence. Vigorous research efforts have been applied to the new forms of trade and financial relations between former communist regimes and between those regimes and the West. Proposals abound for government deficit control, monetary reform, monetary policy conduct, trade liberalization and exchange rate reform. Economists have suggested development of financial and equity markets, encouraged price flexibility and tax system restructuring. To some extent advisors have suggested creation of explicit social contracts including protection of property rights and respect for the law. Much Western advice has been implemented in Central European economies and in the Baltic States, less in the Southern European transition economies and very little in the rest of the former Soviet Union.

Growth Analysis

Within traditional modern growth analysis, there are several major bodies of literature on aspects of growth. These studies fall into two primary categories; one comprises long-range theoretical growth models building on the work of Robert Solow and others in the 1950s. Solow-type models, often referred to as neoclassical growth models, emphasize production and saving. Neoclassical models employ dynamic optimization techniques that are also used in rocket science.[9] Attempts are made to determine the nature of long-range sustainable conditions, called steady states. Steady states are defined as dynamic paths of variables represented in differential equations that satisfy certain conditions such that income, capital, output and the labor force are growing at compatible and sustainable rates. The role of government in these models is generally restricted to budget policy effects on savings and capital formation rates. The three key drivers of growth, all generated primarily by private markets, are labor force growth (measured in quantity and quality), physical capital formation and technological change. Technological change enters into the analysis in a variety of ways but is exogenous in the model. Though in practice the public sector plays an important role through provision of physical infrastructure (for example, roads), education and support for research and development, it is essentially secondary to the private sector as the principal engine of growth.[10]

Empirical applications of this model have led to the conclusion that technological change played a major role, explaining perhaps more than half of growth in the West over the last 50 to 100 years. Growth of human and of physical capital inputs is crucial but inadequate to explain the rate of growth without an additional kick from some unknown factor, called technological change. In terms of this literature, the ratio of output to factor inputs has grown so fast as to suggest that some technological force has been driving production up faster than has input growth. One criticism of this model has been that this important determinant of growth is exogenous to the models; that is, the models do not explain the causes or origins of this significant determinant at all. For this reason, neoclassical growth models are also called exogenous growth models; it is technology that is exogenous.

A second major literature called endogenous growth theory has more recently emerged to enrich the Solow neoclassical model by making technological change an endogenously determined force.[11] In order to allow for endogenous technical change, it was necessary to alter several fundamental maintained (untested) hypotheses of the Solow model. First, either capital formation generates free spillover effects or an industry is required that needs resources to produce knowledge. As part of the growth process, returns due to the spread of this knowledge in the form of spillovers are thought to exceed the return to the initial producers of the new knowledge. (This has required introduction of non-constant returns to scale models and of non-competitive markets. Both of these deviations from the traditional Solow model mean much more complex modeling and at times insoluble optimization functions.)[12]

An important implication of these models is that as more human capital is devoted to creation of new knowledge, economic growth via technical change should accelerate. Recent empirical research has brought the fundamental contributions of this literature into question. Jones (1995a, 1995b) points out that increases in numbers of scientists and engineers, even as a proportion of the whole population, has taken place at times when the rate of technological change was falling. Newer models that are free of this empirical implication have recently been developed.

Another distinct growth literature has been largely empirical in nature and focused on the role of government in growth. Here attempts are made to correlate time series movements or cross-section differences in growth measures to a long list of factors. This literature suggests that the level of government interference in private markets can be negatively related to the rate of growth. Such a conclusion is contentious, but the depressing effect on the private sector of public sector activity has been vigorously supported by Becker (1985a) and by Friedman (1982), among others.[13]

THE BOOK'S OBJECTIVES: FROM MODELS TO REALITY

We have four distinct purposes in this volume, all interrelated. (1) We examine the causes and implications of the collapse of the Soviet Union both by applying standard neoclassical growth theory to its performance and by viewing the collapse as a major aftershock of the economic quake of the industrial revolution. (2) We analyze the transition from central planning to capitalism by linking electoral politics to growth models in which economic reforms impact on various parameters of the models. (3) From the theoretical models we build an econometric model to estimate the interactive effects between reforms, elections and economic performance and politics. (4) We apply our hypotheses, contained in the models, to a six-country sample of reform economies. Tests of the implications of the models take two very different forms. First, we use formal statistical evidence and some econometric tests. Second, we analyze the behavior of economic agents in the post-independence decade of liberalization from historical and heuristic perspectives. The growth models are the central tools with which we integrate these different forms of analysis: economic, political and historical.[14]

Karl Marx, while brilliant in many respects, failed to anticipate the implementation of his ideas by Lenin and Mao. He never intended communism to supplant feudal agrarian societies like Russia and China; instead he thought communism would replace capitalism after its collapse in industrial societies. It now seems evident that capitalism was not fatally flawed and internally inconsistent, and evident that communism would not replace capitalism. Rather, the best that can be said of communism is that it might have served in Russia, and perhaps elsewhere, as a transition away from feudalism (or some other inflexible established order) and eventually toward capitalism. If anything appears historically inevitable, though, it is the collapse of communism, itself fatally flawed and internally inconsistent.

It is not yet clear whether transition from communism to capitalism will work in all countries. Some countries appear to have succeeded, but in general the jury is still out. At the same time, however, we argue that transition from an ossified established order (which for lack of a better term we shall call feudalism) to capitalism cannot succeed without the feudal system undertaking certain kinds of changes. Communists forced such changes on Russia and may have tried to do so elsewhere. We elaborate on this point below.

TWO HISTORIC VIEWS OF THE INDUSTRIAL REVOLUTION

The industrial revolution, like the agricultural revolution, was an economic quake that over time destroyed existing social, political and economic structures. By the eighteenth century institutions had developed in several countries (specifically, England and the Netherlands) which provided incentives that could sustain growth. Furthermore, private rates of return to innovation and application of new techniques were higher and international competition was growing. These realities provided ever more incentives to risk-taking behavior and wealth-creating trade.[15] Nonetheless, feudal systems based on stable hierarchies, strong religious and social customs, and rigid formal and informal relationships between classes of people could not support the labor and capital requirements of the industrial revolution.

The new economic reality required labor mobility, both geographically and socially. It depended on incentives and was impersonal in its selection of winners and losers. The market itself is not capable of sustaining a rigid class system. One of the great questions posed by the intellectuals of the eighteenth century was what type of social organization would work best in an industrial society. Both Karl Marx and Adam Smith had answers to this question,[16] each diametrically opposed to the other. We summarize briefly their analyses of the economic system that they observed – eighteenth-century capitalism in the early stages of the industrial revolution by Smith, and nineteenth-century capitalism by Marx. While intellectual offspring of both Smith and Marx have expanded, revised, modified, improved upon and elaborated these two approaches, it serves our purpose here to focus directly on the thoughts of the two intellectual fountainheads of these paradigms.[17]

Adam Smith

Smith believed in the social virtue of capitalism. He lived during the Enlightenment and his books reflect that period's belief in the greater good being served by the exercise of individual liberty and human rationality. His belief that men may reap the fruits of their labor summed up one major aspect of the moral virtue of private markets. People with marketable skills acquired through training and education would reap rewards under capitalism, and in so doing would inevitably be making other people better off by providing the goods and services called for by consumers in the impersonal marketplace. Voluntary exchange improved the welfare of both parties, thereby increasing social harmony. His remarkable insight in *An Inquiry into the Nature and Causes of the Wealth of Nations* (1776) was the existence of the invisible hand of the marketplace that promoted efficient production and consumer utility. He understood the nature of the division of labor. He perceived the social welfare gains that accrued from a system in which pursuit of enlightened self-interest contributed to social well-being. His most famous book, the aforementioned *Wealth of Nations*, was a defense of free markets, domestically and internationally.

In addition to seeing the normative value of capitalism, Smith also understood that the system worked. He could see both the static optimal results of markets as well as the dynamic ability of market participants, in pursuit of personal gain, to adapt to changing conditions, tastes, technologies and, in general, market forces. This does not mean, as some have claimed, that Smith was a supporter of unfettered capitalism. He felt that the public sector had an important role to play. However, he was less original and forceful here than he was in perceiving and explaining the invisible hand.

Although Adam Smith credited self-interest as being the engine driving human behavior, one must remember that he presumed an institutional environment of clearly defined and defensible property rights and respect for the rule of law. (These are necessary conditions for markets to work efficiently, and they are still underdeveloped or absent in Russia.) *The Wealth of Nations* was his second book and the world too often forgets his first, *The Theory of Moral Sentiments* (1759). There he discussed the ethical forces that bind people together in a workable society, the unique human capability of placing oneself in another person's position, what we might today call empathy; his first chapter is called "Of Sympathy." The self-interest he writes about in *The Wealth of Nations* is not crude greed; a person gets what he wants by honest exchange, not by theft or cheating. According to Smith, a successful capitalist system must encourage "prudence," provide for justice and the rule of law, and allow enough "beneficence" (charity) to prevent relative losers in the system from becoming disaffected. In other words, a workable market system requires a strong civil society.

Karl Marx

In stark contrast to Smith, Marx saw evil in capitalism. Everywhere he looked in nineteenth-century workplaces he saw misfortune and anguish. He thought capitalism was immoral because by definition a few who owned the means of production were rich, while the many who owned nothing were poor. Marx argues in *Das Kapital* (1867) that the collapse of capitalism was inevitable because failure was built into the very nature of its driving force. Inequality in ownership of the means of production and therefore severe inequality between capitalist and worker were natural by-products of capitalism. The capitalist would always exploit the worker in order to increase profits, but profits would eventually be squeezed to zero.

Because workers were kept poor, according to Marx, and because profits were plowed back into businesses, the latter became more and more productive, but meanwhile there would always be insufficient demand for their products. A glut would inevitably occur, and this glut would produce severe recession. Recession would in turn lead to increasing business failures and consolidation. Worsening business cycles would also worsen workers' condition. Eventually the proletariat would rise up, revolt against the capitalists and take over the system. Marx called the subsequent period the dictatorship of the proletariat. He predicted that government would eventually wither away and communism would become perfect socialism, where organized government would be unnecessary. Each person would work for the good of all in a workers' utopia.

Marx did recognize that capitalism was a highly productive system; but where Smith saw it generating social harmony, Marx saw the opposite. Marx and his followers judged capitalism for all times and places based on the peculiarly bad few years in England that he (and Friedrich Engels) had studied – "the hungry '40s."[18] The increasingly interventionist stance of the British government in creating social legislation beginning in the 1840s demonstrates how simplistic was the Marx–Engels view of society. Later Stalin tried to emulate capitalism's wealth by forcing industrialization on Russia, but he withheld the mechanisms that made capitalism work, because it was these very mechanisms that Marx had repudiated. In *The Communist Manifesto* (1848) Marx and Engels summed up their theory in their belief in a single principle, the "abolition of private property."

Who Was Right?

Both Smith's and Marx's ideas were attempts to explain the economic underpinnings of the new industrial world. Based on each writer's normative and positive analyses, can one determine whether they understood the nature of the economic quake that had shaken society? Did they understand that entirely new social relationships would be required so that society could adapt to the requisites of industrialization?

Certainly these two great thinkers were right about many things, and it is with the humility of those standing on the shoulders of these and other giants like Hayek, North and Olson that we reflect upon their work many years later. Smith's vision of the invisible hand, ever present amidst the chaos of market transactions, was clearly brilliant. Marx's vision of the disruptive and inequitable nature of the maldistribution of power, income and wealth arising from unfettered capitalism was equally original. His social and historical analysis has informed modern social science ever since.

Smith's objectives, however, were in a sense more modest than were Marx's. Smith observed that the economic system born in the economic quake contained inherent elements that would make it work – the coincidence of interests implied in every market transaction, the invisible hand in action. He accepted the ethic of this new economy and said little about how humankind should reorganize while adapting to this new system. He presumed a relatively advanced social structure.

Based on his Hegelian notion of dialectical materialism, Marx intended to forecast the long-range outcome of the system. He went even farther, wanting to replace it ultimately with a utopia devoid of inequities and of the opiate of religious beliefs. Convinced that capitalism would fail, Marx planned to mold out of its ashes an ideal communist state. But it now seems evident that he made two mistakes. His forecast underestimated the great productive power of the new industrial system. While it allowed capitalists to enjoy returns, it was potent enough to generate more than adequate incomes for workers as well. Perhaps Marx also failed to appreciate his own influence. Modern flexible democratic political systems have adopted many of his reform ideas. They have been able to adjust to capitalism, to ameliorate its flaws and, in fact to enhance its powers. He missed the possibility of the modern notion of welfare capitalism, prevalent throughout the West in greater or lesser degree, where market systems are modified by measures such as worker safety legislation, trade unions, unemployment compensation and redistributive taxes.

We believe that Marx's intellectual contribution, while enormous, fell short of his ambitious objective, to forecast both the downfall of capitalism and the development of the system that would replace it. Had the opportunistic Lenin not twisted Marxism to fit his own revolutionary goals so that it would apply to feudal Russia, and had Mao and his followers not been enchanted by the siren song of socialist utopia, history might have treated Marx more kindly.[19] After all, the perversities of early British industrialization – child labor exploitation and maltreatment of workers in factories, for example – were concerns eventually addressed by modern democratic capitalism with its tensions between the distribution of political votes and the distribution of money votes, and by rising income levels.

The Economic Legacy of Lenin: The Failure of Central Planning[20]

What had the Soviet Union, and for that matter communist China, to do with Marx? Far less than most people suppose. Communists in Russia under the initial guidance of Lenin and in China under Chairman Mao built communism on the ruins of collapsed feudal systems that were ill equipped to deal with the demands of modern industrial society. That these feudal systems would collapse or at the very least change radically seems obvious to us now. But what type of system replaced feudalism under Lenin, and later Stalin?

Although Lenin was a revolutionary in the sense that he was willing to destroy the prevailing order, he was a reactionary in that he could not tolerate the social, political and economic institutions that the industrial revolution generated and reinforced. Lenin was intolerant of anyone who responded as a self-interested economic agent to the handsome rewards created by competition and innovation. He set out to stifle all entrepreneurial behavior. Everything that made capitalism work – bankers, private property, returns to capital, wage differentials – was destroyed in the Soviet Union.[21]

The Soviet Union was built on resisting, at all costs, the social and economic pressures generated by the industrial revolution. It was created not as a visionary post-capitalist society but rather was a regime designed to resist the inevitable nature of the new and to replace feudalism with communism. It was essentially reactionary, built by people who deplored the social effects of capitalism.[22] Thus their eventual failure was as inevitable as the failure of the hunters and gatherers to withstand the agricultural revolution.

Modern growth analysis explains the inherent flaws in the Soviet system. Quite apart from the immorality of its reliance on murder, torture, intimidation, terror and genocide, the inevitable failure of the Soviet system can be explained on the purely objective grounds of economic analysis. This is important because it means that even if one is willing to tolerate such heavy reliance on negative incentives to get things done, the communist system was flawed. Following Robert Solow, one can think of Stalin's Soviet economic system as one big process by which inputs are combined to produce output. Solow called this process the aggregate production function; industrial production can be summarized by a mathematical function in which inputs, like labor and capital, are combined to generate output.

Marx, Lenin and Stalin all knew that capital accumulation was essential to growth. Whereas they rejected the capitalist incentive system to generate capital formation, they knew that industrialization required capital accumulation. The classic vision of stuffing pigs into a sausage-making machine so that sausages can pour from it illustrates the production function. To produce sausages one requires pigs (raw materials), a sausage machine (capital) and someone to turn the crank on the machine (labor). Though communists repudiated wage differentials as incentives for work effort, they knew that production required labor. They also repudiated a return to capital, but knew too that production required capital. The plan was simple: continually pour more and more labor and capital into heavy industrial production by starving light industry, agriculture, services and consumer goods, and industrial output will continue to increase.

The technical planning mechanisms used in the Gosplan (which set the allocation of workers and machines, and output quotas) can be illustrated by reference to a specific type of aggregate production function – the Leontief production function.[23] Wassily Leontief designed an input–output matrix (described in more detail in Chapter 5) which shows how much of each type of input is required in each industry to produce the output necessary to supply inputs for other industries. All of this production coordination had to be done without the capitalist incentive system, that is, without wage differentials, without a rate of return on capital assets and, most importantly, without profits. Since the plan was a product of the dictatorship of the proletariat, failure to do as told or to meet quotas was a crime against the state and was punished severely.

How is this system flawed? We need first to acknowledge that the Bolsheviks and Stalin did industrialize Russia. They transformed agrarian Czarist Russia, which had been haltingly trying to emulate Western Europe, into one of two world superpowers. They ultimately produced a military machine feared around the world. They challenged the US by sending the first man into space. They built a formidable transportation and educational infrastructure to feed their gigantic heavy industries.

Still, there were two serious and in fact fatal problems. First, modern industry, even assuming a static technological frontier, is far too complex for a single central plan, regardless of the planners' power to enforce compliance. Humankind does not have the tools to devise a successful plan for an entire industrial society.[24] Second, modern economies are highly dynamic, requiring extremely flexible production processes. The mix of inputs and the nature of technology are changing constantly, so that even if one could devise and impose a viable static plan, it would be obsolete by the time it was implemented. How does one build and impose a plan (even using positive incentives) in which participants will constantly alter their behavior and organization in order to adjust to new conditions? It proved impossible to build a viable industrial society able to adapt to changing circumstances.

The Soviets produced a system that became very good at repetitive behavior. Once a plant manager learned to produce ball bearings, he continued production indefinitely, whether anyone needed more ball bearings or not. In terms of production function analysis, output growth came only from input growth.[25] The system encouraged accumulation but not innovation. Everything got bigger but not necessarily better.

Neoclassical growth theory points out that additional inputs will initially raise output. It may rise for quite a while. However, reliance on adding capital to increase output per worker eventually leads to diminishing returns to capital. New increments of capital are less valuable than earlier increments. The growth of output per worker starts to fall. Eventually, unless a mechanism stops capital accumulation, new increments of capital will actually reduce output – production becomes awkward and cumbersome.[26] Plans begin to fail.

Planners become increasingly frustrated at the failures of state-owned enterprises and industries to meet industrial goals.

A malevolent planner like Stalin relies more and more on negative incentives, imprisonment, executions and terror to achieve production targets. At one point Stalin purged the entire industrial sector leadership, thinking that new younger workers, uninfected by old ideas, would follow his orders better.[27] But diminishing returns inevitably set in again. Eventually, the gulags filled up and their administrators were swamped. Stalin's policies aggravated the situation by reducing labor input while capital input was still rising. Diminishing returns to capital set in with a vengeance. In the face of obvious failure, Stalin's followers (Nikita Khrushchev in particular) slowed down the intimidation. For a while this worked because labor supply increased. Still, the essentially static system soon again encountered diminishing returns to capital. In the 1960s, 1970s and 1980s, planners and managers became overwhelmed.[28] Increments of capital, increasingly shoddy, led to declining output, both in quantity and quality. Productivity of new increments of capital was actually negative. Increasing labor and capital inputs no longer increased output.[29]

This analysis makes clear, in retrospect, that the eventual outcomes of the Soviet economic model – chronic overproduction of heavy industrial products, shoddy workmanship, alcoholism, absenteeism, waste, discouragement and cynicism – should not have surprised us. Of course, secrecy, distortion and disinformation were employed by the Soviets to prevent their failures from becoming well known. Putting on a good face with Potemkin villages remained a Russian practice.

In the end, even the planners lost faith. Eventually the leader, Mikhail Gorbachev, turned to glasnost, perestroika and *demokratizatsiya* to try to patch up the system.[30] Citizens of the empire sensed growing opportunities to escape the malaise. They headed for the Wall, in spirit or in fact. Gorbachev and his comrades, thoroughly disenchanted, refused to unleash the military. In the face of people "voting with their feet," the system crumbled. Events in Russia and five other states are covered in more detail in our country studies.

Why had Russia taken the communist path in the first place? Obviously, Lenin and his Bolsheviks were ruthless in imposing their power, but why was Russia fertile ground for their revolution? They failed to export it to Western Europe. What inoculated most Europeans and Americans, but not the Russians? History reveals the significant differences. The people of Russia were ignorant of the Reformation, and they missed completely the spirit of the Enlightenment that influenced Western Europe and the American colonies in the eighteenth century. Russians acquired no notions of the value of individual liberty and private property or of self-determination, no belief in the power of the people to govern themselves, no doubts about the rightness of an all-powerful central authority.[31] Throughout their recorded history, autocracy of one sort or another was all they had ever known. In medieval Russia, the people living on a great landholder's estate came to be seen as property of that estate and its owner. Over time the people of Russia came to view themselves as possessions of the sovereign. The accepted view of the structure of the state was of a household full of servants, each with particular duties. Violence toward the peasantry from state and violence among the peasants themselves had a long tradition in Russia. The horrors of the First World War added to the climate of extreme violence.

Russia was ripe for Lenin. He despised the system that had fostered the results of industrialization in the West – competition, growth, risk and inequality – and in the name of social justice he thereby doomed his system to ultimate failure. Planners did industrialize the Soviet Union rapidly after the First World War, but eventually too many decisions had to be taken by the central authorities, who had too little information. The system was not flexible enough to meet the demands of a vast and increasingly complex economic and political empire.

Russia's autocratic history left the country without a viable civil society, without the basic institutions, such as private property, necessary to nurture a market system. The necessity of social capital for successful economic and political systems has become a popular topic in the West. Most of the former Soviet Union is sorely lacking in social capital.[32]

LESSONS FROM THE COLLAPSE OF THE SOVIET UNION

Our interpretation of the collapse of the Soviet Union leads us to one key conclusion, several new interpretations of events and an unanswered question. The conclusion is that in practice communism, far from Marx's vision of a system that would evolve out of the ashes of collapsed capitalism, imposed industrialization on agrarian society without the incentive structure that would allow capitalism to work. Could Marx have had it backwards? Was communism a transition phase between feudalism and capitalism? More likely it was no more than a tragic detour that contributed nothing positive to humankind's evolution.

Our economic interpretation of the consequences of communism may be too harsh, as we have not made a case for what the communist interval contributed to growth. The communists did destroy the existing feudal structure and social order; the old entrenched interests, the social elite of the old order, would no longer be around. The communists did raise living standards by adopting planned industrialization. Public provision of medical and educational systems, though limited in many respects, was universal. Public goods like transportation systems, energy and other physical infrastructure were developed far beyond anything found in Czarist Russia. Because Russia remained nearly feudal in its economic organization longer than any Western state, the imposition of a centralized system may have helped to move it toward modernism. It may be easier to move from the present state of affairs into the modern world of democratic capitalism than it would have been without the intervening stage of communism, but this is simply speculation.

How did Western states move into the modern age of industrialization and free enterprise? The English moved away from royal governance toward democracy as economic development took place. The Magna Carta, whereby the aristocracy wrested power from the king, the creation of a parliamentary democracy, the Glorious Revolution that gave parliament the power of the purse – these and other steps made England the envy of political freethinkers in the eighteenth century. Parliamentarians read Adam Smith and acted in the interests of capitalistic enterprise. Smith's views coincided with their own.

The bourgeois-driven French Revolution weakened the old order of nobility that might well have been inclined to resist both the industrial revolution and free enterprise. Canada and the United States were fortunate to have no aristocracy or royalty to have to get rid of. Although one could view the American Civil War as the last attempt by agrarian society to hang on to old ways, North America undoubtedly had a huge advantage by building a new society without the weight of an entrenched ruling class.[33] As for Japan, a social structure that supported industrialization and modern capitalism was essentially imposed from without after defeat in the Second World War.[34]

Suppose we are correct in asserting that communism and the Soviet Union were misguided attempts to resist the social and political pressures of the industrial revolution. Suppose further that we are correct in asserting that the democratic capitalism of the United States, Europe and Japan offers successful models of adaptation. These two assertions imply a different interpretation of what has been going on in the Third World during the battle between these two philosophies.[35] Consider the hypothetical example of a member of the political elite – perhaps a landed aristocrat – of the pre-industrial revolution Old World order who now finds himself in charge of a Third World regime. How does he withstand the forces of industrialization with their inherent threat to his hegemony? Society at large may become better off under capitalism and competitive markets, but as a leader of the old order he may be under grave threat once the new middle class begins to recognize the virtues of an economic meritocracy.

The political elite may play one philosophy against the other. Small powerful groups, often backed by the military, may hold reformers at bay by arguing alternately that some aspects of socialism are preferable and that society should side with the communists, or that certain features of capitalism are preferable and society should side with capitalists. These elite groups cling to power by keeping their opponents off balance and thus resisting the inevitable effects of industrialization.

This could explain Latin American oligarchic families who have staved off market reforms and retained political and economic power by adopting anti-capitalist rhetoric. To this day Pakistani leaders, drawn from the elite classes and still referred to as "the feudals," are ill equipped to modernize their economy.[36] Our analysis may also help to explain the resistance of African nations to modern capitalism. Societies enmeshed in old social conflicts, stultifying caste systems and rigid social structures are not well suited to the impersonal and dynamic demands of capitalism for flexibility, adaptation and initiative.[37]

Attempts to bring capitalism to societies in which the old order remains in power have had mixed outcomes. The prevalence of cronyism and corruption, commonplace in Third World regimes, suggests that the old guard is clinging to power in the face of the industrial revolution's tendency to create a middle class that challenges authority. Can societies accomplish the growth of market economies without purging the old ways? Destruction of the old social structure was the target of Lenin's Bolshevik political culture. Stalin's purges finished off the last vestiges of the aristocracy. The landed gentry was eliminated. The outcome was the end of the Old World order that might have resisted adaptation to industrialization.

We do not mean to imply that communism is a necessary precursor to capitalism. Nor do we mean that democracy is a necessary condition for industrialization. Countries like South Korea and Taiwan modernized rapidly without political freedoms common in the West. China is taking a unique approach – trying to adopt free markets without political reform. India, on the other hand, practices democracy but has clung to its own version of socialism. Few in India today benefit from growth.[38] We are arguing that radical leveling of opportunities and greater access to rewards for industrial achievement and innovation are necessary in regimes trying to achieve modern living standards through industrialization.

Our analysis implies that China and many Third World regimes still confront radical social and political changes as modern commercial society imposes its own logic. A good deal of social upheaval is likely as the industrial revolution continues to unfold.[39] How readily these old regimes relinquish power and make the transition to democratic capitalism will determine the degree to which they can raise living standards without excessive bloodshed, violence and revolution.

THE NEW WORLD ORDER

The problem that communism "solved" was to destroy the old sociopolitical power structure built for an agricultural world. It seems doubtful that such destruction had to be as costly as it was. The remaining question is whether democratic capitalism can succeed in regimes where communism held sway for fifty years. It is to this issue that we now turn – the transition to capitalism. In the next chapter we attempt to identify the key collective action problems that will be encountered by a society as it tries to develop a market system. While the allure of Western-style democratic capitalism is undeniable, a serious struggle remains before old social and political systems give way to the kind of society that produces pro-market incentives.

For those persuaded by observations of fledgling market systems that are not working efficiently, for example in Russia, we emphasize here and in what follows that early advisors from the West did not adequately appreciate the absolute necessity for successful market systems of supportive social infrastructure, legal systems in particular.

Chapter 3 reviews the economic benefits that accrue from reforms designed to promote market systems. Chapter 4 contains a heuristic discussion of the economic growth models that structure our subsequent analysis of the behavior of economic agents in newly independent countries. Chapter 5 explores the ways the economic reforms work through the growth model. Chapter 6 introduces a model that connects the economic reforms and their effects discussed in the earlier chapters to voters' reactions, via elections, to those reforms. This integration of the political process and the economic system has a great deal to do with the sustainability of reforms and the likelihood of growth. Individual country studies take up Chapters 7 to 12, and Chapter 13 provides a summary of the book.

We hope our analysis of the transition experiences of six states formerly under Soviet rule will help leaders elsewhere prepare for and adapt to modern market systems. We do not think that there is only one model or one way to adapt to modernization, democracy and capitalism. Democratic capitalism is a broad term, including successful societies as different as Sweden and Taiwan, Canada and Switzerland, South Korea and Italy. However, we do identify important stages along the road to a successful system of private markets.

NOTES

1. We wish to thank Thomas Borcherding, Thomas Hazlett, Charles R. Hulten, M. Ishaq Nadiri and Bernard Saffran for cogent advice on this chapter. They bear no responsibility for errors.
2. Remnick (1994) conveys a vivid picture of the last days of the Soviet regime.
3. See Fukuyama (1992) for an intriguing view of the significance of the end of the Cold War. He argues that serious political ideological differences may be over forever.
4. This notion is explained further in the next section on incremental changes.

5. The earliest information revolution began with the invention of writing; the next began with the invention of movable-type printing.
6. Vernon Smith (1992) provides a superb discussion of the nature of nomadic hunting societies and the disruption brought on by agriculture. Our discussion of the impact of agriculture on hunters and gatherers as suggested by Genesis 2 is based on his work.
7. Among contemporary economists Douglass North is a pioneer of modern institutional analysis. See, for example, North (1990, 1999) and North and Thomas (1973). Co-winner of the 1974 Nobel Prize Friedrich A. Hayek (1944) and Mancur Olson (1965, 1982, 2000) have also made profound contributions to this area of analysis.
8. In recent years growth theorists have been applying models similar to the Solow neoclassical model to explain short-term perturbations about the growth path. This real-business cycle theory has been theoretical, with empiricism mainly limited to simulation models in which attempts are made to replicate cyclical economic performance seen in the data.
9. See Intriligator (1971) and Kamien and Schwartz (1981) for lucid reviews of optimization techniques employed in growth theory.
10. A vigorous debate took place in the US in the early 1990s concerning the potentially independent driving force of infrastructure investment. See, for instance, Alicia Munnell (1991) and Hulten and Schwab (1993).
11. See *Journal of Economic Perspectives*, 12 (2), April 1998, for a set of relevant articles.
12. See, for instance, Romer (1990) and Mankiw, Romer and Weil (1992). Yeager (1999) focuses on the role of government in creating or controlling transaction costs that affect economic performance and growth.
13. See Barro and Sala-i-Martin (1995) and Hall and Jones (1997).
14. The technical aspects of theoretical modeling, econometric design and hypothesis testing all appear in the Appendices, which may be read by those interested in such academic issues. The main text explains in non-technical language the nature of our approach and our findings, summarized briefly here.
15. North and Thomas (1973) cover this subject thoroughly.
16. See Marx (1936) and Smith (1937).
17. Janos Kornai (2000) discusses the criticism that one cannot view the world economic systems of the twentieth century as a simple dichotomy. Also see Brady (1999), pp. 217–33 for the increasingly discouraging analysis of two major pro-market reformers, Yegor Gaidar and Anatoly Chubais. Gaidar describes Russia's 1999 economy as "oligarchical capitalism."
18. According to Boyer (1998), Marx relied on workplace reports from Engels, and their opinions were shaped in the 1840s in the context of a not widely representative period and place. They completely ignored the early stages of welfare capitalism in England.
19. See Courtois et al., *The Black Book of Communism* (1999), for an analysis of the violent behavior of communist regimes, including the Soviet Union, around the world.
20. Remnick (1994) an American author, and both Brovkin (1998) and Volkogonov (1998), Russian authors, have drawn on formerly secret documents to reveal the roles of Lenin and Stalin in the design of the Soviet regime. These authors argue that Lenin was as ruthless as Stalin, and that Stalinism was virtually an extension of the Lenin period.
21. Referring to the regime that Yeltsin first encountered in Moscow in 1986, Aron (2000) reports, "What Yeltsin found in Moscow could be called Adam Smith's revenge. The market's 'invisible hand' – working through thousands of thieving and conniving sales-clerks and trade officials – removed most of the best produce from the shelves of the state stores and distributed them secretly at real prices, paid in bribes, barter, or favours. Even Moscow could never keep up with the merciless efficiency of a market bent on restoring balance between dwindling supply and boundless demand."
22. We do not discuss the details of the political economy of the Soviet system. Kornai (1992) does a brilliant job of this. Brady (1999) presents a vivid picture of the decrepit system encountered by Yeltsin, Russia's first freely elected leader. This included inefficient and surplus capital, ruble overhang, endgame conduct by managers (called Red Directors) and rampant corruption among officials.
23. See Leontief (1951). For a mathematical and statistical explanation of the use of input–output matrices see Dorfman, Samuelson and Solow (1958).
24. Economists were wrestling with this issue in the 1930s; see Lange (1938) and Hayek (1935).
25. Aron (2000) corroborates this analysis in explaining why the 1981 Central Committee plan was doomed: "This stratagem would fail; ever-increasing 'inputs' was the only mode for which the Soviet economy had been designed and in which it could function."
26. After six months in office Yeltsin found that his heavy-handed jawboning was inadequate: "the half-century-old tradition of economic growth based on increasing inputs of raw materials and labor proved virtually impermeable to the slogans of 'intensification' and 'acceleration'. The giant flywheel of the 'plan' ... proved exceedingly difficult to slow down much less to halt." Aron (2000), pp. 170–71. The diminishing returns principle refers to increasing any input(s) when others are fixed.

27. See Courtois et al. (1999) for details.
28. Padma Desai (1989) explains why the 1965 reform efforts of the Kosygin–Brezhnev team failed: "[T]he Soviet economic system that Gorbachev inherited has all the trappings of a rigid institutional structure. Commands from the central planners have left little initiative, and even less incentive, for the performing actors and economic agents. The ill-fitting pieces of shortages, bottlenecks, retarded innovation, and faltering growth have been the inevitable consequences" (p. 25).
29. Easterly and Fischer (1994) provide empirical evidence for collapse of total factor productivity.
30. Desai (1989) explains why Gorbachev's attempts at glasnost and perestroika were inadequate. Gorbachev had to accept the "essential" correctness of the revolutionary history of the Soviet Union. Gorbachev was a good communist. Desai believed that Gorbachev's approach was prudent and necessary. She even seems to feel Gorbachev had successfully reconciled the historic conflict between "Slavophils" and "Westernizers" (pp. 48–9). Later, in an addendum chapter 10, written after the collapse, Desai admits her (and most of our) inability to forecast the rapid turn of events that swamped Gorachev and the communists in the early 1990s. Desai had listed the weaknesses of perestroika's half-measures (p. 53).
31. Even after the collapse, it was evident that, in Aron's words, "The country had no living memory of private economic activity unstigmatized by persecution and unmarred by criminality ... three generations had grown with no memory of family farming on one's own land", Aron (2000), p. 635. Brady (1999) also acknowledges the lack of consensus as a serious problem (pp. 13, 17).
32. On the economic and political importance of social capital that generates trust and ethics, see Abrams and Lewis (1995), Fukuyama (1995, 2000) and Harrison and Huntington (2000).
33. It is interesting to note that, while slavery has a long and sordid history, it was the industrial North that eventually obliterated slavery in the agrarian South. While morally despicable, slavery may also be seen as an ultimately inefficient means of employing labor under capitalism, because it lacks adequate positive incentives needed to induce innovation in the workplace as well as because of the high costs associated with monitoring slaves. It was, however, an economically profitable and viable system in the American South. See Fogel and Engerman (1974).
34. William Manchester (1978) discusses MacArthur's weakening of the power of the Emperor, and the introduction of democratic institutions and the rule of law, including development of labor unions and women's suffrage. He set the stage for Japan to adapt to democratic capitalism. Of course, minimal defense spending and high savings rates played a major role, given the new political and social setting.
35. An important issue to many economic historians has been the role in development of colonialism. Did it retard growth or did it set the stage for growth? We do not comment directly on this issue. It is interesting to note that while it was industrial societies that colonized less-developed societies, this may not reflect the inherent evil of capitalism as suggested by some, but rather reflect the enormous advantages of capitalist societies to generate great wealth, thus creating the enormous disparities that made colonialism feasible. One may ponder the following hypothetical question: had industrial society developed in Africa instead of Europe, would African nations have colonized Europe?
36. See the *Wall Street Journal*, Friday, 7 August 1998, p. 1.
37. See Easterly and Levin (1997) on the growth tragedy of Africa.
38. See Barro (1997) and Hulten (1990). The issue of freedom and growth is discussed further in Chapter 2.
39. In Russia resistance to market reforms was strongest in rural regions. Referring to the elections of 1986, Aron says that "the solidly pro-communist rural areas [were] of the West and Southwest, southern Siberia and the Amur Basin of the southern Far East; and just as firmly pro-reform [were] industrialized North and Central Russia, Siberia, Far East and Urals, and all of the maritime regions" Aron (2000), pp. 631–32. This experience is not unlike the US Civil War between the industrial North and the rural South. Brady (1999) points out that "hardest of all for many Russians to accept was the new unpredictability of life. People had grown accustomed to the attitudes of central planning." (pp. 20–21).

2. The political economy of reform[1]

In the aftermath of the collapse of the Soviet Union, reformers began to transform centrally planned economies into something new. Calls for democracy and for private markets were widespread, but political resistance to restructuring and contradictions inherent in democratic capitalism continue to be evident.

Transforming an economy from socialism into a market democracy is a "public good," something that the private sector will not adequately produce on its own. Success depends on the political system properly setting the stage by passing and enforcing viable private property laws; by creating decentralized, regulated and solvent new financial institutions; and by disengaging itself from ownership and micromanagement of industry. Disengagement requires an unnatural political act – the bureaucracy must self-reform and must voluntarily relinquish many powers while creating and performing unfamiliar new tasks. Needed reforms impose short-term losses before gains begin to appear and citizens, weary from decades of false promises, balk at such losses. All of this makes reform more difficult.

Socialism is alive in Central and Eastern Europe. While some countries have set their sights on US-style democratic capitalism, others prefer a middle path in which private enterprise remains heavily regulated. Whether this middle road is viable remains to be seen. Russia's leaders vacillate between socialism and capitalism, with citizens fully committed to neither one.

NEW POLITICAL AND ECONOMIC CHALLENGES

After the collapse of the Soviet Union, new political entities began to emerge and the evolution away from authoritarian socialism got under way. While Western-style democratic free markets quickly became the stated objective of many new leaders, it was clearly not the ultimate goal of every emerging country. Former communist parties quickly transformed themselves into socialist parties, and in some cases were elected to lead the transition. This polity choice reflected in part the relative political sophistication and experience of the communists. It also reflected voters' reluctance to abandon the known for the unknown.

In some cases communists were overthrown in order to adopt democracy and nascent capitalism; in others, communism, originally imposed from without, was nothing more than an unnatural hiatus in the natural evolution towards modern decentralized systems; in still others, the communists remained a potent political and ideological force. Some of the satellite countries had been closely tied to nearby industrialized Western nations before succumbing to Soviet domination. After the collapse, these countries clearly had become very much poorer than their neighbors to the west had; the immediate intention of reformers was to renew old ties and continue the evolution toward modernity. Others, however, retained socialist notions of evolution toward a "third way," hoping to retain the principles and social support system of socialism while enjoying the benefits of the allocative efficiency of Western-style market economies. In still other cases, communists continue to sabotage reform efforts.

Some countries, after early failed reform attempts, elected former (albeit renamed) Communist party leaders in hopeful attempts to ameliorate and cushion changes brought on by the collapse of the Soviet empire. The variety of approaches and experiences raises the following important question: after a command economy collapses, how does the transition process from central planning work and to what does it lead? In seeking an answer to this question, we report lessons that may be helpful to those in other societies who contemplate or are in the process of conversion towards democracy and market capitalism. There are predictable pitfalls to be avoided, and we believe we can explain why some countries will succeed while others will falter.

Beginning with Chapter 7, we analyze six Central and Eastern European experiences – Bulgaria, Czech Republic, Slovak Republic, Estonia, Hungary and Russia – to shed light on the liberalization process and likely outcomes. We are particularly interested in evaluating connections between political developments (toward democracy) and economic reforms (toward private markets). Opinions on their relationship range from the view that democracy and capitalism go hand in hand, to the view that democracy can impede growth in the early stages and can slow successful capitalist development. Scholarly arguments may be found to support complementarity or incompatibility between democracy and market capitalism. Most scholars de-emphasize conceptual connections and stress instead the importance of particular contingencies or unique local circumstances.[2] Certainly, the astounding economic success of Asian nations like South Korea, Taiwan and Singapore without commensurate political freedom, in contrast to the socialist economic inadequacies of long-standing democracies like India, must give pause to seekers of a simple correlation between capitalism and democracy. One empirical regularity that can be observed across countries is that increases in the standard of living tend to generate a gradual rise in democracy.[3] The experiences of Central and Eastern Europe provide useful natural, though by no means simple, social experiments in which to observe something new: namely, simultaneous attempts at evolution towards democracy and towards Western-style market capitalism across a sizable set of countries.

Table 2.1 lists pairs of countries by row; in each row, countries in the first column have chosen the market path and those in the second have chosen the socialist path. When one thinks seriously of economic development, many causes for different economic performance come to mind: culture, social and religious behavior, natural resource endowments, education and literacy, political history and so on. What makes Table 2.1 interesting is that within each pair, most of the usual suspects for explaining differences do not exist. The Chinese in Taiwan are ethnically identical to the people of mainland China. Austria and Hungary were at one time part of the same empire. In each pair, though, people in the first

Table 2.1 Why do some economies outperform others?

Path	
Market	Socialist
Taiwan	China
South Korea	North Korea
West Germany	East Germany
Costa Rica	Cuba
Austria	Hungary
Western Europe	Eastern Europe
USA	USSR

country are better off economically than in the second. The key distinction is evident. Regardless of ethnicity, climate, culture or religion, countries that adopt private markets (in which property rights are clearly defined and consistently enforced) to determine the bulk of resource allocation decisions uniformly outperform those that adopt central planning.

We turn now to reforms essential to the transformation of a communist economic system into a private enterprise economy. We will explain in detail in Chapter 3 why each of these reforms contributes to economic well-being. Our economic analysis focuses on the goals of five major reforms: (1) to establish well-defined, reliable and enforceable legal private property rights; (2) to adopt a market-driven price system; (3) to impose effective and prudent monetary and fiscal policies; (4) to restructure markets, especially financial markets, in order to remove heavy regulation of productive activity and to reduce central control; (5) to open the local economy to international competition.[4]

Immediately after the collapse of the USSR, influential Western economists quickly identified these reform areas as essential for successful transition to a market economy.[5] It is clear to virtually all Western economists that strong capitalist economies are characterized by well-defined property rights, market-determined prices, relatively stable fiscal and monetary policies, only modest industrial regulation and open markets.[6] A viable tax system, a reliable banking system and relatively efficient financial markets are also known requisite elements of economic health.[7] Unfortunately, it is less clear exactly how to reconstruct a socialist system so that it has or can acquire these features. The political economy of the process is especially problematic.

It is our view that political and economic reforms interact systematically, and this interaction is both complex and subtle. Whereas progress in one area is neither necessary nor sufficient for progress in the other, they are often mutually reinforcing. As private markets generate widespread wealth they begin to create a middle class. The middle class then begins to acquire power at the expense of central authority, whether feudal lords or communist *nomenklatura*. As noted, increasing prosperity tends gradually to generate more democracy. Although we believe that private market decision-making cannot long thrive without a substantial degree of decentralized political power, we believe also that democracy alone does not guarantee economic freedom, private markets and growth.

The tyranny of the masses can hamper and even destroy economic freedom by discouraging capital accumulation and promoting redistribution; representative governments may also be subject to distorting interest-group pressures. It is not clear that the political balance of democratic capitalism is necessarily delicate, but it is subject to perpetual tensions. Democracy, to us, means one person, one vote, and at least one viable opposition party that occasionally wins national leadership. Such a system of allocation of political power is naturally going to conflict with market capitalism in which one dollar generates one vote (for resource allocation). These two voting systems, if you will, that have different distributions of power coexist in the West with tensions, and such coexistence is by no means guaranteed to be successful in the European East.

The former Soviet satellite states in Europe have successfully adopted democratic political practices; even Russia is apparently conducting free and fair elections. The key question for these countries is whether they can sustain functioning democracies and still achieve sustained economic growth via decentralized market systems. The simultaneous changes of both economic and political systems have put great strains on these societies. The dramatic demise of one-party politics and of planned economies was cause for great joy in the West and the source of a flurry of activity among Western economic consultants. These advisors meant well but had a good grasp of only part of the picture. They understood the characteristics of and pay-offs to market systems, but they failed to take adequate account of predictable social resistance to economic reforms at the political level.

Will these newly independent countries be able to sustain economic growth and political freedom? To answer this question, we begin by analyzing the political difficulties of achieving economic reforms in property ownership, market-determined prices, fiscal and monetary stabilization, industry restructuring and trade liberalization. The chapter ends with an exploration of the range of goals of economic development. This last discussion will serve as a warning to those who might have hoped that withdrawal of Soviet tanks would result in smooth and rapid evolution to US-style democratic capitalism.

POLITICAL IMPEDIMENTS TO ECONOMIC REFORM[8]

As we shall see, abandoning central planning and opting for an economic system based on markets have many potential benefits. Why, then, do voters in transition countries resist economic reforms?

Diffuse Benefits versus Concentrated Costs

Any economic reform involves significant social, political and economic costs.[9] By its very nature, reform disrupts the daily flow of doing business and thus raises immediate costs to everyone. To some specific people these costs can be very large, including the loss of power, wealth and influence. Because reform changes the relative wealth and power of different groups, it will encounter resistance. Inevitably, any substantive economic reform produces, at least in the short run, relative losers as well as winners.[10] Every economic system, even a poorly designed one, includes constituent groups that have coalesced around the benefits of the prevailing system. These beneficiaries will become protectors of the *status quo* who will resist effective reforms.

In Central and Eastern Europe the most powerful forces favoring the *status quo* were the Soviet military and civilian officials, the personnel who enforced the system that they had imposed upon the satellite populations. It was not until after people were relatively sure they would not be shot for protesting that any significant political resistance began to take place. Nonetheless, even with the implosion of the Soviet empire, the end of its political domination, the withdrawal of its troops and the collapse of the trading system, local resistance to economic reforms remains in varying degrees in each country. Even reforms understood to be widely beneficial may be resisted if citizens are uncertain about exactly who will enjoy the benefits; they may have a strong preference for the *status quo*.[11]

Local pro-Soviet administrators, secret police organizations, committed Communist Party members, managers of state-owned enterprises and other direct power players in the old regime are likely to resist reform. But many other ordinary citizens who had successfully adapted to the old regime are likely to perceive themselves as potential losers from any reform that changes the old ways of doing things. Such potential losers may include local political leaders, some academics, bureaucrats, managers and technocrats. These people partly retained and increased their power by their access to "insider information." Thus, in addition to being politically connected, they possess a disproportionate share of useful economic information. Different but very important constituents for the old ways are wards of the state such as pensioners, veterans and many public employees.[12] Citizens were accustomed under the Soviets to virtually free utilities, very low-cost housing, free medical care, guaranteed jobs, cheap public transport, free education and assurance, whether true or not, that no one was a great deal better off than anyone else.

The beneficiaries of reforms, as opposed to the losers, are more likely to be hard to identify before the fact. The advantages of a market system are diffuse and only gradually realized. Competition takes time to establish, bringing low prices and more goods. Virtually every consumer may eventually benefit, but until such a system is in place, the gains are not evident to the typical consumer. They are certainly less obvious than the immediate costs to the losers. Furthermore, the individual gains from price liberalization for each product may seem small. Thus potential winners may be less willing or able to coalesce politically than the relative losers whose costs are more concentrated, and this creates a strong political impediment to reform.[13]

Economic Reform Is a Public Good

Economic reforms are not likely to evolve on their own, even after disappearance of overt power of the anti-reform government, for yet another reason. In order for economic reforms to occur after communism, governments must actively establish them. This is because economic reforms have all the characteristics of a public good. After the initial costs of instituting a reform are incurred, the incremental policy cost of adding new beneficiaries is zero, and it is not feasible to exclude additional qualified beneficiaries from enjoying the benefits of the reform. Such goods will not adequately be provided or correctly priced by the market, and consumers are therefore unlikely to signal their desire for these goods via the price of such goods.

Consider, for example, passage of laws to protect the private property rights of landlords. Once a law is passed and the legal apparatus established, including the education and training of judges and lawyers and formation of courts, the set-up costs have been incurred. Now virtually everyone's property is protected by the new legal system. The incremental cost of protecting a new landlord or piece of property is incidental, and exclusion of an individual landlord is not feasible.[14] These two technical features of legal reform – zero incremental cost and non-excludability – mean that socially adequate legal reforms can only be provided by political consensus, and thus with assistance from the government. Such legal systems will not easily evolve out of private markets themselves.

In other words, the government cannot stand aside, do nothing, and expect private markets to form spontaneously.[15] Without laws, protecting private property accumulation is risky, and as one sees in Russia, predatory criminals can feed off the system. A viable legal framework will not simply evolve because there is little private-sector incentive to provide it. Some potential beneficiaries who might have helped in establishment of reform would instead prefer individually to let someone else provide the reform and then free-ride on the benefits. The government must therefore take a proactive role in establishing private property rights laws, just as it must in providing other products with the characteristics of public goods.[16] In some ways, government must expand and change its role in the economy, while disengaging from ownership of capital and from heavy regulation of production and prices.

The same public good features characterize all the economic reforms we are considering. Sound stabilization policy, once enforced, benefits everyone, including free-riders. The benefits of market-determined prices, free trade and industry restructuring benefit everyone, not just those who make sacrifices in order to establish them in the first place. Market-determined prices benefit all consumers, not just a few.[17]

A serious social problem remaining after the collapse of communism, largely a direct result of communist abuses of power, is mistrust of government. This aggravates the public goods problem by lowering the confidence the public has in the willingness and ability of government institutions to adopt economic reforms. The citizenry had very little experience of efficient and enlightened government. Thus, the nature of economic reform after communism has created natural political resistance.

Government Must Self-Devolve

A related impediment to reform is that the overt government action required for successful reforms will inherently weaken the very institutions that install these reforms. Economic reform requires an unnatural political act. Consider, for instance, property privatization. Who will arrange privatization of publicly held property? Some government entity has to be created in order to sell off or give away publicly held property. This entity will set rules for privatization, rules that select among competing interests, rules to settle property disputes and rules to enforce property acquisition and retention. As such an entity begins the privatization task, it engages in its own destruction. This is not a natural act for any bureaucracy; thus, we should not be surprised if such an entity were eventually to lapse into various delaying tactics. These might include setting severe restrictions on new owners, placing financial constraints on ownership, and passing complicated new ownership regulations. These could impede privatization itself and require the long-range involvement, and therefore survival, of the relevant bureaucracy.

A similar natural political impediment is likely to stand in the way of monetary stabilization. The head of the banking system must reduce his own powers in order to create a two-tier banking system with authority devolving away from the center. Fiscal stabilization is even more problematic, because here the polity in virtually every emerging economy must reduce spending and raise taxes or establish new taxing powers, in order to balance its budget. None of the measures to stabilize central budgets is popular politically. Thus one should expect bureaucratic and/or political resistance to responsible stabilization policy.[18]

Restructuring and deregulating industry is obviously painful and difficult politically, since the very agencies whose *raison d'être* is regulation must take on the task of reducing their own influence, power and control. The managers in state-owned enterprises have to abandon all the methods they had learned, thus destroying some of their own human capital, as their firms are restructured. Can one really expect vigorous deregulation by a bureaucracy and business leadership whose very existence and skill base are predicated on regulation?[19] Therefore, we again see natural political impediments to economic reform. Private industry has to be created with some degree of independence before arm's-length regulation can be imposed. This is not to argue that reform cannot occur, but rather to argue that economic reform requires special circumstances and leadership to succeed, and this includes powerful and persistent public support in order to hurdle these strong political impediments.

Delayed Gratification

An economic reform must be established and given time to work before its full benefits can be realized. This creates yet another impediment to reform, the delayed gratification problem. The ultimate objective of any economic reform is to raise living standards, and this takes time. Consider, for example, the need to accumulate capital with which workers can generate more output per unit of labor input. It is such labor productivity growth that leads to higher living standards. But this first requires capital accumulation, and capital accumulation depends on saving (unless foreign capital is imported). Saving, in turn, requires a period of deferred consumption before the capital can be acquired, installed and can begin to generate income. An initial period of sacrifice precedes a period of growth.

Such sacrifice is common to all economic reforms. The key to fiscal stabilization policy in all newly independent European countries is reduction of budget deficits that fund both income-support programs and inefficient state-owned enterprises. Less government expenditure on income support and on state-owned enterprises means short-term losses for program recipients and sacrifices for managers and workers in state-owned enterprises. Unemployment will initially rise as firms face broader competition. Similar problems plague monetary stabilization. Price liberalization and subsequent price-level stability always involve a shock period of rising prices, increased interest rates and scarce credit opportunities before the beneficial effects of monetary stability can be enjoyed. Price liberalization will generate competition and competition will lower prices, but not instantaneously. Similarly, replacing the implicit profit tax on state-owned enterprises with a value added tax implies an initial price shock that lowers real after-tax income before government programs funded by the tax

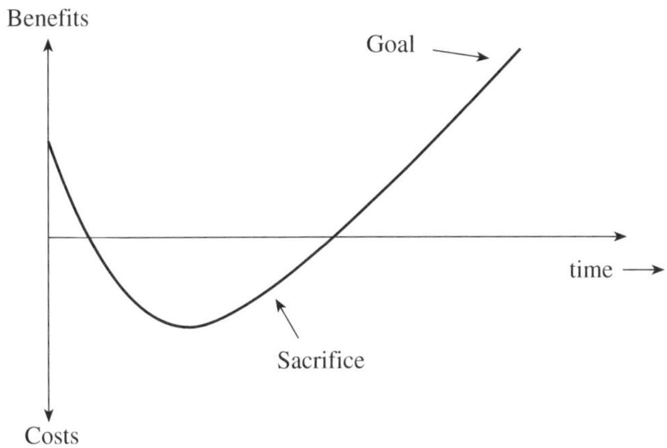

Figure 2.1 Delayed gratification

revenues can generate benefits. Free trade will mean more and better goods via more competition, but some domestic firms will suffer.[20]

In Figure 2.1 we illustrate the basic point that to improve the economic environment by altering economic and social institutions requires an initial period of worsening conditions before benefits kick in. Economic reforms will be tolerated in a democracy only if reforms can be publicly shown to lead to benefits worth the short-run sacrifice, and a sufficient number of people perceive themselves to be potential winners of those benefits.

The process of transition from central planning to market capitalism involves a complex problem in political economy as well as a problem of selecting the appropriate economic rules. Reformers must design political strategies that will overcome resistance from those who perceive themselves to be relative losers from reform, including powerful and strategically placed people as well as a broad range of ordinary voters. Economic reformers must be prepared to make important strategic and tactical political choices. We conclude that a necessary aspect of the reform process toward capitalist markets is for political leadership to build strong popular support for reform policies. This suggests a major role for politicians inclined toward reforms, intellectual supporters of reforms and influential leaders in the press. This is a significant body of pro-market human capital that needs to be developed in virtually all non-market economies.

TRANSITION TO WHAT?

The first important strategic question is this: what should be the ultimate goal of reform? Should a newly independent state's leaders institute reforms that will promote market capitalism of the type practiced in the US, or should they adopt a Nordic model with private markets, significant redistribution, a heavy dose of regulation and centralized cooperative decision-making? It is important to realize that the removal of Soviet power and the collapse of the trading system, the Council for Mutual Economic Assistance (CMEA), left a vast

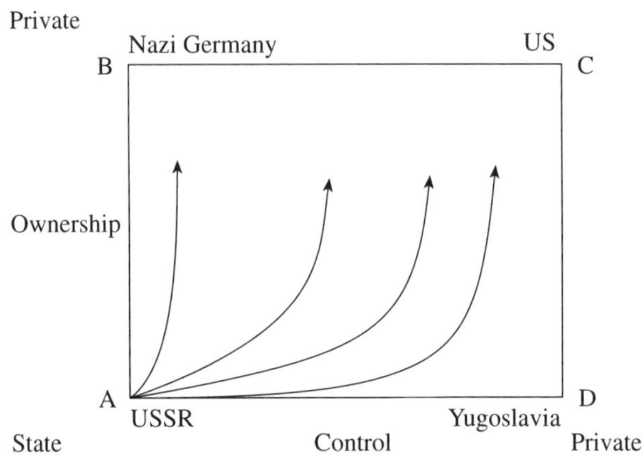

Figure 2.2 *Tableau of ownership and control*

vacuum which some new economic and political arrangements would have to fill. Change was inevitable. The real question was not, "Will change occur?" but instead, "Will change lead to a new communist regime under a different name, to US-style market economics, to Nordic-style welfare capitalism, or to something altogether new?" European affection for market socialism is not dead.[21]

Figure 2.2 illustrates the range of economic systems from which these countries must choose. In this figure each point in the two-dimensional box represents a potential economic system; two characteristics determine the nature of the system, one based on ownership and the other on control. Who owns the means of production and who makes economic decisions are two distinct issues. Ownership runs along the vertical axis upward from complete state ownership at point A to complete private ownership at point B. A kibbutz in Israel may best illustrate points at the bottom of the box, like A, in which the government (or collective) owns all the important property. As one moves up the vertical axis, ownership spreads away from state ownership towards a system of broadly held, legally protected and well-defined private property rights.

Even during Soviet domination, the state permitted private ownership of a few individual properties, though not for business purposes. Small private residences were in some cases left in the hands of private owners; however, even this was not a right, but was rather allowed at the discretion of the state. Moreover, the homeowner never owned the land under the structure. All land belonged to the people; that is, to the state. The state typically owned all means of production including capital, natural resources and all land.

At the other extreme, at the top of the box all property is owned by private individuals and protected by property right laws that limit the power of the state. There are no real-world examples of this, though obviously the US, Canada, the UK and Japan are close. Even in the US the state owns parks and public lands, there are many common properties and property can be taken by eminent domain (purchased by legal right of the state).

The horizontal axis measures control, ranging from the left – central control by the state, an autocracy or dictatorship in which all economic decisions are made at the center – to the right, where there is no state control of resource allocation. The Soviet Politburo with its Gosplan clearly made many detailed allocation decisions by setting production targets and quotas for industries. For the Soviet Republic of Estonia, for instance, control resided in Moscow. Similar but somewhat less completely centralized plans were made in the satellite countries.

Classic competitive markets in which no one individual or agency has power over price decisions exemplify the far right of the box. Decisions are made in impersonal marketplaces in which all economic agents take prices as given. Economists call this atomistic competition because each individual's and each firm's influence is relatively small, like an individual atom. Again, no real-world economy reflects this extreme point, but in some Western and some Asian economies relatively high degrees of private decision-making are common. In the US, Hong Kong, Canada, the UK and Taiwan, most production decisions are privately made. Even in these cases, though, much is decided (like military allocations, education expenditure, infrastructure construction, banking regulation, environmental rules) by various levels of government.

Any economy can be located on some point in the Figure 2.2 box. Point B, for example, is a private-ownership economic system in which decisions are made by the state. An extreme example of this case would be Nazi Germany during the Second World War. While individual families and stockholders owned the capital stock, a central plan governed all major wartime allocation decisions. Nazi Germany was a command and control economy with private ownership of the means of production.

Point D is another interesting case. Here the state owns all property, yet private individuals make economic decisions. This is called market socialism: even though the state owns everything, decisions are supposed to be made by individual producers in response to price signals, mimicking a capitalist price system. One version of state ownership with private decision-making was Yugoslav worker participation and control before the breakup of the state.

Virtually all economies lie within the interior of the box, not on a boundary. Clearly one would place the pre-1991 Soviet Union close to point A at the lower left-hand corner. The state owned all important property and controlled all important decisions. Conversely most observers would place the US, Canada, Hong Kong, Japan and many European states very close to the upper right-hand corner, point C, where private property dominates and private decisions govern resource allocation.

Economies like Sweden, Finland, West Germany, the UK and France lie closer to point B, characterized by private ownership with many economic decisions made by government or determined cooperatively at the center by major power groups. High marginal tax rates, heavy regulation, detailed labor laws, incomes policies and various government–business entities suggest a good deal of concentration that differs substantially from the private market ideal.

The question we pose is, where are the newly independent European countries heading as they move away from A? This is an important question, because not all regimes are structuring reforms to accomplish the same ends, and there is a significant debate going on in these countries as to the ultimate objective of economic liberalization. In fact, we argue that some countries in our study are adjusting at very sluggish paces; they have muddled objectives and they are moving toward different outcomes altogether.

In brief, we believe that the Czech Republic is moving in the direction of C, the US model. The Estonians, who would be expected to mimic Finland, have instituted some of the most liberal reforms in Europe and are moving toward C as well. Hungary seems intent on staying in the middle of the box, with some state control of decisions and some regulation, even as it moves away from the bottom half in terms of ownership of property. Slovakia's goals were not clear while Slovakians were distracted by nationalistic concerns and uneven leadership until a change in direction with the 1999 elections. Before that, it seemed unlikely that they would aim toward C, but the jury is still out.

Bulgarians cannot decide whether they want to give up socialism or not. They may end up viewing Hungary as their role model. Russia is struggling with a new paradigm for its economic model, evidently unwilling or unable to relinquish authoritarian state control and faced with a failing economy without the social infrastructure necessary to support markets.[22]

Thus, even as European and former Soviet countries abandon communist central ownership and control, they have not achieved consensus on adopting American-style democratic capitalism. The debate in Central Europe involves many possibilities: the American model, the European welfare state "middle way," managed Hungarian gradualism, old-style centralization. Voters in many places are loath to give up the old guarantees, and politicians override voters' wishes at their electoral peril.

PROBLEMS IN POLITICAL ECONOMY

Economic reformers face considerable political resistance. We have identified four distinct political impediments to economic reforms. These are summarized in Table 2.2. (1) The benefits of reform are spread widely and occur incrementally. Some groups and individuals, however, will clearly perceive themselves to be absolute or relative losers of reform. Potential losers include those most successful in the old system, such as managers of state-owned enterprises, high-level bureaucrats, communist intellectuals and ideologues and some military leaders. They also include wards of the state like veterans and pensioners. (2) Reforms to transform a socialist state into a successful private market capitalist system will not occur on their own; reforms are public goods – the government must install them and then enforce them, at least until they become firmly established. This requires a capable and committed polity. (3) The public entities that must create economic reforms will themselves be relative losers, as they disburse power; thus economic reform is an unnatural political act. (4) Economic reform requires an initial period of sacrifice before benefits can be enjoyed and thus the political system must create a climate in which people will accept delayed gratification.

Table 2.2 Why societies resist reforms

1	Benefits are diffuse and costs are concentrated.
2	Economic reform is a public good.
3	Government must self-devolve, an unnatural act.
4	Gratification is delayed: costs now, benefits later.

Mistrust of government, widespread after the collapse of the USSR, has hampered reform by exacerbating these political problems. Communists had perpetually preached that short-term sacrifice would eventually lead to better living conditions. The abject failure of the communist system has caused people to become jaded about government promises of a better future.

Finally, most new countries are not likely to convert to US-style capitalism, but may instead move toward a system in which the public sector will retain significant control over industry and distribution of resources. This outcome reflects residual socialist influence that will retard economic growth and could lead to stagnation.

Advocates of reform toward Western private markets must surmount these many political difficulties. To do so, they must determine their ultimate goals, make them clear to constituents and then convince constituents that benefits of reform will exceed the costs. This makes economic reform a problem in public choice[23] and a task involving a great range of complex economic issues.

At the same time, economic analysis must play a central role in designing reforms; in order to sell reforms, reform advocates need to understand what each reform will achieve and they must understand why such achievements are worth the costs. This brings us to the purposes of the next three chapters: first, to analyse the intended consequences of economic reforms, and second, to design an economic model that will capture the crucial consequences of these reforms for rising living standards.

NOTES

1. For an excellent survey of economic policy reform literature, see Rodrik (1995b). Both political scientists and economists have contributed to the growing field of political economy in analyzing the reform process: See Bates and Krueger (1993), Haggard and Webb (1994), Krueger (1993) and Przeworski (1991).
2. See Barro (1989, 1996a), Haggard and Kaufman (1995), Helliwell (1994), Huntington (1993), Olson (1991, 1993), Przeworski and Limongi (1993), Scully (1988), Sirowy and Inkeles (1990) for a range of arguments, some empirical. Barro (1997) provides an excellent survey.
3. Barro (1997), p. 52.
4. As early as April 1991 Yeltsin identified these reforms as imperative first steps. According to Aron (2000) Yeltsin "listed … a 'sharp tightening' of the state budget to preserve the viablitity of the ruble; de-etatization and privatization of state enterprises; the creation of an independent banking reserve system; land reform; and foreign investment. Most important and most urgent, however, was price liberalization within a 'sufficiently short' time" (p. 427).
5. An important example arguing that these reforms are key is Blanchard et al. (1992). Other examples from a large literature include Gelb and Gray (1991), Hare (1991), Hillman (1991), Murphy et al. (1992). Dewatripont and Roland (1995) offer a formal argument for gradualism that depends upon correct sequencing of reforms. Murrell (1995) points to the limitations of the approach that starts with the desirable ends without adequately allowing for the historical and cultural context. Williamson (1994) polled "techno pols" but could find no consensus that necessary political conditions for successful reforms.
6. Monetary policy here includes a monetary system with price stability and a fully convertible currency.
7. Not only Westerners understood the need for these reforms. Igor Gaidar's autumn 1991 "programme was a drastic diminution of state ownership of the economy … To effect this tectonic shift, Gaidar counted on far-reaching liberalization (liberation from state control) through an extensive privatization of the economy, on agrarian reform (which would permit the selling and buying of land), on the opening up of foreign trade and, most of all, on freeing from state control the prices of almost all products, goods and services … He was especially adamant about … a drastic reduction in the budget deficit and the introduction of a strict monetary policy", Aron (2000), pp. 486–7.
8. Tom Hazlett provided numerous useful suggestions on the political economy of the transition process. We even adopted some of his ideas.

9. For two perspectives on the costs of reform, see Milanovic (1993) and Winiecki (1990).
10. Brainerd (1998) provides a superb analysis of the winners and losers in Russia. Her analysis is based on data from cross-section household surveys. Losers tend to be older, less educated, and those with shorter expected lifespans. These characteristics are all consistent with our voter growth models developed in Chapters 4 to 6.
11. Fernandez and Rodrik (1991).
12. Ham et al. (1998) attribute much of the political resistance to reforms to unemployment. They show how the Czech Republic managed rapid privatization and growth of services. Meanwhile the Slovak Republic suffered much more unemployment, partly as a result of different policies but partly because the military factories lost most of their business.
13. The economist largely responsible for developing this approach to collective action analysis is Olson (1965).
14. Some of the gains and enforcement can be captured by property taxes, so the public sector is able to spread the costs even to those who may try to "free-ride" on the system.
15. An important complication is that government itself results from a market. This market forms various coalitions and laws that accomplish ends attractive to the governing coalitions. We do not develop this fully, but believe that election results set the stage for market reforms.
16. For a thorough introductory treatment of public goods, see Rosen (1999), Chapter 5.
17. Some consumers will prefer controlled prices, low quality and little variety, but net gains from market prices will be positive.
18. Offsetting these forces is the countervailing force that democracy puts on bureaucracies. Voters, elected officials and political parties have interests in these outcomes as well and can, perhaps only crudely, impose their will on public-sector entities.
19. Miles Kahler (1990) discusses the "orthodox paradox" of reform processes in less-developed countries, the fact that government agencies and officials must design and implement changes in their own functions and the nature of the state itself.
20. Yeltsin and his Minister of Economy and Finance Gaidar were well aware of the need to move fast. In their view "further procrastination would be suicidal," Aron (2000), p. 488. The Russian parliament endorsed the Gaidar–Yeltsin reform package by a vote of 876 to 16. At the same time they allowed one year to achieve reforms via decrees. See Aron (2000), p. 491. It was widely recognized that Yeltsin was taking a political risk in instituting reforms.
21. For the basics of market socialism, see LeGrand and Estrin (1989). Kornai (1990) analyzes the Hungarian version and the transition process away from it. Bardhan and Roemer (1992) present the case for its rejuvenation. Oskar Lange (1938) and Abba Lerner are credited with the analytical development of the concept of market socialism; path-breaking essays are in Kowalik (1994), and Stiglitz (1994) provides a critical comparative analysis. See also Easton and Walker (1997).
22. The Russian presidential campaign for the June 1991 election revealed the deep divisions on economic policy. Yeltsin's most formidable opponent, ex-Prime Minister Nikolay Ryzhkov, called "for a 'regulated market economy'" and referred to the anti-capitalism position as "...the choice for which our forefathers fought." "Ryzhkov "absolutely opposed private ownership of land." Yeltsin called for radical economic reform and a "'new market model' of the economy... 'within the shortest possible time'", Aron (2000), p. 433. Note that opponents of capitalism stressed the historical high ground in this debate.
23. We define the public choice approach as the economic analysis of collective actions and decisions; in other words, economic analysis of the political process.

3. Why private markets work

In order for reforms to be sustained, citizens must appreciate their benefits. Economic analysis demonstrates the value of five economic reforms. (1) Price liberalization is essential for the creation of a market system in which prices reflect social costs and in which these costs are paid by those who receive the benefits. (2) Private property is essential for capitalism. If property rights are well defined, the private owner is the residual claimant and therefore acts as the consumer best able to satisfy his own wants and as the producer inclined to satisfy consumer demands while husbanding resources and minimizing production costs. (3) Well-designed fiscal and monetary institutions and policies ameliorate business cycles, reduce crowding out and promote price-level stability. This last facilitates private decision-making by not allowing inflation to vitiate price signals. (4) Industry restructuring and deregulation reduces bureaucratic rent-seeking and empowers producers to maximize profits, which minimizes costs while satisfying consumer demand. (5) International trade liberalization exploits countries' comparative advantages, maximizes the benefits of specialization and fosters technology transfer. Free trade also eliminates the rents that local monopolies would otherwise enjoy and thus reduces the concentration of power in the hands of former *apparatchiks* and state managers.

Even though the political system may resist these reforms, each will improve economic efficiency. Inefficiencies are "failures" in both private markets and in government. Central and Eastern Europe continue to be troubled by the evident failure of planners to deal with environmental degradation and by their tendency to exacerbate monopoly power by protecting state-owned monopolies. Replacing planning with private markets and replacing the state banking system with an independent private banking system may free government officials to deal more effectively with such failures of the market system and of the political system.

WHY THESE REFORMS?

We have seen that reforms needed to achieve competitive markets are likely to encounter serious, persistent political resistance when introduced into socialist states. Consequently, economic reformers need to build a mandate in order to overcome these political impediments.

Table 3.1 Five generic economic reforms

1	Price liberalization
2	Property privatization
3	Macroeconomic stabilization
4	Industry restructuring
5	Trade liberalization

A necessary ingredient of such a mandate is clear understanding of the potential benefits of each reform proposal. In this chapter we analyze the consequences for private markets and for social welfare of five reforms, listed in Table 3.1.

We provide economic justifications for these five generic economic reform proposals.[1] One can show that regardless of local political or social conditions, each reform will lead to improved social welfare; that is, better living conditions for the typical citizen. Although local political and social conditions will have a big effect on whether or not a particular reform can be implemented and sustained, we first consider the economic efficacy of the reforms themselves.[2] We explain why successful modern market systems work better with each reform than without it. There are many reasons to justify each reform, and many reform consequences have interactive effects with other reforms. We highlight the key points favoring each reform in its own right and comment briefly on some of the interactive effects.

Even though almost everyone in newly independent European countries pays lip service to private markets, actual reform measures often encounter considerable resistance. Thus, it is essential to understand exactly why certain reform measures will lead to a better way of life in formerly socialist societies. We briefly define each reform and explain how it will improve living conditions; specifically, how it will change the rules of the system and how the new rules lead to a superior economic outcome. We will also review the sources of political resistance that each specific reform is likely to encounter.

PRICE LIBERALIZATION

Socialist planning involved highly centralized administered prices rather than a decentralized market-determined price mechanism. Socialist states had overtly set relative prices that held the costs of necessities (as defined by the bureaucracy) low, and the costs of luxury goods (also defined by the bureaucracy) high. Consequently, the prices of foodstuffs, energy for heating, rents, medical care and public transportation were low, while prices of radios, televisions, holiday rentals, entertainment, foreign travel and other consumer exotica were high.[3] Price rationing was by fiat.

Administered prices meant distorted relative prices, so that the price system was unable to serve its allocative function. In a private market system, the unimpeded interaction of buyers and sellers determines the price of each product. Prices act as the signals that cause resources to move to their best uses in an economy; they generate the phenomenon that Adam Smith called the invisible hand. On the supply side, productive inputs are drawn to their most efficient uses as producers strive to maximize profits. On the demand side, consumers allocate their incomes among products so as to maximize satisfaction. Given the existence and protection of clearly defined property rights, consumers and producers interact freely in the marketplace to determine prices. This interaction is voluntary and makes both economic agents better off. Decentralized markets function to improve social welfare, as if guided by an invisible hand, operating without the help of a central planning committee.

In a centrally planned economy, planners establish quotas for production levels of necessities. This was necessary as the administered prices were too low relative to incremental costs to bring forth adequate supplies. Production quotas were often not achieved, so that additional means of allocating scarce goods and services were also employed. Several methods were common. One was to restrict demand by limiting access to outlets that carried desired products. To shop at certain stores or to visit certain resorts or to attend certain events required membership in an elite group such as the Communist Party, the Central Committee or the Academy of Sciences.[4] Allocation among competing buyers was accomplished by extensive reliance on queuing, given excess demand at fixed prices.[5] Another method was to raise the price of a good via a "turnover tax," a tax with the purpose of giving planners some price flexibility in order to respond to shortages or surpluses.

Price liberalization amounts to relying on the impersonal forces of supply and demand to determine relative product prices. One obvious virtue of a market price system is that a product's price serves the allocation function by seeing to it that supply and demand are equal at a market-clearing price. Central plans are not needed to determine supplies, and demand need not be controlled by artificial limitations.

Do market-determined prices in fact lead to superior allocation in some meaningful sense, or are markets merely a different way to allocate? Market-determined prices have several distinct social advantages over administered prices. First, the market-clearing price of the product generates enough revenue to cover costs of production, including opportunity costs. Opportunity costs include the market value of all resources employed, even those already owned by the firm; they are inevitably higher than accounting costs. No other means are needed to get producers to provide the amount demanded by the market.

Second, the cost of producing the good is paid for by the consumer who reaps the benefits of the good. This allocation method places the cost of production on the consumer who gets the goods. The person who benefits pays the costs. Costs are not arbitrarily shifted to some third party. This means also that one knows at the point of consumption the costs incurred. This links costs directly to benefits, so individuals automatically are made aware of the full opportunity costs of consumption. When costs are separated from benefits in time and space, inefficient (that is, not least costly) allocations are likely to result.

There is a third and perhaps most important, yet subtle, reason that market-determined prices improve social welfare (well-being). Consider the effects of price liberalization on the price ratio, P_b / P_c, of any two arbitrarily chosen goods, *b* and *c*. Suppose that good *b*, say bread, was set by the central planners below its market-determined price relative to the price of good *c*, say cheese. This is equivalent to saying that the administered prices distort the relative prices of the two goods compared to the relative prices that consumers in a private market would set on the basis of their own personal preferences for the two goods. Based on the distorted relative prices, set administratively, consumers will be encouraged by prices to buy too much bread (the cheap good) and too little cheese (the expensive good) in terms of their own preferences. They will be worse off.

This means that, after price liberalization, the price of bread will rise relative to that of cheese:

$$(P_b / P_c)|_{Administered} < (P_b / P_c)|_{Market.}$$

The higher relative market price of bread and the correspondingly lower relative price of cheese will induce consumers to increase their consumption of cheese at the expense of bread, and they will do this precisely because it is in their own self-interest to respond to price signals. Since consumer preferences now are driving the price system, the reallocation of resources away from bread consumption toward cheese consumption must represent *ipso facto* an improvement in social welfare, or well-being.

The mix of goods in the consumer bundle will represent an improvement in the utility (satisfaction) that consumers obtain from a given level of expenditures after price liberalization. In heuristic terms, price liberalization leads to a new market price structure intended to reflect tastes of the sovereign consumers, whether bourgeois or not, rather than the tastes imposed by some bureaucratic agency. This result drives our treatment of price liberalization in the growth model in Chapters 4 and 5; we argue that price liberalization increases the utility of a given level of consumption expenditures enjoyed by the representative consumer in the growth model.

This social benefit of price liberalization coincides with a reallocation of resources that results from a change in relative wages. While prices of frequently purchased items like bread were artificially low and shortages common, liberalization of prices means that some whose incomes go primarily to basic foodstuffs or other so-called necessities now find these goods less accessible. Counteracting this effect is an increase in wages of those who produce these necessities. Thus, for some consumers the purchasing power of their earned income from wages falls after price liberalization whereas for others it rises.

This result may explain the perception of some that after price reform, people went from a world where goods were cheap but unavailable to a world where goods were plentiful but unaffordable. In a functioning market economy this cannot be true in equilibrium. High prices of goods coincide with high incomes for the producers. These producers include farmers, clerks and other workers engaged in the production and distribution of the goods. They earn income to improve their own living standards. This reflects Say's Law: supply creates its own demand. In a transitory disequilibrium stores could be abundant with goods that people cannot afford, but in a market economy the prices would have to fall or the mix of goods change, and a fundamental point of markets is that they evolve toward equilibrium. Producers cannot make money if they do not sell goods. Especially in Central and Eastern Europe, at least until the collapse of the Soviet Union and the CMEA, basics like bread, heating oil, rents and public transportation were cheap and, while perhaps of low quality, plentiful. Some of those on the margins of existence, the very poor whose incomes go mainly to necessities, would be worse off immediately after price liberalization, especially before higher prices generate more competition and therefore lower prices.[6] We emphasize that the benefits of price liberalization take effect because production becomes more competitive. Where privatization did not lead to more competitive behavior, for example, where powerful individuals effectively stole companies, the result was often monopoly capitalism. In many cases in Russia price liberalization meant higher monopoly prices without the pressure of competition to lower prices and increase output.

PROPERTY PRIVATIZATION

Transfer of the means of production from state to private ownership dramatically illustrates the transition from socialism to capitalism. According to Karl Marx, capitalism is most fundamentally defined in terms of the ownership of the means of production.[7] Capitalists are called such because they own the capital stock; the proletariat owns none. They are employees of the capitalists. Marx argued that the social destructiveness of capitalism and the basis of its inevitable end derive from exploitation of the working class by capitalists. The two classes are by definition opposed, and power lies with control of the means of production. As conditions deteriorate through recurrent and worsening depressions, the proletariat will eventually revolt and take over the system. Privatizing property as a step toward economic liberalization must deliver something beyond symbolism or it too will encounter political resistance. What exactly is the economic virtue of private property?[8] Certainly, it has the political advantage of disseminating power away from the state toward private individuals; but is there an economic justification for unequal private distribution of the ownership of the means of production?

The answer lies within the fundamental nature of capitalism. Private ownership of productive property makes the owner, whether it be one individual or a host of stockholders, the residual claimant of returns to the property.[9] This fact makes property owners operate as Adam Smith asserted they would, in the best social interest. That is, owners have an incentive to see to it that their resources are put to the most desired social use, as expressed by consumers in the marketplace. Increased productivity and competition in labor markets combined with the ability of capital accumulation to create wealth led naturally to higher wages and better working conditions in every Western country. This unambiguously improved the lot of workers after the early stages of the industrial revolution. Producer surplus additionally allowed funding of welfare programs to raise the living standards of others.

The *deus ex machina* of this process is the profit motive. Driven to maximize their profits, owners of productive assets seek to maximize the rate of return on those assets. They do this by producing at least cost and by producing the goods most in demand. Thus, private property leads to important social advantages over state ownership. For any given level of output, costs are minimized; given cost conditions, output is maximized and producers respond to consumer demand in choice of products.

An important result of this interaction between producers and consumers is that private markets produce higher-quality products, a greater range of qualities and a greater variety of products than do central planners. One of the truly startling features of Western market economies to outsiders is the rich range and variety of products produced.

This advantage of private ownership applies to allocation over time as well. A private owner will, in response to changes in market prices and market interest rates, use assets between time periods in a socially optimal way. He also does this in response to the profit motive. If he will earn more by storing his assets for future use, he will do so. If not, he will use the assets for current production and thus consumption. This applies to assets in the form of natural resources, as well as to capital stock.

Despite the important advantages to private property rights, they are by no means easy to introduce into a socialist society. Privatization can be complex, tendentious and sensitive. The rights of private property owners must be legislated, and workable enforcement mechanisms must be devised. For instance, can a private owner of rental property evict tenants? Does the owner have the right to set rental rates, determine maintenance and repair policies, determine safety features for the property? These issues are controversial even in the United States; they are more so in countries formerly controlled by the Soviet Union with their socialist tradition of guaranteeing the rights of tenants.

New legal codes are required, along with new training for lawyers and judges who will enforce the codes and adjudicate disputes. Privatizing property is an expensive and ideologically subtle public undertaking. Transfer of ownership rights is especially controversial, and numerous rules and regulations often restrict and accompany such transfers. This reflects partly a Marxist fear of concentration of power among a few capitalists and partly the belief that the public sector must set standards that protect relatively weak tenants or consumers. As a practical matter, transfer of property can hurt innocent bystanders, especially in the case of restitution policies. Consider a residence in an urban center that was decades ago converted into a restaurant. Suppose the pre-war owner comes back to claim the property. He may have sound legal rights to the property, but if he reconverts the property into his residence, the workers in the restaurant lose their jobs.[10] Such events can cause people to oppose property reform.

A practical problem in transferring ownership to the private sector is choosing mechanisms and criteria for transfer. Who should get the property? How do they pay? And who decides these things? In their approach to privatization, Central and Eastern European countries have treated three types of property differently: (1) residential property, both houses and flats; (2) small retail shops, stores, farms and medium-sized firms; and (3) larger state-owned enterprises in manufacturing, chemical production, mining, telecommunications, energy, transport and large-scale agriculture.

The state sometimes permitted individuals to own small residences, though not the land under them. After the Soviet collapse, privatization of small retail shops and firms and small farms occurred without much difficulty. Acquiring adequate funding was evidently not a prohibitive problem for potential merchants, sometimes borrowing in groups, and many small private enterprises now characterize the retail markets and produce markets of most of Central and Eastern Europe. This part of the privatization process has been rapid and thorough.

Factories, utilities and other state-owned enterprises have been harder to privatize for a variety of reasons. This has been especially true of the very large state monopolies. Among the most important reasons has been confusion over asset values, liabilities, contracts and property rights. This problem is naturally more complex for large enterprises than for small properties in which physical assets are easily defined. Natural intransigence on the part of ministries, management and workers has contributed to the problem, as has the complex web of interlocking debt obligations woven into the financial structure of firms and the banking system.

Finding legitimate buyers for large state-owned enterprises has not been a trivial task, aggravated by the lack of clear accounting measures of value and a clear notion of what a new owner's rights would be. Who locally has enough financial capital to buy such large firms? There has been considerable variation among countries with respect to their methods of privatization and their willingness to welcome large foreign buyers. Several types of candidates emerged initially – fewer than had been expected, because of the poor condition of firms, the uncertainty of legal structures and high degrees of political risk in some places. Some foreign companies that bought firms proceeded to close them down, lay off the workers and cannibalize the physical capital. This was not anticipated and was obviously unpopular, making it hard to convince local citizens that transferring ownership from the state to foreigners was an improvement. It was difficult to argue that shutting down major firms was in the best interest of workers.

A second potential set of buyers included the criminal element and former party bosses and plant managers; in many instances such buyers undertook "spontaneous privatization." They stripped saleable assets, stole saleable products and shut down what was left of firms.[11]

Reformers tried to find local funding sources, often by developing local stock markets and creating mutual funds (typically investment funds based on government vouchers) that would allow access to ownership rights to citizens. The degree of success of this approach is subject to dispute. Developing local financing took time, which allowed solidification of entrenched resistance to reform. It also exposed the damages of financial shenanigans like pyramid schemes.[12]

The mass privatization schemes employed in Czechoslovakia more directly involved the people, giving them a political stake in property ownership from the start.[13] The Czech government distributed vouchers in the privatization process that people used to buy ownership rights in firms or in investment funds. Difficulties in initiating the system may have contributed to the Velvet Divorce in which Slovakia split off from the Czech Republic. In the case of vouchers gathered into investment funds, state ownership of banks seriously hindered the privatization process when the funds were held and administered by those same banks. The dilution of ownership also left managers with too much control, which often resulted in sluggish restructuring.

Bureaucrats, managers and workers had yet another reason to resist privatization. Even though many of these firms were comparatively inefficient and in some cases virtually worthless, some individuals had been the residual claimants of monopoly quasi-rents – returns that had resulted from short-term monopoly power and accrued to strategically placed bureaucrats, managers and workers. Entrenched in these firms, people undertook non-productive activity in order to redistribute gains toward themselves. Such unproductive activity is called rent-seeking. Rent-seeking activity stalled early attempts at privatizing large firms. Since initial attempts at privatizing often led to dissolution of the firms with cannibalization of the remaining capital assets, the powerful forces of entrenched special interests found time to array their forces against privatization.

Financial interconnections have proven an even tougher nut to crack in trying to privatize large state-owned enterprises. In the old regimes, the means of transferring intermediate product between enterprises had been financed through banks by a Byzantine system of credits and debits, often determined in part by the state-run central bank in negotiations with various plant managers and financial officers. Toward the end, some of these financial arrangements were casually ignored because the officers of state-owned firms, including banks, knew the system was likely to collapse and that their firm's financial obligations would then become someone else's problem. Financial obligations were typically maintained on the books without transfers of financial capital ever occurring. Permanently bad debt was endemic in Soviet-run European banking systems and it remains so in a few.

After the Soviet collapse virtually every country's large firms held debt instruments from many other large firms. Some of this debt was counted as assets to the firm or as assets to the banking system. This system of interlocking debt created a serious problem for the privatization process. The existence of large debt obligations incurred by former managers put off many potential buyers.

Another impediment to privatization of large firms emerged. If a firm with many financial obligations was seen to be worth less than these obligations, this could threaten the solvency of its creditors even if they were otherwise healthy. In other words, reformers feared that privatizing large enterprises could spillover into failures that would affect healthy enterprises along with unhealthy ones. It is one thing to accept the worthlessness of a failing business, but quite another to see healthy firms damaged in the process, especially if this could trigger a larger financial and industrial collapse. Thus, a legitimate debate emerged between those who wanted to privatize quickly to overcome political resistance and those who counselled caution and a slower path. This, in addition to resistance from rent seekers, has in some countries slowed privatization, especially of large state-owned enterprises.

Residential privatization encountered an entirely different set of problems. These were due in large part to visceral fear of homelessness and lack of experience of, or information about, property values. Disputes about historical property claims and debate over exactly what rights landlords should have also slowed the privatizing. Even in Western Europe and the US, rent controls and legal restrictions on eviction imposed by local government entities are not uncommon. Some Czechs claim that rental property rights in Prague are more liberal in the classic sense than in New York, and we tend to agree with them.[14]

Despite all these practical difficulties, the basic point, that the purpose of privatizing the means of production is to improve the productive efficiency of capital and other non-labor inputs, still holds. Privatization completely alters incentives for producers.[15] Efficiency in production and improvements in products pay off. Analytically, privatization reform amounts to improving the productive efficiency of non-labor inputs. In the growth analysis that begins in the next chapter, we treat privatizing property as increasing the level of output derived from any set of inputs; that is, privatizing acts like an increase in society's technological capacity to generate output from a given level of capital inputs. We also believe that privatizing the means of production leads to an increase in the marginal product of capital. In Chapter 5 we link these effects to the growth model.

MACROECONOMIC STABILIZATION

Macroeconomic stabilization has two principal components: fiscal policy and monetary policy. Fiscal policy refers to budget decisions of the government, and monetary policy to management of the money supply and interest rates by monetary authorities, typically the central bank. Apart from financing public sector outlays, the economic goals of these two policies include stabilizing the average level of prices, maintaining high employment, smoothing the business cycle, targeting interest rates and managing international exchange rates.

The two policy tools, fiscal and monetary measures, can be jointly set or can interact less formally. In the US and Germany they operate on two usually cooperative yet distinct tracks, since the central banks are quasi-public and independent of control by the elected executive or legislative branches of government. Regardless of policy structure, though, sound fiscal and monetary policies must provide an essentially stable environment in order for private markets to flourish.

Practical implementation of sound stabilization policy in the emerging states requires significant institutional changes in the banking system and the government. Perhaps most important of these institutional changes is the redesign of banking systems from state monopolies into two-tier systems that privatize commercial and industrial lending decisions while leaving regulatory supervision and money supply policy in the hands of independent central banks. Another major institutional change is replacing revenues provided by the old state enterprises with a viable tax system. A third thorny problem needing careful institutional adjustment involves purging the banking system of the bad debt obligations that resulted from the egregious inefficiencies of years of central planning and its consequently poor-quality capital stock. That the assets of the banking system consist in some cases of financial obligations of non-performing state enterprises does not bode well for workers, veterans, pensioners and others whose wealth consists of bank liabilities. Governments, increasingly sensitive to the power of the electorate, in many places are hesitant to let banks fail, further slowing the potential benefits of liberalization.

According to John Maynard Keynes in *Essays in Persuasion*, Lenin said that the best way to destroy a country is to debauch its currency. Indeed the history of hyperinflation in Europe and the former Soviet Union means that price-level stability is the top priority of stabilization authorities in nearly all emerging countries. Inflation, especially virulent hyperinflation, will destroy any attempts at reform.[16] The economics literature has focused a great deal of attention on this issue. We should not, however, miss the underlying conflicts inherent in stabilization that result from the desire of officials to meet competing and often conflicting goals related to growth, employment, cyclical stability, exchange rate and interest rate targets.

Fiscal Policy

Fiscal policy reform on both the expenditure and the tax sides has been important in the new Europe for four major reasons. First, sound fiscal rules tend automatically to adjust the difference between spending and taxes, the deficit or surplus, countercyclically. Such rules were not in place under the Soviets. Second, most governments' budgets were in substantial deficit at the time of the Soviet collapse, and central banks frequently funded these deficits by printing money, thus generating inflationary pressures. Reducing budget deficits became a top fiscal priority.

Third, reducing deficits in turn meant that spending had to be cut and taxes raised. Unpopular under the best of circumstances, these changes had to take place during severe slumps caused by the structural shocks of the demise of the USSR, by the collapse of the CMEA, and in part by the worldwide recession of the early 1990s. Spending cuts had two unpopular distributive consequences: government withdrawal of financial support from poorly run state-owned enterprises accelerated their demise and resulted in losses of jobs and worker incomes, and payments to various wards of the state such as pensioners and veterans had to be reduced. Both measures inevitably alienated significant blocks of voters.

As industry was privatized, governments had to create new revenue sources with new tax systems.[17] Tax collection was especially difficult as personal income taxes and effective business income taxes were unknown, and as former governments had lost the confidence of the people. Most new regimes adopted value added taxes (VAT), which are hard for firms to avoid and easy for states to collect. Unfortunately, a short-term consequence of VAT is to increase prices.

Finally, government deficit spending, even in a regime in which public debt instruments are not marketed, competes directly with the private sector for savings. Profits of healthy firms drained off in taxes to finance income support programs or to prop up inefficient firms are earnings that cannot be invested in productive capital. This is classic "crowding out" of private domestic investment, which slows growth. Thus, reducing the deficit reduces the extent to which the public sector competes with the private sector for savings. A decline in crowding out could be expected to lead eventually to more private domestic investment and thus more economic growth.

The basic purpose of fiscal stabilization, then, is to reduce the government's direct allocative role in the economy and to reduce deficit spending. From the point of view of our growth analysis in the next two chapters, we treat fiscal stabilization as reducing government spending and transfer payments to wards of the state. Less government spending also implies lower implicit tax burdens, but a lower deficit means taxes fall less than the sum of transfers and spending.

Monetary Policy

Sound monetary policy, an essential ingredient of successful private markets, has been difficult for some new governments and surprisingly easy for others. Two first structural steps were required before monetary policy as practiced in the West could be undertaken. First, as noted, two-tier banking systems had to be created to replace monopoly state banks. Central banks in the former communist states had monopoly power over all financial transactions, including normal central bank responsibilities and all activities of financial institutions (usually savings banks of some sort).[18] In new two-tier systems, one tier is made up of private commercial banks that compete with one another for both deposit and loan customers; the other tier is a central bank with arm's-length supervisory, inspection and regulatory duties over the commercial banks while acting as banker to the central government.

Equally important, the new central banks (except in countries with currency boards) are responsible for managing the money supply, and this brings up the second necessary structural change: the monetary authority must be somewhat independent of the fiscal authority.[19] The central bank must be free to determine monetary policy without being under the control of fiscal authorities. Whether executive or legislative, fiscal authorities are by definition subject to political pressures. They should not be able to force the monetary authority to finance budget deficits by printing new money; such measures lead inevitably to inflation pressures. This point is currently less relevant to countries with currency boards (for example, Estonia and Bulgaria) and may be less relevant also to countries that are joining the EU and subsequently adopting the euro.

Establishing true central bank independence has proven politically difficult in some countries in the last decade, and the result has been a few monetary disasters, for example in Bulgaria in 1996 and in Russia in 1998.[20] To understand why monetization of budget deficits leads to disaster, one must recognize that a monetary authority has economic policy goals besides serving as banker for the government. One is to help stabilize the economy by leaning against business cycle forces, by slowing the growth of money and credit in expansion and by speeding growth in contraction. Another is to keep the growth of money steady enough and low enough to prevent price-level instability and inflation. The control of inflation is important in order to maintain convertibility of the currency within a viable exchange rate regime.

Apart from international currency implications, price-level stability is valuable for two distinct domestic reasons. First, central banks are responsible for seeing to it that government-issued money can perform its basic functions as a medium of exchange, a unit of account and a store of value. If money's value relative to goods is falling through inflation or if its value is unstable as a result of price-level fluctuations, then money ceases to perform its task of facilitating transactions and saving. This alone can wreck every other reform effort, and it can destabilize a banking system.

Second, without price-level stability the system of relative prices is unable to perform its allocative function. If the price level is unstable, then buyers and sellers cannot easily distinguish relative price changes from absolute price changes, so that the signaling function of prices is vitiated. This again strikes at the very heart of a capitalist economy and can cancel all reform gains. Indeed, a growing body of evidence argues for the view that inflation leads to slower economic growth, and that growth rate response to changes in the rate of inflation is large.[21]

Monetary stability is obviously very important, yet money plays only an indirect and implied role in the growth model developed in Chapter 4. Without a formal monetary instrument in the growth model, we infer monetary and fiscal stabilization as operating mainly through the government budget.[22] Country-specific monetary issues are discussed in each of the country case studies of Chapters 7 through 12.

INDUSTRY RESTRUCTURING AND DEREGULATION[23]

One of the most difficult reforms in the newly independent European states has been industry restructuring and deregulation. Regulation of all business formed the very soul of socialist regimes, and the structure of finance, accounting, management and control were all in deference to central control. Communist economies incorporated extensive commercial, financial, industrial and social regulation – for example, in the form of job guarantees, wage controls, tenant rights and landlord obligations. In some countries heavy regulation is not perceived to be a social or an economic problem. Where the role of the state in managing lives and controlling business conduct is simply assumed and accepted, the costs of such regulation are not widely discussed nor well understood.

Those who benefit from regulations always defend them, and this includes bureaucrats who enforce the regulations. This rent seeking on the part of government officials who obtain financial and non-pecuniary returns from regulation is common in the West as well as in the East. While much regulation merely reflects inefficient rent-seeking behavior, much regulation also reflects well-intentioned social goals to protect worker safety, encourage worker input into decisions, insure fairness in hiring, provide various kinds of social insurance and so on. Every Western nation has modified the effects of the market system to a degree by the passage of social legislation – for example, unemployment compensation, harassment laws, child labor restrictions, minimum wage levels. Such regulations in Soviet regimes stifled market activity, except perhaps for small rural produce markets. In the West economists recognize that while regulations may reduce market efficiency, some regulation is inevitable and useful (for example, financial market regulations and bankruptcy laws). Getting the balance right is a constant battle. Democracy keeps the disagreements open and public, and makes their results generally tolerable.

Some countries (like Bulgaria, Hungary and Slovakia) may privatize state-owned enterprises and other property or at least decentralize ownership to sub-national governmental entities, while maintaining invasive government regulations and control. In our judgment privatization without significant deregulation can be a poor halfway approach to achieving private markets. Nominal private ownership without private control and independence of action can lead to distortions and economic inefficiencies.

For instance, if a plant manager is unable to choose his own workforce and set his own wage policy, his key tools for managing labor input in order to achieve optimal market outcomes are removed. If firms are forced to modify decisions in order to meet some ancillary social objectives rather than to maximize profit, then they will be unable to perform the function that Adam Smith envisioned for producers, that is, to provide goods that consumers want at least cost. Adam Smith's invisible hand can be crippled, even with private ownership of the means of production, if deregulation is not undertaken at the same time. Most economists agree that a major reason for persistently higher Western European unemployment (compared to the US) is rigidities in labor markets due to heavy regulation.

Regulations to enforce rules that foster competition and rules that control managers who have taken ownership of companies may actually have to be increased during the transition period. Someone has to constrain state managers who have perverse incentives to pilfer the firm's property. This problem has been widespread in transition economies. Many large state enterprises were virtually stripped of assets before legal privatization could take hold. Minority stockholders need to be protected from well-connected majority owners who have obtained stock interests without guarantees for the minority holders. The detail of restructuring and regulation requires extensive analysis to see to it that it promotes market competition, rather than supporting entrenched interests.

Growth models do not formally include regulatory mechanisms and are inadequate to analyze regulatory costs on a case-by-case or industry-specific basis. However, there is little doubt that regulation impedes production and we therefore model it as an effective tax burden on capital that raises the costs of doing business. Viewed in this way, regulation's costs to growth can be represented as a direct burden on the user-cost of capital.

Obviously, some regulation imposed on industry is worth the cost to society, but these costs should be taken into account in deciding whether regulations are worth maintaining. This raises the more general and complicated issue of the role of government in market economies, which we will turn to after discussing trade liberalization.

TRADE LIBERALIZATION

The classic benefits of free trade based on Ricardo's theory of comparative advantage are well known and compelling. The larger the trading region, the greater the degree of specialization and the larger the production possibilities set. Trade expansion is invariably a win–win situation for both trading parties. (There may be winners and losers within a country as trade grows, but comparative advantage theory tells us that net gains will be positive.) Even in a more realistic world where products are made up of components from many countries, the social welfare arguments for free trade hold.

A second benefit of free trade, causing economists to advocate it in overwhelming numbers, is that it fosters technology transfer. Most research and development takes place in a few of the world's advanced countries. Once a new idea is discovered, it is readily available to anyone who chooses to use it.[24] Why, then, do many less-developed economies fail to adopt new technologies? In Chapters 4 and 5 we argue that it may be because the local firms do not have to. They can continue to operate below an efficiency frontier if they are protected from foreign competition. Increased exposure to foreign competition can lead to faster and easier adoption of new technology.

Another distinct advantage of free trade in Central Europe and other emerging economies is less obvious than comparative advantage and technology transfer, but is perhaps as important. This has to do with limiting the gains from local monopoly rents and from those who illegally acquire state-owned enterprises. Some countries like Bulgaria and Russia have been victimized by a good deal of spontaneous privatization.[25] In other countries like the Czech Republic, Hungary and Slovakia, large state-owned monopolies have had the political power to resist privatization or breakup. This need not be a problem if these firms are forced to compete internationally. If free international trade is realized, then even large firms will be forced to become more efficient in order to compete. Furthermore, the rents captured from state monopolies by insiders will be limited once these new firms have to compete with outsiders. Such competition militates against the existence of insider trading and commercial theft.

A fourth important benefit of free trade is financial. The need to convert currencies, implicit in free trade, imposes discipline on monetary and fiscal authorities. Regimes that fail to stabilize their currencies are quickly exposed when international financial markets assess the risks of holding such currencies. Trade generates incentives for monetary authorities to control the money supply or to consider a regime with a non-convertible currency. A non-convertible currency seriously hampers trade because it either reduces trade to barter or forces traders to work through the financial bureaucracy.

AN ACTIVE ROLE FOR GOVERNMENT

We have shown that price liberalization, property privatization, macroeconomic stabilization, industry restructuring and trade liberalization, while politically difficult to implement and sustain, are essential elements of an efficient market system. However, we have also shown that political realization of these reforms is problematic. The problem is that government officials, elected and appointed, are required to decentralize and therefore relinquish power.

This problem can be explained in terms of principal–agent analysis. Voluntary sacrifice by officials is in the interest of their principals, the private citizens whose power increases as the authorities' power declines. Still, it is at odds with the immediate self-interest of the agents themselves, the very government officials who are overseeing dissolution of the old central authority and the reshaping of responsibilities.

As difficult as this public choice problem is, another rather subtle aspect of the relation between the public sector and the private sector in a market economy makes transition even more complex. While private markets must seem attractive to those who have lived under central planners, private markets are by no means perfect. A central tenet of modern economics involves the concept of "market failure," the inability of markets, under certain conditions, to perform efficiently. For our purposes, three impediments to efficient private sector market performance – monopoly, externalities and public goods – are most important.[26]

To understand market failure, one must first recall the key concept of market success. Driven by decentralized decisions that are guided by market price signals, producers satisfy the wants of consumers, given constraints on resources and technology. Consumers maximize utility, given constraints on incomes and prices. Under competitive conditions, these private decisions lead to an optimal (efficient) allocation of scarce resources. An optimum is not achieved, however, in instances of market failure. Monopoly, the power of one economic agent to influence price rather than to have prices set in the competitive marketplace, illustrates market failure. The monopolist fails to achieve a social optimum by restricting output and raising prices.[27] Historical examples of monopolies include public utilities like telephone services, refuse collection, gas and electricity, water and possibly transportation systems like roads, railways, and airlines. In some cases these are enterprises with large economies of scale; that is, unit price continues to fall as the scale of production grows. This provides an incentive to create a monopoly, as more producers mean higher costs of production. Such companies are called natural monopolies.[28]

Externalities, a second well-known source of market failure, occur when social costs that result from the action of an economic agent are external to the cost calculus of that agent; that is, social costs exceed private costs.[29] A familiar example is the social cost incurred when a factory pours toxic waste into a river. Unless a charge is imposed for use of the river as a disposal device, this cost is external to the allocation decision of the firm. Consequently, in his optimization problem, the factory manager undervalues the river relative to its true social worth and so pollutes the river beyond the social optimum. Other river users incur costs they did not create: fishermen catch sick fish, children swim in polluted water. Note that there are no market incentives leading the factory manager to internalize these costs.

The concept of a public good, used in Chapter 2 to explain the difficult politics of reform, is a third important market failure. Public goods have two technical properties: marginal costs are small relative to fixed costs; and once fixed costs are incurred, users cannot easily be excluded from receiving the services. A national defense system designed to defend an entire country is the classic example. Once installed, most costs have been incurred; the army is trained, equipment and capital are acquired, missiles are built and troops are deployed, and it is no longer feasible to exclude from protection anyone who refuses to pay his share of the costs. Individual agents, whose self-interested motives are appropriate to success in a private market, have an incentive to free ride, that is, to pay less than they value the service on the assumption that others will pay for them. Due to free riding, private markets will underfund provision of public goods.

Instead of relying on private markets, the political system decides how much defense to provide and then compels citizens to pay for it. Public goods, or largely public goods, include inoculation against contagious diseases, construction of hydroelectric dams and construction of road systems. Left to its own devices, the private market system provides suboptimal amounts of public goods' services.

Assuming that market failure is possible under well-known conditions such as monopoly, externalities and public goods, what role can the government play to correct these failures? Solutions are varied and controversial. They range from the government taking over the economic activity itself to prohibitive laws, taxes, fines and subsidies, to government setting new laws that provide incentives for producers to correct the market failure. National postal services are examples of governments producing services that are not adequately supplied by the private market because they are largely public goods.[30] Some cities provide refuse collection. A less intrusive government solution allows production by a private monopoly that is regulated by a government agency to constrain abuse of monopoly power. Public utility regulation in the US illustrates this approach. While private firms provide water, electricity and gas, they are regulated by public agencies.[31] The Public Utilities Commission and the Federal Trade Commission in the US are examples of government regulatory agencies designed to constrain natural monopoly powers.

A third approach to market failure is to devise new rules that simulate conditions in which private markets work well. An example is the creation and enforcement of private property rights for a resource where its use would otherwise be external to the cost calculus of users. For instance, assigning property rights to a river to an environmental group or to the owners of adjacent property would then give these owners an economic incentive to charge the appropriate "simulated" market price for use of the resource. This would result in optimal use of the resource in the same sense that ownership rights of cows assures the optimal social use of cattle or ownership rights of oil reserves assures the optimal use of oil resources. The principle is the same in the assignment of transferable pollution permits by a government agency.

The question that arises is which if any of these government solutions is the best for dealing with any specific market failure. This question is not resolved in conventional economic analysis. The appropriate role of regulators is a major area of research, as is the optimal method of dealing with externalities. Which goods are public goods and how to provide for them is also controversial. Some economists argue that government regulations can make matters worse, even if the private market results in inefficiency. Put another way, one cannot in general guarantee that the public sector dealing with a market failure will improve social efficiency. Policy analysts should at least try to compare the outcomes among various strategies before settling on an approach to market failure. A theorem does provide a guide to the use of government when market failure occurs: select a public government solution only if it improves on the outcome generated by the private market.

Public choice analysis explains why there is no guarantee that government can correct market failures efficiently. When we expect the public sector to outperform the private sector we sometimes slip into an "optimal policy" presumption; namely, that the government can efficiently select, implement, monitor and enforce an optimal policy. We lapse into the comforting notion that there exists a rational entity called government that has the public interest at heart.

Mainstream economic analysis is based on the generality that individuals behave rationally – that is, that humans are self-interested, and within the context of the rule of law, we behave in order to maximize our own objectives, subject to whatever constraints we face. Government is an aggregation of individuals, grouped into agencies or parliaments or bureaucracies or committees. Each has its own agenda and priorities. Pressures on decision-makers come from interest groups, political constituencies, colleagues, the public press and other media, political parties and bureaucracies. We should not be surprised that the public sector can be inefficient, too; there is such a thing as "political market failure," or "government failure."[32] This analysis should encourage us to examine carefully every government solution to instances of market failure, looking for a restructuring of incentives that will generate voluntary efficient behavior.

FAILURE: MARKETS VERSUS PLANS[33]

The previous section explored the notion of market failure, the unintended failures of private markets to work efficiently. Without any deliberate actions, monopolies, externalities and public goods arise in market systems. These failures provide one rationale for an economic role for government in a free enterprise economy, although the precise nature of the government's role is a hotly contested issue. Communist systems relied heavily on the public sector, centralizing nearly all economic functions.

With this sort of deliberate planning, we might expect the Soviet system to work better in some ways. For example, Westerners agonize about methods for achieving incremental reduction in levels of air pollution; a thoroughly centralized planning bureaucracy ought to be able to set, implement and enforce policy more easily. In fact, in some cases of market failure, socialist regimes actually performed more poorly than decentralized systems. Environmental degradation in particular was worse in centrally planned economies than in the private market economies of the West. This outcome requires some explanation, but surely standard market failure arguments will not do. Why was the Soviet environmental regime so disastrous?[34]

Market failure problems and solutions complicate the transition from central planning to markets, because they imply some legitimately larger roles for government even after a market economy has been established. The key questions are what the government should do, and how. Simply withdrawing government from the economy, while difficult to implement, is an easy task to conceptualize; but shifting government out of many traditional activities and then shifting it into others is more complex. To accomplish this shift in the face of tendentious ideological disputes is politically tricky.

The basic ideological disputes were discussed in Chapter 2. Marx criticized accumulation of private wealth because it generates economic disparity between people. It also enables capitalists to exploit workers. Communists predicted a better government by the proletariat after workers took over the economy. The government could be counted on to improve labor conditions, to provide safe and healthy living conditions for all and to redistribute wealth and income fairly (according to needs). That was the intention.

An enigma for analysts of reform in Europe is why planners failed so thoroughly to deal with some areas of traditional market failure. It is clear that they failed to perform the enormously complex allocational tasks that markets undertake; but where the theory of market failure calls for central action as a solution to a particular problem, then should one not expect planners to perform better than minimal-intervention market economies? Why did they not?

There are ambiguities. Was the East competitive in the public goods sector, such as in defense and public transportation? Here the record is mixed. The Soviet military held the West at bay for a long time, though direct US–Soviet combat never took place. A proxy war in Korea and showdowns in Berlin, Turkey and Cuba were standoffs.[35] Public rail in Central and Eastern Europe is often very good, but some air transportation is less reliable than in the West. Failures like Chernobyl suggest inferior infrastructure.

In the case of monopoly, the central planners performed rather worse than Western economies. Concentration of production was excessive in the Soviet Union even where it could not be justified by increasing returns to scale. Bureaucrats found huge, highly integrated single plants more convenient to control and operate than many smaller firms.

In the case of environmental standards, the West clearly has the better record. Environmentalists and economists were shocked to see the terrible condition of natural resources – land, forests, rivers and air – behind the Iron Curtain.[36] Problems that the Western economies had struggled with for 30 years had gone unrecognized by central planners in the East. Why did the central planners allow the environment to become so degraded relative to conditions in the West? There are several possible answers. One possibility is that the general failure of the economy to perform well resulted in lower living standards so that the demand for a clean environment was less than in the relatively affluent West. This view is hard to reconcile with the aggressive role environmental issues played in the 1980s grassroots protests against Soviet projects that would have affected the environment. In Bulgaria, for instance, Greens spearheaded the anti-communist ecoglasnost dissent that eventually led to collapse of the one-party regime. The first mass movement in Estonia in the late 1980s was organized to protest against a Soviet water project.

A second possible answer is that public sector failure in the East exceeded public sector failure in the West. That is, the structure of the political system in the East contributed to the failure of the public sector to solve externality problems. There are two competing subhypotheses here. One is that quite distinct from the socialist system's failure to manage the economy, a one-party political system fails to respond adequately over time to the wishes of the population, due to severe principal–agent problems. Another is that the central planners failed to correct market failure situations precisely because in a socialist system, it is the planners themselves who are culpable in undervaluing and exploiting resources. To resolve such a failure the planners would have had to admit that they were the source of the failure in the first place. The *mea culpa* approach was never popular in the Soviet world. If the authority in a police state is the polluter, to whom does one complain? It takes dissidents to protest against the *status quo*, but a one-party system tends to stifle dissent. Externalities are problems for market economies and may require government intervention, but environmental conditions may well be even worse under near absolute government control. In addition, environmental measures are one of many demands on government funds, one that is easier to cut than others (such as pensions or education).

In our view public sector tolerance of monopoly, poor-quality infrastructure and environmental degradation reflects inherent flaws in one-party central planning. Government failure in the form of severe principal–agent problems, absence of checks and balances and unlimited power of a single-party leadership contributed to poor government even where one may have expected the government to be relatively efficient. Furthermore, when the government bureaucracy itself is culpable, a single-party central system cannot easily redress the problem without admission of guilt.

If public choice analysis explains the failures of central planning in solving problems that Westerners see as the result of inefficient markets, then perhaps public choice analysis can suggest solutions as well. Getting government out of businesses on economic efficiency grounds will free public sector energies to focus on problems it handles relatively well. This suggests a rarely recognized cost of inappropriate government intrusion in the private sector. It distracts public officials from doing what they are capable of doing well (for example, postal delivery services, tax collection, public health protection, law enforcement, national parks preservation) and prevents them from recognizing and solving problems that they cause. The movement toward markets and reduced government influence in areas in which private markets excel may result in better government performance in areas of conventional market failure.

Our task in Chapter 4 is to develop an economic growth model to which we can link the five reform measures and thus formalize our argument that economic reforms lead to economic growth.

NOTES

1. By "generic" reform proposal we mean the general concept of each reform, such as establishing market-determined relative prices rather than administered prices. We do not discuss in this chapter, except in an occasional example, the specific legal and political nuances that apply in a particular country. Local considerations will be taken up in subsequent individual country chapters.
2. Blanchard, Froot and Sachs (1994) contains eighteen analyses of the reform process after two years into the transition. The authors, some prominent in advising on reforms, discuss many of the countries we review as well as other former Soviet Union countries and other Central European countries. We are building on the Peter Murrell (1995) critique of these papers as well as presenting our own analysis of events in individual countries.
3. In Warsaw at the time of the takeover by Solidarity a color television set cost more than four months' rent. In market economies without rent controls, color televisions run closer to one-fifth of one month's rent.
4. Hedrick Smith's *The New Russians* contains numerous examples of such favoritism. In Budapest, the authors attended banquets held at special restaurants formerly reserved for members of the Academy of Arts in Hungary.
5. The authors learned that Central Europeans had adapted so well to standing in queues that they missed the queues after private markets developed. The queues had become social gatherings. This is an excellent example of human resilience; people adapted by turning a waste of time into a social event.
6. The term "necessity" is of course subjective. Many people living on the margin of existence in the US may have color television sets even though they may not have indoor plumbing.
7. Some scholars contend that the Soviet system was no longer influenced by Marx, but consider the following: "Deputy [to Yeltsin's communist opponent in the presidential elections, Zyuganov] Valentin Kuptsov noted 'ruefully' in May 1986, 'the abolition of private property is one of the main tenets of Marxism' and 'still causes the most arguments'", Aron (2000), p. 599.
8. Good contemporary sources on privatization are Estrin (1994), Frydman et al. (1999), Frydman and Rapaczynski (1994), Frydman et al. (1993a, 1993b) and Brada (1996).
9. Yeltsin clearly understood the importance of private ownership. In 1996 he stated: "From the very beginning

it was clear to us that there will be no progress if we retain the state's, that is nobody's, property and if people are denied the right to own the means of production ... Privatization was a matter of vital importance." Aron (2000), p. 620.

10. Locals told the authors of imminent removal of restaurant managers in Prague, Bratislava and Tallinn. Courts had to deal with conflicting rights on a case-by-case basis in each country.
11. Georg Winckler, professor at the University of Vienna, told at a conference on Eastern Europe of cannibalization by managers of large state-owned enterprises in Bulgaria. He found radically different movements in producer and consumer price indexes hard to explain. Inflation according to the consumer index was rising rapidly. At the same time, prices according to the producer price index were falling or stable. How could these two sets of prices move so differently? It seems that producer prices were low as managers of large state enterprises sold assets and products to satellite firms that were surreptitiously owned by the managers themselves. These firms then sold the product at inflated prices on the open market, reaping the difference between low producer prices and high consumer prices as profit. This scam is just one illustration of how insiders could exploit the transition from public to private ownership.
12. Such pyramid schemes became nationally known in both Russia and Albania. The Czech Republic also suffered from illegal insider activity while trying to privatize. It is still difficult to know to what extent illegal activity was taking place, how far complaints of such activity reflect a socialist dislike of capitalists, and whether such activity reflects judicial incompetence or ignorance of private property rights. Ponzi schemes in borrowing come up later in our discussion of monetary policy. Such schemes appear to have happened in fairly localized financial markets, at the central government level and in banking systems.
13. Schroder (2000) analyzes the difficulties in principal–agent issues associated with the specifics of mass privatizations.
14. Jiří Schwarz of the Liberal Institute in Prague has made this point to us as well as to an economics conference in Hong Kong in 1996.
15. Frydman, et al. (1999) shows that privatization to insiders tends to be ineffective in generating (at least immediate) efficiency gains. Their horizon is three years and they find that only firms privatized to outsiders tended to become more efficient, and these only on the revenue side of the ledger. By insiders they mean both workers and existing management. This problem has been especially pronounced in Russia.
16. An interesting historical note is that the Supreme Soviet retained control of the central bank until October 1993. This central bank approved loans to enterprises at annual interest rates of 20 to 30 percent at a time when the rate of inflation was 2500 percent in 1992 and 880 percent in 1993. It appears that the communists continued to undercut capitalism as Lenin had advised.
17. See Martinez-Vazquez and McNab (2000) for a detailed analysis of tax policy measures in newly independent states of the Soviet Union and its satellite countries. They reinforce our view that history has a serious influence on new-regime tax policies. They also note that enforcement of tax policy is often more difficult than passing laws to set up tax systems. Finally, they observe a tendency to exploit tax policy for special political ends rather than to opt for neutrality, simplicity and efficiency.
18. The first commercial bank in the Soviet Union was established in Tartu, Estonia in 1988.
19. The issue of central bank independence is explored thoroughly in Willett et al. (1995).
20. The financial system in Russia was worse than in the satellite countries. Russia actually used two distinct systems of money. One was the ruble. Large firms were permitted to use the ruble only to pay wages. Financial transactions for products exchanged between enterprises did not involve transfer of rubles, but only the recording of charges according to the financial arrangement worked out with the central bank. Thus, two entirely distinct monetary mechanisms were operated simultaneously. Unfortunately, the non-ruble system continued within many state-owned firms in Russia well after the collapse. This system effectively permitted firms to "purchase" inputs and intermediate goods from other firms without actually paying anything. Thus, firms all have a set of books containing various promises to pay with no effective mechanism to insure payment. Failing state enterprises continue to operate.
21. See Barro (1996c), Fischer (1991) and Willett et al. (1995).
22. Integration of money into the growth framework is beyond our capacity here. There is an extensive and important literature on financial reform in newly independent European countries. See, for example, Hochreiter (1995) and Thorne (1993). For inflation and growth in the former Soviet Union see Fischer, Sahay and Vegh (1996).
23. Some refer to this reform as microrestructuring.
24. Two exceptions to this point are restrictions on export of sensitive military analysis and new ideas that require expensive new capital assets in order to transfer them.
25. The "oligarchs" in Russia are notorious for exploiting the system. This may reflect in part that the authorities do not know how to deal with such lawless capitalists.
26. These phenomena are described in Rosen (1999) or in any other modern public finance textbook.

27. Competition in some instances (for example, natural monopolies) can lead to higher prices. Even in these circumstances, one can show technically that monopoly is inefficient in a Pareto-optimal sense.
28. In recent years economists and policy makers have recognized the distinction between a natural monopoly in infrastructure (like telephone lines and pipelines) and in provision of service flows utilizing a competitive environment.
29. Positive spillover effects can also be external to a private decision.
30. Technological advances are rendering many publicly provided postal services obsolete.
31. Here too new arrangements are being developed to allow greater competition among service providers in markets that have traditionally been viewed as natural monopoly industries.
32. As in the case of "market failure," these expressions imply inefficient or suboptimal outcomes, not failures in the usual sense of the word.
33. This section explores the likelihood of political (government) market failure; that is, the sources of inefficiencies in processes involving collective choice in the public sector. This is an important element of the public choice approach described in Johnson (1991).
34. Roemer (2000) analyses the relation between the level of public bads and the degree of egalitarian focus in democracies.
35. More recent military conflicts involving Russian hardware and tactics against US forces and proxies (for example, Afghanistan and Iraq) revealed the Soviet conventional military tactics and equipment to be much less effective than previously thought.
36. While walking on the Charles Bridge over the Vltava River in the middle of Prague in 1989, one of the authors asked a Czech why no one was boating on the river. As we walked nearer to the water, the stench gave the answer. The river was so polluted that no one could bear to be near it. However, unlike the Cuyahoga River in Cleveland, the Vltava has never caught fire, and in fact boating is now popular again.

4. Growth models for assessing reforms[1]

The social value of reforms is reflected in their influence on growth of income, consumption and utility (consumer satisfaction). Both neoclassical and endogenous growth models provide a number of specific channels for reforms to affect consumers and for subsequent policies to influence growth. These models focus attention on the need to accumulate physical capital. Such accumulation in turn requires saving. Growth models provide a number of insights as to how policies may enhance or retard growth. For reforms to succeed, they must assist in the process of reorienting resources into optimal new technologies embodied in new capital that requires in turn development of domestic human capital. The best solution to a growth model is called the optimal steady state, the best of the economy's long-run equilibria. It is shown to consist of three conditions: the marginal decision rule of the optimizing forward-looking consumer, the marginal decision rule of the optimizing forward-looking producer, and the dynamic time path of capital.

Growth models provide lessons for reformers; for example, savings must generate enough productive capital to hurdle replacement requirements, population growth and labor quality improvements for growth in living standards to be enjoyed. Social gains from capital formation may exceed the private returns on capital as a result of technological spillovers embodied in new capital. Free trade promotes growth by fostering adaptation of new technologies from advanced economies. Policies to encourage savings and forward-looking behavior and policies to foster new technologies and orientation of savings to productive capital will contribute to growth.

REFORMS LEAD TO GROWTH

The *raison d'être* of economic reform is growth – higher living standards for the typical citizen. In a democracy, reform policy failure exposes reform candidates and parties to electoral defeat. Consider the example of stabilization policy. While it is easy for outsiders to insist that local political officials balance budgets and manage money growth to prevent inflation, achievement of these reforms consumes considerable political capital by local incumbents and can result in defeat.

The politics of stabilization reforms are especially tricky in societies where many workers hold jobs in the obsolete military equipment field or in inefficient state-owned enterprises and where many voters (who may also be pensioners, veterans or other wards of the state) depend on public largess. Raising taxes is problematic when public sector legitimacy has collapsed amidst social chaos. This has been the case in some former Soviet states. If a cabal of wealthy entrepreneurs captures the governing apparatus, sensible and legitimate taxation is unlikely. Printing money may be the only way left for a government to cling to power. Transition regimes are tempted to run budget deficits that they finance by printing money. In such states, responsible central government budget and monetary policy is at best problematic. Sound stabilization policy exemplifies the public choice problem of reforms; unless a compelling case can be made showing that stabilization will lead to improved living standards, transition governments will be unlikely to sustain the reform.

In this chapter we develop and explain a conceptual model linking each of the five essential economic reforms to improvements in living standards.[2] Whereas in Chapter 3 we explained the role each reform plays in an established market economy, here we present a model that will show how each reform contributes to improved living standards via growth. This will allow us to place each reform in a dynamic context in which it promotes growth. We discuss the specific features of growth models and then develop more descriptively the implications of those features for emerging economies. We specify in Chapter 5 the parameter set of the growth process through which reforms will operate.

This modeling demonstrates intuitively how each reform, operating through a unique channel, can improve living standards. One also sees how different societies with different demographics, initial conditions and prospects may be inclined either to favor or reject certain reforms. This analysis reveals the root causes of the difficulties reformers encountered in the first decade after the collapse of the USSR. The linkage of reforms to growth provides the first building block of the political economy model that integrates reforms, economic outcomes and elections. In Chapter 6, we model elections and tie election results to economic performance; political events and economic reforms interact, so that politics influences economics and economics influences politics.[3] It is this simultaneous and interactive nature of political decisions and economic performance that we believe best explains the transition processes in post-communist societies.

The growth modeling here will achieve three specific objectives. First, one can understand intuitively and with minimum mathematics how a simple private economy grows. Second, one can evaluate the impact of various fiscal policies on the growth process. Third, one can see links between each reform and specific features of growth. In the next chapter, each of the five specific economic reforms (property privatization, price liberalization, macroeconomic stabilization, industry deregulation and restructuring, trade liberalization) is seen to change key parameters of the decision-making process. Specifically, growth paths that characterize the outcomes of the models are influenced in a particular way by each reform; consequently, improved living standards are directly influenced by reforms.

Among the insights our model provides is that the likelihood of support for a reform, based purely on its possible economic consequences, depends upon initial conditions (history). History also plays an important role in the creation or destruction of institutions that will support or resist reform. The importance of history in growth modeling is often neglected, since in growth models consumers are forward-looking. Nonetheless, rational consumers are influenced by their past because history informs tastes and expectations, and consumer decisions depend on tastes and expectations. History tells us about the development of institutional arrangements that provide incentives for all economic agents, including consumers.[4]

From the perspectives of different individuals during various stages of life and with certain demographic characteristics, each reform has different consequences. Different people's living standards will be influenced in different ways by each reform. This follows *ipso facto* for different groups of voters. This analysis helps to explain the varying degrees of success that countries are having in achieving reform. It also suggests the tendencies for voters to return socialists to power when reform efforts seem to stall economic activity. We argue that varying degrees of success result partly from different initial conditions (histories) and different distributions of political power across certain demographic groups, and partly from different political strategies adopted by reform leaders in each country.

GROWTH MODELING: DESCRIPTION, PURPOSES AND LIMITATIONS

Economic reforms, obviously not an end in themselves, are means to a healthier economy and a better life. They are intended to change economic institutions and systems in order to create an effective incentive system that induces individuals and institutions to behave constructively. This in turn means that reform changes the environment, and that success can occur when economic performance has improved and brought about better living standards. Better living standards – increased income, consumption and utility – can occur only through economic growth.

To evaluate a reform we must show that it will improve economic circumstances. To do this, we link reforms to the decision-making process that generates income growth, more consumption and increased utility. Growth models are natural vehicles for this analysis.[5] We develop the technical rudiments in Appendix A, where reforms are linked to specific outcome parameters. In Chapter 6 we model the political process and tie this process to the economic process with a model of elections.

The models that we describe are intertemporal representative-consumer growth models that are highly stylized, imposing very strict assumptions to insure precision. They have significant analytical virtues that make the suspension of disbelief, inevitably associated with such modeling because of necessary simplification, worthwhile. For example, in the usual growth model analysis, the key decision-maker may be thought of either as a benevolent dictator or as a large number of identical economic agents, each acting in his own self-interest as a rational optimizer subject to a budget constraint. In the former interpretation, the benevolent planner maximizes social welfare as defined by the present value of the consumer's future utility stream subject to various resource constraints.[6] In the latter interpretation, consumers maximize the present value of their future consumption streams. Both interpretations lead to the same consumption plan. On the production side, we have either the same benevolent planner who maximizes profit, or numerous identical profit-maximizing producers. Regardless of whether the decision-maker is characterized as a dictator or as a set of private producers, production is constrained by technology. Technology is represented by a one-to-one correspondence between inputs and output, that is, an aggregate production function, a single well-defined function relating inputs and output for the whole economy.[7]

For simplicity, there are only two inputs, capital and labor. Labor's growth rate is an exogenous constant – the model makes no attempt to explain the growth of population or of the labor force, which are assumed to be the same. The two inputs, capital and labor, combine to generate output according to rules imposed by the production function, which specifies technical relationships between inputs and output. The actual requirements are flexible in that different combinations of labor and capital can combine to produce a given level of output. Thus, the producers choose the mix of inputs based in part on the technological constraint imposed by the production function and based in part on the costs of the inputs (wages and capital user-costs). All producers and consumers take prices as given, since the equilibrium price set is endogenously determined.

Output in the private economy goes to one of two uses, consumption or investment.[8] Investment is the amount of output not consumed (that is, saved) that is added to the stock of capital. Thus, the production decision amounts to choosing the combination of labor and capital to generate output. Output goes to consumption or new capital investment. The capital input depreciates so that given labor force growth and the rate of capital depreciation, the overarching plan involves choosing the path of capital growth over time that maximizes the present value of utility from the future stream of consumption.

In the decentralized agents interpretation, there are two sets of economic agents, consumers and producers. Consumers maximize the present value of the future flow of utility from consumption, subject to the flow of income from wages and from the net yield on capital. Producers maximize profits subject to technology, resource constraints and input prices. Under certain restrictive (but well-known and plausible) conditions, the outcome under decentralized competitive behavior is the same as under the benevolent central planner. We explain intuitively the solution system of the model below, after discussing its purposes and limitations.

Specific Advantages of Growth Models

When economists study aggregate economic performance over time, they begin by decomposing intertemporal economic changes (indicated, for example, by GDP) into components reflecting the two principal empirical realities observed in data. First, economies tend to swing in cycles over time periods of expansion followed by periods of contraction. Problems associated with cycles are the focus of short-run economic models that deal usually, though not exclusively, with demand forces. These include Keynesian and monetarist models that highlight causes of cyclical fluctuations as well as fiscal and monetary measures intended to ameliorate such fluctuations.

The second type of intertemporal movement in economic models is the long-range secular trend that is revealed once cycles are smoothed out, perhaps by constructing multiyear moving averages of the data. Growth models focus on these long-range trends. An active and rich literature deals with the cyclical aspects of the transition process in emerging economies in Europe, and a robust literature deals with structural aspects of reforms.[9] This book addresses the hiatus remaining, the analysis of long-range consequences of the structural reforms. To analyse long-range consequences it is best to employ a long-range model – that is, a growth model. The evolution of transition economies has involved significant structural shocks, calling for a model capable of evaluating long-range, as opposed to cyclical, consequences. These long-range consequences require changes in the allocation of resources over time. Such changes can be seen, at least partly, through an intertemporal growth model.

Movements from a one-party system toward democracy and away from central planning toward capitalism imply a philosophical change in favor of decentralized decision-making and ownership. The key decision-maker no more is a dictator (or single decision-making body like a Politburo). Instead, numerous individual economic agents, each without individual power to set prices, wages and capital costs, act in their own best interests subject to prices, wages and certain government policies. Growth models are well suited to deal with a change in authority (from central planning to decentralized decisions) because typically in these models decisions are made either way. Such models also accommodate a public sector with budgets, including deficit spending, which can be used to assess the consequences of changes in fiscal policy.

A stubborn problem confronting the post-communist leadership has been the residue of bad debt left over in both the banking and non-banking sectors. Debt was incurred by firms and banks (and carried by other firms and banks) without debtors or creditors ever expecting repayment. Growth models can accommodate borrowing. State-owned firms may borrow beyond their means in what Blanchard and Fischer (1989) call Ponzi schemes. That is, they borrow to finance short-term spending while perpetually shifting the eventual tax burden into the future. (Or they sell financial assets and pay yields out of revenues from ongoing sales rather than from real net earnings.)[10] Eventually, of course, Ponzi schemes collapse and the last-period claimants suffer. A Ponzi scheme is illogical as an ultimate outcome in a growth model because it has no unique close-ended solution – there is no steady state. It may, however, provide a *deus ex machina* to explain financial policy in the USSR and the satellite states shortly before and immediately after the collapse of the old planning and trading system.

As a society shifts institutionally away from central planning, where the interests of individuals are incidental, to a system in which decisions are driven by individual utility optimizers, social goals change as well. Outcomes suddenly depend on consumer tastes for goods rather than on the central planners' abstract interpretation of the social good. Thus, it is useful to trace the implications for consumer well-being of economic reforms in an economic model, albeit a stylized one.

We consider two types of growth models. In the terminology of Barro (1997), we analyze growth using the neoclassical growth models of Solow (1970), Ramsey (1928) and others. These models are sometimes called exogenous models or neoclassical models. We also analyze more recently developed models, endogenous growth models of economists such as Barro and Sala-i-Martin (1995) and Mankiw, Romer and Weil (1992). In these newer models technological change is determined within the model; it is endogenous.

Exogenous growth models, initially developed in the 1950s, are relatively straightforward. On the demand side, a rational, forward-looking representative consumer maximizes the present value of a future utility stream subject to labor earnings and capital income constraints. On the supply side, a rational, forward-looking representative producer, constrained by technology, acts as a competitive price taker. The producer selects the mix of inputs that maximizes the present discounted value of a future profit stream. Wages and capital user-costs are determined in the market.

The public sector, represented by a government budget, uses up some output in its expenditures, transfers income and imposes various taxes. Transfer payments include disability benefits, government pensions and the like. Taxes are imposed on various private sources of income. Optimization by the two private economic agents, the consumer and the producer, creates paths for capital formation, income, consumption and utility. It is these paths which characterize the outcomes of the models. Examination of the nature of these paths and how they are influenced by various reforms comprises the analysis that follows in the section on the structure of growth models.

Technological change in neoclassical models enters the story in several ways. It may be a shift variable that raises output for any given combination of inputs.[11] Or, new technology may be brought in as a variable that augments labor by raising its contribution to output for each level of capital input.[12] Or new technology may come embodied only in new vintages of capital.[13] Neoclassical models treat technological change as an exogenous force that adds to output without costs and without using up inputs. Since it is viewed as free, it is sometimes referred to as manna from heaven.

Endogenous growth models, developed during the 1980s and 1990s, treat the rate of technological change as a variable whose value is determined within the model itself; hence the term "endogenous." Once produced, such technological change usually augments the labor input. While endogenous growth modeling has of late become a virtual cottage industry, differences between exogenous and endogenous models are actually rather modest.[14]

The driving force behind development of endogenous growth models was the prevalence of empirical evidence pointing to the importance of technological change in the growth process. Empirical research undertaken during the 1960s, 1970s and 1980s for the US, Europe and Japan indicated that technological change may explain from one-third to over half of productivity growth since the Second World War.[15] Even though technology was important, it was widely viewed, in a term coined by Edward Denison (1962), as a measure of our ignorance. That is, after researchers accounted for the contributions of observable factors like increases in the labor force and in capital stock, a large residual of growth remained unexplained. This residual was attributed to technological change. Despite, or perhaps because of, this ignorance, such a large role for technology spurred economists to try to explain the causes of technological change and then to integrate them into growth models.

The singular advantage of endogenous growth models, then, is that a key source for growth, the rate of technological change, is determined within the model. This modeling has enriched understanding of the development of new technologies and its relationship to costs, social organization and development. In other words, the growth process can be better understood and the consequences of technology can be better explained. This in turn fosters better policy analysis related to technological change.

How is one to model production of new technology? A distinctive assumption of endogenous models is that production of technological change is costly. Society must devote resources to its production; it is no longer manna from heaven and, like other investments, requires forgone consumption. These costs have been associated with research and development expenditures and with the proportion of workers involved in science, research and engineering. Sometimes the focus is on human capital inputs and sometimes on investment-specific technological change.[16]

One key difficulty in endogenous modeling is highlighted by the argument that the benefits from technological change, *ipso facto*, spill over to economic agents besides those who incur the direct costs of production. That is, if a producer invents a new design, the benefits of the concept behind the new design become ubiquitous – these benefits cannot be fully captured by the original producer who had borne the cost of production. For example, once Descartes discovered calculus, it could be used by everyone, and the marginal cost of adding a new user is zero. By its very nature new technology, in the absence of protective laws such as patents, can be applied by anyone who wants to apply it. This inherent feature of new technology means that its level of production, if handled by a private market, will be socially suboptimal. This is a classic market failure. Thus, in order to internalize technology in models, one needs to model an additional sector; even harder, the sector that is going to produce the technology has got to be organized as some kind of non-competitive firm or as a government agency.

One of the empirical implications of the early endogenous models was that significant scale economies caused increases in resources in R&D to lead to greater increases in growth rates. Has this been the case? Charles Jones (1995a, 1995b) has argued that endogenous models, as descriptors of technology in advanced growing economies, may be flawed; this important empirical implication does not hold. For about half a century, the proportion of technological workers (scientists, researchers and engineers) and the level of R&D expenditures have risen in the US, but meanwhile productivity growth has fallen. As Jones points out, increases in the proportions of labor and capital devoted to the design of new technologies should induce sustained increases in growth rates according to the increasing scale properties of the endogenous models. Jones (1995a) shows that this result is not reflected in the data; modern industrial societies have added to growth-oriented inputs throughout a period when the rates of growth have slowed down. He concludes, "the 'scale effects' prediction of many recent R-&-D-based models of growth is inconsistent with the time-series evidence from industrialized economies" (p. 759).

Jones (1998) develops endogenous growth models that do not carry the unfortunate empirical flaw described above. We utilize both exogenous and endogenous modeling here. We follow Jones in the endogenous models. Most of the endogenous growth literature has dealt with the production of new technology in advanced industrialized countries like the US, Germany and Japan. These contributions of the endogenous models are somewhat tangential to our analysis. However, Jones suggests that a simple extension of these models can provide a vehicle by which technology is transferred to developing economies. We employ this model below.

Endogenous models suggest policies such as strengthened property rights, increased investment in human and physical capital and encouragement of international trade. Some of these ideas flow from our interpretations of both neoclassical and endogenous models. Of course, many changes in economic organization called for in newly independent Europe would not require loss of consumption to bring in new technologies beyond that associated with acquisition of new capital. New inventions themselves seem less important for transition economies compared to application of existing technologies. In short, adopting well-known practices from existing capitalist democracies does not require reinventing the wheel.

The direct costs of new technologies roughly equal the costs of acquisition of new physical capital and new human capital. There is of course the need for new labor skills and new modes of production, thus both research and education will be required. But new technology can be freely adopted from elsewhere, provided local workers know how to use it. We model this effect below. Our analysis also suggests that successful economic growth requires significant political and social disruption. Political modeling in Chapter 6 incorporates these elements. We think that political and social costs are crucial barriers to successful transition.

Limitations of Growth Models

While growth models are essential in order to assess reforms properly, one should clearly understand their limitations and should be cautious in drawing inferences from them. We shall nonetheless draw some inferences that do not strictly derive from formal growth models alone. For instance, representative-consumer models contain only one type of consumer, so any possible distributive effects can only be inferred. In order to discuss the effects of reforms on different individuals, we interpret and apply the growth model in a somewhat unusual fashion.

We view each consumer as if she were at a particular stage of life (for example, she may be a new entrant to the labor force); or as if she had certain demographic characteristics (for example, she may be retired and on a government pension). In each case, we assess the effects on such individuals of particular reforms. For instance, the consequences for a consumer of tax increases or transfer payment decreases, both intended to reduce government budget deficits, will be very different depending on whether the consumer pays taxes or receives transfers. Similarly, if a policy lowers wages of some workers while lowering production costs, the effect on certain consumers will differ from that on certain workers. One's position in the society will influence whether one supports reforms that induce such changes.

To accommodate these issues, we assume each voter in our political model bases her choices on her particular self-interest.[17] Each is assumed to vote for or against a certain reform, based only on how that reform is perceived to influence that individual's personal well-being. To assess a reform, each voter views herself as a representative consumer whose tastes are hers and who bears her own particular demographic and social characteristics. In order to portray different types of individuals as winners and losers of a particular reform in the political model based on outcomes of the growth model, we extrapolate beyond the power of the growth model itself. We do this by assuming that each voter acts as if she assesses possible reforms from her personal perspective as the representative consumer.

Growth models are abstract; their bare bones are without much "real world" flesh. Our connections of reforms to growth get around this shortcoming to some extent. When we deal with removal or restructuring of burdensome regulation, for instance, we do not model a formal regulatory mechanism. Instead we include a parameter which can sensibly be thought of as representing social and economic costs of inappropriate regulations. By inappropriate regulations we mean those that cannot be justified by a market failure in which the possible regulatory (or government) failure is less than the (private sector) market failure. Excessive regulations imposed inappropriately result in increases in effective capital costs over competitive levels.

Growth models focus on physical inputs and outputs and rarely contain formal financial sectors. The government can have a budget with taxes, expenditures and transfers, but in our models there is no monetary instrument, no banking system and no monetary authority *per se*.[18] While this may seem like a fatal flaw if one wants to evaluate reforms like macroeconomic stabilization, we think it is not. A great deal of scholarly research has been devoted to the problems of newly independent European economies in the context of short-run cyclical stabilization.[19]

Many researchers have built models with monetary sectors and banking systems and reviewed the short-term cyclical stability consequences of various policies. A great deal of research also deals with price-level stability and the role of the monetary system and the monetary authorities. These efforts have generated useful policy insights. There is no question that monetary stability is an essential element of a thriving market system.

Severe instability has characterized the Russian ruble since 1991. Whether this reflects intended communist policies or not is unclear. What is clear is that refusal to adopt sensible monetary and fiscal policies has hamstrung any attempt at market reform. This is obvious to anyone who understands basic monetary theory. Our objectives here, however, go beyond explaining monetary policy failure.

In our view, the basic problem facing the transition economies is not one of short-term cyclical instability, but instead is one of significant structural change. It is necessary to analyze this situation as one in which large structural shocks hit a long-run growth model forcing shifts in capital stocks, income levels, consumption levels and utility. In particular we are concerned with the role of saving in the growth process and the remarkable difficulty that saving poses for these economies. It is not necessary to add a monetary sector and financial system in order to analyze reforms from this long-term perspective.

Both neoclassical and endogenous growth models confine themselves to one representative consumer and to one final-sector product. In such models, therefore, the consequences of price liberalization are not obvious, because price liberalization alters the relative prices of various goods, which in turn will alter the mix of goods that consumers purchase. However, a parameter can sensibly reflect the consequences of decontrolling prices and shifting to a system in which relative prices are set in private markets according to private preferences. In particular, we argue that for a given level of consumption expenditures, utility would be lower in a controlled-prices regime because such controls generate a suboptimal mix of goods from the individual consumer's point of view. This means that the benefits (utility) consumers receive from a given level of consumption expenditures will rise with introduction of a market economy in which consumer sovereignty determines relative prices.

Finally, our formal models deal with closed economies, that is, where there is no formal trade sector. This excludes direct analysis within the models of the terms of trade, exchange rates and currency regimes. Again, this may seem a serious defect, especially since one of our five reforms is trade liberalization. However, the models do not prevent the telling of this important part of the story. We will demonstrate in Chapter 5 that a model without a formal trade sector, money market or exchange rates can, with reasonable inference, be used to reveal a good deal about how various financial reforms may lead to a different set of growth conditions.

In the next section we explain heuristically the key assumptions and workings of the models. We summarize the setup of a simple model, identifying the players, their motivations and constraints, and we summarize the outcomes of the model, showing the nature of the growth paths implied by the behavior of the players.

THE STRUCTURE OF GROWTH MODELS

Demand reflects decisions of one representative consumer whom we call Robinson, whose choices generate final product demand. Supply reflects decisions of one producer, called Crusoe, who generates final output.[20] These are the only two private players in exogenous models and both act as if they are operating in a competitive economy, taking prices and costs as given and optimizing either utility or profits subject to constraints. Endogenous models add new players, producers of new designs whom we call researchers. The unique nature of technology (discovery of new ideas) requires that different rules govern the behavior of these researchers. Government will provide patents to protect the researchers' intellectual capital. The government also enters the models as a user of final product represented by a budget policy, expenditures and various taxes.[21]

The Consumer Robinson

Robinson may be thought of as an individual, as an infinitely lived household or family, or as an infinite number of identical households. He is assumed to be forward-looking, self-interested and infinitely lived. This means that Robinson considers only future consequences of policies for his personal utility; he is interested only in benefits that he expects to reap personally from now on as a result of his own rational decisions made within the confines created by the economic environment and by policies.[22]

Robinson's utility at each moment in time depends only on his consumption at that time. While utility is Robinson's subjective index of personal benefits received from consumption, he is rational, so that this index obeys certain obvious properties: utility increases with increases in consumption, but the increment to utility from an added unit of consumption declines as the level of consumption rises.[23] Choice in the consumer growth model amounts to choosing a path for consumption over time. The key parameter for such a choice is called the consumer's elasticity of intertemporal substitution. It can range from zero to infinity. We can think of two extreme examples. Rigid consumers are unwilling to exchange consumption today for more consumption tomorrow. Highly flexible consumers are willing to shift consumption between periods in order to maximize utility. Utility can be expressed by functions, just like production processes can. These functions contain an explicit parameter for the degree of flexibility of the consumer. We can all think of people we know with high and low degrees of flexibility.

At any moment in time, Robinson makes choices that maximize the present value of the future stream of utility, which is the weighted sum of utility he will receive at each moment in the future from his consumption stream. Since he is evaluating a future utility stream from today's perspective, he may discount future consumption relative to current consumption.[24] The discount factor is another parameter that distinguishes types of consumers. The discount rate can vary from zero to one. A low discount rate is associated with a patient individual who does not have to get everything right now. A high discount rate reflects an impatient individual. We may think of patient individuals as the industrious ant of Aesop's fable, and the impatient individuals as Aesop's carefree cricket.

To summarize, Robinson chooses the consumption path that maximizes his entire future utility stream, the present value of the discounted sum of utility from consumption throughout the future, where the weight assigned to each future moment's consumption is determined by the subjective rate at which Robinson discounts future utility.[25] Notice that three factors influence Robinson's decision: consumption at each time t, his subjective utility from consumption at each t which includes a value for his elasticity of intertemporal substitution, and the subjective rate of time discount. Reforms operate on these parameters, and the values of these parameters help to explain how different citizens, looking to their own best interests, will vote on certain proposed reforms.

Robinson's utility maximum is constrained by his command over resources. He receives income from two sources, labor (the product of the wage rate and the quantity of labor supplied) and capital (the after-tax rate of return on the capital stock, which he owns). He is allowed to borrow or lend on an open bond market, so that his wealth equals his human capital plus his capital wealth minus (plus) his monetary debt (monetary assets).[26] The budget constraint adds parameters through which reform proposals influence the consumer: the wage rate, the after-tax rate of return on capital and his monetary position (debtor or creditor). It also includes his tax or transfer status.

Robinson selects the consumption–savings path throughout the future, given paths for wages and after-tax capital returns. He chooses the path that maximizes his utility subject to his intertemporal budget constraint. Since he may either consume or save his after-tax income, any disposable income not consumed is saved and therefore is available to Crusoe for capital formation. This simply states that at each point in time the sources of income, wages plus capital earnings,[27] equals the sum of the two uses of income, consumption and investment.

The Producer Crusoe

The producer Crusoe, also a rational, forward-looking, self-interested agent, maximizes profits (the present value of his future income stream). He discounts the future profit stream by the rate of return on capital, because this rate reflects the opportunity cost of tying resources up in production. Profits are defined as the difference between revenues and costs. Revenues derive from sale of output after two types of costs, labor and capital, are incurred. Price of product is normalized at one.

Output derives from production in which technology is represented by the production function. The production function must obey certain reasonable rules: production requires positive inputs, an increase in inputs results in an increase in output, and an increase in one input, holding the other fixed, results in increased output (product) at a diminishing marginal rate.[28] Output per worker (labor productivity) rises at a declining rate as capital per worker rises.

As noted above, both exogenous and endogenous growth models allow technological change to intervene and alter the relation between the inputs and output in several different ways depending on how one wants to tell the technology story. The cleanest approach analytically is to assume that technological change augments the productive efficiency of the labor input.[29]

Assuming constant returns to scale (a proportionate increase in both inputs leads to a proportionate increase in output) makes analysis much more tractable because output per worker depends only on technology and capital per worker. Under constant returns, living standards depend on the ratio of capital per worker, available technology and on technological shocks.

Labor supply (or what is the same thing in this model, population) is assumed to grow at an exogenous constant (geometric) rate. At any moment in time, the quantity of labor in production is the product of the initial stock of workers and the growth rate of labor over time to that moment.

Given exogenous labor growth, the choice variable in production is the amount of capital per worker. This choice is constrained, because capital has an important natural characteristic: it depreciates, that is, a given unit of capital per worker declines in quantity over time because it is worn out in production. This means that output (per worker) derived from each unit of capital (per worker) declines over time. It is conventional to assume that the rate of capital depreciation is a constant (geometric) rate.

The Public Fisc

Government expenditures, which use final product, can be thought of as military expenditures or subsidies to inefficient state-owned enterprises, two important budget items that transition governments have to reduce.[30] This means that when government is in the model, final output goes to three uses: personal consumption, private investment and government spending.

The government also transfers a certain amount of income to wards of the state. These transfers include retirement and veterans' benefits, welfare payments and other direct social outlays to individuals.[31] Government transfers, unlike expenditures on goods and services, do not use final product directly but are a source of income for some citizens who may then spend the income.

Government spending on goods and services plus transfer payments are financed, at least in part, by tax revenues. We consider two sources of tax revenue – taxes imposed on each consumer's income and taxes on capital; in addition to a general tax on everyone, the cost of using capital includes a tax imposed on capital by the government. Thus, the government budget deficit (or surplus) is defined as the difference between total outlays (expenditures on goods and services plus transfer payments to individuals) and total tax revenues (direct income taxes plus capital taxes).

To finance its deficits the government borrows funds from the private savings pool. This pool also finances private investment expenditures. Thus the difference between total government expenditures (on goods and services plus transfers) minus revenues (direct income and capital taxes) equals the amount of government borrowing (or lending) on the open bond market. Normally one assumes the government, like private individuals, borrows only up to the point at which it can eventually pay off its debt.[32] This restricts deficit growth to the growth rate of the tax base.[33] It turns out that with such a constraint on long-range borrowing, deficit spending only avoids taxes in the short run. Thus the deficit has no permanent independent effects on equilibrium growth conditions apart from the effects of government spending levels.

Government fiscal activity influences Robinson's budget because sources of income are wages plus after-tax capital income minus income taxes net of transfer payments. Crusoe's profit-maximizing production decision is also influenced by the government fisc because government taxes returns on the capital input. This tax distorts the private sector away from capital formation. Finally, the time path of consumption falls as a result of government use of final output. This leaves less to be shared between consumption and capital formation. The level of government spending, total taxes and the form of taxes all alter some aspect of private after-tax income, relative input prices or the levels of consumption and utility.

Human Capital and Technological Change

We now introduce two forces that augment the labor input. One is human capital, a force related to two parameters, the level of education of the workforce and the effect of education on worker productivity. We assume that the level of human capital reflects the level and quality of education.[34] Empirically, the years of schooling or the degree of on-the-job training of the workforce are potential measures of the level of education. The productivity of this education (its quality) reflects the impact of a year of schooling on output per worker for a given level of capital input.

Technological change also augments the labor input. The origins and nature of this change are subjects of much speculation. In exogenous models, technology grows at a constant rate, so that the efficiency of workers simply improves with time. Endogenous models provide causal stories for the evolution of technology. One approach is that researchers discover new ideas that can be implemented by bringing new designs of capital on line. The rate of discovery may be a function of the existing stock of knowledge and the proportion of the labor force engaged in research instead of producing final product. Exactly how these variables, the state of knowledge and the intensity of research effort, influence advances in technology is not well understood.

How do new technologies get transmitted to transition economies from advanced societies where they are being discovered? Jones (1998) argues that new technologies are filtered into developing economies depending upon the extent to which local firms are required to compete in international markets. Without free trade, a protected local monopoly (or oligopoly) can operate below the world technology frontier because it need not compete with more advanced foreign firms. One of the basic reasons economists advocate free trade is to force local producers to compete with foreign firms. This competition, in turn, creates a mechanism for the adoption of new technologies. The rate of this adoption is restricted, however, by the level of human capital in the local developing economy. Free trade provides the channel for new ideas to transfer from advanced societies to transition economies. The level of domestic human capital in the transition economy limits the effectiveness of this transfer.

THE WORKINGS AND OUTCOMES OF GROWTH MODELS

Technology that governs production is still a two-input, constant-returns-to-scale function as described above. Now, however, the labor input is measured in "effective efficiency units of labor." The quantity of labor now reflects three features. One is the constant growth in the number of workers over time. The second is the level of human capital in the society. Even with the same raw number of workers, a workforce with more human capital will be more productive. We refer to a measure of the labor input corrected for the level of human capital as the quantity of "effective labor." The third is the growth rate of Harrod neutral technological change that makes each worker more productive. Thus the measure of labor input is augmented by new technology. We refer to measures of labor input corrected for technological change as the quantity of "efficiency units of labor." Combining these concepts, our measure of the labor input corrects the raw number of workers for the level of human capital and the rate of growth of technological change that improves labor output at each level of capital stock. Output is a function of the capital stock and the stock of "effective efficiency units of labor."

Analytically, bringing in human capital and technological change as augmenting labor makes solving the growth model relatively simple. We solve for output per effective efficiency unit of labor. Once we solve for steady-state values of output, consumption and capital in effective efficiency units of labor, we can go back and solve for the per capita values simply by exploiting the definition of effective efficiency units of labor.

Under conditions described above, private decisions made by Robinson and Crusoe produce paths for consumption, savings, investment and income. The economy so designed will achieve a dynamic equilibrium or point of rest, a steady state. A steady state describes a path over time where key variables – income, output, capital and the labor force – are growing at compatible and sustainable rates. It is characterized by three rules that define the paths of income, consumption, capital formation and utility. Two of the three rules reflect decisions by Robinson and by Crusoe, and the third reflects the dynamic properties inherent in capital as it evolves over time.

The Consumption–Saving Rule of the Forward-Looking Consumer

The first rule governs the consumer's consumption–saving choice:[35] it guides consumer Robinson in choosing the best consumption path available to him; that is, he maximizes utility over time subject to the budget constraint (governed in turn by the evolution of capital). If the consumer is flexible and patient and if he thinks he will gain more by capital accumulation than by current consumption, his pattern of consumption over time will increase. An impatient, inflexible consumer will not save much and his consumption will fall over time. The growth rate of the economy and of living standards depends on the consumption–savings choice rule, which reflects the consumer's flexibility in terms of shifting consumption between periods. If the consumer is a rigid fellow, he will not be a saver. He is unwilling to sacrifice current consumption for future consumption regardless of potential gains from capital accumulation. A very flexible consumer is willing to sacrifice pleasure today for pleasure tomorrow provided there are gains to be made. Robinson's willingness to sacrifice current consumption depends in part on the net efficiency of a new increment of capital in generating increases in future consumption. Intuitively, he will save if the saving leads to enough future consumption. This in turn depends on having an economy characterized by efficient production of quality capital in excess of the growth of population.

The savings–consumption choice (which determines how much current output the consumer is willing to put aside for capital formation) depends on consumer tastes, the efficiency of the production process, the growth of population and the durability of the capital stock. *Ceteris paribus*, flexible consumers will be more willing than rigid consumers to substitute consumption between periods in order to accommodate capital acquisition. For the impatient consumers (crickets), the savings rate is low. Farsighted consumers (ants) do not discount the future, so they will save more. Rapid population growth and shoddy (rapidly depreciating) capital both discourage savings, because more of the gross marginal product of capital has to compensate for population growth or for more rapid depreciation. These forces can each reduce the net benefits from sacrificing consumption now.

We believe that consumer patience and flexibility to some extent reflect historical and social, as well as economic, influences on consumers. Older, inflexible consumers and carefree crickets will resist policies with short-run costs and long-range benefits. Young, flexible consumers and industrious ants with foresight will tolerate sacrifice for future consumption.[36]

Fiscal conduct by the government will influence the budget constraint at each moment in time, because consumption plus asset accumulation (saving) must equal disposable income, or wage income plus capital income plus transfers minus taxes. The main effect on consumer choice of government activity depends on the level of government spending and, under disciplined government fiscal conduct, not on timing of taxation.[37]

Marginal Product of Capital Rule

Profit-maximizing Crusoe employs capital per effective efficiency unit of labor up to the point at which the marginal product of capital equals the after-tax rate of return on capital plus depreciation. Given his optimization decision, Crusoe's marginal product of capital must cover the gross yield, including depreciation and taxes, on capital income. Positive taxes on capital income means that the marginal product of capital has to be higher than it would be without such taxes. Given the diminishing marginal product of capital, the quantity of steady-state capital must be lower than it would be in the absence of capital taxes. Thus, the tax on income from capital acts as a drag on the growth rate of capital and therefore on the economy. In Chapter 7 we exploit this fact by equating excessive regulation with an implicit tax on capital.

Time Path of Capital

There are four uses of final product: consumption, government spending, spending on replacement capital sufficient to maintain capital per worker given depreciation and population growth, and spending on (net-of-replacement) new capital per worker. The steady-state rate of growth in capital expenditure maintains new capital at a level that equals income minus consumption, government and capital replacement spending. In other words, new capital formation must compete for final product not only with consumption and government spending but also with the need to cover capital replacement requirements per person.

The time path of capital, like the other two steady-state conditions, provides vehicles through which reforms influence growth. The size of government spending directly enters the time path of capital by competing with the private sector for final product.

This analysis produces a practical conclusion about economic behavior and growth for transition economies. If savings and thus gross investment are inadequate to replace depreciating capital and to supply the new capital needed to accommodate increases in the number of workers, then growth will be negative; living standards will decline. Positive growth requires that gross investment exceed the sum of depreciation plus labor force growth. If consumers discount the future, then savings will be inadequate to lead to a maximum level of consumption per person.

Put another way, the growth in capital per worker at any time (and thus improvements in living standards) equals the difference between total income (from labor and capital) and the sum of consumption expenditures, government expenditures and total replacement requirements. This result means that capital per worker and therefore output per worker can grow only if income per worker is large enough and if savings (the excess of income over consumption and government spending) exceeds labor force growth plus the rate of depreciation.

From a policy perspective, saving which leads to gross investment must be at least enough to cover both the labor force growth rate and the rate of depreciation if living standards are not to deteriorate over time. This has implications for consumers, for the financial system, for government and for producers. Consumers must be willing to forgo current consumption and save. This may be painful if income is low. Government must restrict its inefficient spending. The financial system must effectively channel savings into formation of capital goods rather than housing or consumer durable goods, because consumer goods do not increase capital in the production function.[38]

The Optimal Consumption Rule[39]

Whereas consumers who do not discount the future will maximize utility by maximizing consumption, consumers who do discount the future will maximize utility at a lower consumption level and a higher rate of capital formation. Because the marginal product of capital is larger when consumption is below the maximum, the optimal levels of capital and consumption are both lower than their maximum values. This result implies that societies populated by patient consumers (ants) will eventually enjoy higher living standards than the impatient crickets.

SAVING: THE ESSENTIAL INGREDIENT

To summarize, the economy will achieve an optimal steady state when several rules hold. First the consumer chooses the consumption–savings path where he balances the return on capital (the interest rate) against the yield needed to offset population growth and economic depreciation plus his subjective rate of time preference. If he will be better off accumulating capital for future consumption, he sacrifices an increment of consumption at time t for savings and capital formation. If, on the other hand, he feels that the present value of an increment of marginal utility from current consumption exceeds the benefits of accumulating a unit of new capital, he consumes an additional increment of output.

The second condition reflects the profit-maximizing requirement that the marginal product of capital equal the net after-tax rate of return on capital plus depreciation. The third condition characterizing the optimal steady state is that the growth rate of capital per worker equals the difference between income per worker and the sum of three terms: consumption per worker, government spending per worker and per-worker capital replacement requirements to offset depreciation and to accommodate labor growth.

The fourth condition requires that savings and capital formation must increase until the incremental return to capital, in terms of new product, just offsets consumers' time discount plus depreciation plus labor growth.

The preceding analysis implies several important policies, rarely acknowledged by reformers, for transition economies. These policies are necessary to ensure that reforms in fact lead to higher living standards. Most importantly, for positive economic growth, savings must lead to adequate formation of productive capital. Our model points out that saving must be large enough to hurdle both population growth and capital replacement requirements, before capital per worker can grow. As the initial capital stock in Soviet-dominated Europe was developed to serve a central plan, a significant proportion of total investment will have to go to replacement capital for some time in order just to sustain existing output levels. Before capital per worker can rise, capital formation must exceed replacement requirements and must also exceed the growth rate of the labor force.[40]

If a safer, less hostile environment creates more optimism, then labor force growth in the new Europe may accelerate. This would put added pressure on savings rates, as a higher growth rate of labor means more capital is needed to sustain capital per worker, before growth in capital per worker can be realized. High savings rates are critical to sustained growth in emerging economies. This has a wide variety of policy implications for reformers, ranging from installing efficient financial markets to endorsing policies that favor savings and accumulation of productive capital. It also suggests a flash point politically. Increased savings, given income, implies lower consumption, a social burden that some of these countries may be unwilling to tolerate.

The more forward-looking the population, the less consumption is required out of a given level of output to maintain the same level of utility. A more forward-looking population is likely to accept a higher savings rate and lower consumption rate, which means they will save more and accumulate capital faster and reach a higher living standard more quickly. Thus, reformers have an incentive to foster an optimistic and forward-looking population.

Crucial growth parameters will be affected by government fiscal policy, demonstrated when we introduce the government budget into the model. Enlightened government policies will recognize the importance of fostering savings, encouraging productive capital formation and urging citizens to be forward-looking.

NOTES

1. A technical treatment of steady-state equilibrium of a neoclassical growth model is contained in Appendix A.
2. Technical aspects of the growth model appear in Appendix A.
3. Murrell (1995) points out that some Western economists were disappointed in the reform progress of some countries studied in this volume. Many of those disappointed analysts were actively engaged in promoting reforms as advisors to transition regimes. Murrell argues that the dissatisfaction of certain Harvard economists with the pace and direction of reform may reflect their shared biases, rather than any flaws in the behavior of countries' leaders. In particular, he notes that history and local institutions played almost no role in the policy analysis of those economists. The distinctly mainstream model we develop here can, by linkage to a public choice framework, pull in history and local political nuance that are critical to understanding the reform process in different countries.
4. North (1990) is the father of the new institutional economics and argues cogently that history matters. Yeager (1999) provides an accessible case for the necessity of appropriate institutions to support and sustain

growth. Olson (1982) emphasizes the importance of institutional influences and provides a useful analytical framework for incorporating institutional arrangements.

5. The neoclassical model we develop is based on Blanchard and Fischer (1989) and the endogenous growth models are based on Jones (1998).
6. This is merely an analytical device and is not to be taken seriously in a public choice sense.
7. The idea that the processes of production for an entire economy can be represented by a production function is due to Robert Solow (1970).
8. Sometimes such an economy is referred to as a corn economy. Corn is produced and may be either consumed (by being eaten) or invested (as seed corn). See Appendix A.
9. For good surveys, see Corbo and Fischer (1995) and Rodrik (1995b).
10. Many of the financial problems that bedevil privatization of state-owned enterprises and that threaten monetary collapse, especially in the more centralized systems like Russia and Bulgaria, reflect this type of Ponzi scheme borrowing.
11. In the first edition of *Value and Capital* (1946), Sir John Hicks introduced this form of technological change as an element of the choice calculus of producers.
12. Sir Roy Harrod (1939) developed growth models in the UK; at the same time, Evsey Domar (1946) was developing growth models in the US. The famous Harrod–Domar model was the predecessor of the Solow models of the 1950s.
13. See Solow (1970).
14. Bernard Saffran (1998) discusses differences between endogenous and exogenous growth models.
15. See Maddison (1987), Denison (1962), Jorgenson (1995), Jorgenson and Griliches (1967) and Hulten (1990, 1992).
16. Paul M. Romer (1990) develops a model with human capital as the key resource needed for production of new "designs" of capital goods that are technologically superior to older designs. Greenwood, Hercowitz and Krusell (1997) analyzes investment-specific technological change. Hulten (1992) analyzes the social accounting implications of endogenous versus neoclassical models.
17. In a telephone conversation in September 2000, economist Tom Hazlett made the point that if one weights the outcome times the probability of one being the deciding vote, the importance of economic outcomes becomes moot. People must then be voting based on ideology rather than rational economic analysis. We take up this issue in Chapter 6 when we discuss voting behavior.
18. Monetary sectors can be introduced but are not necessary here. See Blanchard and Fischer (1989).
19. See Corbo and Fischer (1995), Portes (1993) and Willett, et al. (1995).
20. While we find it rhetorically useful to refer to one two-dimensional individual, Robinson Crusoe, these models may also be interpreted to contain an infinite number of identical consumers and identical producers.
21. Government budget policy is an exogenous control variable here, but is endogenous in the political model of Chapter 6.
22. This is sometimes referred to as a greed model because Robinson is interested only in his own well-being. It is true that this rules out altruism, taken here to mean including benefits to others in one's utility function. It is worth noting that this also rules out venal motives, reaping utility from another person's suffering. Perhaps our assumption that economic agents operate in their own interest and behave neither benevolently nor malevolently is about the middle of the ethical scale. In any case, it serves as a useful predictive device.
23. In mathematical terms, utility at time t is a continuous, twice-differentiable, non-decreasing function of consumption at t with positive first and negative second derivatives, that is, diminishing marginal utility. See Appendix A for details.
24. Shortsighted individuals (crickets) would discount future utility a good deal relative to current consumption, whereas the farsighted (ants) may not discount the future as much. We shall see that this attitude toward sacrificing the present for the future plays a major role in determining attitudes toward certain reforms and in determining the likelihood of success in growth via savings.
25. Appendix A shows the mathematical formulation of this stream expressed in continuous time.
26. Robinson may buy bonds in some models. The return on bonds must equal the after-tax return on capital so that he is indifferent between ownership rights of physical capital and bonds. Borrowers are limited by their ability to pay off the debt – this means debt growth cannot exceed growth of interest earnings on capital. A similar condition will be applied to public sector debt issue when appropriate.
27. Net private bond holdings sum to zero unless the government runs a deficit.
28. Production functions can be of many different types. The simplest, the Leontief, named after the Russian-born Harvard economist, imposes fixed proportions on the inputs so that if two workers operate one machine, then six workers operate three machines, and marginal products are always zero. More common models allow for factor substitution, so that one can increase output by increasing one input and holding others constant, but output rises at a decreasing rate. When changing the scale of production, that is, altering all inputs in proportion, a simplifying assumption is constant returns to scale in which output must change in

the same proportion. This assumption focuses on ratios such as output per worker (labor productivity). Vintage capital models assume that each vintage of capital has embedded in it a particular technology (which may increase over time), so that each vintage of inputs has its own vintage production function. In some models, different types of labor or capital are allowed, for instance, skilled and unskilled workers. The text tends to deal with generic results from many models. Details are in Appendix A.

29. Capital-augmenting technological change can be, but need not be, embodied in new vintages of capital.
30. The Yeltsin regime cut defense "appropriations by 90 percent between 1992 and 1996[.]" Still, soft loans to state-owned enterprises continued to absorb large portions of the budget. Firms were provided "free" electricity. Gas, electricity and water were state provided, but inefficiently. See Aron (2000), p. 647.
31. In Soviet Russia the welfare state was gargantuan. All women over fifty-five and all men over sixty were paid pensions. Medical care and education were provided free of charge. Housing subsidies exceeded defense expenditures; see Aron (2000), p. 647. Clearly a decline in government outlays and transfers would have a major impact on many people's lives.
32. Even under Yeltsin Russia's government deficit finance, through short-term, high-yield bonds, drained loanable funds from the private sector. Aron (2000) refers to these bonds, GKOs (Gosudarsvennye Kommercheskie Obligatsii) as a "pyramid scheme[.]" The rate of return could not be matched by the private sector, thus slowing private capital formation and impeding tax collection (p. 648).
33. This assumption is dropped when we consider financial shenanigans that lead to financial collapse usually via hyperinflation and reversion to a non-convertible currency.
34. See Appendix A for details.
35. This choice rule is called the Euler condition; it is explained further in Appendix A. Leonhard Euler is the eighteenth-century mathematician who derived the optimization methods.
36. This is not to say that all young consumers are flexible and old consumers inflexible. These are just illustrative extreme examples.
37. As long as government must offset budget deficits in the future with equivalent future taxes, consumer choice will be independent of the timing of taxes. This rules out deficits financed by excessive money growth and potential eventual default.
38. Lest this sentence conjure up thoughts of early Soviet industrialization, the reader is reminded that investment here is presumed to foster optimal technological change.
39. This condition refers to the modified golden rule. The term "modified" reflects Robinson's decision to require the steady-state increment of output from capital to cover his subjective discount rate as well as the rates of depreciation and labor force growth. The latter is measured in efficiency units given labor-augmenting technological change. Efficiency units take into account not only the number of workers but also the efficiency of each worker, which will be enhanced as available technology improves.
40. For some emerging economies, foreign direct investment is an important part of total spending on new capital goods.

5. How each reform promotes growth

> Each economic reform has unique effects on growth prospects. With growth models we can show how each reform changes behavior of optimizing agents or parameters on which their behavior depends. These changes in turn alter steady-state values of income, capital, consumption and utility. Price liberalization directly raises utility by improving the mix of consumer goods, but it reduces effective incomes of those who had benefited from low administered prices. Property privatization improves growth prospects by raising output per set of inputs and by fostering formation of both physical and human capital. Macroeconomic stabilization lowers the cost of the public sector by eliminating waste; lower military spending and fewer subsidies for inefficient state-owned enterprises leave more income for consumption and accumulation. Lower taxes and transfers help some people and hurt others, while improving incentives to produce. Industry deregulation reduces effective burdens on capital, which increases growth. Free trade improves the mix of goods, ameliorates local monopoly power, enhances competition, disciplines the authorities responsible for stabilization and fosters technology transfer. All of these reforms generate relative losers who will resist the reforms politically.

THE ECONOMIC CHANNELS OF REFORM

If citizens understand the relationship between market-oriented reforms and improved living standards, then voters are more likely to allow reformers to impose the necessary structural shocks on the body politic. In Chapter 3 we explained the theoretical benefits of each of the basic reforms needed for a market economy to thrive. In Chapter 4 we developed models to explain how private market economies with a public sector grow. We now link the two. Our modeling will bring to light additional methods by which policy can foster growth, apart from the five reforms we emphasize.

Our five generic economic reforms are: (1) price liberalization, the ending of government determination of prices; (2) property privatization, including small and medium-sized enterprises, large companies and residential properties; (3) macroeconomic stabilization, emphasizing the importance of a balanced government budget; (4) industry restructuring and deregulation, changing government's role away from running business and toward building appropriate institutional environments for commercial and financial activity; and (5) trade liberalization, encouraging competition, greater product variety for consumers and technology transfer that raises productivity. We argued in Chapter 2 that these reforms will meet significant ideological resistance in states formerly ruled by the Soviet Union. Indeed, each of these reforms requires a radical departure from the socialist system imposed by the Communist party, and each underlies a defining element of virtually every successful market system. In this chapter we show how each reform alters the basic parameters of growth models, thus changing the determinants of private decisions. We show how the outcomes of growth models are changed by each reform, given the channel through which each influences the parameters of the models. Finally, we explain why specific types of individuals, given their circumstances and tastes, will support or resist each reform.

Each of the five reforms has multiple aspects to it. None can be imposed in a simple one-step procedure. Price liberalization, for instance, while undertaken quickly for most retail products, has been harder to realize for various administered prices, including utilities. Similarly, freer trade has been realized in many markets but has been especially difficult in some, such as agriculture. Markets have been opened up to the West by most Eastern European countries, in some cases before the collapse of the Soviet Union. However, certain restrictions remain, especially on financial capital flows. The nature and degree of property privatization has been mixed. We discuss each reform in some detail.

Table 5.1 illustrates, very generally, channels through which reforms, according to our analysis, can alter steady-state variables and growth. These channels fall into three categories: consumer decisions, producer decisions and the government budget. Some parameters directly influence both production and consumption decisions and some also influence the government budget at the same time. Nonetheless, partitioning the effects by decision-maker is useful in focusing on voters in Chapter 6.

Table 5.1 Channels for reforms' influence on growth

The consumer: utility maximization
Consumption
Utility function
Subjective rate of time discount
Disposable income
The producer: profit maximization
Production function
Technological change
Human capital
After-tax cost of capital
The government: budget policy
Expenditures on goods and services
Transfer payments
General tax levels
Taxes on capital

PRICE LIBERALIZATION

Price liberalization allows prices to serve their proper signaling function, reflecting tastes of sovereign consumers and relative scarcities of supply rather than the decisions of bureaucrats.[1] Successful price liberalization results in an improved mix of products in terms of private wants and of social costs. In the growth models this amounts to a sustained increase in utility per unit of consumption. *Ceteris paribus*, this effect will make the consumer better off and voters, who are also consumers, will favor price liberalization because it will make them better off. Utility from each level of consumption will rise because a superior bundle is consumed.

There are nonetheless political impediments to price liberalization. Our model reveals an important offsetting effect of price liberalization that will make some persons worse off. Price liberalization results in changes in relative prices as an administered price set is replaced by market-driven prices; some prices rise and some fall. In the growth models, rising prices translate into falling wages; purchasing power falls for consumers whose bundle is weighted toward products with rising prices.[2] Each economic agent will weigh the gains from a better mix of goods against losses from lower effective purchasing power of income resulting from higher prices. How each consumer comes out after this calculation will depend on the mix of goods purchased.

Consider, for instance, a consumer at the margin of existence. Suppose she consumes primarily goods like heating fuel, basic foodstuffs, rental property and public transportation. These items were undervalued by administered price setting. When liberalized, these prices tend to rise, reducing the purchasing power of the marginal consumer. Longer-range market improvements in the allocation of rental units, foodstuffs, heating oil and the like take time to materialize. In the meantime, the marginal consumer will be worse off, and so the unemployed, marginal workers and welfare recipients may well resist price liberalization. Virtually all of the price liberalization laws in transition countries initially excluded many goods thought to be necessities, such as housing and public transport. Attempts at liberalizing rents, heating oil and other utilities have often met with political resistance.[3]

Consider economic agents with promising earning potential, like young educated workers, entrepreneurial and adaptable individuals. If they perceive improved earning potential from a decentralized market economy, then they will see price liberalization as a good thing. The gains from utility accruing from a superior mix of goods will exceed possibly perverse income effects.

Price liberalization has supply-side effects as well. Facing prices that reflect market demand, producers will alter their product mix toward the goods and services consumers want to buy. As with privatization, this results in an increase in effective output for every combination of factor inputs and may be modeled as an increase in technological change that shifts the production function up. Thus, three parameters of the growth decision-making process are influenced by price liberalization. Utility from each level of consumption rises. Purchasing power of income goes up for some workers and down for others. And the production function shifts upward so that output per worker is greater at each quantity of capital per worker.

PROPERTY PRIVATIZATION

Regardless of intent, the most important consequence of property privatization is improved productive efficiency in enterprises. This is expected to happen primarily because privatization changes the incentive system driving decision-makers. In particular, establishing private ownership with well-defined property rights and connecting that ownership to management link the key agents to the principals who are the residual claimants of private enterprise. The key agents are the plant managers, financial officers and chief operating officers of the firms. Their principals are the owners for whom the decision-makers work. The organization that connects the stockholders (in the case of publicly held firms) and the managers or decision-makers may be subtle and complex, involving various institutions (boards of directors, financial intermediaries) and processes (elections, shareholder meetings). Potential ownership-versus-control problems are endemic to the corporate form of business enterprise.

How Privatization Works

Improved productive efficiency reflects four distinct forces.[4] First, the output mix, driven by the profit motive, will be more responsive to market needs, so that the output itself, from any set of inputs, will be more likely to be that desired in the marketplace. In the old regimes, producers either responded to a plan or simply continued to produce goods whether demand was there or not.[5] Output decisions tied to profitability result in production of goods that will make the most money, the very goods in demand. This means that output per worker[6] will rise at every level of capital per worker.

Second, efficiency will improve from better technical uses of inputs. This reflects the fact that earnings will be tied directly, again through the profit motive, to performance. As Adam Smith understood, people who work for their own benefit are apt to be more productive than those working for the state; this idea extends to management as well as to conventional labor inputs. Thus privatization should lead to an improved technological relation between inputs and output.

Third, privatization fosters acquisitive behavior and this can translate into improved human capital. A large portion of income in any market economy is income earned by the labor input. Labor with more human capital earns more income. In our models the development of human capital reflects the amount of time people spend in acquiring education and skills. Since the gains to such education will now accrue to the private owner of the human capital, each person has a greater incentive to learn more. The quality of education also should improve. By quality we mean the translation of education and training into generating a more productive worker. As the residual claimant of the gains from applying education to production, the student now has a greater incentive to learn useful and productive information.

The fourth source of improved productive efficiency has to do with the choice of capital. Managers, driven by profits, have an incentive to choose the right capital, that is, the least costly capital–labor mix to produce each level of output. At each level of capital, then, one would expect the marginal product of capital to be higher. These gains from privatization influence two aspects of decision-making in the simplest growth model. Output from each combination of factor inputs rises in two ways: increases in the exogenous rate of technological change,[7] and increases in the marginal product of capital.

Privatization is, in part, manna from heaven – gains without costs. This result suggests that privatization reform should be unambiguously popular. Yet, even after collapse of the communist dictatorship, privatization has met political resistance, especially when attempts have been made to privatize large state-owned enterprises. We turn now to explaining why this is so.

Resistance to Privatization

A public choice approach to the results of a policy change emphasizes incentives of winners and losers. Three distinct negative responses to privatizing property can be expected. The first derives from envy; in a society dominated by the philosophy that no one deserves to have more than anyone else, resentment of the winners of privatization can dampen enthusiasm among voters.[8] This is why it is important for privatization to be undertaken in a way that gives voters a sense that the process is fair and, if possible, that everyone has a shot at being a player. If capitalism is seen to be benefiting only favored insiders, then voters are likely to resist privatization.

A second source of distaste for privatization derives from some of the methods used to bring it about. People resent individuals who acquired their property by unethical and possibly illegal means. This resentment is especially harsh when the individuals exploiting the system had been placed in positions of trust. Spontaneous privatization, insider theft of property by plant managers, executives and the like, casts private ownership into a negative light. When elected officials or their appointees are exposed handing state property to friends or to foreigners in return for kickbacks, voters get angry.

This reaction to privatization is exacerbated when foreign-owned firms buy domestic state-owned enterprises, dismantle them and sell off the assets in pieces, creating unemployment in the process. Such actions, while perhaps rational,[9] generate fear and anger in a populace unaccustomed to such sudden shocks to the business environment.[10] Even Prime Minister Vaclav Klaus in the Czech Republic suspended sales of state-owned property to foreign interests if plans for this dismantling (derisively referred to as cannibalization) were suspected.[11]

Third, privatization does produce relative and absolute losers. Some people will be fired, and this stirs fears among workers in state-owned enterprises. Managers and bureaucrats who, entrenched in the old regime, perceive themselves to be potential losers, are willing to exploit these fears. This situation presents a classic public choice problem: whereas the winners, who individually may receive small benefits, are many, the losers are few but their losses are directly perceived and potentially large. This can lead to political resistance to a reform even though the reform leads to a socially superior outcome.

Additionally, individual properties can be the object of different property rights claims. This was certainly true in Central Europe where, after the collapse of communism, property owners from the pre-Second World War era returned to lay claim on their former homes. Especially in restitution cases, privatization got tied up in lengthy legal disputes.[12]

We conclude that privatization should lead to unambiguous social gains by improving growth prospects and the levels of output, consumption and utility at the steady state. However, certain groups will resist privatization; but given the fact that net social gains are positive, reformers should be able to compensate losers and assuage fears among voters. For reform to be undertaken successfully, these problems in the political economy of privatization have to be addressed by reformers.

MACROECONOMIC STABILIZATION

Macroeconomic stabilization has two distinct interactive components, fiscal policy and monetary policy. In the case of post-Soviet economies, both fiscal and monetary policy reforms required structural and institutional change as well as change in the conduct of the authorities. Both have proven elusive and politically difficult.

Fiscal Policy

Fiscal policy refers to the government's budget. Budgets for the satellites were in deficit long before the Soviet system failed in 1991. There were three types of government expenditure in post-Soviet Europe that had to be seriously re-evaluated. Warsaw Pact military spending, which became largely obsolete with the collapse of the Soviet Union, clearly had to be reduced. Financing of state-owned enterprises, expected to evolve downward as privatization proceeds, would have to fall. Financial support for wards of the state (veterans, pensioners and so forth) was large and probably unsustainable. The first two items appear in the growth models as government expenditures on goods and services, and the third appears as transfers. Thus, three items in the government budget of the models will be altered by fiscal reform: government expenditures, taxes and transfers. Given the government budget constraint, reducing spending or transfers will either reduce the deficit or allow a decrease in taxes, as deficit spending equals government expenditures plus transfers minus taxes. How do these forces influence growth?

This analysis of fiscal reforms in Europe is not meant to be a broadside attack on the role of government. It is certainly vital to stress that capital in the (parsimonious) growth models includes public infrastructure. In a similar vein, human capital, which will later be seen to play a significant role in adoption of new technologies, is developed to a large extent by public education. We also noted earlier the new role government will have to play in establishing and enforcing the rule of law including property rights, contracts and the many rules of appropriate conduct needed by a private market economy. The public sector also is legitimately involved in dealing with externalities and public goods.

The total level of government spending and taxation influences the steady state. Capital's growth path will shift upward as a result of less output going to government use. However, steady-state capital and output will not change, because technology, the rates of time preference, labor growth and depreciation are given, and these factors determine the steady state. Even though steady-state output and the capital stock are not changed, consumption rises because less final output is consumed by government expenditures. Reducing unnecessary Warsaw Pact spending and support of inefficient state-owned enterprises would seem to be an obvious benefit to consumers.

Suppose fiscal reform reduces both taxes and transfer payments. Recall that taxes net of transfers enter the budget constraint, but taxes and transfers do not appear independently. Significant redistribution had been forced on productive workers and inputs under the old regimes, and under reformers one would expect less redistribution to occur; thus groups who are recipients of transfers and those with whom they do business will resist fiscal policy reform.

Stabilization reform should be popular since it increases consumption per worker at every level of capital per worker. This is especially true if cuts in spending reflect smaller subsidies for inefficient state-owned enterprises and the military.

However, obvious groups will resist reductions in military spending, removal of subsidies and reduction of the safety net of transfers. In particular, direct beneficiaries will resist loss of government funds. Entrenched bureaucrats and managers in large state-owned enterprises are very likely to resist withdrawal of government funding and firming of soft budget constraints. In addition, to the extent they produce military matériel, such firms have to downsize significantly or convert to consumer goods or new export goods, probably for markets outside the old trading group.

Specific households for which transfers exceed taxes will oppose reduction of transfers, whereas those for whom taxes exceed transfers will favor these same reductions. One would expect pensioners, veterans and the poor to resist reforms, and the relatively well-to-do and young, skilled workers to favor them.

Monetary Policy

Monetary reform requires both substantial institutional revisions and changes in the conduct of policy. These are discussed at length elsewhere in the transition literature.[13] Structural reforms deal with partitioning the single government-run banking system into two parts: a private, competitive commercial banking system, and a central banking system that manages the money supply, supervises the commercial banks at arm's length, and acts as banker for the government. The relation between the central bank and the fiscal arm of the government has been an important topic of research; Willett et al. (1995) and others have argued that central bank independence fosters price stability, an important goal of monetary policy.

The conduct of monetary policy determines monetary variables: price level, inflation rate, nominal exchange rate, interest rates and so forth. Central banks find it easier to achieve success in stabilizing prices and nominal exchange rates if they are free from financing excessive or chronic budget deficits. This means that responsible monetary and fiscal policies are both important to assure a stable environment for successful private markets.

INDUSTRY RESTRUCTURING AND DEREGULATION

One of the most difficult reforms for former socialist states is industry restructuring and deregulation. The tentacles of the state reached very deep into all sectors so that prices were controlled, production quotas were imposed and the means of production constrained. Furthermore, firms had little discretion in hiring and managers were little more than state bureaucrats. In the absence of private ownership, managerial incentive systems were grossly inadequate.[14] The financial system was among the most abused, given the Marxian labor theory of value that implies the inappropriateness of a return to capital. In fact, intra-firm transactions took place in Russia with shadow money. Firms and financial institutions relied instead on bookkeeping entries. Currency was used only to pay wages.

The law of unintended consequences, perverse outcomes of well-intentioned policies, set in with a vengeance. Entrepreneurial behavior was stifled, independent thinking and innovation discouraged. Many industries became ossified and their products shoddy. Resources were badly allocated and goods were produced that had no final market. Capital production was so rigid that some useless products continued to be produced even after production quotas had been satisfied. The monopoly bank that was investing forced deposits of workers funded all of this inefficient activity. Inefficient state enterprises were not generating enough real output to justify the implicit financial claims of pensioners and other savers in the state banking system.

When the Soviet system collapsed, most state-owned enterprises were in debt, usually to one another, and the levels of this debt were in many cases too great to be paid off in the foreseeable future. The central financial institutions had made loans to these firms that had become non-performing. This meant that financial institutions could not meet their own obligations (often to wards of the state and retired workers) and that many state enterprises were broke.

This was partly a consequence of poor production outcomes, which reflected the collapse but also reflected the implicit method of finance – obligations were recorded on the books and little attention was paid to the viability of these obligations or the risk of holding obligations of a firm likely to fail. Risk was not a reality because the government was always there to subsidize state-owned enterprises.[15] This is how the concept of the soft budget constraint operated; firms would be bailed out if they failed to meet their budget constraint guideline. Financial transactions among firms were often merely bookkeeping activities.

Many firms and financial institutions continued borrowing and lending even after the collapse of the Soviet regime. These financial practices, widespread and interactive across industries and even across national boundaries, resulted in massive financial obligations between state-owned enterprises. This legacy of interlocking debt created two problems. First, if one state-owned enterprise failed, it could pull down other firms that were healthy except for holding the first firm's debt obligations. Second, potential buyers would have to deal with the firm's debt obligations, which could exceed its profit prospects.

This situation reflects a classic public choice endgame problem. When a player knows the game is coming to an end, the incentives to cooperate based on future dealings begin to collapse. Until a reliable set of new commercial laws, including protection of property rights and bankruptcy laws, is established and enforced, and until a viable set of fiscal institutions is in place, firms will continue to finance their activities as they have in the past without much concern for future consequences. Regime changes may be accompanied by financial chaos precisely for this reason – the normal constraints limiting inappropriate conduct have been removed and not yet replaced by new ones. Such a situation is ripe for Ponzi scheme financing, borrowing beyond the eventual capacity to pay back loans.

This socially perverse behavior of borrowers and lenders was exacerbated when transition took place slowly. Officers of state-owned firms, uncertain about the future, felt compelled to continue to operate in the old ways even though they knew firms they were dealing with, possibly their own organizations, were insolvent. Not knowing what future penalties, if any, would accrue after failure of the soft budget constraints system placed managers in a position of moral hazard; even honest individuals have an incentive to chisel when no one is accountable. While personally rational, such behavior, stimulated by a failed institutional structure, is socially destructive.

Graft, corruption, malfeasance, absenteeism and cronyism became commonplace. Only after some time did the full extent of the damage to morale, work ethic, labor skills, financial stability and product quality become evident. The eventual degeneration of the environment and the squandering of precious resources under the Soviets were astounding.

How does one model this regulatory morass? One consequence we can demonstrate is that interventionist regulations placed an effective burden, or tax, on capital, which distorted production away from the unimpeded competitive equilibrium, the steady state. We model removal of onerous regulations as a reduction of the "tax" on capital. A burdensome tax on capital raises the equilibrium marginal product on capital and so capital and output per worker at the steady state are lower. Reversing this process through deregulation raises steady-state capital, income and consumption.

The government budget constraint changes if we view capital taxes in the model as reflecting a regulatory burden on capital that does not generate government revenues. Under this interpretation, capital taxes do not contribute to revenue, so the budget is simply expenditures plus transfers minus taxes, generating deficit spending. This changes capital's path to the old path minus the deadweight loss due to inefficient state regulation, and raises the steady-state values of consumption and capital per worker.

Economic Depreciation

A decline in the rate of economic depreciation is one likely consequence of reform, especially of deregulation and privatization. An improved market-oriented economy with decentralization, privatization and deregulation should result in a decline in the rate of depreciation of capital and thus reduce replacement requirements. This key parameter enters all steady-state conditions, as well as the steady-state levels of capital, income and consumption. The steady-state growth rates of both capital and output increase. This is important because it is not just a shift in the level of output, but a sustained increase in the growth rate of output.

Slower depreciation means a larger quantity of capital per worker. Capital's path also shifts upward as a result of a decrease in depreciation because at each level of capital per worker, replacement requirements are smaller. Therefore, given technology, more output from capital is available for consumption. This is another reason for the increases in consumption.

Marxist Ideology, and Structure and Regulation

As damaging and oppressive as obsolete structures and inefficient regulations are, one might expect widespread support for restructuring and deregulation. However, three groups may well resist this type of reform even if it can lead to increases in output, consumption and utility. First, regulations reflect the socialist view that positive social outcomes will result from each specific regulation. Institutions are subservient to this regulatory view. Certain workers may believe that they will lose relatively if they, as a group, had been favored by regulations. Academics and teachers were supported and regulated by the communists, but also carefully monitored. National academic societies carried regulatory control along with perks for membership.[16]

Furthermore, regulations and their supporting institutional arrangements reflected Marxist doctrine, and an ideology does not simply evaporate when old regimes fall. There are two significant dimensions to this doctrine. First, the importance of the collective (the state) supersedes that of the individual. The distribution of income is thought to be at least as important as the aggregate level. For many in the new Europe this egalitarian ethic persists, and one consequence is that issues of distributive justice can dominate issues of economic efficiency and growth. Resentment of success is not uncommon. As restructuring and deregulation are likely to cause redistribution of gains and losses, and as competitive markets will likely lead to less equal distribution (or at least to more open and obvious inequality), many fear and dislike reforms. Nevertheless, such an outcome of private markets is to be expected; growth spurts may be accompanied by less equal income distribution.

A second thread of thinking in Marxism–Leninism disputes the very goal of higher consumption that is assumed in our model to drive the consumer's utility. Consumption to some ideologues is a social evil, not a social good (hence the communist aphorism, "property is theft"). This repudiation of the legitimacy of consumption reflects two arguments. First, consumption requires exploitation of workers, because capital receives a return that is deducted from wage compensation by the capitalist. Under the labor theory of value, any positive net return on capital implies labor exploitation. Second, consumption satisfies bourgeois tastes, which are anti-socialist. Thus, deregulation can be expected to encounter ideological resistance.

Many rent-seekers of the old regime who ran the institutions of control and who gained from regulations oppose restructuring and regulatory reform. For very pragmatic personal reasons, these beneficiaries of control resist change even though it may well improve utility for the representative consumer and living standards economy-wide. Such rent-seekers include government bureaucrats, managers of state-owned enterprises and political leaders in the communist governments.

TRADE LIBERALIZATION

Free trade has three primary advantages. It exploits comparative advantage by enlarging the trading group, thus fostering more specialization. This means the mix of output improves, because efficiently produced goods are produced locally and traded for goods produced more efficiently elsewhere. An immediate consequence of free trade is to improve the mix of the consumer bundle and, in our model, improve utility at each level of income and consumption.

A second advantage of free trade is brought out in the endogenous growth models. It provides a vehicle for the transfer of new technology from advanced developed economies to developing economies. This transfer depends on the development in the domestic economy of the transition country of human capital. Advanced technologies often require workers with high levels of education and skill development. This means that opening an economy to foreign trade forces domestic firms to compete on international markets with the most efficient firms of advanced societies. As human capital develops in the domestic economy, the local firms are able to adopt more advanced technologies and compete with high-technology and high-value-added firms.

Another major benefit of free trade is the political discipline it imposes on domestic producers and the entrenched political elite. Growth in many developing countries is hampered by the simple fact that the local political elite, whether a caste, tribe, dictator, family or Mafia, may see its own interests threatened by economic development. After all, economic growth tends to generate many wealthy people from all walks of life, and it can be difficult for a small cabal to cling to power when many different groups gain economic power.

Under free trade, domestic producers must compete in open markets. This reduces the power of local monopolies and reduces monopoly rents. In addition to improving product quality and raising output, this international competition, by reducing monopoly rents, lowers the ability of local industries to capture regulators and government officials, thus contributing to reduction in corruption. An important social benefit of free trade is that it imposes constraints on government, forcing officials also to act more efficiently.[17] Survival of a local elite depends in part on the ability to bribe supporters and punish opponents. These methods require in turn either control of police and the military or command over financial resources. Both are hampered by the presence of many financial powers distributed across the society.[18]

SUMMARY: REFORMS AND GROWTH

Three tables in this section illustrate the mapping of reforms into changes in steady-state values of key variables. Table 5.2 shows the channels through which each generic reform measure influences growth. We note that privatizing property has numerous positive effects on many elements of the decision-making process in growth models. Price liberalization, on the other hand, primarily improves the mix of products and thus does not improve growth of measurable outputs; it does, however, make the representative consumer better off. Stabilization *per se* operates primarily through the freeing up of final product for consumption. Restructuring and deregulation, which means removing burdensome regulations on capital formation, improves production and lowers costs.

Table 5.2 Channels for economy-wide reforms

Reform	Discount rate	Production function	Costs	Utility function	Budget constraint	Gov't. budget	Path of capital	Tech. change
Free prices				↑				
Privatize	↑	↑	↓				↑	↑
Stabilize					↑	↓		
Restructure		↑	↓			↓	↑	
Open trade		↑					↑	↑

Table 5.3 Long-range effects of reforms

Reform	Income	Capital	Consumption	Utility	Technology
Free prices				↑	
Privatize	↑	↑	↑		↑
Stabilize			↑		
Restructure	↑	↑	↑		
Open trade	↑			↑	↑

Table 5.3 explains the next step in the chain of events by which reforms influence steady-state values of economic outcome variables. Each reform, operating through different channels, changes different outcome variables. We see again the importance of privatizing and of opening up to foreign trade. Perhaps these results explain why most academic economists support these two reforms. Stabilization and industry deregulation each involve an important social trade-off. The appropriate level of government spending has to be a public choice and the degree of regulation has to be decided on a case-by-case basis. We can see that a cost of government spending is less consumption. We can also see that regulation is a burden that can lower the long-range values of the capital stock, income and consumption.

We know that different people have different attitudes to reforms. We know that some reforms are more popular than others.[19] One can understand these attitude differences among citizens by imposing different behavioral assumptions and different initial conditions in the growth models. We separate effects on attitudes of citizens into two groups: variables like innate tastes that influence the behavior of individuals, and variables like wages that influence the initial context in which economic agents make choices. Table 5.4 illustrates some of these factors. We believe that flexible and patient consumers are much more likely

Table 5.4 Attitudes toward specific reforms[20]

	Taste parameters				Initial conditions						
	Flexibility		Discount rate		Wages				Tax/transfer		
Reform	Loose	Rigid	Zero	Large	SOE	Retired	Young	Entre.	Military	Tax	Ward
Free prices					no	no	yes	yes			no
Privatize	yes	no	yes	no	no		yes	yes			
Stabilize					no	no			no	yes	no
Restructure			yes	no	no			yes			
Open trade	yes	no	yes	no	no			yes			

Notes:
Entre.: An entrepreneur.
Military: One dependent on military spending.
Tax: A net taxpayer.
Ward: A net recipient of transfer payments.
SOE: A state-owned-enterprise employee.

to be willing to forgo short-term gains for long-run benefits. Those who are less rigid and more patient will be more likely to accept privatizing property and deregulating enterprises than those who tend to be rigid or myopic (meaning that they largely discount the future).[21] Terms like myopic and rigid are not necessarily pejorative. Old people without offspring may be rational to discount future potential gains steeply.[22]

Given tastes, an economic agent's initial conditions have a lot to do with his attitudes toward reforms.[23] Reducing taxes and reducing transfers have the opposite effect on wards of the state and taxpayers. There are many existing wards of the state in the former Soviet Union and they are unhappy to see their promised income threatened by less government income support. Similarly, one's source of wage and non-wage income would seriously influence one's attitude toward privatizing state-owned property. Workers in military factories and other state-owned enterprises were sensibly quite fearful of privatization. Young and entrepreneurial agents would be likely to support privatizing because it provides them with opportunities from which they can reap benefits.[24] The political implications of these types of differences are a subject for the next chapter.[25]

Government policies have three important effects on growth. As we will be looking for these in the analysis of each country in our sample, we summarize them here. First, a major push toward growth of the private economy can be made if the government will reduce its spending on both unnecessary military goods and on inefficient state-owned enterprises. Lower government spending with comparably lower taxes leads to a higher level of disposable income. A higher income level in turn permits a higher level of both consumption and capital formation.

Second, deregulation and restructuring industry will lower the cost of capital, foster capital formation and increase the rate of growth. This follows from our view that regulation imposes a cost on the ability of owners of capital to generate output, and directly impacts upon the efficiency of the economic system. Improving the efficiency of the system in transition economies acts like an upward shift in technology in a world in which new technology acts like manna from heaven: output increases without any increase in costs.

A reduction in transfers and a corresponding reduction in taxes offset one another in the models, but certain obvious redistribution effects are to be expected. Wards of the state will have less income so such declines should be rejected unless efficiency effects outweigh declines in income transfers. Owners of productive inputs will be better off if taxes are lower. This suggests that the latter are more likely than the former to endorse stabilization reform measures that lower transfers and taxes.

Finally, we believe that some financial officials and managers of state-owned enterprises played Ponzi scheme games in which they accumulated worthless debt instruments knowing that they would not be held accountable once the old system collapsed.[26] The legacy of these games includes serious financial impediments to reform, especially to privatization of state-owned enterprises and banks. These problems have plagued all post-communist governments to varying degrees.

This completes the description of economic reforms and the growth model that projects their effects on countries moving from central planning to markets. In Chapter 6 we combine the activities of policy-makers with the responses of voters to consider sustainability of reforms.

NOTES

1. See Alexeev (1991), Hillman (1991), Murphy et al. (1992) and van Wijnbergen (1992a) on price liberalization.
2. Brainerd (1998).
3. Many US cities impose rent controls, and public utility prices in the US are often regulated.
4. Appendix A contains specific details linking each reform to parameters of the growth models. Property privatization turns out to be one of the most important reforms. It alters the production function and shifts the function upward via a Harrod-neutral technological change. It improves effective human capital and improves the quality of non-human physical capital. Price liberalization we treat as a one-off Hicks-neutral technological change.
5. Michael Intriligator, a UCLA economist who specializes in the Russian economic system, spoke at a Claremont conference on the Soviet collapse. He told of large volumes of capital assets that simply disappeared during the Soviet period, and of large volumes of goods that were produced whether or not there was a final demand for them.
6. This means a proper index of output will rise, because the market value of the output will be higher.
7. Harrod-neutral technological change captures both improved output selection and improved management leading to increases in "effective" output per unit of actual labor.
8. Envy is inconsistent with our model. We assume that each consumer cares only about her own utility. Some critics of modern economics dislike this assumption because it implies that people are selfish and thus rules out altruism. In defense of economics, the model also rules out envy.
9. By "rational" here we mean that dismantling poorly organized enterprises and selling off the remaining capital may be the best use of resources.
10. This is a problem in the West as well. Presidential candidate Jesse Jackson argued for government to bail out failing Chrysler Corporation. He felt that it was such a large firm that society could not afford the job losses that would result from its collapse.
11. A Hungarian economist told us of plants that, if privatized, would be worth about 2 percent of their current book value. In his view, this meant privatization was not feasible. This is a perfect example of the importance of having an economic system in which the shutdown problem can be solved. If society cannot cease worthless activities, then resources are wasted and, in the case of state-owned enterprises, subsidies are needed which drain resources from productive alternatives.
12. According to sources in Prague, Klaus fired his first privatization minister for allowing conflicting legal claims to tie up the privatization process. Klaus is said to have blamed stalled privatization for the separation of Slovakia from the Czech Republic.
13. On banking reform, see Thorne (1993), van Wijnbergen (1992b), Hochreiter (1995), Bonin and Székely (1994) and Willett et al. (1995).
14. Winiecki (1989) discusses rent-seeking in large state-owned enterprises.
15. Kornai in *The Socialist System* (1992) provides a brilliant analysis of the role of the "soft budget constraint" in business and financial decisions under the Soviets in Europe.
16. Bergson (1984) addresses inequality in the Soviet system.
17. In the mid-1990s Los Angeles reduced its regulatory burdens on industry because many firms were moving out of the city. The same pressures apply to states in the US that compete with one another to attract business and workers. Free trade merely extends the region of competition and thus forces more efficiencies on governments.
18. Currency convertibility acts as a discipline on the conduct of monetary policy. It is difficult to disguise inflationary stabilization policies if one's currency is convertible. For this reason, if a currency is declared non-convertible, trade flows dry up quickly.
19. See Brainerd (1998) and Ham et al. (1998) for local evidence of such differences in Russia and in the Czech and Slovak Republics respectively.
20. Appendix A gives precise definitions to these heuristic terms. "Rigid" and "myopic," for instance, refer to limiting values of two parameters of utility.
21. Brainerd (1998) presents the interesting argument that old men are likely to discount the future heavily because life expectancy for males is falling.
22. Aron (2000), pp. 626–9 provides evidence that supports our analysis. Most resistance to adopting a system to accommodate the industrial revolution, that is, capitalism (see Chapter 1), came from rural areas and small towns: "Polls showed Yeltsin well ahead in large cities, especially Moscow and St Petersburg". Our notion that resistance to the economic quake comes from relative losers is borne out by this mix of votes. Just as hunter-gatherers had resisted agriculture, Russian farmers now resist capitalization.
23. Yeltsin supporters, according to Aron (2000), p. 628, consisted of demographic groups that our model

predicts will be proreform: "'pro-Yeltsin' demographic groups did, in fact, support him overwhelmingly: the young, the educated, the urban, who had benefited most immediately from political and economic liberties and from the economic revival inspired by the dramatic decrease in the rate of inflation from 135 per cent in the previous year to 22 per cent in 1996. University students preferred Yeltsin 84 per cent to 7 per cent."

24. Aron (2000), p. 582 notes, "Yeltsin's potential electorate [in January 1996] seemed especially solid among younger Russians. In poll after poll, with a uniformity that excluded accident, Russians between twenty and forty-four years old (38 percent of the population) rejected communism by a very wide margin – no matter how questions were phrased."
25. Aron (2000), pp. 629–30 shows that in the Russian election choice between Yeltsin the reformer and Zyuganov the communist, the outcome was 54 percent Yeltsin, 40 percent Zyuganov and 5 percent "against all." Whereas Zyuganov led Yeltsin in the agricultural red belt, Yeltsin won the regional capitals. Both Moscow and St Petersburg "gave Yeltsin astronomic leads: 77 per cent to Zyuganov's 18 per cent in Moscow, and 74 per cent to 21 per cent in St. Petersburg."
26. Aron (2000), p. 638 notes that "most managers sought 'rent' from the asset and political connections … Their response … was not restructuring … but stripping and sale of assets, profligate and reckless borrowing, withholding of taxes and the accrual of enormous inter-enterprise debts." This was complicated by the fact that the Supreme Soviet controlled the central bank and approved loans at 20 percent rates "when the rate of inflation was 2500 per cent in 1992 and 840 per cent in 1993." We interpret this as classic endgame rent-seeking and Ponzi-type fiscal shenanigans.

6. Challenges facing reformers

A change in political orientation from communist centralization to democratic decentralization has great economic consequences. Bureaucrats are more insular under a one-party political monopoly than under a multi-party democracy. One-party regimes are less responsive to dissent; entrenched bureaucracies can avoid corrective mechanisms and ignore changing circumstances. Periodic elections force eventual responses to public interests.

We develop a model that links politics to the economic model presented in Chapters 4 and 5: economics affects politics through polls taken by candidates and through decisions made by voters, and politics affects economics by establishing the legal rules of the economic regime. Before an election, politicians allocate their human and political capital between four activities: setting goals, designing strategies, winning supporters and debunking opponents. These activities are optimally chosen to maximize political success.

One purpose of the model is to analyze similarities and differences among countries. Local historical distinctions imply different prospects in transformation. A history of well-being and liberalism gives some countries clear goals to attain through reform. Situations under the Soviets also influence longer-term prospects: the Estonians viewed the Soviets as foreign military occupiers, whereas the Bulgarians enjoyed unprecedented economic improvement under the Soviets. These historical circumstances have shaped consumer attitudes and thus how voters will assess reform proposals.

WHY A POLITICAL MODEL IS IMPORTANT

In Chapter 2 we argued that certain powerful political forces would resist the economic reforms needed to move a society away from central planning toward private markets. Such resistance is to be expected because of the ideological history of socialist societies, because reforms create winners and losers, and because economic reforms have public goods characteristics that make implementation politically difficult. Furthermore, market-oriented reforms place natural burdens on public sector officials, creating a kind of moral hazard that causes additional resistance.

In Chapter 3 we justified certain reforms needed to achieve Western-style market economies on purely economic grounds, showing how each of five generic reforms can improve the ability of the economy to deliver the goods and services that consumers want. We connected each reform to a specific parameter set of the growth model in Chapters 4 and 5, and argued that self-interested, forward-looking rational individuals will favor reforms that improve their lot.

The reforms discussed so far are economic in nature and the models we have used to trace their effects are economic growth models; but to ignore political considerations in assessing the likely impacts of economic liberalization would be a great mistake. Politics is the vehicle for establishing the "rules of the game" under which economic agents will operate; the laws, institutions and customs within which economic agents interact depend on political decisions. However, the political system itself follows a particular set of political rules. Economists use public choice models to approach the latter issue by assuming political agents are driven by the same forces of self-interest that characterize the behavior of individuals in private markets. Officials under a one-party system (or what is the same thing, a party that rejects the legitimacy of democracy) will behave radically differently from those under democracy. Our argument is simple: political officials are constrained by the cauldron of democracy to consider constituent interests even when these are in conflict with the politician's personal ideology. This constraint operates through the threat and the reality of elections. This election mechanism significantly limits the power of politicians, and the political structure determines the nature of principal–agent problems encountered by politicians in dealing with bureaucrats.

New forces are unleashed when democracy replaces autocracy, just as when competitive markets replace central planning. Both democracy and private markets foster competition by creating many different players who can influence outcomes. Democracy fosters competition in the political arena because voters, in the final analysis, can "throw the rascals out." Likewise, private markets foster competition because consumers can move their dollar votes from one producer to another. This force of competition is the crucial distinction, both in politics and economics, that causes both political and economic producers to take into account the interests of voters and consumers respectively. The relationship between political and economic systems is discussed further below.

A second reason for the emphasis on politics is that the political system is the arena in which sociopolitical stresses brought on by economic reform influence the progress of reforms. Either these stresses must be mitigated so that reforms can proceed, or else they may be powerful enough to slow down or derail reforms. The political model must allow for the possibility of both outcomes. Finally, the political system is a mechanism linking historical economic experience to contemporary political events and linking contemporary political events to future economic policies. The model developed in this chapter captures these historical connections and characterizes the essential political features of each country we examine. Like the growth model in earlier chapters, it will shape the analyses of individual countries that begin with the next chapter.

We review a set of economic challenges that were common to the newly independent European states in the early 1990s. The end of the Cold War brought with it changes in the external environment, changes that were not conducive to reform. The Eastern European trading bloc disintegrated, removing most traditional markets for both inputs and outputs. The collapse of the perceived military threat of the Soviet Union in the West caused significant structural changes along with a simultaneous widespread recession due to a collapse of Cold War sources of (military) demand. This meant that just at the time when reformers in the East needed to open new markets to the West to replace old trade ties, the West failed to rush in with new buyers. Furthermore, in the wake of the collapse of the communist political monopoly, the bankrupt financial position of the large state-owned enterprises, the state budgets and the state-owned banks became evident. New political parties had to design new institutions during a period of serious domestic and international economic weakness. Companies were saddled with obsolete or worn-out capital stock and many were turning out non-competitive products. Even pro-reform regimes, with little practical experience with either democracy or capitalism, faced huge challenges that hampered reform efforts. Few emerging political parties had personnel skilled and trained in private market business practices.

While common problems are one basis for pursuing liberalization programs, post-independence countries differ in many important respects one from another. Significant unique local features go a long way toward explaining variations in countries' reform success rates. Two important distinctions are the historical experiences before the advent of Soviet control, and the relationship between local communists and the central authorities in Moscow during the Soviet period. This chapter ends with a discussion of key differences among our six countries and their implications for reform outcomes. This is the last preparatory step before launching into country studies in Chapters 7 to 12.

INTERACTION OF POLITICAL AND ECONOMIC SYSTEMS

Chapter 1 was devoted to the decline and ultimate failure of the Soviet empire. The explanation was based on the nature of a highly centralized system. Our view is that poor economic outcomes reflect not only the endowment of resources, human or otherwise, but also poorly designed political and economic systems. This view suggests that new systems can generate new outcomes. We believe that appropriate political and economic systems can lead any society to economic well-being, subject to constraints. But scholars do not agree about the exact connection between systems and outcomes.

Some scholars have argued that certain types of economic systems systematically foster certain types of political organization, that causation runs from economics to politics. For example, Marx argued that capitalism generates exploitation of workers, which will inevitably generate revolution. Only a proletariat revolution could destroy the enormous political and economic power concentrated in the hands of a relatively few capitalists. Destruction of capitalism would then provide the opportunity for the workers to create a new state. The problem was who would control the new state. Hayek (1944) argued that socialism eventually chokes innovations and freedom, leading to autocracy.

Milton Friedman (1982) argues that capitalism is conducive to democracy, since competition generates personal initiative that creates many sources of power which compete with one another for leadership. John Kenneth Galbraith (1967) claims that under capitalism the political system evolves into a corporate state in which corporate leadership supplants power of the individual. He believes that political power must break up corporate power centers and redistribute economic and political power among the population. According to Francis Fukuyama (1992), capitalism reinforces democracy by raising living standards that satisfy the citizens and by deflecting headstrong and power-hungry individuals towards generating wealth through leadership of large corporate enterprises, rather than through domination of the political system.

Many scholars have argued that the political system influences the economic system and its outcomes, that politics shapes economics. A question among Western economists since the Bolshevik revolution has been whether it is feasible to plan an economy centrally, as the Soviets tried to do. Oscar Lange (Kowalik, 1994; Stiglitz, 1994) designed decision rules for central planners and managers to follow in order to mimic private markets, in an early attempt to design a market-system outcome with socialist organization ("market socialism"). The input–output matrices of Wassily Leontief (1966) were useful tools of the central planner. Yugoslavia was long seen as an experiment in socialism with some private markets. While certain obvious failures of Soviet planners were well known (for example, overly large, heavy nails to meet planners' weight quotas, or poor-quality denim jeans to meet the demand for Levis), most economists in the West agreed by the 1950s that the Soviet system was working. After Stalin, living standards in the Soviet Union appeared to be higher than under the Czars.

Other Western economists believe that too much democracy can slow economic growth. Robert Barro (1989, 1994) argues that democracy, by allowing demands for egalitarian distribution measures, may stifle market incentives and slow economic growth. Gary Becker (1985) argues that growth rates are inversely correlated to the growth of government in democracies. The fact is that no one has demonstrated a direct causal link between democracy and economic growth.

We think that political systems and economic systems influence one another. In our view, any philosophy that produces a sustained political monopoly is unlikely to build an economic environment that maximizes the utility of individual citizens given constraints on talent and resources. Sustained centralization of power is a dangerous political outcome from the point of view of economic well-being. One-party systems create extreme principal–agent problems; the principal (the consumer) becomes unable to control his agent (whether bureaucrat or elected official) once a political monopoly is firmly entrenched over a long period of time.

This long-range concentration of political power, while a danger in a democracy, is a more likely outcome in a socialist system, although we do not think that some limited degree of planning (as in Sweden, for instance) is fatal. The concentration of power is the problem. Whereas a regime may start out as a benign religious state or be guided by well-meaning socialist ideologues, long-range concentration of political power will corrupt because the principals (consumers) lose control of their agents (political officials). This explains why failures in the Soviet Union became so overwhelming before the system collapsed. This completely concentrated system became ossified over time, a classic case of Mancur Olson's (1982) institutional sclerosis.

Democracy by no means resolves all principal–agent problems, but it does ameliorate them. Elected officials are not completely controlled by their constituents, and bureaucracies can function with a lot of slack before elected officials gain control. However, when elected officials have ultimate control over budgets and when voters can turn the rascals out, there is at least some control of agents, both bureaucrats and elected officials, by their principals, the voter–consumers. Even a democracy requires a significant mass of constituents that benefits from capitalism, a middle class. Otherwise property rights exist at the mercy of political elites and consequently are inherently insecure. This insecurity reduces incentives to invest and accumulate. The mass of beneficiaries from market economies provides a feedback loop by which these principals are strong enough to keep their public sector agents in line, supporting the market system.

One can think of elections as the backstop technology of the principal–agent problem in which voter–consumers can, in the final analysis, break up concentrations of power by replacing agents who consistently fail to satisfy the principals. Within a democratic system, political agents have an incentive to design regimes that will promote social welfare. Of course, not everyone agrees on which set of policies will lead to higher social welfare. Furthermore, most policies create some winners and some losers. This is why policy conflicts have to be worked out in the competitive political arena.

A MODEL OF ELECTIONS AND POLITICS

We turn now to modeling how politicians in a democracy set rules for the economic system. How does the political system cope with stresses so that market-oriented economic reforms can move forward or be slowed down? We believe that communism was abandoned only when citizens became convinced that they could organize and express political opposition without risk of being shot. The decision by Mikhail Gorbachev to restrain Soviet troops in 1989 was the precipitating event that allowed overwhelming repudiation of the communist political monopoly to begin. In Chapter 1 we analyzed why Gorbachev felt forced to abandon the old system.[1] One can only speculate as to the exact dynamic of how he came to this decision. The voting model in this chapter becomes relevant once open dissent becomes possible and more than one party is allowed to compete effectively for power. It links voting behavior and political decisions to the performance of the economic system via changes in the rules of the game.

Regimes and Elections Defined

This political linkage model represents a vehicle for passing reform laws. We define an economic regime as a set of rules that govern economic players. A regime consists of rules and enforcement procedures that govern property ownership, price determination, stabilization policy, business regulation and international trade. A regime is the product of a political event, as elected officials make rules. A regime consists of the environment within which economic actors behave until a new regime is established by a new political event. In our model, all regime changes are created by an election, but not every election leads to a regime change.

The political event that establishes a regime is an election. The outcomes of elections consist of reform packages or regimes. Given a regime, the economy performs as our growth models predict, subject to the parameter values that reflect the reforms that comprise the regime. When a new election occurs, voters and candidates decide the next economic regime. The political system puts policy-makers in place; they set the rules and create the institutions which govern the economic model, so that politics shapes the economic system. As the new election is influenced by the economic realities of the previous regime, causation also runs from economics to politics.

The Agents

The political model contains two types of agents, voters who "demand" regimes and candidates (politicians) who "supply" regimes. Campaigns, precursors to elections, provide the information flows used by both sides of the market as they prepare decisions – what voters will support and what parties will offer and be prepared to provide. We view the election event in which people actually vote as the market-clearing mechanism that determines the future regime.[2]

Voters

It is popular among many students of political economy to view voting as either irrational or ideological. The argument is that the likelihood of any one voter actually changing the outcome is too low to justify the cost of voting (time plus information gathering). In the US, with a population of 275 million people, this makes a lot of sense. We suggest several caveats to this view. First, people do vote in reasonably large numbers and economic variables explain a lot of outcomes, even in US presidential elections. To chalk up the enormous resources in political activity and voting behavior to ideology and irrationality is going too far. Size matters too. In ancient Greece, the cradle of Athenian democracy, citizens took their role as voters seriously. The voting population was small and the government was a direct democracy, so it was clear to all that every vote mattered. European countries are smaller than the US so individual votes are more likely to influence outcomes. With continuing ambivalence in the populace between socialism and capitalism, election outcomes are likely to have much larger effects on people and firms. A model linking economic outcomes to voting behavior seems interesting and perhaps even relevant.

Viewing themselves as "Soccer moms" or "blue-collar workers" or "stockholders" and then acting as part of a group helps people to become more involved in the electoral process even though they may not view their votes as making a difference. Furthermore, one can separate the decision to vote from the decision of how to vote. Suppose it is irrational to vote. Once one decides to take the time to vote for whatever reason, deciding for whom to vote may be rational. Finally, the amount of time devoted to political activity, of which voting is a small fraction, varies considerably among people. We think that economic models contribute to explaining this variance.

In our model, each voter views herself as the representative consumer in a growth model. She is a rational, self-interested and forward-looking individual who bases her vote on certain specific information. First, personal and national history informs her tastes, her flexibility regarding intertemporal substitution, and her subjective rate of time preference. Heuristically, her control would extend to any parameters of her utility function. For instance, she knows if she is a carefree flexible cricket, a rigid inflexible ant or whether she has some other set of well-defined tastes. Each consumer knows how much to discount the future.

Second, each voter is aware of her budget. She may be a wage-earner in a state-owned enterprise. She may be a young, well-educated self-employed worker. She may be a retired citizen who, as a ward of the state, receives much of her income from transfer payments. She may be a young shopowner and taxpayer. She may hold vouchers for stock in the production process. These factors will influence how she assesses proposed reforms when she prepares to vote.

Third, each voter knows current economic performance before the election, which she attributes to the pre-election regime. She receives information from the campaign regarding the options presented by the candidates in the upcoming election. To keep matters simple, suppose she is presented with only two options: candidate A proposes reforms[3] and candidate B proposes the opposite of A's reforms. In other words, she votes thumbs up or thumbs down on reform.

Fourth, she knows how each reform operates on the steady state via the parameters described in Chapter 5. Under these circumstances, she uses the growth model to calculate the present discounted value of her expected utility stream, acting as if she is certain of outcomes under reform and under no reform. She votes for or against the proposed reforms based strictly on which option provides the highest utility according to her analysis. In other words she votes according to her self-interest.

Consider some illustrative cases of how certain voters will react to certain reforms. Suppose that reformers propose cutting military spending to reduce the size of government. As shown in Chapters 4 and 5, a stabilization reform that reduces the size of government will raise living standards by shifting the steady-state per capita income up. This follows from the fact that lower government spending leaves more income aside, at every level of capital stock, for consumption. Utility and consumption rise. Still, military employees, directors of firms that produce military equipment and immediate suppliers to such firms may all vote against the proposal because their own primary source of income may derive from a plant to be closed. The loss of wage income and the loss of "residual claimant" income from the state-owned enterprises are likely to have the largest effects on this voter.

As a second case, consider privatization that involves shutting down an inefficient state-owned enterprise. We have argued that in theory such a reform has lots of positive consequences for growth, shifting out the steady-state level of per capita income. Recall that privatization improves productive efficiency by acting like a Harrod-neutral technological shock. It also lowers the depreciation rate of capital and improves the mix of consumer goods. These are serious improvements in well-being. But consider such a proposal from the viewpoint of an employee in the targeted enterprise. If she reacts to the implications of plant closure for her own well-being, she may well perceive herself as a loser and so will vote against the reform.

The same privatization reform, viewed from the perspective of a young worker with a low discount rate, may be attractive. She may calculate that, despite immediate loss of income from the plant closure, the future gains in utility justify the sacrifice.

Finally, consider a reform proposal for freer trade. While this will enhance the transfer of new technology from abroad, it may reduce the rents that the local monopoly had been enjoying. Thus, domestic monopoly economic agents will resist or vote against reform even though it improves per capita living standards. In short, the model linking reforms to growth to voting behavior provides a host of testable hypotheses regarding voters' reactions to reform measures.

Candidates

Candidates also are rational, self-interested, forward-looking agents whose ideology informs their tastes regarding various reform proposals. They do three things. They poll voter–consumers for information about their attitudes regarding the previous regime. Given polling results and personal ideology, each candidate then develops and proposes a regime. Each candidate is constrained by his supply of political and human capital as well as by his ideology. Political capital refers to reputation, credibility and claims on support groups such as unions, academics or pensioners' organizations. Human capital refers to the capacity of the candidate (whether individual or party) to run a government. This includes formal education and political experience (in other words, personal training and skills in politics and economics) and the number of members of his party, as well as their skills, knowledge and training. We introduce these two measures of political prowess because an important constraint on many reform movements in emerging countries appears to be poor-quality leadership both in terms of personal capabilities and in terms of power. Finally, given political capital and partial information about consumers' views and ideology, politicians determine their proposed regime and begin a campaign.

Modeling the supply side of this process in more detail, we assume that a candidate applies his scarce human and political capital to four intermediate products, in two broad categories. The first category is products related to economic analysis. (1) He sets goals for his regime. A goal is an outcome that his reform package is designed to achieve. A goal might, for instance, consist of achieving a given living standard or growth rate. (2) The candidate designs a strategy for achieving his goals. A strategy consists of a model linking specific economic reform measures to the goals that the candidate claims his regime will accomplish. These two intermediate products involve using the growth model to analyze alternative reform packages affecting targeted voter groups.

The second category of intermediate product is political effort. (3) A candidate campaigns by explaining and justifying regimes to supporters. Every campaign must reinforce the enthusiastic backing of strong supporters while it works to enlarge its constituency. Good campaigners toss rigorous reforms to the hard-core supporters (to overcome possible free-rider problems) while they target a softer message to marginal voters in order to enlarge their base. (4) Each candidate must devote some scarce human and political resources to repudiating potential opposition to a proposed regime. Opposition to reforms can take many different forms. Some candidates may not campaign on any specific regime at all, but emphasize instead national or ethnic issues. Some may propose measures in the interest of fairness or equality that amount to *de facto* opposition to the reform movement. Liberals who favor strong versions of market reforms must be able to deal with all of these kinds of implicit and explicit opposition.

Figure 6.1 illustrates the choices facing candidates in allocating their scarce human and political capital between various intermediate products. The final product is the regime proposed in the election. As production in each of the intermediate products requires depletable human and political capital (the key inputs available to candidates), each candidate must decide how best to allocate these scarce inputs between competing intermediate products so as to maximize the chance of winning the election. We argue that some reform-minded parties have been unable to win elections precisely because their limited human (and at times political) resources were inadequate to produce enough of these intermediate products to be successful. In some cases so many human and political resources were needed to accomplish certain political ends that little could be expected in the way of reform despite the opportunity to change.

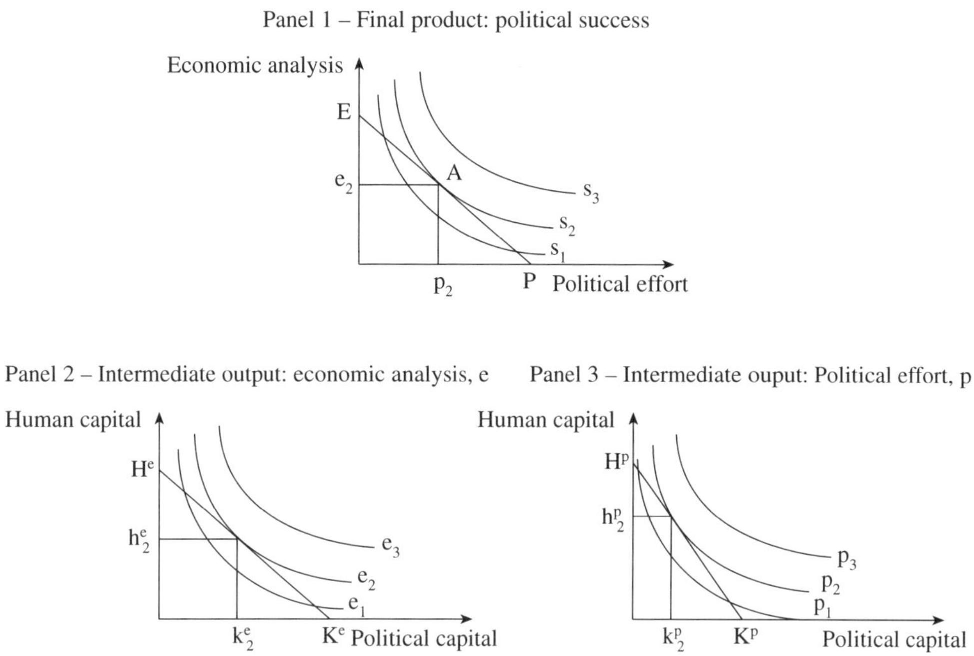

Figure 6.1 Two-stage decision-making process

As political capital and human capital are limited, each candidate chooses how to spread these resources between alternative categories of intermediate products. Figure 6.1 illustrates this two-stage production process assuming only two intermediate products: economic analysis, e, and political effort, p. Assume a candidate wants to produce the highest possible level of political success. Panel 1 illustrates the situation. Each combination of two inputs, e and p, produce a given level of success. Suppose his resources constrain him to line EP. If he employs all his resources in economic analysis, he is at point E, and if he employs all his resources on politics, he is at point P. The levels of political success are represented by the curves s_1, s_2 and so forth. Each curved line represents the combinations of analysis, e, and effort, P, that can produce unique success levels (s_1 , s_2 or s_3). The farther the s-curve from the origin, the greater the degree of political success. In the figure, the campaigner maximizes political success at point A, where he achieves success level s_2 using the pair (e_2, p_2) of economic analysis and political effort.

Each candidate is endowed with a certain level of primary inputs, human capital and political capital. This is represented by the line HK, the constraint on this candidate's ability to achieve a given level of an intermediate good, either economic analysis in panel 2 or political effort in panel 3. The curved lines represent different levels of economic analysis and of political effort in the respective panels. Curve e_1 represents a lower level of economic analysis than $e_{2,}$ and so on.

Panel 1 shows how changing the mix of economic analysis and political activity leads to different success levels. This in turn is accomplished by shifting amounts of human and political capital between panels 2 and 3 to produce various levels of economic and political effort. In this illustration, the producer's optimal political success involves applying h_2^e and k_2^e primary inputs to economic analysis, and h^p_2 and k^p_2 primary inputs to political effort.

One might think of political success as maximizing votes or as maximizing the probability of winning the election and thus being able to install one's regime. In our example, the candidate chooses mix (e_2, p_2) of economic analysis and political effort. This puts him on the highest success plane possible and thus maximizes his chances of success. Note that the slope of H^e K^e is the rate of transformation of human and political capital in establishing a viable economic regime (producing the best level of economic analysis), and the slope of EP is the rate of transformation of economic analysis and political effort in achieving the final output, success.

Elections as Market-Clearing Devices

Campaigns that precede elections amount to attempts by candidates to inform voters about the implications for the future of various proposed regimes. The main political event is an election in which candidates run and individuals vote. The election is basically the market-clearing device that determines the winners. This political event sets up the next regime.[4]

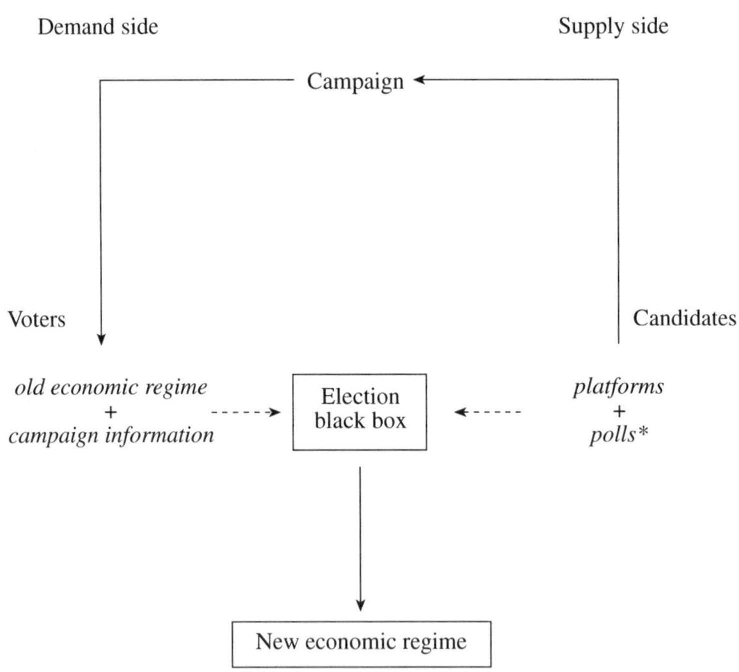

* The platforms and polls reflect, in addition to ideology, voters' reactions to the old economic regime.

Figure 6.2 Election process

The winner of an election is determined by a majority rule.[5] Because politics is clearly far more complex and subtle than this, we view the election as an event in which candidates and voters enter a black box, the voting booth, out of which emerges a winner and thus a new regime. Figure 6.2 depicts the election process. The final product of the political process is the regime, or reform package. The platforms and polls reflect, in addition to ideology, voters' reactions to the old economic regime.

The Interaction of Politics and Economics

Politics affects economics and economics affects politics. We use a simple schematic to illustrate this in Figure 6.3. Assume time is discrete and an election is going to take place in period t; this is represented by an election black box. Voters in period t base their choices on the period t–1, economic regime R_{t-1}, and on information set I^p_t (information about politics and platforms) obtained in the campaign. Candidates base their proposals on polling information I^e_{t-1} (information about expectations), obtained from consumers in the previous period. The economic regime in t–1 affects politics in period t in two ways. Voters in period t have experienced the t–1 economy and its regime and candidates poll

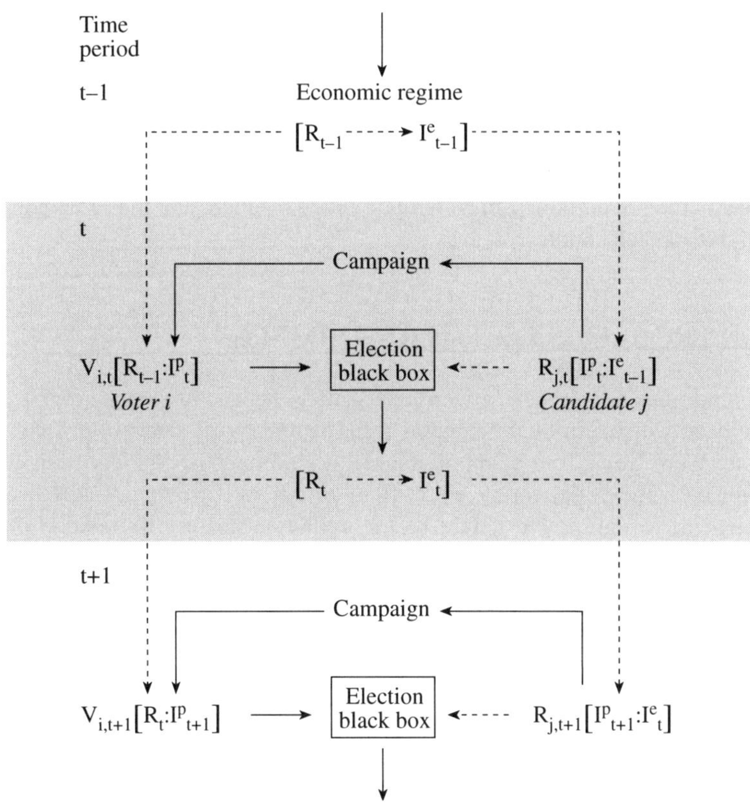

Figure 6.3 Interaction between politics and economics

the period t–1 consumers, and this informs (though imperfectly) the proposed economic regimes for period t.

Period t politics affects the contemporary economy because each voter views himself as the representative consumer in the growth model for period t. As a consumer, each individual maximizes his expected utility from the future stream of consumption subject to the parameters of the growth model. As a voter, he votes for the regime that maximizes his utility. Parameter values in the growth model depend on the regime chosen in the period t election. Thus, the outcome of the period t election will be a new economic regime R_t, and a new information set for the period I^e_t that the candidates will poll for the period t+1 election. Each election depends on the previous economic regime and each economic regime depends upon the outcome of the election.

To summarize, there are two transmission mechanisms from economics to politics: the economic reality that informs the voter's tastes and time preference for his optimization problem and the poll that informs the candidate's regime choice. Two transmission mechanisms run from politics to economics. One is the campaign that informs voter–consumers about the proposed regimes. Second, the election determines the new economic regime; that is, the election sets parameter values for the growth model. Note that both information variables, I^p and I^e, are stochastic variables, as campaigns are not perfect information flows and neither are polls.

The models developed in this chapter and in Chapters 4 and 5 are used as the framework for examining six different countries' performances since independence and their likelihood of long-run economic success. The technical analysis appears in Appendices A and B. Models alone, however, are not sufficient to provide an adequate explanation for a country's performance to date or a prognosis for its future. Two other elements will be important: the set of problems that faced policy-makers upon independence, and the local conditions and histories unique to each country.

COMMON PROBLEMS FACING REFORMERS

Economic conditions facing new governments after the end of Soviet domination could hardly have been worse, but their problems were natural by-products of crumbling centralized systems. Were Soviet-run economies healthy and had the Soviets been winning the Cold War, the collapse would not have occurred, or at least it would not have been so rapid. It is important to recognize the nature of the collapse, because its residue placed many burdens on the new government leaders. We identify six major economic problems that accompanied the end of the Soviet empire, each of which presented new governments with the task of imposing major structural changes. There were many other consequences, of course, but we are interested in those problems that had immediate and significant impacts on attempts at reform. Each of these six structural problems required costly political and economic responses in each country in order for any reforms to go forward.

Collapse of the CMEA

The trading system of the Soviet empire, including trade within the Soviet Union itself, disintegrated. The Council for Mutual Economic Assistance (CMEA) established all the rules, guarantees, terms and institutions governing trade between the countries within the Soviet bloc. When the Soviet regime collapsed, and as local communist dictatorships disappeared, the established trading system was crippled.[6] It continued to function to a limited extent, partly through inertia; but clearly new sets of trading relationships had to be created quickly.

This trade collapse was especially hard on satellite states and the Baltic nations because, as a result of a quirk of central planning, the terms of trade before the collapse seem to have favored them at the expense of the Russians and other Soviet republics. Of particular importance were the supply and the price of oil. The Soviets had held the price of oil well below world prices, evidently believing that world prices were artificially high and excessively volatile as a result of speculation; they determined current prices as a weighted average of past prices. This meant a very gradually changing price of oil charged to energy users in the Eastern bloc that lagged well behind the higher world level. This resulted in a subsidy for the satellite countries in the form of inexpensive oil. It ended when trade with Russia stalled, and energy costs, among others, increased following the collapse of the trading system.

Difficulties in the West

A second structural shock that accompanied the end of the Cold War reflected the elimination of the Soviet and Warsaw Pact military threat to the West. This new pacific reality led to a significant downsizing of military economic activity in the West as well as in the East. This had both cyclical and structural manifestations. The West, from Germany to the US, was in a deep recession made worse by the loss of demand for military goods and services. Certain regions (such as southern California, Texas and central Germany) confronted major structural changes as a result of the sudden collapse of government military spending. It was painful in both the East and the West to hammer swords into plowshares.

At the time when new liberal regimes in the East wanted to turn westward for trade and development support, the West was unable or unwilling to help because it was struggling with its own problems. Economic assistance and trade access initially were not generous.

Inadequate and Inappropriate Productive Capital

Whereas the slump in the West represented a negative demand shock, the third problem confronting new governments was a major supply-side shock. For two distinct reasons the productive capacity of the capital stock collapsed. This meant that the ability to provide goods and services was limited and that a period of lower output, especially in heavy industry, could be expected. Once Western firms and potential investors were able to look closely at the physical plant and equipment in Central Europe and the former USSR, they realized that the state of the capital stock was deplorable. In some cases, investors purchased factories only to cannibalize them. In other cases, state-owned enterprises could not be sold for more than 2 or 3 percent of their accounting values. These were not isolated instances. First, a large proportion of industrial production in many regions of the Soviet Union went to military goods. With the end of the Cold War these goods were no longer in demand. Capital goods can have uses in many different production processes; to the extent this is so, capital is general. But some capital is useful for only a specific task or production process. Such capital loses its value when the products it is designed to produce are no longer demanded. Thus, the proportion of capital that is specific rather than general determines the extent to which the capital stock falls when a shift occurs in the demand for product type.

In some cases, capital can be designed, built and installed to be flexible if that is desirable, but in many instances in the Soviet system, capital was locked into specific uses with little adaptability to others. This reflected the bureaucratic decision-making process that seems to have driven capital design; factories were designed to facilitate central administrative control. Flexibility, adaptability and fluid design do not seem to have been important. Instead, very large plants were built to produce specific products for use across the entire Soviet empire.

For example, Slovakia is sprinkled with huge factories designed to produce heavy products for the Soviet military. Railway lines run directly out of these factories into Ukraine, an efficient capital design for shipping tanks and other heavy equipment directly to the Soviet military. With the end of the Cold War, this capital was suddenly worth far less. Factories, the machines designed to produce military ordinance and the transportation system linking these heavy industries to the Soviet Union consisted largely of task-specific capital. Thus, the capital stock was depleted after the Cold War in part because the products it was designed to produce were no longer in demand.

A second feature of the design of capital in the former communist countries reflected one of the most economically destructive aspects of the political system. Marxism is based on the idea that capitalists exploit workers. Capitalists do this, in the Marxist view, by expropriating some of the earnings of the workers in the form of profits. This idea is based on the labor theory of value, which holds that the value of any product reflects only the value of the labor effort that went into producing it. If any portion of the earnings from a product go to some source other than labor, these sources are taking advantage of workers by paying them less than they deserve. In a capitalist system, the return to capital is the interest rate or net rate of return on capital. If one believes that capital deserves no return because it gets this only at the expense of labor, then one does not believe interest rates are appropriate. Thus, the interest rate that plays a vital role in determining the cost of capital, its yield and its allocation, was basically non-existent in the Soviet system. Interest rates allocate the financial capital that is used to pay for physical capital stock.

How does one allocate capital in a system without interest rates? The short answer is, badly. The longer answer requires a description of central planning. The Soviets knew that physical capital was important. As a result, they produced a great deal of it. In fact, the great strides of the economic system under Stalin reflected production of large volumes of capital. However, without a private financial capital market driven by interest rates, planners determined capital allocation. The public choice problem, when capital allocation is left up to planners, is overwhelming even if the planners are benevolent. It became evident as Central and Eastern Europe opened to the West, that a good deal of the physical capital produced by the East was useless because it was produced by state-owned enterprises that had no real interest in demand, and because it was of poor quality.

At the end of the Cold War, the capital stocks of the former Soviet states were dilapidated, misallocated and depleted. The poor quality of cars, trucks, roads, machinery and equipment as well as the misallocation of this capital meant that new government would have to set the stage for major capital production and renovation. The productive capacity of the new countries was extremely low as a result of the wrong capital stock, badly built, functioning in industries producing products without potential markets. The conversion of military industry in the West was simple in comparison.

Poor and Inadequate Private Financial Markets

In addition to the low physical capital stock, most countries had no viable market for pricing financial capital assets. Many new governments hired Western accounting firms to value their capital assets. The problem with this was that these accounting firms valued capital at book value without knowing what the future demand for the capital or the products it produced would be. In other words, accountants provided historic estimates of value because forward-looking market-determined values were unavailable. Perhaps the only aspect of the economy in worse shape than the physical capital stock was the financial system needed to value and allocate this stock.

This brings us to the fourth common problem faced by virtually all post-independence governments. The financial system that had governed exchange among enterprises was essentially a Byzantine mess of interlocking financial obligations. Many state-owned enterprises were bankrupt according to their own books. Some state-owned enterprises were clearly going to be unable to compete in the absence of government-assured monopoly power. Many other firms held financial obligations of the failed or failing enterprises. Much inter-firm trade had become virtual barter. Many companies were supposed to have received payments for deliveries, but no payments occurred. It looked as if the financial managers of many firms, knowing that the end was near, failed to reconcile their books and failed to see to it that debt obligations were met. This meant that even when new governments wanted to shut down or sell inefficient state-owned enterprises, they could not.

Who would buy a company that had large debt obligations and at the same time held assets of other state-owned firms that were bankrupt (or nearly so) themselves? And shutting down a big firm could create problems elsewhere. New governments feared a general economic collapse. An otherwise healthy firm with a potential future market may be impossible to sell if its assets include obligations from other failed firms. It was not simply a case of an unavailable private market in financial instruments to finance capital purchases, but the system that was in place was an interdependent mess.

Government Budget Deficits and Outstanding Debt

A fifth problem, related in part to the poor quality of financial systems and physical capital of state-owned enterprises, was the poor state of internal government fiscal affairs. Most governments were broke and continued to operate in the red for some time after the collapse. Government budget deficits reflected two major spending categories that were out of hand.

First was the need to continue to prop up failing state-owned enterprises. For example, managers of an enterprise producing military ordinance that was no longer needed wanted to keep workers employed and to protect both suppliers to the firm (who may not have been paid) and those holding debt obligations of the enterprise. Governments often felt compelled to prop up such firms with subsidies. In the absence of adequate income generated by other state enterprises, governments simply ran budget deficits which were then monetized (debt instruments were purchased by the government bank, which issued money to the government), fuelling inflation.

A second government expenditure item was also difficult to reduce. This consisted of numerous social support programs for veterans, pensioners and others in need. Cutting these expenditures would lead to considerable misery and consequent political turmoil, especially if citizens were able to express their displeasure in the voting booth. Thus the government budget was a problem itself for most of the new governments: failure to prop up state-owned enterprises contributes to a general economic collapse, and reduced social payments alienate many voters.

One-Tier Banking Systems

The sixth problem confronted by all new governments in the region was redesign of the single-bank financial system into a two-tier banking system with a central bank and commercial banks.[7] The single-bank system common to socialist regimes was ill suited for private markets. As more of the GDP is produced by private businesses, a parallel privatizing of the financial system is necessary. There are many good reasons for this, but one of the most important is to foster competition in banking, so that banks serve as effective devices for allocating savings in the form of financial instruments among competing investment needs. It is extremely difficult for a central bank to serve this function. A second reason is that banks assess and distribute risk associated with capital allocation and investment. The discipline needed in a system of risk assessment requires competition. Thus, before any government could begin to correct its own budgets and privatize production, it had to create a two-tier banking system.

UNIQUE LOCAL CONDITIONS

We have seen that similar challenges faced reformers in each newly independent country after the collapse of the Soviet Union. Some of these difficulties were purely economic. The trading system collapsed. The West, suffering widespread recession, provided little more than advice. The productive capacity of domestic industries had fallen, lacking good specific physical and efficient human capital. Financial markets were non-existent, and both governments and enterprises were deep in debt.

Other problems involved political weaknesses. Political systems were institutionally and practically ill equipped to lead the transition. Each country had to define private property rights, since they did not exist under communism except at the pleasure of the state. This involved adjudicating property disputes involving restitution claims by owners from before the Second World War, establishing rules for transfer of ownership, establishing constraints on ownership rights and creating enforcement systems. Some countries found this relatively easy for small shops, stores and farms, difficult for land and residential property and extremely difficult for some large enterprises.

Most national government budgets were in very poor shape. Long entangled in financing state-owned enterprises and long the source of financial support for so many wards of the state, most governments were running substantial budget deficits and had accumulated debt, including in some cases extensive foreign-held debt. How could reformers deal with all these problems as they tried to chart an entirely new course for their people?

The answer turns out to differ in important ways among states, because each state's economic and political environment differed. Important local distinctions go a long way toward explaining different degrees of success in implementing and sustaining reforms that lead to Western-style market capitalism. We identify two crucial distinctions that contribute to explaining different outcomes by country: life in the golden era of each people, and life under the Soviets.

The Days of Glory

A natural reaction to new-found freedom after the collapse of communism was to look to the past for a period that might serve as a pattern for the future. Consider, for example, the state of affairs in the Czech Republic before the disasters of occupation by the Nazis and then by the Soviets. Before these dark periods, the Czechs were among the more successful industrialists in Europe. Some claim that Czech living standards exceeded those of the Germans before the First World War and of the Austrians before the Second World War. The inter-war golden era was retained in the collective memory so that, once the yoke of foreign domination was removed, Czech reformers could point to a successful past that was again possible. They could also look across their borders to Germany and Austria for models. Estonia too seems to have a clear sense of what is achievable with private markets. Though its inter-war period of independence was short, its economy was thriving and comparable to the economies of Finland and Denmark. Reformers could look back to better times, and could model themselves on their closest cousins, the Finns.

In the cases of Bulgaria and Slovakia the past provides no memory of a particular period of good times. Bulgaria, long dominated by Turks and others, was a relatively poor agrarian society, victimized by foreign invasions and social struggles. The Soviets brought higher living standards than Bulgarians had ever known. Similarly, Slovakia was a poor rural area before the Soviets took over, and would not consider reversion to the past an attractive alternative. Under the communists Slovaks enjoyed much improved industrial strength and a standard of living on a par with the Czechs. Hungary, a cosmopolitan trading state before the Second World War with historical ties to Austria, had always been dominated by stronger states. And finally, Russia had never experienced either political democracy or a market system.[8] The glory days were glorious only for the aristocracy.

In short, each country's experience before the Soviet period was different and these differences have two effects: they inform the consumer's attitudes toward change by recollection, and they determine the degree of difficulty reformers encounter in explaining and selling the goals of transformation to constituents.

Life under the Soviets

A second important distinction involves experiences under communist rule, particularly the treatment of the local population and its traditions by the Soviet rulers. In some cases, most notably Estonia and the Czech Republic, communism was imposed from outside and was viewed as foreign occupation. The Baltic States, including Estonia, were captured by the Soviets and made part of the USSR. Occupation included brutal treatment. Deportations and executions of tens of thousands of Estonians accompanied pacification and integration into the USSR. Estonians cheered when the Soviet military withdrew from their homeland; it was not emotionally difficult for them to reject the socialist economic system in which their economy was a mere outpost run by the economic engine in Moscow.

The Czechs had initially welcomed Stalin's tanks that drove the Nazis away. A famous replica of a Soviet tank, displayed as a monument in Prague, celebrated the arrival of the Russian liberators to that lovely city. Even after 1990, some Czechs felt this tank should remain as a symbol of Russian support in 1945.[9] After Soviet tanks crushed the Prague Spring of 1968, the communist puppets held power mainly via Lenin's "barrel of a gun" policies, and virtually all major decisions had to be approved in Moscow. As in Estonia, the Czechs were eager to abandon their Soviet-dominated economic system; it was associated with harsh foreign control and with a lack of freedom. Communism in Estonia and the Czech Republic was a foreign import imposed on the local population by foreign administrators and by soldiers.

In other cases, Russia and to some extent Hungary and Bulgaria, communism was homegrown. The Hungarians, like the Czechs, cheered as Stalin's troops drove the Nazis out, and today some still credit Stalin with having saved historical sites on Buda from total destruction by limiting the use of heavy artillery in their campaign. Monuments to Russian soldiers and to Marx still stand in Hungary. After the Hungarian revolt in 1956, the relationship between the Soviets and the communist leaders in Hungary eventually improved. Perhaps concerned with instability in nearby Czechoslovakia, the Russians allowed local decisions in Hungary that moved the products of small agriculture plots and retail shops through private markets. As long as the Hungarians remained politically and militarily loyal to the Warsaw Pact agreements, they were allowed considerable economic autonomy. By the 1960s, domestic political and economic policies in Hungary increasingly reflected local decisions by Hungarian communists, and some of these decisions resulted in private market forces operating on a small scale. This ameliorated some of the worst results of central planning in Hungary and became known as the Hungarian way or Hungarian goulash. The pragmatic nature of the Hungarian communists through the 1970s and 1980s made Hungary a relatively successful Eastern European country. At the time of the Soviet withdrawal from Central Europe, the Hungarian economy was in better shape than the others were: per capita GDP was higher than in any other satellite country. As reformers, the Hungarians remained gradualists during most of the next decade.

Bulgaria, long a poor and rural country with an uneducated peasant workforce, found life under Soviet control an improvement. The Russians brought some industrialization, education, finance and more international trade. It is hard today for reform-minded Bulgarian leaders to capture the imaginations of voters. The Soviet past, relative to anything else the Bulgarians had experienced, was actually an improvement. Many older Bulgarians, fearing the future and change, are resistant to moves toward Western markets. Political fissures are apparent in Bulgaria, especially between pro-reform politicians and socialists. Younger, urban and better-educated voters appear to be more willing to adopt new ways than are their older, agrarian and less-educated compatriots.

Conditions in Slovakia before, during and immediately after the Russian occupation were not unlike conditions in Bulgaria. Both were rural and agrarian; both populations were largely uneducated and unsophisticated; both did relatively well under communism. Moscow planners industrialized Slovakia and often favored Slovaks over their urbane Czech counterparts. Heavy military industry was located in Slovakia and local resentment against the Czechs may sometimes have been more important to the population than discontent with the Russian occupiers. The collapse of the Soviet empire did not elicit the great joy in Slovakia that it did among the Czechs. Many celebrated new freedom, but many mourned the passing of Soviet support and guarantees.

In Russia, the power center of the Soviet Union, communists have retained the most influence, even after a failed coup. In fact, coup leaders were elected to the state Duma shortly after the attempted coup. Only in Russia do the former communists still refer to themselves as communists. Everywhere else in the satellite states the parties renamed themselves socialists. Aleksandr Prokhanov, editor of the pro-communist hard-line weekly *Zavtra* and close confidant of Gennadiy Zyuganov, felt that "'Russian patriots' supported the Communist party because 'for Russian patriots the very idea of communism is Russian.'" Zavtra thought "Russia was an occupied country; democracy and the market economy had been imposed on it from outside." The nationalistic high ground was captured by the communists and Yeltsin had to make a case for imposing a "foreign system" on Russia.[10]

In summary, we believe that a country's pre-Soviet history informs its view of the future, and that its experience under the Soviets shapes its liberalization efforts. Both influence the likelihood of long-term economic growth. The next chapter is the first of six country studies, each organized in terms of these historical periods and each built on the framework of the growth model of Chapters 4 and 5 and the political–economic interaction model of this chapter.

NOTES

1. We analyze the underlying causes of the collapse of the Soviet system in Chapter 1. Our political model in this chapter is not intended to explain events that led up to that collapse. We argue that the collapse of such a rigid anti-market regime was inevitable. We also acknowledge that China has yet to reform its authoritarian communist political system.
2. A more complex model would distinguish between election outcomes that select parties and candidates, and the process by which elected officials create actual programs, laws and new institutions.
3. This could be a continuation of reforms if the prior regime was reform-oriented and the reform candidate is the incumbent. In this case, the alternative candidate proposes to retract reforms.
4. We do not model here the complex process that occurs between an election and establishment of an actual set of measures that amounts to a new set of economic rules.
5. We abstract here from the necessity to form governing coalitions, to work out political compromises and to set up minimum voting requirements, different types of political systems, upper and lower houses and other aspects of the democratic process.
6. See Rodrik (1995a, 1995b) on trade issues during the early transition period.

7. Hochreiter (1995) and Hochreiter and Kowalski (2000) provide good summaries of the issues and institutional arrangements in banking reform in Central and Eastern European countries. See also Bonin and Székely (1994).
8. Boris Yeltsin's 1996 communist opponent for the presidency, Gennadiy Zyuganov, felt that Russian history supported both empire and socialism. According to Aron, "Gennadiy Zyuganov believed that Russia was a 'unique civilization': embodied first in Kievan Rus, then in the 'tsardom of Muskovy', then in the Russian empire, and finally in the Soviet Union ... two [historical] features were crucial to the Russian–Soviet civilization: empire and socialism ... Capitalism was 'inconsistent with the flesh and blood, with the being, with the habits and with the psychological make-up' of Russia", see Aron (2000), pp. 595–6.
9. This tank, a replica of the first 1945 tank to challenge the Nazis in Prague, became a symbol of change. On 28 April 1991 a student, David Cherny, painted the tank pink. Law officials arrested Cherny and had the tank repainted army green. In defiance of persecution of Cherny, some members of parliament on 16 May 1991 painted the tank pink once again. Amidst renewed controversy, the government eventually removed the tank to a military museum in Kbely, where it is now green.
10. Aron (2000), pp. 593–4.

PART II

Country Chapters

Introduction to Part II

Part I emphasized the connections between economic reform measures, growth prospects and political decisions. Chapters 7 to 12 use the conceptual connections built in Part I to analyze the economic performance and prospects of six countries: Bulgaria, the Czech Republic, Estonia, Hungary, Russia and the Slovak Republic. Chapter 13 summarizes Parts I and II.

The countries vary greatly with respect to their historical experiences, political backgrounds and economic development. Estonia and Russia were republics of the USSR (Estonia by military conquest), and Russia was the political and economic control center of the Soviet empire. The others were satellite states. Bulgaria and Slovakia were poor and underdeveloped before the Soviets, whereas the Czech Lands were relatively rich and compared favorably with the wealthier states of Western Europe. Hungary was literally taken apart between the World Wars, losing over half its territory. The choices these countries have made and the determination with which each has pursued democratic capitalism reflect their unique histories.

We argue that a country's economic transition goals are influenced by citizens' notions of their "golden era," the key period that shaped their hopes for the future and their vision for themselves. This means that one must look at their histories before Soviet domination to understand their behavior today. In the framework of growth models, consumers act according to their tastes. Their national histories tell how those tastes have been formed. Consumers' tastes in turn determine whether individuals will behave in ways that promote growth. Another important historical element of economic success is whether there is any societal memory of institutions that make growth feasible; for example, legal structures that protect property rights.

The determination with which people pursue liberalization after independence also depends in great part on their treatment during the Soviet period. The deeper the antipathy for the Soviets, the more disciplined people are likely to be in moving toward market systems. We review each country's history prior to and during Soviet rule before analyzing the implementation and effects of the five basic economic reforms. We conclude each country study by reporting on our quantitative econometric analysis of economic progress as a result of political and economic interaction. This all contributes to our prediction about the likelihood of sustained growth.

7. Bulgaria: impatient but indecisive*

> We failed to explain to our people – because we didn't know – that in order to build a society with a market economy and mature democratic institutions, we needed to go through the valley of tears.
>
> (Petar Stoyanov, President of Bulgaria, May 2001)[1]

> So … you had no bidders other than worker/management buyouts. Most of these enterprises are garbage. People can make them work for a while but investors are not interested.
>
> (Georgi Ganchev, Centre for Liberal Strategies, May 2001)[2]

Bulgaria has for centuries been a battleground between East and West, swamped by sea changes of foreign conflicts and overrun by powerful neighbors. Prior to the late nineteenth century Bulgaria was under Ottoman Turk domination for 500 years. During most of the twentieth century it was controlled by either Germany or the Soviet Union. In spite of the long period under the Turks and communist oppression of the Muslim minority in the 1980s, Bulgaria is peaceful and enjoys good relations between the Bulgarian majority (85 percent) and the Turkish minority (9 percent). Bulgarians are tolerant people; they provided shelter to Armenians in 1915 and they protected their 50,000 Jews in the 1940s.

In the 1990s Bulgarians again found their fortunes largely driven by outside forces, primarily the collapse of the Soviet empire. Prospects for Bulgarian reform toward a healthy Western market democracy are uncertain. Its long history of foreign domination, the effects of its communist period and its upheavals in reaction to Gorbachev's perestroika and glasnost that forced reform on the Bulgarian Communist Party (BCP) suggest a difficult transition to capitalism. The Communist Party, renamed the Bulgarian Socialist Party (BSP), remains a formidable political force, dominant in five of eight immediate post-Soviet years. Only the 1991–1993 period saw a non-socialist coalition government until 1997; in February of that year the BSP was driven from office among street protests, recession and hyperinflation. In April 1997 the non-socialist Union for Democratic Forces (UDF) took over. Ivan Kostov (an economist) became Prime Minister.

Unfavorable political, philosophical and economic preconditions in Bulgaria have conspired to impede requisite changes toward viable market reform. While incipient fascination with the United States offers a glimmer of hope, the legacy of Soviet egalitarian philosophy slows progress toward capitalism. Marxist–Leninist ideology instilled the conviction that maintaining one's relative economic status is more important than attempts to improve one's absolute well-being. This egalitarian philosophy leads inevitably to resentment of those who are most likely to succeed in a competitive market economy. This impedes attempts to convert the system to a market economy because initially market economies inevitably generate significant inequalities in incomes. When people perceive these inequalities as

* We thank Dragan Manoev, Simeon Nesterov and Victor Penev for their contributions to this chapter.

inequities, then they may resist the very policies that lead to growth and eventually to broader dispersion of income at higher levels of income.

Lenin ordered the destruction of kulaks based on this egalitarian philosophy.[3] To Lenin, the term "kulak" came to refer not only to the wealthy landowning farmers who were his first victims, but to anyone with entrepreneurial spirit. He bolstered his destruction of the successful classes in Russia by exploiting peasant and worker envy of the well-to-do. This version of egalitarianism had natural appeal to the poor; it is easier to accept the view that one's poverty derives from exploitation by the successful than from one's own limitations. The wealthy are rich because they have exploited you (the worker) by expropriating the fruits of your labor. Lenin labelled kulaks "blood-suckers" and called for their slaughter. He incited the masses to a frenzy of hatred resulting in the extermination of habits of acquisitiveness, self-improvement and thrift. Older Bulgarians whose lives were indeed improved under Soviet domination seem to have absorbed this view. Hope for reform lies in the young. A new generation of Western-educated leaders can turn the country away from the envy built on the egalitarian model, but this will take time, education and effort.

Bulgaria's historical agrarian legacy (agriculture still accounts for 27 percent of employment) includes centuries of oppression under the Turkish Ottoman empire. It was the Russians who liberated Bulgaria from Ottoman rule in 1878. Bulgarians still admire pre-communist Russian culture but distrust the Russian state because they hated the imperial imposition of Soviet rule. However, given Bulgaria's relative stability and economic well-being under communism, its Marxist–Leninist indoctrination and its peoples' penchant for subservience (born of necessity), it is not surprising that capitalism was an alien concept. Bulgarian socialists resisted every reform toward a viable market system until recently. After a doomed effort in the early 1990s by a coalition government, the country reverted to socialism in 1994, which led to hyperinflation and real-output collapse in late 1996. In 1997 Bulgaria at last began to move away from "the dictatorship of the proletariat" toward democracy and away from central planning toward private market decision-making. Progress has been uneven and voters are ready for change again. An examination of the past will help us understand the indecisiveness of the Bulgarians today.

HISTORY BEFORE COMMUNISM

In 681 Bulgarian tribes united with Danube Slavs to defeat the Byzantine empire, forcing it to pay tribute to the Bulgarian Khan. This marked the beginnings of the kingdom of Bulgaria, the third great European power after Charlemagne's kingdom and the Byzantine empire. Bulgarian coinage was issued in the tenth century. For three centuries the kingdom of Bulgaria prospered, until 1018 when the kingdom disintegrated and the Byzantine empire conquered the territory.

Bulgaria's more recent history consists of centuries of foreign domination punctuated by short and relatively unsuccessful episodes of independence. Economically, Bulgaria was an agrarian society until the late 1870s. From 1878 until the First World War, Bulgaria enjoyed a brief flowering with development of some modern infrastructure. This short period of development provides the only recent period of relatively successful independence. Bulgaria never really knew democracy or capitalist-style markets. The past provides little guidance to the populace for successful democratic capitalism. Bulgaria was a serfdom of the Byzantine empire during the eleventh and twelfth centuries and was then subjugated by the Turkish Ottoman empire for another 500 years.

Under Turkish rule, all land belonged to the Sultan though peasants could work land inherited from their fathers. The state treasury allocated land to the Ottoman military and to the administrative and religious aristocracy. Further, Turkish domination isolated Bulgaria from European advances of any sort and also severed Bulgarian ties with Balkan neighbors.

Bulgarians had only one golden era of home rule, the 300 years prior to the eleventh century, crowned by the rule of King Simeon during the tenth century. This era (from 681 to 1018 plus five good years in the thirteenth century) are the only periods prior to 1887 when the country was run by independent Bulgarian powers. The fact that a language, a currency, a national identity, a literature and a culture evolved and has been sustained is remarkable.

As was the case for many Central and Eastern European peoples, most of the twentieth century was a disaster for Bulgarian independence and economic well-being. From 1878 until the Balkan wars that preceded the First World War, Bulgaria was independent, though largely still agrarian and feudal. Under Stefan Stambolov (1887–1894) Bulgaria enjoyed a brief independence and flowering. Stambolov developed Bulgarian infrastructure: roads connecting the major cities, libraries, government structure and a coherent agriculture policy. Bulgarians could boast 330 industrial enterprises, nearly 1000 kilometers of railways and a substantial telegraph system. Bulgaria entered the twentieth century with a relatively sound agricultural sector, a promising start at development and living standards about half those of Hungary.

Bulgaria began to swing from one political extreme to another as Europe became engulfed in the ideological wars between fascism, communism, socialism and capitalism. Severe and destructive turns toward political extremism, communism and fascism distracted Bulgarians from serious industrial development until they fell under the yoke of the Soviet empire. In August 1919 the Bulgarian Agricultural National Union (BANU) emerged as the leading political force. Heavily influenced by Marxist–Leninist thinking, it soon mutated into a totalitarian regime. Then, in an equally radical response, a pro-fascist government under Alexander Tsankov replaced the BANU in a 1923 *coup d'état*.

Twice choosing Germany as its principal ally, Bulgaria was devastated by the two World Wars and weakened by the depression in between. The Red Army rolled into Bulgaria in September 1944, and local communists easily imposed absolute control within a few years. A history of foreign domination and rural poverty gave the communists a pliant population willing to accept hardships and social constraints for the promise of eventually rising living standards.

HISTORY UNDER COMMUNISM

By the end of the Second World War Bulgarians had formed a loose amalgamation of political groups called the Fatherland Front (FF) which pledged to bring peace to the region. On 8 September 1944 the Soviet military entered the country. Bulgaria had declared war against America, but not against the Soviet Union, when siding with the Axis powers. The Russians had helped to liberate Bulgaria from the Ottoman Turks. The Bulgars and Russians shared the Greek Orthodox religion and the Cyrillic alphabet. Thus, when they entered Bulgaria in 1944, Soviet troops were welcomed as liberators. It did not take long for them to help local communists capture the FF and to begin the purge of non-communists.

The 12,000 Bulgarian communists, some of whom had formed the core of the underground forces resisting the Nazis, were the most militant and cohesive group within the Fatherland Front. They controlled the Ministry of Justice and the Ministry of the Interior in the newly formed government. Promising democracy (their members who were Social Democrats and Agrarian Party (BANU) members were hoping for democracy), the FF won 70 percent of the vote in elections to 30 percent for the opposition groups. The people were tired of conflict.

The communists were poised for a violent takeover. They began to exploit their positions in the Ministries of Justice and the Interior. It was a cautious and classic communist subversion of a budding democracy. After banning civil service educational restrictions, they began to infiltrate the bureaucracy. The Ministry of Justice dissolved the police and started a series of purges of the police, the army and state and local administrations. The position of Deputy Political Commander was introduced; his task was to force political compliance on each unit of the military. The same thing was done throughout the administration and the police. The communists soon controlled all unions, syndicates, cooperatives, the army, the bureaucracy and the police.

Eventually opposition political parties were ruled unpatriotic and stripped of all legal protections. Communist party membership exploded from 15,000 to 300,000. Resistance from opposition forces in the military was crushed. The Ministry of Justice decreed the creation of People's Courts. Communist purges of the opposition, disguised as war trials, began. After removing all conservative forces, the communists turned on their left-wing allies. The members of parliament were arrested and most non-communist members executed.

By 1947 the Agrarian Party was the only opposition force to have survived the purges. Following the Yalta formula agreed to by Churchill and Roosevelt, 75 percent of Bulgaria was given over to Stalin's influence and 25 percent to the West. Thereafter the French and British paid little heed to matters in Bulgaria. The reparations imposed by a regulatory commission expired in 1947, and soon after that the Agrarian Party leader was accused of espionage on behalf of the Americans, arrested and executed.

Another familiar pattern followed, with the Stalinists consolidating power in the Fatherland Front through purges of fellow communists. Party member Georgi Dimitrov won an overwhelming majority and began to purge his communist rivals, setting the stage for domination by his brother-in-law, the notorious Vulko Chervenkov. Under Chervenkov, 20 percent of the party members were purged. In 1950 he forced 250,000 ethnic Turks to emigrate. Jews were encouraged to migrate to Israel. Chervenkov mimicked Stalin with a cult of personality, five-year plans, massive resources devoted to heavy industry and brutal repression of opposition, including all non-communist political forces, organized religion and even dissidents within the party itself.

With the fall and disgrace of Stalin, the Soviets under Khrushchev replaced Chervenkov in 1953 with Anton Yugov. But Todor Zhivkov, who proved to be a far more effective, charming and youth-oriented leader, ascended to General Secretary of the Communist Party in 1956. Zhivkov threw out the old guard, replacing them with new young communist leaders. He presented himself as a humorous, pleasant public persona without the cult of personality that had characterized his predecessor. Still, like his predecessors, Zhivkov ruled Bulgaria as a completely loyal satellite of the Soviet Union for the next thirty-eight years, albeit as a Khrushchev loyalist rather than a Stalinist. Zhivkov nevertheless purged his opponents and by 1971 had assumed full control of all organs of government.

When in 1989 Mikhail Gorbachev began to open up the Soviet regime with *glasnost* and *perestroika* and tried to achieve international acceptance, the repressive Zhivkov regime became an embarrassment; Zhivkov, for example, had permitted the brutal public beating of ecoglasnost demonstrators in the presence of the Western press. Perhaps sensing the Soviet Premier's displeasure, the BCP Central Committee prepared for Zhivkov's removal. Petar Mladenov, following a visit to China in November 1989, met with Gorbachev in Moscow. On Mladenov's return, Zhivkov was stripped of power and in November 1989 a new communist regime assumed authority.

For Bulgarians the best economic times were experienced under communism with local leaders who, while devoutly loyal to Moscow, had earned the credibility of true Bulgarian partisans during the war. As argued in Part I of this book, this does not augur well for reform toward democratic capitalism. History does not provide the collective memory with a guide to the virtues of a decentralized system versus central planning. The communists who brought relative economic well-being were Bulgarians and their relations with the Russians had long been positive. Communism was not seen, as in the Czech Republic, as a system imposed by a hostile foreign power.

The Soviets succeeded in industrializing a devastated agrarian society that had chosen the wrong side during both World Wars and had suffered from the intervening depression. Nonetheless, the communist rulers of Bulgaria, while homegrown, were totalitarian and thoroughly dedicated to socialist economics. The Soviet model dictated state ownership of all means of production, central planning of major industry, communization of agriculture and police-state methods of asserting control with intolerance to opposition, religion and independent thinking of any type. Forced industrialization may be communism's contribution to the transition from agrarian society to capitalism (a point demonstrated in Chapter 1).

Although it is difficult to trust the accuracy of data covering the entire interval, Table 7.1 shows Western calculations of Bulgarian GDP growth for 1961 through 1999. These data

Table 7.1 GDP growth, 1961–1999 (average annual percentage changes)

Period	% change real GDP	Period	% change real GDP
1961–1965	6.6	1989–1990	–9.1
1966–1970	4.7	1991–1992	–9.5
1971–1975	4.5	1993–1994	0.2
1976–1980	1.2	1995–1996	–3.6
1981–1985	0.9	1997	–6.9
1986–1990	–1.8	1998	3.5
		1999	2.5

suggest success under the communists in the 1960s and 1970s, followed by stagnation up to 1989–1990.

In 1982 Todor Zhivkov, initiating a drive to bring new technologies into Bulgaria, declared Bulgaria's goal to become "the Japan of the Balkans." It did have some successes in some industries, competing effectively in international markets. Its ash soda chemical industry served much of Western Europe. Its large trucking firm SOMAT (International Auto Transport) served the Middle East and Central Europe as far west as Germany, Austria and Italy. Bulgarian canned produce was exported to the East and to Italy, Austria and elsewhere in the West. In 1989 SOMAT was purchased by German trucking czar Willie Betz for $50 million. The Belgians bought a Bulgarian wheat, maize and flower enterprise for $100 million. The ability of Bulgarians to compete in international markets was recognized in the West.

The burden of bureaucracy and central planning took its toll, and the Bulgarian economy slowed significantly, starting in the late 1970s. It ground to a halt in the late 1980s. As elsewhere in satellite Europe, the implosion of the Soviet empire was the last straw for the Bulgarian economic system. No longer propped up by cheap Soviet energy, Bulgaria could not recover from the loss of CMEA trade.

POLITICAL TRANSITION, ECONOMIC CHANGES

The beginning of the end of the communist dictatorship came in November 1989. Gorbachev's apparent decision to stay out of Bulgarian affairs placed Soviet loyalist Todor Zhivkov in harm's way. Evidently given a green light, the Bulgarian Central Committee undertook an internal party *coup d'état* to remove Zhivkov from office.

In fact, stresses had been developing within the Bulgarian command system for some time. A major fracture was developing between business directors on the one hand and the political *nomenklatura* on the other. Disputes within enterprises between management's business decisions and political directives from local communist committees were increasingly frequent. Through various internal struggles and exaggerated promises, with only modest attempts at political and social reform, homegrown communists managed to hold on to power from November 1989 until December 1990 despite widespread social and political unrest. While the BCP had to change its stripes by becoming the BSP and had to replace its aging *apparatchiks* with young communists, it continued to compete successfully for political power and remains a potent political force in Bulgaria today.

The tidal wave of Gorbachev's *perestroika* and *glasnost* rolled through the loyal Bulgarian puppet regime as it did elsewhere in the Soviet empire. As in all of the former Soviet states, Bulgaria had to rebuild its economy after the collapse of the Soviet regime and the trade system, CMEA. In Bulgaria initial local protests dealt with concerns that had much less to do with anti-Soviet or even anti-communist feeling than they did with minority rights, environmental degradation and labor market conditions. Only later in 1990 when the Russians withdrew energy supplies did economic reform move toward the front burner of public concern.

In terms of public displays, one may trace the beginning of the end of the communist monopoly to February 1985. Todor Zhivkov initiated a policy of forced integration of Turks into Bulgarian life. Public Muslim religious services were curtailed, the chador was outlawed and many Turkish books were forbidden. Official hostility toward Muslims and Turks continued for some time. In January 1988 the Independent Society for Human Rights focused protests on the maltreatment of the Turkish minority. After five centuries under the yoke of the Turkish Ottoman empire, Bulgarians still resented this 10 percent minority. Turkish terrorist Ahmed Dogan led an underground campaign in defense of Turkish and Muslim rights. Brutal police suppression in which Bulgarian Turks were beaten (some even killed) during rallies held in the summer of 1989 led to the exodus of 300,000 Turks. More social unrest was to come.

Concern among human rights activists for official maltreatment of the Turks, however, was soon supplanted by broader social concerns. Most notable was the ecoglasnost movement objecting to urban chemical pollution in the cities, especially the industrial and chemical center of Rousse and the spread of radiation from Chernobyl. Capitalizing on an international environmental forum held in Sophia, the Bulgarian capital, the ecoglasnost group held a protest rally in October 1989. Like the Turkish protest, this too was brutally suppressed by the police. This time the public response was massive outrage toward the communist power structure and even more political unrest.

This outrage, in the context of Gorbachev's withdrawal from Central Europe, forced internal Communist Party reforms and subsequently generated numerous public protests, rallies and labor strikes. The unrest reflected years of pent-up frustration with the arrogant BCP monopoly, with economic recession and with poor working conditions. The trade unions and environmentalists were major organizing forces for opposition to the communist regime. Unlike elsewhere in satellite states, pressure for private property, Western-style markets and traditional economic reforms played a relatively insignificant role in Bulgaria's swing toward pluralism.

In the wake of the Soviet collapse in 1989–1990, the Communist Party (BCP) felt compelled to loosen central authority somewhat on both political and economic fronts. Struggles led to various power changes within the party and the executive was forced to share more power with legislators. The communists, desperate to cling to power in the late 1980s, had passed a Labor Code in 1986 that allowed workers to be fired for cause. In 1989 they also approved an important privatization measure, Decree 56, permitting small-scale private property ownership of businesses. These partial measures, born more of desperation to retain power under public pressure for reforms than of a coherent philosophical change, proved to be insufficient for the BCP to retain power. The winds of perestroika and glasnost and the collapse of the Council for Mutual Economic Assistance simply proved too powerful for the communist incumbent party, despite modest reforms.

In December 1990 a weak coalition parliamentary government of mainly non-communists assumed power. This was the first multiparty government in Bulgaria. Headed by Dimitar Popov, a compromise leader agreed to by the still-dominant BSP (47 percent of parliament) and the opposition Union for Democratic Forces (UDF), the new government initiated modest reforms. Driven largely by external events, especially the collapse of the Soviet internal trading system, and spurred on by outside experts from the International Monetary Fund, the European Union and the World Bank, this first non-communist regime proposed reforms in February 1991. The UDF had taken a step toward market liberalization; the coalition was a weak one, but UDF reformers favored Polish-style "shock therapy" reforms.

During the interval in which non-communists held limited power, roughly from the reform decree of February 1991 until the socialists' reascension to power in the December 1994 elections, some price liberalization occurred. Some privatization efforts in the form of property restitution were launched, and tougher stabilization measures were installed. The socialists, fully back in power by 1995 (winning 43.5 percent of parliament to the UDF's 30.7 percent), began to turn the reform clock back to state guarantees, price supports and continued public ownership of large state-owned enterprises.

Even the socialists, though, had accepted the notion of some privatization. Private shops, offices and farms sprang up following BSP Decree 56 in 1989, by which the Bulgarian Socialist (former Communist) Party legalized small-scale property ownership. Unfortunately, Decree 56 actually prohibited larger-scale private ownership of the means of production. Large-scale privatization was largely spontaneous, basically theft of capital assets and cannibalization of enterprises by employees and management. This type of privatization was formally outlawed in 1990. Under Popov's hybrid government, a new effort to privatize the state-owned enterprises was launched by forming the Agency for Privatization in February 1991. A new Act on Ownership and Use of Agricultural Land was passed in March of 1991 and a liberalizing Trade Act was passed in May of that year.

Table 7.2 indicates the state of the economy in 1989 and 1990 when the coalition government took over. GDP fell in 1989 by 1.9 percent, in 1990 by 9.1 percent and in 1991 by 11.7 percent. Bulgaria suffered negative economic growth from 1989 to 1993 and 1996 to 1997. These figures demonstrate the inability of Bulgarian policies to turn the economy around. For all of the Soviet trade partners in the CMEA, 1991 was a bad year: a massive collapse in GDP was common to all countries in our sample. What is unfortunate is the evident inability of Bulgaria to recover. Estonia and the Czech Republic enjoyed positive economic growth while imposing significant political and economic reforms, and Hungary and the Slovak Republic at least slowed the downward spiral by liberalizing. Bulgaria, however, remained mired in depression.

Table 7.2 Growth and inflation, 1989–1999

Year	Real GDP – % change	CPI – % change
1989	–1.9	—
1990	–9.1	23.8
1991	–11.7	338.5
1992	–7.3	91.2
1993	–1.5	72.8
1994	1.8	96.0
1995	2.1	62.1
1996	–10.9	123.0
1997	–6.9	1082.2
1998	3.5	22.3
1999	2.5	0.3

Although the UDF began to splinter in 1991, a comparatively radical pro-reform group actually won the October 1991 elections with 34 percent of the vote. The communists won 33 percent. Philip Dimitrov was elected the first non-Socialist Prime Minister of post-Second World War Bulgaria. He began aggressive economic reforms. Even under Dimitrov, though, the reform-minded group was relatively weak. The UDF itself was little more than a loose coalition of 16 parties whose primary common cause was opposition to the old regime. Most key ministries were retained by the still powerful BSP. From the beginning non-communists were unfocused, splintered and weak, so that the kinds of economic reforms needed to achieve private market growth were only vaguely connected to social forces for change.

The notion that the principal social complaints – environmental degradation, low wages, poor working conditions and lack of civil rights – could be addressed by resorting to a decentralized market system is barely understood in the West, much less in Bulgaria. In fact, the necessity of economic reform was forced on Bulgaria externally by the collapse of the Soviet trading system. It did not spring from local sources. Cheap energy from the USSR suddenly evaporated, along with established product markets. This forced new approaches to economic organization.

Alas, badly designed reforms, an economically ignorant population, poor economic performance relative to the Soviet era, political corruption and impatience with reforms brought the Bulgarian Socialist Party (BSP) back to power in parliamentary elections in December 1994. As predicted by our models in Chapters 2 and 6, consumer–voters were too impatient to allow reforms to take root. It was, in the final analysis, myopic anti-capitalist sympathies that doomed early reform. The reform process ground to a halt. Bulgarians remained ambivalent about removing the government from micromanagement of labor relations, pension funding, large-scale agriculture and heavy industry. Wage and employment conditions were controlled by centrally planned incomes policies even during the relatively liberal 1991 reform period. Given their experiences, Bulgarians were reluctant to abandon the ersatz promises of the welfare state.

ECONOMIC REFORMS: THREE STEPS FORWARD AND TWO BACK

Responsible fiscal and monetary stabilization measures which had begun to take effect from 1991 to 1993 were eroded in 1994–1995. Full financial collapse hit in 1996. Phony pyramid schemes erupted in Bulgaria. Stabilization policy had been modified toward structural decentralization, giving the central bank (BCB) some independence. Under the UDF, stabilization policy had been relatively responsible, with serious efforts at deficit reduction and control of money growth. The new Prime Minister, Zhan Videnov, and the BSP began to reverse these advances.

Dysfunctional interest rate policies (real rates were highly negative, possibly –80 percent) discouraged private savings and impeded legitimate accumulation of wealth throughout the early 1990s. Soft budget constraints for marginal state-owned enterprises were reintroduced. Knowing they would not be held responsible (the government backed financial transactions between banks and state-run firms), bankers bypassed restrictive monetary policy by supplying unsupported bank credit to large firms. The government's budget deficits had to be financed by printing money, which led to accelerating hyperinflation in late 1996 and early 1997.

On the real side of the ledger, Bulgaria did not fare much better. The late 1980s and early 1990s saw Bulgarian output shrink as inflation raged. With a real rate of increase in GDP of 1.4 percent, Bulgaria was at the bottom of the growth table for the European transition economies in 1994. After a slight upturn in 1995 fed by output of the state-owned enterprises, the economy began to decline again. The banking system was near collapse with two-thirds of the country's banks insolvent. With foreign debt 75 percent of GDP, the Bulgarian lev lost 25 percent of its dollar value in the first half of 1996.

In a desperate effort to curtail deficit-funded support of inept state-owned enterprises, the government eliminated about 30,000 jobs. As if failed policies and a return to socialism were not enough, the lag in privatizing public property fostered organization of criminal cartels evidently established in association with BSP leaders to exploit the eventual privatization of state-owned enterprises. The cartels – Multigroup, Orion, Tron, VIS2 and SIC – all with some form of official government backing, began to position themselves to take over the remains of the state-owned enterprises. The utter failure of the BSP to restructure left Bulgaria a sad illustration of the costs of deferred liberalization.

The BSP government collapsed in February 1997, having debauched the currency and turned the country into one of the poorest states in Europe. In the April 1997 elections the UDF won 52.3 percent of the vote and the BSP got only 22.1 percent. President Petar Stoyanov selected new interim Prime Minister Stefan Sofiyanski, the popular Mayor of Sofia. For the second time in post-Second World War history Bulgaria's Prime Minister was a member of the UDF, the non-communist Union of Democratic Forces.

The importance of the change in government from socialist to market-oriented exceeds the importance of a return to economic reform, important as that is. It also signifies that the former communists have voluntarily relinquished power according to democratic rules. This augurs well for the political transition from authoritarian rule to democracy.

The marked reluctance of government action toward reform reflected the people's underlying feelings of ambiguity. In the first decade of transition Bulgaria changed government six times. This hardly allowed for coherent time-consistent intertemporal reform. By January 1997 Bulgarians were in the streets protesting against the decay in living conditions and failure of the government to move the country forward. The Videnov government was compelled to resign amid public displays of outrage against official corruption. The UDF won the April 1997 elections with 52.3 percent of the vote (and with 137 of 240 seats in parliament); the BSP got 22.1 percent. Bulgaria was poised for a serious attempt at sustained reforms.

Now the UDF had a second and better chance at initiating reforms. The socialists had debauched the currency and generated recession and the UDF had a political mandate to clean up the mess. Stefan Sofianski was transition Prime Minister and Petar Stoyanov was President. (Later Ivan Kostov, leader of the UDF, became Prime Minister.) The new government agreed to the IMF push for a currency board, and monthly inflation fell from 243 percent in February to 5 percent in April. The new government announced intentions to privatize 40 percent of the state-owned enterprises and to prohibit the central bank from monetizing government debt. Will the people allow the UDF to institute the serious reforms that we have shown are needed to create a successful market economy? Our earlier chapters stress the role of history in informing tastes of forward-looking consumer–voters. We turn now to an appraisal of Bulgaria's efforts toward transition to a market economy.

Progress made in the five reform areas of price liberalization, property privatization, macroeconomic stabilization, industry restructuring and deregulation, and trade liberalization during the relatively brief period when Bulgaria was not under the control of the communists, December 1990 to December 1994, was mixed and not entirely coherent. While serious and partly successful efforts at fiscal and monetary stabilization were made and while many prices were liberalized, privatization was stymied by poor design and ineffective administration, and industrial restructuring was largely ignored. New trade relations were opened to the West. But as a consequence of ineffective administration and mediocre support, reforms failed to stave off depression and instead appear to have worsened the economic condition of too many people. This poor economic performance combined with parliamentary democracy did not allow reformers enough time and power to generate adequate support for private markets. They were not able to capture the imagination of the public with the potential gains to be appreciated under capitalism.

In February 1991 Popov began to introduce reform packages. As noted, these were undertaken amidst considerable political uncertainty by a weak coalition government. Reforms were initiated under pressure and with guidance from the International Monetary Fund. The Reform Act initiated formal privatization, liberalized many prices and set the stage for subsequent pieces of legislation throughout 1991. These included the National Banking Act in June and a Commercial Code and a Foreign Investment Act in May. Significant advances were made once the more reform-minded UDF leader Dimitrov became Prime Minister in late 1991. Agreements were made with the World Bank and with the International Monetary Fund, resulting in major loans. Private property restitution was introduced into both agriculture and small urban stores and shops in the Privatization Act of April 1992. Our reform index peaked in 1992–1993, then fell until a new peak in 1997 when the UDF resumed reform.[4]

Unfortunately, the UDF proposed a level of openness that worried too many middle-level technocrats. Proposing to audit newly privatized state-owned enterprises and proposing to open secret security files threatened the former *nomenklatura*. As our model in Chapter 5 indicates, this group is most likely to resist reforms; they may be relative or even absolute losers unless they can "spontaneously privatize" state-owned property for their own gain. Torn between economic progress with corruption and a desire to establish social legitimacy, the radical UDF took on more than it could handle.

President Zheluy Zheleva tired of the UDF and with support from the now legal Turkish party, Movement for Rights and Freedoms (MRF), the BSP took over with Lyuban Berov as Prime Minister. The reform process stopped and the economy began to stagnate. After two years of squabbling, the Berov government resigned. The BSP under Videnov took control with an absolute majority in December 1994 and began to reverse the reform process.

The socialist government had proved unable to sustain stabilization policies consistent with *glasnost*, *perestroika* and *demokratizatsiya*. The reform index moved from 105.5 in 1993 to 96 in 1996 (the base year 1995 was set at 100). Table 7.2 shows that the economy fell into a severe recession with GDP growth at –10.9 percent in 1996. Hyperinflation followed the inevitable attempt to monetize budget deficits driven by government costs of propping up state-owned enterprises and subsidizing non-productive activities. The consumer price index rose 1082 percent in 1997. The currency collapsed. Foreign direct investment and trade with the West fell. Soon the socialists were unable to sustain power.

The UDF took power in April 1997 and a new era of reform began. The UDF immediately initiated a currency board. They pegged the Bulgarian lev to the Deutschmark and inflation fell to less than 25 percent in 1998. Restitution rose to nearly 80 percent of agricultural property. Bankruptcy law was tightened and other reforms were on the way.

Price Liberalization

The method for setting petroleum and agricultural product prices was relaxed somewhat as early as 1990; in February 1991 the Popov coalition government liberalized many consumer product prices. The annual percentage rate of change in the consumer price index peaked at 338.5 percent in 1991, then fell to under 100 percent until the currency collapse in 1996–1997 (see Table 7.2). The loss of low-cost oil from the Soviet Union meant significant relative price increases in energy. Energy prices and prices of foodstuffs remained under government control and monitoring. Nevertheless, by 1992 the government administered only 18 percent of consumer prices. In 1993 the government stepped back in and tried to cover up economic difficulties with new regulations, including minimum wage and pension laws, agricultural subsidies and indexed state employee wages. Administered prices rose to 45 percent of consumer goods prices by winter 1994. The price liberalization reform subindex, 125.4 in 1993, fell in 1994 to 100.

Unfortunately, egregious mismanagement of stabilization policies led to hyperinflation and collapse of the lev. This made price liberalization under the socialists virtually moot. Relative prices cannot be detected during hyperinflation and flight from the currency tends to render it useless as a medium of exchange or as a unit of account. This explains why the first task of the UDF in 1997 was to stabilize the currency.

Property Privatization

Privatization has taken four forms in Bulgaria: small-scale, Privatization Agency sales of state-owned enterprises (SOEs), restitution and spontaneous. Given the Bulgarian penchant for egalitarian values, none of the four was wildly successful. Though property has been privatized, the process was uneven, seen as unfair and even found to be criminal in some instances. Other than for small retail stores, the process may have succeeded mainly in building public resentment.

The first sort of privatization started with Decree 56 in 1989. Bulgaria began to permit small-scale private property holdings of shops, stores and farms; modest enterprises began to spring up. One problem of legitimacy arose from the question of who could afford the properties. All too often, those with the necessary financial capital were either former *apparatchiks* or criminals. Still, this sector has proven to be the most vibrant of the economy, which suggests that private ownership, provided it can be socially legitimized, can be a source of growth.

In February 1991 the Popov government started the second type of privatization by forming the Agency for Privatization, whose task was to sell off state-owned enterprises and to permit larger-scale privatization than under Decree 56. Unfortunately, the design of the process was perverse. Before the agency could sell large-scale state-owned property, it had the power first to approve of the buyer but had to obtain permission of the ministry that owned the property. The incentives of course led the ministries to sabotage the process. They benefited by unloading non-performing assets, the SOEs that were worthless or nearly so; they retained SOEs that generated revenues. It is obviously harder to find willing buyers to privatize failing enterprises than successful ones.

Another serious problem was the determination of a suitable price for a state-owned enterprise. Without understanding the forward-looking nature of private markets, bureaucrats in the Privatization Agency valued assets at a markup over historical costs. Potential buyers predictably had no interest in buying junk, especially at high predetermined prices.

In addition, the Privatization Agency itself felt no urgency to sell off state property. In the words of Agency Director Alexander Bezhkov, "we have a whole set of requirements for all potential buyers." Clearly Mr. Bezhkov felt more reluctant to sell to an inappropriate buyer than to hold onto state property indefinitely. The bias was toward retention, not sales. This bias was the logical result (explained in Chapter 2) of a state bureaucracy charged with an unnatural act – turning state property over to private owners. Public choice theory leads us to expect bureaucrats to find ways to avoid doing this, and indeed this form of privatizing SOEs has largely failed.

When the BSP took over in December 1994, it began to stymie the privatization of state-owned property. The socialists also reinstituted many price controls. Our computed price liberalization sub-index for Bulgaria fell from 125 in 1994 to 100 in the 1994–1996 period.[5] The government subsidized failing state-owned enterprises, presumably to maintain employment. They encouraged loans from banks to inefficient enterprises. These policies would lead eventually to financial collapse.

The third method of privatization involved the courts dealing with private legal claims for property taken by the state in the 1940s. In our view the early UDF reformers made the mistake of focusing too much on restitution as a means of privatizing property. Some of this worked. Small firms, restaurants, retail stores and small farms were returned to owners whose property had been expropriated in the 1940s. Some small-scale economic expansion resulted. Although this method is justifiable by an appeal to the legitimacy of private property, it proved too cumbersome for rapid economic development. A great deal of viable business and farm property was tied up by restitution claims that were eventually recognized and honored in the courts. As in other emerging European states, excessive reliance on this means of determining ownership causes property allocation decisions to be made in the judicial system rather than in the markeplace. Courts became bogged down trying to sort out competing and conflicting claims going back forty or fifty years.

This tied up the courts, tied up the Privatization Agency and, most costly, tied up property. Many of these claims were made by former Bulgarian citizens who had left the country during or immediately after the Second World War. Rather than reinforcing the virtues of private property, the Bulgarian government may have succeeded in further tarnishing the image of private ownership. Rather than private property leading to more efficient resource allocation, the courts stalled economic development with extended legal squabbles over property rights. There is still not a functioning market for land in Bulgaria.

This leaves the fourth and most ethically problematic method of privatization, spontaneous privatization or decapitalization. This is little more than theft of state property by insiders. Managers of large firms, for example, would sell capital stock and inventories at low prices to fictitious small satellite firms near their state-owned factories. The managers themselves then took over ownership one way or another of these satellite firms. Thus the managers acquired both capital stock and products below cost. These were then resold at competitive prices. While this spontaneous privatization, along with some restitution, resulted in a shift of property ownership away from the state, it generated a high correlation between personal wealth and corruption. Moreover, 90 percent of the means of production remained in government hands. The result was a bitter populace resentful of private property and an economy largely controlled by state managers who continued to operate under perverse incentives.

Major progress was made toward the end of the 1990s. In late 1997 and early 1998 a new voucher privatization scheme was developed. The US Library of Congress country study for Bulgaria reports that 70 percent of the economy was privatized by December 1998. The European Union's *Bulgaria 2000* report notes Bulgaria's good progress, especially with respect to privatizing banks.

Macroeconomic Stabilization

For a time macroeconomic stabilization was relatively successful, but the progressive UDF policies to decentralize the economy and to use conservative monetary policy measures to stabilize the currency were undermined by BSP policies from 1994 to 1997. The levels of government spending, taxes and subsidies of state-owned enterprises were lowered in 1991. Subsidies had fallen from 15 percent of GDP in 1990 to 2 percent in 1992. A value added tax (VAT) began to replace state enterprise profits as a source of government revenues only in 1993. Nonetheless the budget deficit grew from 9.2 percent of GDP in 1990 to 15.7 percent in 1991. The deficits resumed growth in 1993 to 10.9 percent. Under the BSP budget discipline was loosened, and deficits and monetization of the debt exploded in 1996 (see Table 7.3).

Table 7.3 Central government budget policy (deficit/surplus as a percentage of GDP)

Year	Deficit/surplus (%)	Year	Deficit/surplus (%)
1989	–0.6	1995	–5.6
1990	–9.2	1996	–11.5
1991	–15.7	1997	–2.9
1992	–5.8	1998	–2.8
1993	–10.9	1999	–1.5
1994	–5.8		

Pent-up demand and a significant monetary overhang in 1989 were absorbed by price rises following price liberalization. This one-shot increase in prices took place in 1991. Monetary stability ended in 1993–1994 as government debt began to soak up personal savings, and bank loans to state businesses, encouraged by the government, put pressure on the Bulgarian Central Bank to monetize the debt. This was all part of the impending financial crisis that struck in 1996 with bank failures and the fall of the lev. In 1996 the stabilization reform sub-index fell to its nadir, 76 percent, as low as it had been in 1991.

The government deficit exceeded 11 percent of GDP in 1996, a higher proportion than for any of the other European transition economies. The rate of year-to-year inflation in 1994 was around 80 percent. In 1995 it fell to about 60 percent but increased in 1996 to an average of over 100 percent reaching hyperinflation proportions in early 1997. In April 1997 the new UDF government established a currency board and stabilized the currency and got the budget deficit under control. Foreign debt, however, was about 80 percent of GDP in 2000.

Industry Restructuring and Deregulation

Bulgaria desperately needs investment, but the legal and regulatory climate must be improved to attract businesses; bureaucratic barriers are high.[6] Bulgarian socialists have been among the least willing of transition European regimes to restructure. They maintained wage and price controls throughout most of the 1990s. Although the UDF established a serious bankruptcy law in 1998, it is not being adequately enforced. Soft credits continued to prop up inefficient state-owned enterprises. These were reduced only in 1997 and 1998. The Bulgarian stock exchange was opened in 1997 but financial intermediaries are weak. Bulgaria's financial system is seriously underdeveloped and restructuring is halting and slow.

Trade Liberalization

Until late 1997 Bulgaria had difficulty attracting direct foreign investment. This flow is more volatile than for any of our other transition economies, but it has increased dramatically since strict monetary reforms in 1997. Bulgarians now enjoy a fully convertible currency and this has fostered trade with the West. Table 7.4 presents some international statistics that indicate recent improvements in trade activity and international financial arrangements. Foreign direct investment, while modest, has grown to 5.8 percent of GDP. Imports are above 40 percent of GDP and there are no serious balance of trade problems. The exchange

Table 7.4 International trade and finance (selected years)

Year	FDI* (%) of GDP	Imports (% of GDP)	Balance of trade (% of GDP)	Exchange rate (Lev/$)
1990	0.1	17.2	−1.2	0.8
1995	0.7	43.5	−0.1	67.2
1997	5.0	48.5	−0.4	1677.0
1998	3.3	41.0	0.0	1754.4
1999	5.8	40.8	—	1836.1

Note: * Foreign direct investment.

rate indicates the severity of the currency crisis of 1997. In 1995 67.2 lev purchased one US dollar. By the end of 1997, it took 1677 lev to buy a dollar. This statistic helps explain the collapse of the socialist government and re-election of the United Democratic Front.

In 1997 and 1998 Bulgaria joined the IMF and WTO. The free trade and restructuring sub-indexes both peaked in 1997 and 1998. The macroeconomic stabilization index was low, 76 to 88, as a result of hyperinflation, bank failures and collapse of the currency on international markets. Bulgaria ranks just ahead of the Russians in various indicators of economic freedom, liberalization and corruption. In other words, Bulgaria has a long way to go.

When the electorate returned the socialists to power in December 1994, it virtually ended reform efforts until 1997. The BSP quickly stalled privatization, reintroduced subsidies to state-owned enterprises and began to monetize the state budget deficit. In 1994 price regulations of gasoline and staples were renewed. Like their ideological forefathers of the BCP, the BSP proved unwilling to wean society from administered prices, wage controls, state pension support and continued subsidies of ineffectual state-owned enterprises in heavy industry. As a consequence Bulgaria suffered severe fiscal deficits. Forcing the banking system to prop up ineffectual state-owned enterprises led to a serious monetary crisis in 1996, including major private bank failures involving two-thirds of the country's banks, currency devaluation and re-emergence of hyperinflation.

CONCLUSIONS AND RECOMMENDATIONS

Data on reform indexes and economic variables over election intervals in Bulgaria are presented in Table 7.5. We consider the UDF and its coalition members to be more staunchly pro-reform than the Socialist Party and its coalitions. Based on this, the percentage of votes received by the more reform-oriented parties was only a plurality in the 1997 election. However, the UDF did form a weak government in 1992. Socialists were in power twice, 1990 to 1992 and 1995 to 1997. We computed an annual average reform index (base 1995 = 100) for each election interval. The index was highest during the UDF periods and lowest during the socialist intervals.[7] Reforms and votes for reforms are closely correlated. Economic performance is less clearly linked to political regime. Table 7.5 presents average

Table 7.5 Elections, reforms and economic performance, 1990–1997 (all variables cover election intervals)

Year	Votes for reformers (%)	Reform index (1995=100)	GDP % change		Inflation rate		Unemployment rate	
			After	Before	After	Before	After	Before
1990	43.0	91.0	–10.8	–4.3	233.6	14.1	8.0	0.8
1992	49.5	104.0	–2.3	–10.8	86.7	233.6	14.8	8.0
1995	45.4	98.0	–4.8	–2.3	233.9	86.7	12.1	14.8
1997	59.7	120.6	–0.5	–4.8	11.3	233.9	14.0	12.1

annual GDP growth, inflation and unemployment before and after each election interval. Unemployment figures, as in all transition economies, have drifted upward. In 2000–2001, Bulgarian levels are worryingly high at 18 percent. Part of this reflects the decline in importance of the huge state-owned enterprises and some reflects statistical procedures coming into line with international standards. The inflation measure does correlate with reforms and reform parties, reflecting the more prudent macroeconomic policies under the UDF. The socialists were unable (or unwilling) to rein in government spending. The resulting deficits were then monetized by the central bank.

Pro-capitalist reforms have been relatively unpopular in Bulgaria; liberalism has had a hard time establishing itself there. In earlier chapters we have stressed the importance of social consensus on the goals of reform. In Bulgaria the society is deeply divided over the choice between socialism and capitalism. What model will Bulgarians choose? Much depends on the success of pro-reform liberal forces in the UDF.

To sustain reforms, liberals will require a substantial infrastructure of think tanks and academic institutions capable of bringing together serious academic intellectuals with a market bent to focus on Bulgarian socioeconomic issues. In addition, liberals must design reforms that give the public a stake in the future. A more direct approach to rapid privatization, perhaps using vouchers, would help reformers bring the populace along by making them active players in the private ownership game. Private ownership of the means of production is necessary to provide the profit motive that successfully drives markets.

Through stocks and creation of mutual funds, focused decision-making in firms can be reconciled with widespread private ownership and public inclusion. Investment is a lower proportion of GDP in Bulgaria than in any other transition state. The key point of our growth analysis in Chapter 4 is that private savings translated into accumulation of private productive capital is essential for the survival of capitalism.

Both the elimination of chronic government budget deficits and creation of banking independence are necessary to assure a stable currency. Without price-level stability, private markets cannot work effectively. With UDF leadership, Bulgaria has begun to enjoy success on this front. The National Bank of Bulgaria (BNB) was freed of the requirement to finance government debt in 1997.

Finally, open trade with both the East and the West augments competition even for the former state-owned monopolies. The government should withdraw from dominating private market forces by letting wages and prices move freely and by allowing businesses to compete and either succeed or fail. Bulgaria's government can be an active participant in balanced economic growth by promoting incentive schemes to prevent environmental degradation, enforcing basic laws that protect property and persons, and by adjudicating property disputes in a sensible, forward-looking way. Most important, it must sustain its reform programs and it must undertake microeconomic restructuring efforts to improve the business climate. Everything we know about growth emphasizes the crucial role of investment.

NOTES

1. Kraler, Nicholas (2001), "Royal wave that is rocking a leader's boat," *Financial Times*, 2–3 June.
2. McAleer, Phelim and Theodor Troev (2001), "Bularia looks to privatization of state hotels to give tourism a boost," *Financial Times*, 24 May.
3. See Remnick (1994), who persuasively shows that the terrorism of modern communism in the Soviet Union began with Lenin, not with Stalin. Courtois et al. (1999) confirms this point.
4. Appendix B contains details in Tables B.1, B.2 and B.3 on reform measures from 1989 to 1999.
5. See section 5 of Appendix B for details on the construction of reform indexes for Bulgaria.
6. Corruption is still a serious problem, and the judiciary is weak and ineffectual. EU, *Bulgaria 2000*.
7. Index construction is described in Appendix B, section 5.

8. Are the Czechs capitalist superstars?*

> [M]icroeconomic, institutional, structural and social rigidities ... impose a substantial constraint for the future, as they are likely to develop and disseminate disequilibrating tendencies in the course of the transition process itself.
>
> (Miroslav Hrncir, Chief Executive Director, Czech National Bank, 1992)[1]

> We are listed among emerging markets. Forget it ... We have already emerged.
>
> (Karel Dyba, Czech Economy Minister, 1994)[2]

> The Czechs underestimated the importance of the legal framework from the beginning.
>
> (Jan Svejnar, Executive Director of the William Davidson Institute, University of Michigan School of Business, 1999)[3]

The Czech Republic has existed as a sovereign state only since January 1993; before that time it was joined with Slovakia as Czechoslovakia. It was a single republic, a democratic market-based system between the World Wars. During the Second World War the Nazis took control but were eventually thrown out by the Soviets. Communists won political power in 1948 and retained it until the Velvet Revolution in 1989. Czechoslovakia became a federal state in 1989, comprising the Czech and Slovak Republics, until it separated into two independent republics in 1993.

The Slovaks and the Czechs developed over centuries within different traditions; Czech culture was from early days influenced by the Austrians and the Germans, while the Slovaks languished as a neglected part of the Hungarian empire. The Czech Lands were industrializing before the turn of the twentieth century. They had for decades experienced more balanced industrialization than the Slovaks and were following a Western European development path until 1939, when the Germans took the reins of government. After the withdrawal of Soviet power in 1990, the Czechoslovaks hit the ground running, but reaction to the new conditions was different in the two parts of the federation. The Soviets had treated Slovakia as a rural area in need of development, and that development had proceeded via promotion of heavy industry. (The Slovak story is told in Chapter 12.)

The Czech Republic is considered to be among the most successful of the transition economies. In June 2000 the United Nations Human Development Report placed the Czech Republic thirty-fourth among the forty-six countries included in the "high human development" group. Criteria included income per capita, literacy and life expectancy. Its 10 million people, over 80 percent ethnic Czechs, are aware of their centrality in any optimistic scenario for post-communist Europe. They occupy Europe's geographic center, bordered by Poland (north), Germany (west), Austria (south) and the Slovak Republic (east), and they identify closely with Western Europe. They have joined NATO and the OECD and are in the

* We owe thanks to Jan Hanousek for his assistance with this chapter.

first group of EU applicants. Most of them view the Soviet period as a time of foreign occupation, a long detour from their road back to equal status with their developed neighbors to the west and south. In 1910 the Czech Lands produced more than half of the Austro-Hungarian empire's industrial output; Czechoslovakia was one of the world's ten most developed economies up until the 1940s, and the only democracy east of the Rhine in 1938, until German occupation in 1939.

Based on the careful design and zealous pursuit of macroeconomic reform policies, the Czech Republic has attained considerable success since independence in 1989. Real GDP has very nearly reached its reported 1989 level. As has been the case in every emerging market economy in Europe, the Czechoslovak economic performance measures slumped after independence. Table 8.1 shows that GDP growth was negative in 1990, bottomed out in 1991 and turned positive only in 1994. It grew at around 4 percent in 1995 and 1996, but the economy turned sluggish in 1997 and fell into recession by 1998. GDP growth was virtually flat in 1999 but rebounded to over 3 percent in 2000. The long recession ended in 1999.

Table 8.1 Real GDP growth rates, 1989–1999 (average annual percentage rates of change)

Year	% change	Year	% change
1989	4.5	1995	4.8
1990	–1.2	1996	3.9
1991	–14.2	1997	1.0
1992	–6.4	1998	–2.7
1993	–0.9	1999	–0.6
1994	2.6		

Appropriate macroeconomic policies are in place and are clearly understood by politicians and the public, an achievement envied by others in emerging Europe. According to the international statistical agencies, Czech income is relatively high among transition economies. The government's budget has been kept under control (deficits, though persistent, have been small), and inflation has been held down. Inflation was around 3 percent in the year 2000. Despite these stabilization achievements, growth slowed dramatically in 1997. What went wrong? Vaclav Klaus and the Civic Democratic Party (ODS) were blamed for the recession and for legislative lethargy, as well as for fraud. The Czech Social Democrats (CSSD) took office in 1997 after eight years of ODS rule, a record in the European transition countries.

The source of problems lies in the area of microeconomic institutional change – what we call restructuring and deregulation. Among all economic reforms undertaken, the outstanding performer was widely considered to be the voucher privatization program that gave 80 percent of Czechs a personal stake in the success of the new capitalism. The program turned out to be flawed, however. The Czechs' light (central government) debt load allowed implementation of a plan based on virtually cashless internal voucher privatization. Most company shares ended up in bank-run investment funds, and banks were not in fact extensively privatized. The results were poor corporate governance, falling profits, alleged fraud in some companies and a financial crisis at leading banks, due in part to an asymmetric bankruptcy law that favored debtors over creditors. Corporate governance is still a problem area. The Czechs persistently ignored the importance of restructuring of legal frameworks. However, the last two of the four big state banks have been sold, going a long way toward eliminating soft loans.

There is room for a great deal of improvement in legal and financial sector structures, in implementation measures for various reforms (including privatization), in incentives at many levels, in industrial restructuring in general and in judicial and civil service regulations and practices in particular. Czechs recognize that corruption and economic crime are still both social and economic problems.

In spite of the challenges that remain, we fully expect the Czech Republic to continue toward regaining its position as a front-runner among the former communist economies. We base this judgment in large part on our hypotheses about a country's economic success that are central to this volume. Historical experience can provide a people with a viable model, a memory of the past that shapes a vision of the future; this in turn enables policy-makers to implement enlightened reforms and enables voter–consumers to be forward-looking enough to support and sustain those reforms. Experience informs the utility functions of the citizens who choose whether or not to sacrifice short-run for longer-run gains, who choose whether to embrace risk or retreat to demands for social guarantees, who can or cannot see competition and market incentives as opportunities for a better future.

We argue that the significant historical influences that predispose politicians and voters to be forward-looking are, first, the recognition of and strong identification with a "golden era," for the Czechs a period of liberal democracy and capitalistic markets; and second, a strongly negative experience of domination by the Soviets. The Czechs were a part of Western Europe before the war, and they want to be again. The brutal period of Soviet domination was imposed and managed not, primarily, by homegrown communists, but by outsiders, and with brutality. The Czechs' past has helped to generate politicians who understand what it takes to get their economy back on track, and voter–consumers who understand what it takes to sustain economic progress. Now that macroeconomic reforms have largely been accomplished, restructuring requires serious attention. The EU accession process has made this obvious.[4]

HISTORY BEFORE COMMUNISM

Although the Czechoslovak Republic did not exist as a nation until 1918, Celtic ancestors of the Czech people lived in Bohemia before the birth of Christ, and the first Slavs arrived by the sixth century AD. The Czech Lands and Slovakia followed different historical paths from the time of the Magyar invasions in the tenth century and for the next thousand years. Throughout this period, the peoples of the Czech Lands leaned culturally and economically toward German and Austrian influences, whereas the Slovaks were drawn southeast toward the Danube; in the late nineteenth and early twentieth centuries, Slovakia was called "Upper Hungary."

In 1355 King Charles IV became Holy Roman Emperor and made Prague the political and cultural center of the empire. He founded Charles University and built some beautiful structures still standing in Prague, including the Charles Bridge. By this time the country had undergone an urban transformation on a par with development in the Netherlands and in Flanders. The Czech silver groat was the primary currency in Europe; Czech silver mines and woven textiles were famous throughout Europe.

In the sixteenth century Ferdinand I of the Austrian Habsburgs became the King of Bohemia and Hungary, making the Czechs and Slovaks his subjects. The Hapsburgs ruled from Vienna, with the exception of Emperor Rudolph II (1576–1617) who ruled from Prague Castle. He granted the Czech Estates (the nobility) a charter and guaranteed religious freedom to all inhabitants of the kingdom, including serfs. The favorable economic development path of the country was interrupted when Ferdinand II, a Habsburg, became the Czech King. He was an uncompromising and absolute ruler and recognized only the Catholic Church. In 1618 the Czech Estates revolted against him, starting the Thirty Years' War that ultimately spread all over Europe. The noblemen of the estates lost, the country was devastated and the population reduced by about half. For nearly a century – until 1775 – there were peasant revolts that reflected desperate living conditions.

Habsburg monarchs Maria Theresa and Joseph II introduced pro-industry legislation in the eighteenth century, and Joseph guaranteed religious freedom and abolished serfdom. The Constitution of 1867 granted the Hungarian people a status equal to that of the German-speaking population, at which time the empire became known as Austro-Hungarian. By this time the Czech Lands had experienced considerable economic development and had become the workshop of the empire, producing about 65 percent of Austro-Hungarian industrial output before 1900.

The Austro-Hungarian empire disintegrated at the end of the First World War; the Czechoslovak Republic was created in October of 1918. The Treaty of Versailles established boundaries of the nation in 1919. Tomas Garrigue Masaryk, a Czech philosopher, was the first President. Czechoslovakia's reputation for fiscal and monetary conservatism was reinforced in 1919 when the Finance Minister, after having already put measures in place that saved the country from the hyperinflation raging throughout the empire, temporarily closed the border. He had all Austro-Hungarian currency circulating within the country stamped and he declared it the only legal tender. Hyperinflation went on all around the stable island of Czechoslovakia. This streak of conservatism was in evidence throughout the democratic period of the 1920s and 1930s, and in fact continues to serve economic reformers well.[5]

The country enjoyed democracy and prosperity throughout the 1920s and 1930s, with a per capita income that approximated those of Austria and of France before the Second World War. In those days, the Czech GDP per capita was higher than Austria's, but Slovak per capita income was lower than Austria's. The differences between the industrialized Czech Lands and Agrarian Slovak Lands persisted throughout the inter-war period. The Czechs had been part of the Austrian empire for centuries, then part of the Austro-Hungarian empire, finally becoming independent two decades before the Second World War. Their history and their development path put them among the leading democratic societies and capitalistic economies of Western Europe during the 1920s and 1930s. From long historical experience, the people of the Czech Lands related to their immediate neighbors to the west and south, to German and Austrian culture, more than to any others outside their own.

Nazi Germany occupied the Czech Lands in 1939 and during the Second World War made Slovakia a separate state dependent on Germany. The whole country was liberated in May

1945. The first Czechoslovak parliament after the war was democratically elected, with a ruling coalition made up of two Slovak and four Czech parties, dominated by the communists.[6] The Prime Minister was a left-leaning social democrat, and one Deputy Prime Minister was a Slovak communist, the other a Czech communist. Key ministries were balanced between communists and other parties, although the civil service was professional and therefore supposedly not subject to political pressures. The communists were the strongest political party in the Czechoslovak state. Had the non-communist parties maintained solidarity, they could have outvoted the communists, but they did not. Nevertheless, the communists were initially pursuing socialism through democratic political means.

By mid-1947, Soviet pressure drove the Czechoslovak communists to give up their own path to socialism and the process of Stalinization got under way; one early move was to force Czechoslovak withdrawal from Marshall Plan negotiations. Eventually all non-communist ministers were forced to resign from the government, and a party-organized demonstration was staged to get the President to accept their resignations and appoint a new communist national government. All this was done according to constitutional rules, ostensibly through appropriate political channels and completely peacefully.

A Central Action Committee and local action committees were organized to purge the country of "reactionaries and traitors."[7] Electoral laws were changed and by the 1948 general election, parliament existed in name only. It was in fact so intimidated by the communists that it gave an overwhelming vote of confidence to the government, knowing that this would be the end of democracy. Thereafter, single candidates were nominated by the National Front, and much of the power of parliament was transferred to a Presidium, which looked strikingly like the Supreme Soviet. All non-communist political parties were abolished and their leaders either escaped the country or were arrested. The judiciary was severely modified, with the constitutional and the supreme administrative courts abolished.

In 1945 over 60 percent of the total Czechoslovak industrial workforce was already employed in nationalized enterprises, and another 15 percent was employed in "confiscates," enterprises taken away from German and Hungarian owners after the war.[8] But about 25 percent of the labor force was employed in cooperatives and private enterprise, and markets were still working. Nationalized enterprises were committed to employee participation in management through factory committees. The economy had a large state element but was still mixed, and the ruling Communist Party plans initially allowed for considerable freedom and competition. In other words, the economy was not so deliberately centralized as was the Soviet planning system. This changed with the Stalinization of Czechoslovakian political and economic systems.

HISTORY UNDER SOVIET RULE[9]

Two results of the 40 years of Soviet domination of the Czech economy are particularly striking. First, the economy was changed from one of the more advanced in the world to a poor and underdeveloped one. Right after the Second World War, markets were still functioning in Czechoslovakia, although industry was already partly nationalized, along with banking and insurance. After the communists took over in 1948, the economy was soon centralized and subjected to planning, enterprises were all nationalized and emphasis moved to heavy industry. Reported growth rates were high during the first five-year plan (1949–1953), but that did not last. Initially, the centralized system could mobilize resources rapidly, and plenty of inputs were available via CMEA trade. However, the limitations of a centralized system soon became evident and overwhelming: perverse incentives, limited innovation, inefficient allocation of resources, rigidities. Growth slowed in the later 1950s and stagnated in the early 1960s. Reforms improved the situation by the latter half of the decade, but also led to the Prague Spring in 1968. Growth slowed significantly from the mid-1970s (the oil shock changed the terms of trade within the CMEA, and agricultural output fell) and stagnated in the 1980s.

From the onset of central planning, Czechoslovakia was forcibly removed even farther from world trade than Poland or Hungary. The extensive dependence on CMEA trade promoted progressive technological backwardness. Furthermore, any disruptions in CMEA markets were reflected back into the Czech economy. In 1990, per capita income in Czechoslovakia – close to Austria's before the war – had fallen to about one-fifth of Austria's.

The second striking result of the Soviet period was that by 1990 there was negligible difference in GDP per capita between Slovakia and the Czech Lands. There had been policies in place during the period of independence to promote integration and industrialization, but the Soviets increased the pace of Slovakian industrialization significantly by transferring financial and physical capital and technical resources from Czech industries. They promoted industrial "integration processes" between the two areas by emphasizing the development of Slovak power, mining, heavy engineering and defense industries, and by converting agriculture into communes.

By 1958, the Slovakian share in national industrial output had grown from 8 percent before the war to 17 percent, and its share of national income had risen to over 20 percent.[10] In 1948 Slovakia's per capita income was about 60 percent of that of the Czech Lands; in 1968 it was approaching 80 percent, and by 1970, it was near parity. This accounts in part for the Slovaks' lesser antipathy toward socialism compared to the Czechs. More of the explanation can be found in the milder form of "normalization" imposed on the Slovaks after 1968.

The reforms that were undertaken during the early 1960s were initially designed to promote economic growth. They culminated in the Prague Spring of 1968. This refers to a time when the reformed communist government under the leadership of Alexander Dubcek, a Slovak, instituted a series of new policies called "socialism with a human face." These included worker participation in management of firms, some autonomy for firms themselves and some price liberalization. Significantly, there were plans to separate economic from political policy-making. All the plans came to naught. The Soviets reacted to the reforms by sending Warsaw Pact troops and tanks into Czechoslovakia in 1968. The Dubcek regime was split, purged and crushed. Central planning was reinstituted and the Soviets made certain that notions of economic reform were suppressed thereafter. The army stayed. The only idea from 1968 that was implemented, in 1969, was the introduction of a federal structure. Instead of one parliament and one government, there were three – Federal, Czech and Slovak. In practice, however, all key decisions continued to be made by the Czechoslovak Communist Party Presidium, tightly tethered to Moscow.

"Normalization" was the term used to encompass the Soviet policy response to the Prague Spring reforms, which were equated with counter-revolution. The normalized regime rested on three principal processes. The first was a purge of all major social and economic institutions, including the party itself, of anyone associated with the pluralistic reforms initiated in 1967. Nonconformist behavior was controlled with severe punishment or with threats of it. The second was the strict control over the spread of unacceptable ideas, and involved a purge of institutions engaged in the dissemination of knowledge and culture, especially the media. This helped the leadership institutionalize and ritualize agreement and public acts of compliance with normalization policies. The third was centralization of the economy.[11]

These three processes established centralized control and institutionalized social conformity. Normalization was less severe in the Slovak region, partly because counter-revolutionary activity was less in evidence there. Czech opposition to the regime was stronger and was shared within a community of dissidents. From 1968, political repression was thorough. Officials who ran the system were now from outside; the Czechoslovak people had no control over their political system or their economy. The policies of normalization were continued up to the time of the Velvet Revolution, when Czechoslovakia separated itself from Soviet domination.

THE VELVET REVOLUTION

The Czechoslovakian state won independence from domination by the Soviet Union late in 1989. The evolution of the independence movement centers mostly on political activities in Prague. (For this reason, that movement is dealt with here rather than in the Slovak chapter.) The major events reviewed involve dissident activities, open conflict with authorities, mass protests and a symbolic general strike that finally caused the Soviet-controlled regime to bow to the will of the people.

Opposition to the government can be traced back to the early days of normalization; the high level of public conformity during the twenty years of its existence only repressed open dissent. This does not mean that the regime went unchallenged. Blacklisted writers were publishing underground and were obtaining and circulating forbidden foreign books, and they established contacts with representatives of the other main source of dissident activities, the youth counter-culture. The first public trials of opponents to the regime occurred in 1972, and this sparked the founding of Charter 77, the eventual source of Civic Forum and Public Against Violence, the two key groups that created the Velvet Revolution in the late 1980s. This pioneer organization described itself as "a free, informal, open community of people of different convictions, different faiths and different professions united by the will to strive individually and collectively for the respect of civil and human rights in the country and throughout the world."[12] This statement proclaimed the courage of the individual member to resist conformity to the mores of an amoral state.

The mushrooming of dissident groups after the formation of Charter 77 and the emergence of public demonstrations by the late 1980s undermined the notion that the government was beyond criticism. The three primary sources of threat to the normalization regime came to a head by 1988. Two were internal, the growth of public criticism and the increasing economic difficulties; the third was external, the changes under way in Soviet Europe. The first major public demonstration was made up mostly of young people and took place in

Prague on 21 August 1988, the twentieth anniversary of the Soviet invasion. After this, more public protests occurred, and the authorities responded with force and by imprisoning leaders. This stiffened resistance domestically and raised public consciousness abroad. Dissident groups based on human rights, religious and ecological concerns, proliferated.

The government was facing serious economic difficulties at the same time that the political scene was heating up. Costs of production were increasing and the central planning system was in obvious need of structural change; a number of leading Czechoslovak economists advised that a market economy was the only answer, but the authorities were unwilling to deal with the social changes that market reforms would involve. Political pressures were growing; from late 1988, Poland and Hungary were accelerating their radical reforms toward market economies and political pluralism. The Berlin Wall came down in November of 1989. All of this stiffened the resolve of the reformers in Czechoslovakia.

The Velvet Revolution of November 1989 started with Prague university student protests and demonstrations that led to significant declarations by the Academic Forum (academic staff) and then the Civic Forum (OF).[13] The Civic Forum was led by playwright Vaclav Havel and formed in Prague in November 1989, at about the same time as the Public Against Violence (VPN) was founded by actor Milan Knazko in Slovakia. The OF and the VPN were two branches of the same organization. This was deliberately not a political party in order to gain the trust of the people, who had developed a wariness of all forms of political organization, typically associated with state violence. It was rather a group intent on opening discussion with the authorities, and it took responsibility for coordinating protests and demonstrations as well as negotiating with the government.

The event that signaled the end of the communist regime was the general strike of 27 November 1989. It represented the overwhelming support of the general public for the opposition. The Communist Party leaders had counted on the industrial and agrarian working class to ignore the appeals of university students, OF and VPN activists. The party had preached that strikes were a form of economic sabotage, and there was certainly no public perception of a right to strike. Although the general strike was originally the idea of the students, it was designed and planned by Havel and his associates, who understood the reservations of the workers, especially those outside Prague. The general strike was designed to be unlike any strike that had gone before it, to be an opportunity for the public to register protest and to be an informal referendum on the role of the Communist Party. The OF and VPN coordinating committee was non-directive, but functioned instead as an information center for the preparations for and execution of the strike; the general public was distrustful of political agencies ready to give orders. Importantly, individuals identifying themselves as democratic socialists and reform communists had broken with the controlling Communist Party and joined the OF and VPN. This calmed fears that the opposition movement would jeopardize the future of socialism. This informal and careful management carried the day, and the general strike was a massive success; three-quarters of the Czechoslovak labor force participated. The communist authorities got the message.

By the end of the first week of December 1989, the basic organizational structures of the ruling Communist Party had been dissolved, Marxism–Leninism was abolished as the official ideology and 25,000 party members had resigned. The formation of a new government based on a political coalition marked the end of the revolution as an opposition movement. A few weeks later, just before Vaclav Havel became the first democratically elected President since the Second World War, the Communist Party apologized to the people of Czechoslovakia for "the mistakes and injustice" it had caused. Democratic parliamentary elections were held in June 1990; twenty-three parties or coalitions entered the contest for seats. Civic Forum and Public Against Violence, transformed into one political party just after the November revolution, trounced the Communist Party at the polls.

First Steps on the Road West: Czechoslovakia 1989–1993

The newly elected Federal Assembly immediately set about legal and institutional restructuring by codifying civic and political rights, reaffirming commitment to human rights, and establishing a Constitutional Court designed to interpret and protect the constitution and to enforce a system of checks and balances. The basis of a clear civil structure was in place by 1992.

The plan for radical economic reform was announced in September 1990, and it closely resembled Poland's approach to rapid transformation. Its main backer was then Minister of Finance Vaclav Klaus. Agreement about transforming the economy to a market system was virtually universal but there was disagreement about the methods for accomplishing this, and about how they should be applied. There was some support for considerable state intervention and a slower pace of transition, to avoid troublesome social effects. The September plan had social and economic sections, and in the social part the priorities were social security and justice, employment, wages and protection from the possibility of serious declines in incomes. Proponents of such protections lost out in the subsequent debates, and the emphasis was placed on economic reforms. Before those reforms could be implemented, however, parliament had to work very hard to push through masses of supporting legislation. The program was officially launched on 1 January 1991.

The arguments of the radical reformers against gradualism reflected a relatively sophisticated level of understanding of market mechanisms. They stressed that macroeconomic stabilization, mostly through aggregate demand restriction, was an absolutely key goal in the earliest phases of the transition to markets. These policies would involve fixing the exchange rate and setting targets for the money supply and possibly for wages and incomes. In fact anti-inflation policy dominated all other macroeconomic objectives. Reformers recognized that real resources could be used most efficiently throughout an economy only if decentralized markets determined prices. They believed funds for capital formation, whether for private investment or public infrastructure, would best be allocated if accompanied by wholehearted and consistent political commitment to economic transformation. They turned to unrestricted trade and a convertible currency to gain the benefits of free trade for exporters and for consumers and to stimulate supply-side responses to competition. They adopted privatization of enterprises and the principle that reduced state involvement in economic decisions is essential for efficiency.[14] Havel hesitated for some time before deciding to support the radical reformers, who thereafter quickly set about getting programs in place under his leadership.

The strategies adopted – to achieve macroeconomic stability, transfer property rights from the state to the private sector and open the system to competition – reflect the conventional wisdom of neoclassical economics that is mirrored in conditions typically imposed by the International Monetary Fund on countries that want to borrow. We elaborated on reforms necessary for a successful economic system in Chapter 3. Hrncir (1992) argues that the diagnosis behind the policy recommendations was somewhat misguided, emphasizing the costs of macroeconomic instability based on analysis of countries with markets already in place, rather than emphasizing the peculiar problems of a system without markets. This in Hrncir's view has led to overemphasis on macroeconomic stability and insufficient attention to the "microsphere": to needed changes in behavior patterns, to institutional and structural rigidities and to the absence of market institutions. This has generated higher transaction costs, including delays in accomplishing real restructuring. Hrncir believes in the existence of an "asymmetry between the progress of macroeconomic stabilization and liberalization measures, on the one hand, and the microeconomic and institutional spheres on the other."[15]

The reform plan began with price liberalization for retail goods and a start to phasing out subsidies. The government continued to exercise its conservative fiscal tendencies by controlling budget deficits. Gradual tax reform was begun. The koruna was made internally convertible. The first phase of privatization succeeded in privatizing most small businesses. Various plans were made available for the privatization of larger enterprises, and citizens were encouraged to buy vouchers with which they could participate in the process.

Before examining major reform programs in greater detail, it is appropriate to note the political separation of the Czechs and the Slovaks in 1993, at a time when the two might have been closer than at any period of their coexistence. Why did it happen, and why was separation chosen by the weaker of the two states?

The Velvet Divorce, 1993

The market reform programs that followed independence revealed the economic and political inequalities between the two parts of the federation. Slovak political leaders linked the negative impact of economic reforms to their inadequate power in the decision-making processes. They felt that major decisions were made in Prague without sufficient Slovak input. The degree of sensitivity to disparities was evident in the lengthy and acrimonious "hyphen debate" in March 1990. The result: the word "Czechoslovak" would be hyphenated in Slovakia but not in the Czech Lands. This dispute, foolish in the eyes of outsiders, signaled the existence of a more serious underlying problem.

The removal of Soviet political controls allowed for the re-emergence of the Slovak question. Nationalistic issues had not been permitted a hearing during the Soviet period. Historically one can view the formation of two new states as a continuation of the disintegration of Austria-Hungary into nation states. This was finally made possible by the collapse of the Soviet empire. It was another instance of emancipation of a minority ethnic group and the mobilization of a community into a nation. This social phenomenon was one of the powerful forces of the twentieth century.

The formation in 1918 of a single Czechoslovakian state was doomed because it rested on overly simplistic notions of statehood. Czechoslovakia was a foreign attempt to join two very different peoples into a single state. In retrospect it seems evident that the economically and educationally more backward Slovaks, mostly deeply religious farmers, would not combine effectively with the more developed, secularized and urbanized Czechs.[16] By the late 1980s the two communities had become similar by many measures and the cooperative experiment apparently was working well. But serious political fissures lay beneath the surface.

The dissolution process occurred not because of strong public feelings, but rather because there were not sufficiently strong political forces on either side that were able to create a viable notion of a single state and work out ways to share their vision and make it operational. Although the Slovak general public had little idea of the options under discussion after independence, they suspected that they would lose out as a result of the new reforms. The Czechs, on the other hand, apparently harbored a growing suspicion that they were carrying a bigger part of the burden for which the Slovaks should have been more grateful. Public opinion was not the decisive factor in the separation process because civic participation was nearly absent. Public opinion polls at the time suggested that a great majority of both Czechs and Slovaks preferred to retain the federation, but the same polls also revealed that only 17 percent of Slovaks were satisfied with economic reform, while 37 percent of Czechs were satisfied. Most Slovaks, 64 percent, wanted more gradual reform, while the Czechs favored radical reform by a margin of 52 percent.[17] In the final analysis, while the public never voted on separation, the politicians were unwilling to avoid it.

Just after the parliamentary elections in June 1990, negotiations began on the division of powers between the federal and the national governments. Some Slovak politicians wanted to continue the federation while others (notably Vladimir Meciar, the Slovak Prime Minister) wanted a separate and sovereign nation. In the face of intractable disagreements about the relationship between the Czech Lands and Slovakia, the Federal Assembly approved a law allowing a referendum nationwide or in one of the countries. The Slovak politicians who were determined to separate the two republics had seen the public opinion polls favoring confederation and so would not allow a referendum. They ordered the Slovak National Council, the country's legislative body, to adopt a declaration of sovereignty and a constitution not based on the federal constitution. The Council refused to vote on the proposals. Havel tried to break the stalemate by proposing early elections, a referendum and even dismissal of the Federal Assembly. Slovak politicians, with help from some Czech colleagues, blocked those efforts.

During this time Czechoslovakia was experiencing political fragmentation on a grand scale. Parties and movements were splitting and re-forming. After the June 1991 election, six parties were represented in the Assembly, and OF and UPN held 168 of 300 seats. Before the June 1992 election there were 15 parties in the Assembly and the largest group held 43 seats. The 1992 election revealed surprisingly divergent results in the partner states. The overwhelming winner in Slovakia with over 37 percent of the votes for the National Council was a nationalist and leftist party led by Meciar. He was pressing for more independence but had stopped short of demanding separation. His party wanted to slow down market reforms and increase the role of the government in the economy. Klaus's party was the most popular in the Czech Lands and had garnered nearly 30 percent of the votes for the Czech National Council. Klaus took this as a clear mandate for radical economic reform.

After the election, negotiations continued between Meciar and Klaus. They agreed to reduce the size of the federal government. Soon thereafter the Assembly failed to re-elect Havel as President twice, mostly because he was so strong in his support of unification. In July the Slovak National Council adopted a declaration of sovereignty but claimed it was symbolic, and not really a declaration of independence. A few days later, Vaclav Havel, the most powerful symbol of a united Czechoslovakia, resigned (although he returned later). Klaus and Meciar agreed to set processes in motion to divide the state into two. In October both government delegations agreed on legislation that would end the single state with "the passing of 31 December 1992" and establish two new states, the Czech Republic and the Slovak Republic.[18] In November the Federal Assembly voted to dissolve the federation, and thus itself and all other federal institutions as of 1 January 1993. That ended the seventy-four-year-old federation.

The split of the Czechoslovak federation was handled in a civil and businesslike fashion with respect to division of assets and liabilities.[19] An initial monetary union collapsed early in 1993 when both countries introduced their own currencies. This was necessitated by a very large outflow of foreign currency reserves in anticipation of the January 1993 introduction of a value added tax in both countries, and as a result of the general uncertainty surrounding their separation.[20]

ECONOMIC REFORMS

Price Liberalization

The whole system of price subsidies began to be dismantled in 1990 with the elimination of subsidies on retail prices. In January 1991, 85 percent of producer and consumer prices were liberalized. Czech statistics show the 1989 inflation rate at 1.4 percent, although according to the OECD (1991), hidden inflation added another few points.[21] In 1990 inflation was 9.7 percent. With widespread price liberalization in 1991, the consumer price index jumped over 50 percent. In 1992, most remaining prices were freed. The rate of increase in the consumer price level dropped to 11 percent. Inflation spiked to over 20 percent annually following the Divorce, but fell until 1998 (see Table 8.3). Price liberalization proceeded smoothly and was virtually complete within a few years, with some important exceptions, for example, electricity, gas, telephones and water. The prices of 18 percent of goods in the consumer price index basket remained controlled in 1992; by 1999 that had dropped to13 percent.[22]

Privatization

Of all the transition peoples, the Czechs (along with the Hungarians) show the largest ratio of private sector output to GDP, at 80 percent.[23] In common with the other emerging market economies, the Czechoslovaks began the privatization process with a restitution scheme – a way to restore to owners land and real property confiscated (nationalized) after 1948. There were time limits on the program, and it has been completed.

Privatization proceeded with small enterprises and was based on legislation that went into effect at the end of 1990. Auctions began in early 1991; the first round was limited to Czechoslovak nationals, but foreigners could participate in any subsequent rounds. Eligible establishments had been sold off by mid-1993 and the program was terminated.[24]

The first wave of large-scale privatization began in 1992, although some joint ventures with foreign firms had already taken place in 1991. The Large-Scale Privatization Act specifies that ownership can be transferred by several methods: competitive public tenders, public auctions, direct sales, unpaid transfers (for example to municipalities) or voucher privatization. They all require creation of a "privatization project" statement, outlining plans for upgrading, for employees, for production and so on. Any domestic or foreign individual or group can submit projects. Firms can also be privatized with vouchers where citizens bid for shares with their vouchers, or investment funds bid with vouchers.

The voucher system was one of the most noteworthy of the Czech reforms.[25] Each citizen over 18 was given an opportunity to buy a book of vouchers for 1035 koruna (Czech crowns), about one week's wages. (This was called the "first wave" of voucher privatization, and there have been two more.) Each booklet represents 1000 points that can be used to purchase shares in companies, or they can be used to invest in a fund or to buy residential property. The average book value of assets per voucher booklet was estimated at 30,000 crowns between the second and third waves (*Trade Links* October, 1993, p. 22). More than two-thirds of voucher holders had transferred their points to an investment fund by that time; such funds have become the dominant owners of enterprises in the country.

In connection with the first wave of voucher distribution, some 450 investment companies were established. They operate like mutual funds or investment trusts, by issuing share certificates that entitle holders to a share of the company's assets and to participation in the yield on assets. They may be open- or closed-end funds. No one of them can hold assets valued at more than 10 percent of total investment company or fund assets; no fund can acquire more than 20 percent of a company. Banks run the larger funds, and some funds have made loans against voucher book collateral.

The first two privatization waves succeeded in transferring more than half of the assets of state enterprises to private hands, and the ten largest investment funds obtained more than 40 percent of all vouchers – over 70 percent of all vouchers held by funds. The privatizing reform sub-index for Czechoslovakia peaks in 1992–1993 as a result of voucher privatization.[26]

The voucher scheme earned considerable positive attention worldwide. It stimulated development of capital markets by promoting some institution-building that can serve these markets in the future. It created a huge body of stakeholders in the system, a broad array of citizens who became risk-takers and who care about the performance of the private sector and therefore the success of economic reforms. The state, through the National Property Fund, still holds stakes in many "strategic" companies – in energy distribution, mines, steel mills and banks.[27]

The voucher system came under criticism after 1996. The negative implications of investment fund activity for corporate governance, for profits and for capital markets were increasingly obvious. Fraud within companies was reported in the press, along with insolvency of some leading banks.[28] Investment funds trade blocks of shares among themselves and sell to other investors. The funds could become the "cornerstone of financial infrastructure essential for capital allocation and corporate governance in a market economy."[29] But the fact that large banks still own considerable portions of the funds can create conflicts of interest in lending practices, especially where firms are in trouble. This is one serious consequence of weak legal and regulatory frameworks, and it has retarded the restructuring process. We shall see below that design flaws in the voucher privatization program have serious consequences for restructuring and therefore economic performance.

Macroeconomic Stabilization

The principal outcome of effective macroeconomic policy is price-level stability. As Table 8.2 indicates, the Czech inflation rate peaked in 1991 at 56.6 percent. It fell to single-digit annual rates from 1995 on. (The 1998 rate hit 10.7 percent but inflation fell to 2.1 percent in 1999.) The means for achieving low inflation is essentially slow monetary growth. However, slow monetary growth is difficult to accomplish if the central government's budget deficits are large, because this deficit spending creates pressure to monetize government spending by printing more money. More money leads in turn to higher inflation. Since monetary authorities often conduct their policies with an eye toward exchange rates and trade balances, problems in international trade can also have deleterious effects on monetary stabilization. The Czechs did a good job in conducting effective stabilization policies. This accounts in large part for their being placed in the mid-1990s at the top of the ladder of success in transition. Unfortunately, by 2000 fiscal deficits were rising again, as was public debt.

Table 8.3 shows that budget deficits were usually between 0.5 and 2 percent of GDP, reaching 3 percent by 1992. Any pressures to turn on the monetary spigot derived from the

Table 8.2 Inflation and unemployment, 1989–1999

Year	CPI (% change)	Unemployment rate
1989	1.4	0.4
1990	9.7	0.8
1991	56.6	4.1
1992	11.1	2.6
1993	20.8	3.5
1994	10.0	3.2
1995	9.1	2.9
1996	8.9	3.5
1997	8.5	5.2
1998	10.7	7.5
1999	2.1	9.4

Table 8.3 Central government budget policy (deficit/surplus as a percentage of GDP)

Year	Deficit/surplus	Year	Deficit/surplus
1989	–1.2	1995	–1.2
1990	–0.2	1996	–1.9
1991	–1.9	1997	–1.4
1992	–3.1	1998	–1.4
1993	–0.7	1999	–1.6
1994	1.3		

foreign trade sector, not from fiscal policy. The Czechs decided to hold down the exchange value of the koruna; some international agencies argued that the koruna was held to 50 percent below its equilibrium value. An undervalued koruna provided a kind of cocoon around Czech businesses – their products were cheaper to foreigners, thus stimulating demand for Czech exports and domestic demand for Czech products. This cozy environment gave Czech firms the chance to familiarize themselves with the new competitive environment following the CMEA and Soviet collapse, and it bought time for state-owned enterprises to adapt to a newly competitive environment. This meant fostering labor productivity, installing effective accounting procedures, tightening financial controls and establishing effective management practices – in short, firming up corporate governance. The Czechs could also more easily handle the move away from trade primarily with the East to trade primarily with the West.

The Czechs launched stabilization reforms in January of 1991. They devalued the koruna and pegged it to a basket of currencies (mostly the dollar and the Deutschmark). They introduced internal convertibility of the koruna and a 20 percent import surcharge. They controlled wages and activated a social safety net.[30] Low wages helped competitiveness and reinforced price-level stability. These measures were buttressed by a continued commitment to a balanced budget. Other objectives were to attract foreign capital, decrease subsidies to enterprises, promote privatization and generally reduce the role of government in the economy. These measures were akin to those that Poland had implemented earlier and the Czechs seemed to adopt them naturally.

The trough of transition economic activity was 1991, when real GDP growth was –14 percent and inflation was over 55 percent. Goals for 1992, in addition to limiting inflation, included stopping the decline in GDP and real wages and holding the budget deficit level. Meanwhile, the government was launching the privatization scheme for large enterprises, trying to improve the banking sector and liberalize trade. Monetary policy continued to be restrictive, but tight fiscal policy was harder to sustain. Enterprise profits declined during the hard years 1991–1992, government social expenditures went up, and the deficit grew. Since 1992, however, it has been held to less than 2 percent of GDP. (Even after the split of the federation in 1993, both the Czech and Slovak governments continued to practice conservative budgetary policies.)

These tough stabilization measures in the early years were carried out under challenging circumstances: the country was in the process of shifting trade flows from East to West, CMEA trading relationships had in most cases disappeared, and a worldwide recession was under way, which did not help trade flows.

By the mid-1990s the Czechs appeared to have pulled their economy out of the doldrums into modern growth. The peak year, with growth at 4.8 percent, was 1995. After that the growth rate fell. No other Central European countries were in decline at the time. The growth rate fell in 1997 to 1.0 percent, and by 1998 the Czech economy had stalled, with GDP falling 2.7 percent. What happened to the superstar?

The collapse in growth does not appear to have resulted from reckless stabilization policies. The government managed to control its deficits even through the recession and the financial crisis that began in 1997. Full convertibility was implemented in October 1995; the currency peg to the international basket held, and the koruna remained stable until late 1996.[31] By that time the economy was slowing, the exchange value of the koruna was falling and foreign investors were pulling out of the Czech Republic. The central bank decided to protect the currency. It intervened several times, driving interest rates up over several weeks. In May 1997 the bank officially abandoned the fixed exchange rate regime. The sharp increase in interest rates and the shortage of liquidity slowed the domestic economy further. Recession ensued.

Nor can one attribute the slump to excessively generous wage policies. The authorities kept labor costs down in the early years of transition, and while this restricted living standards of ordinary people, it contributed to price-level stability. Boeri and Burda (1995) argue that the Czech government pursued active labor market policies to keep unemployment low, for example by tightening up the unemployment insurance system and subsidizing private sector employment and job creation schemes on a large scale.[32]

A hint of the nature of the causes of the collapse arises from the financial practices of state-owned enterprises. Despite tight macro policies at the federal level, few state enterprises failed. Why? The answer is that inter-firm debt and unpaid obligations between firms and banks rose. A large part of the industrial sector is heavily in debt to the domestic banks that own it. The state is still extensively involved in the economy insofar as it controls companies or subsidizes bad debt for banks.

Evidently the Czech government, while setting the stage with tight stabilization policies, had not exploited the undervalued currency period to tighten up microeconomic business practices and rules. Czech enterprises failed to use the period of stabilization to reform either. State-owned enterprises, including banks, continued to operate under the old rules. The government resisted cracking down on inefficient enterprises and banks continued to provide loans to firms that were not adopting new competitive practices.[33] Through the banks the government continued to insulate poorly run businesses from failure. This prevented the threat of collapse from propelling individual firms toward microeconomic and structural reforms.

As we noted in our modeling efforts of Chapters 4 and 5, stabilization policies alone do not guarantee growth. While price-level stability is essential to a healthy economy, it is not sufficient. Growth of living standards requires capital accumulation. Capital must grow faster than the labor force and faster than replacement requirements for depreciating capital. Savings must be large and channeled into productive capital. In Chapter 3 we stressed the importance of private property and market-determined prices. The same point applies to the cost of capital. Capital market prices are signals to investors where to invest savings so that it leads to productive physical capital formation. Poorly designed financial markets, inadequate controls from poorly designed voucher programs, and poorly designed incentives in enterprises prevented effective allocation of savings into productive capital. Despite a stable environment and a weak currency, Czech firms and the government failed to make the necessary structural changes to foster growth.

Foreign investors began to figure out that Czech firms were operating on borrowed time. Economic efficiency was not improving. Neither old firms nor inefficient workers had been replaced. By 1996–1997 wages were rising faster than productivity gains, contributing to poor economic growth rates. After many foreign investors withdrew, the central bank tried to stem the tide by raising interest rates. Unfortunately the problem was not one that monetary measures could solve. Essential reforms such as withdrawing government subsidies and creating incentives for producers to behave constructively had been neglected. Even though the Czechs were successful in fiscal and monetary stabilization, they had not made the structural changes necessary for sustained growth. One result of this failure was the 1997 defeat of the Klaus regime.

The economy began to recover in 1999 and was growing again by 2000. Inflation and the government's deficit are also rising. Transfer payments are over 50 percent of government spending and are 20 percent of GDP. This is a potential threat to macroeconomic stability.

Restructuring and Deregulation

Enterprise restructuring may be the Czech Republic's biggest single task. For industrial restructuring to proceed successfully, civil administrative and judicial institutions must be in place and functioning efficiently. The Czech Republic has been criticized by EU officials for lack of appropriate administrative structures; for poor enforcement of existing legislation; and for unsatisfactory training and supervision of civil servants, including state attorneys and judges. Whereas both government and private sector restructuring have begun, measures look better on paper than they do in practice: central government administration lacks functioning internal financial controls, environmental problems continue, law enforcement is weak, workplace health and safety legislation has stagnated. The Czechs have plans in place to overhaul the judiciary and to introduce a new civil service law.[34]

The Czechs have not yet institutionalized adequate monitoring, supervision and regulation of the financial system and of corporate governance.[35] Norms of fiduciary responsibility are weak, and shareholders are not yet adequately protected by reasonable oversight of fund activities. This problem extends to the Czech stock market, which has had no strong supervision to deter insider trading or inadequate disclosure. Capital markets are underdeveloped in general and do not act as a source of capital domestically. There has been not a single Initial Public Offering in the Czech Republic since the stock market opened in 1993. Financial markets are not providing an adequate framework for business activity.[36] The Czech equity market is underdeveloped, liquidity is low and supervision is inadequate; however, the new Securities Commission has performed well and has somewhat improved the general atmosphere in financial markets.

In 1996 foreign investors bailed out of the Czech stock market in large numbers, citing poor regulation, widespread fraud (or at least the perception of it) and lack of interesting investment opportunities.[37] This signaled the onset of recession. Our privatization reform sub-index is lower for 1997–1999 than it was for earlier years. According to the IMF, recent poor performance of the private sector reflects in large part weak corporate governance that has resulted from ownership structures established in the voucher privatization program.

Much of the work yet to be done in getting incentives right for the long-term benefits of markets involves getting the government out of industry and seriously revising its role. The government is not yet willing to leave wages to the market and productivity has been low. Firms will need to shed workers more readily if productivity is to improve. Reported unemployment was unrealistically low until the recession years; it may still be underreported.

Inter-firm indebtedness is still high but the government is apparently not willing to let firms fail at an efficient rate. The structure of industry ownership has hampered companies' ability to restructure and to modernize. Some measures were passed in 1999 to address the bad debt problem, but thousands are probably technically bankrupt; in 1999 over 31 percent of outstanding debt was bad. The overly bureaucratic judiciary is slow and enforcement of bankruptcy law is poor.[38]

Capital markets are dominated by banks, reflecting the fact that the Czechs have patterned their financial system after Germany rather than the United States. The biggest investment funds are run by the biggest banks, which are also the lenders to the companies in which the investment funds hold equity. When firms are in danger of bankruptcy, banks may have conflicts of interest. Financial markets reacted favorably to plans announced in 1999 to privatize remaining state-owned banks.

Rent controls are still in place, and this reduces labor mobility. The labor market is relatively tight in Prague, but unemployment is much higher in the countryside (over 15 percent in some areas).

Trade Liberalization

The Czechs made impressive progress in reorienting their trade away from former CMEA partners. In 1989 almost two-thirds of Czech trade was with communist bloc countries, and now they account for less than 20 percent. At least two-thirds of Czech trade is now with advanced economies, mostly EU countries. About one-third of Czech exports go to Germany, a level of integration that surpasses that of Germany's main EU trading partners. In 1990 in all of Czechoslovakia there were fifty-two firms trading with foreign countries; now, in the Czech Republic alone, there are tens of thousands.[39]

When the government undertook to move to markets, the decision was made to liberalize the domestic and external spheres at the same time, in hopes that the benefits would outweigh the costs. The benefits to liberalizing trade included attracting foreign competition that would dilute the power of domestic monopolies, "importing" foreign price ratios, and reallocating resources toward more efficient outcomes.[40] The sustainability of open trade required nearly 90 percent devaluation of the exchange rate, accomplished in three episodes in 1990.

The shift from CMEA to Western trade resulted in a serious deterioration in the terms of trade for Czechoslovakia. In the early years of independence inflation was high, consumption and investment spending was low, exports were low and import prices were high; there was a current account deficit in 1990. Devaluation raised exports and reduced imports and made a positive contribution to GDP. According to Sujan and Sujanova (1994) this added to inflation pressures. In 1991 the current account moved back into a small surplus of 0.3 percent of GDP. Trade was nearly balanced for the next three years.

The Czechs experienced a rapid increase in the trade deficit and capital inflows in the first half of 1995. Falling exports and rising imports contributed to sluggish economic growth, with only 1 percent growth in real GDP during 1997.[41] According to the Czech National Bank (1994) capital inflows were financing the current account deficit, and the service balance (tourism) was large. But in 1996 and 1997 these trends began to reverse. The Czech economy was moving into a recession by 1997 and did not recover until late 1999. By 1999 foreign direct investment was rising again, which suggests that the Czechs were beginning to respond to calls for serious structural improvements (see Table 8.4).

Table 8.4 International trade and financial statistics (selected years)

Year	FDI* (% of GDP)	Imports (% of GDP)	Balance of trade (% of GDP)	Exchange rate (koruna/$)
1990	0.2	20.1	–1.0	18.0
1995	5.0	49.8	–1.4	26.6
1997	2.3	48.1	–3.2	31.7
1998	4.9	52.4	–1.0	32.3
1999	7.5	54.0	—	34.6

Note: * Foreign direct investment.

ECONOMIC PERFORMANCE AND THE FUTURE

By the mid-1990s the Czech Republic was credited with being one of the most economically liberalized of the emerging market economies. Inflation had decreased persistently since 1991 and real GDP growth had improved steadily. The Czechs had not yet recovered to the (reported) 1989 income levels, but they had been very successful in their liberalization efforts, and most people were better off each year.

The Czechs avoided mass unemployment after Soviet withdrawal. The unemployment rate moved up from zero in early 1990 to 4.1 percent by 1991. Unemployment rates were persistently higher in Slovakia, in part because of unemployment compensation and other labor policy differences.[42] Other explanations are based on the nature of Slovakian production and the slump in demand for its heavy industrial products, and on the greater number of people employed in small businesses in the Czech Republic. The Czech rate appears to have been kept low in part because Czech citizens could easily travel across the border to work in Germany and Austria. Also, the Czech Republic is home to fewer Roma (gypsies) than is Slovakia, and Roma comprise a large proportion of the unemployed in Slovakia.

By 1996 clouds were on the horizon. In 1997, economic activity slowed and foreign investors were feeling less optimistic about Czech prospects. Growth in GDP fell from 4.8 per cent in 1995 to 1 percent in 1997. In 1996 the European Bank for Reconstruction and Development (EBRD) argued that the failure of industry to restructure lay at the heart of the economy's inability to grow faster, citing the necessity for revival of the industrial sector.[43] The EBRD has urged changes in the tax system and in regulations that allow majority shareholders to siphon off company profits that should be shared with all shareholders. There is insufficient pressure from shareholders for companies to restructure, and it is proving difficult to get managers to take the initiative without better incentives. The Klaus regime was unwilling to adopt appropriate but unpopular reforms.

The trade deficit was growing, productivity was in the doldrums and wages were rising. The government was under pressure to increase spending and pensions were already taking up 27 percent of the budget. In mid-1997 many observers believed that the Czech Republic was standing at the brink of a financial and political crisis. Prime Minister Klaus claimed that these gloomy forecasts were "overplayed and overdone."[44] By 1998 the economy was in recession and GDP growth fell by 2.7 percent.

The fundamental lesson here is that avoidance of structural changes and deregulation of enterprises eventually catches up with the economy. Governments that do not design incentive structures that induce competitive behavior by firm managers and limit central government bailouts are promoting stagnation. Without market-allocated investment spending, effective capital per worker will not grow and eventually growth will slow down. The task before the Czechs is to turn to controversial microrestructuring measures. The future is dependent on how effectively they do this. If they continue to choose not to adapt their government, legal system and corporate governance to enhance private property rights and to attract private investment, they may lapse into comparative stagnation. If they assault these problem areas aggressively, they could again become the capitalist superstars.

The Czech Republic has been among the most stable of the former communist countries in Europe. Prime Minister Vaclav Klaus was in power longer than any other transition country leader. By 1997 the economy was slowing and Klaus was in danger of losing his position. His zeal for reform had softened. Some political analysts detected a lack of dynamism politically and this was reflected in the sluggishness of the economy.[45] They referred to institutional and legislative paralysis. According to this point of view, the Czech people were either ready for a change in government or apathetic and indifferent. The Civic Democratic Party seemed to be running out of ideas for moving forward. Klaus argued that all this was exaggeration, but he recognized that the country needed to attract more foreign capital. The Social Democrats began to attack Klaus's ODS as unwilling to grasp the nettle of restructuring. In 1997 the Czech Social Democrats (CSSD) defeated the ODS, and re-elected President Havel appointed Milos Zehman Prime Minister, ending Vaclav Klaus's eight-year tenure.

Table 8.5 summarizes election results, reform indexes and economic data on growth, inflation and unemployment for election intervals. The ODS was clearly a reform party in the early years. However, its reformist zeal began to decline in the middle of the decade. By 1996 it was no longer the strong reform advocate it had been in the early 1990s. This reflected two forces. The earlier reforms, while including the dramatic privatizing of property and price liberalization, focused mainly on macroeconomic stabilization. These

Table 8.5 Elections, reforms and economic performance, 1990–1999 (all variables cover election intervals)

Year	Votes for reformers (%)	Reform index (1995=100)	GDP % change After	GDP % change Before	Inflation rate After	Inflation rate Before	Unemployment rate After	Unemployment rate Before
1990	51.5	101.7	–9.0	2.6	33.5	4.2	2.9	0.5
1992	36.7	96.4	1.6	–9.0	12.1	33.5	3.2	2.9
1996	33.3	90.1	–0.2	1.6	9.1	12.1	5.0	3.2
1998	49.0	100.4	–1.3	–0.2	5.0	9.1	8.8	5.0

reforms were successfully adopted under the Klaus regimes of 1990 and 1992. The Czechs tamed inflation, but unemployment drifted upward. Measured GDP growth has been sluggish.

The next stage of reforms is politically more costly; for example, government regulatory measures of the financial sector are bound to rankle the financial elite. They involve dismantling large state-owned enterprises that employ many voters. The ODS resisted these reforms and the recession of 1997–1998 was the result. In our reform index analysis we treat the 1996 and 1998 ODS as non-reformers as a result of the sluggishness of reforms by that time, and reform indexes for the second two election periods are comparatively low. The improved reform index under the CSSD in 1998–1999 reflects increases in foreign direct investment, expansion of trade and currency stabilization. Given our definitions, votes for reformers tend to be followed by more reforms.

One hopes the Social Democrats will take up the reform mantle, and perhaps the ODS will find its reformist zeal again. In either case, microeconomic restructuring is clearly in order. It is hardly surprising that an economic system that came so far, so fast under one leader began to discover that markets are complicated and that it will take effort and ingenuity to institutionalize appropriate incentive structures. The fundamental liberalization of the Czech economy has been accomplished. While the system is up and running, nobody said it would be easy to sustain.

NOTES

1. Hrncir (1992).
2. "The new Bohemians," *The Economist*, 22 October 1994, p. 23.
3. Reed, John (1999), "Explaining the Gap," *Wall Street Journal*, 27 September.
4. See European Union, *Czech Republic 2000*.
5. Svejnar (1993), p. 23.
6. Bradley (1991) is an excellent source on Czechoslovak politics after the Second World War.
7. Ibid., p. 27.
8. Selucky (1991), p. 161.
9. This section draws heavily on Jan Svejnar's (1993) work and on Dyba and Svejnar (1991).
10. Selucky (1991), p. 167.
11. Wheaton and Kavan (1992), p. 6.
12. Ibid., p. 12.
13. The narrative on the Velvet Revolution is based on material from Wheaton and Kavan (1992).
14. Hrncir (1992), pp. 166–7.
15. He expressed concerns about shortcomings in Czech microeconomic restructuring at a Conference on Economic Performance and Financial Sector Reform in Central and Eastern Europe, in Tallinn, September 1996.
16. See Butora and Butorova (1993); these authors are particularly good on sociological issues and have drawn on Czech and Slovak literature in the formation of their judgments.
17. The United States Information Agency published this result in a research memorandum dated 3 February 1992.
18. Pehe (1992a).
19. Pehe (1992b). Pehe details the agreements drawn up at the time of separation.
20. See World Bank (1994).
21. Czech statistics from the Federal Statistical Office and Czech Statistical Office are reported in Svejnar (1993).
22. European Bank for Reconstruction and Development (2000), p. 156.
23. European Bank for Reconstruction and Development (2000).
24. In discussions with Jeri Schwartz, President of the Liberal Institute, we learned that Vaclav Klaus felt that

turning to the courts of restitution had slowed the privatization effort and stalled the large-scale voucher privatization method. Klaus felt the sluggish pace of privatization contributed to the breakup of Czechoslovakia. As a result, he fired his first Privatization Minister.

25. For an overview, see Aghion and Blanchard (1994) and Blanchard et al. (1994).
26. Construction of the reform indexes are discussed in Appendix B, section 5.
27. See European Union, *Czech Republic 2000.*
28. Hanousek and Kocenda (1998a) discuss some of the implications for corporations of the voucher privatization scheme.
29. World Bank (1996), p. 56.
30. See Svejnar (1993), p. 29.
31. See Hanousek and Kocenda (1998b) on currency issues.
32. Svejnar (1993), pp. 46–8, describes unemployment insurance provisions, both the initial 1990 scheme and the 1992 program revisions.
33. Kutan and Brada (2000) explain that banks continued to control non-financial enterprises through bank ownership of investment funds. This arrangement led to a "proclivity to make loans to unprofitable firms in which [the bank's] investment funds hold large stakes," p. 32.
34. European Union, *Czech Republic 2000.*
35. IMF Staff Country Report No. 99/90, *Czech Republic: Selected Issues*, expresses serious misgivings about enterprise performance in the Czech Republic. Without better implementation of reforms, they expect matters to deteriorate. They attribute many problems to flaws in the design of the voucher privatization program; it limited ownership by strategic investors and created incentive problems for investment privatization funds.
36. European Bank for Reconstruction and Development, *Transition Report 2000.*
37. *Financial Times*, 3 April 1997.
38. European Bank for Reconstruction and Development, *Transition Report 2000.*
39. *Trade Links*, July 1993, pp. 58–9.
40. Hrncir (1992), p. 170.
41. *Financial Times*, 3 April 1997.
42. Svejnar (1993).
43. *Financial Times*, 3 April 1996.
44. *Financial Times*, 3 April 1997.
45. These arguments are made by Jiri Pehe in the *Financial Times* (1997) and by *The Economist* (1997a).

9. Estonia is headed West*

How did a former Soviet republic end up with one of Eastern Europe's best growth stories, and the most liberal economy west of Hong Kong?
(Matthew Brzezinski, *Wall Street Journal*, 9 December 1996)

In spite of foreign domination since the thirteenth century with the exception of a few decades of independence between the World Wars, Estonians have maintained a strong sense of national identity. They provide a clear case for our hypotheses about historical determinants of success of the transition process: namely, that success depends heavily on a country's vision of itself in the future (based on its best period in the past) and on its experience under Soviet domination. The better and more prized a country's "golden era," the clearer are its goals for the reform process. The more repressed and mistreated the society during the Soviet period, the more eager are people for complete change and for self-determination. The Estonians have, since independence in 1991, demonstrated a remarkable degree of social cohesion on the direction and nature of the economy. They continue to be committed to market reforms and a future wherein Estonia once again approximates Finland in its standard of living. Their experience of Soviet occupation has united them in their determination to depend upon markets to allocate resources. Some indexes rank Estonia at the top of the class of emerging market economies with respect to degree of liberalization and economic freedom.[1]

Estonia lies south of Finland, less than fifty miles across the Baltic Sea and, like Finland, against Russia's western boundary. The Baltic States – Estonia, Latvia and Lithuania – were integral parts of the Soviet Union, with no control over their economies during five decades of occupation. Other than being former Soviet republics, the Baltic States have little in common, culturally or linguistically. (With a view to EU and NATO membership, they continue efforts to forge cooperative Baltic trade and defense arrangements.) Estonia was the most developed republic of the USSR with the highest per capita income; it is the only one of the countries examined in this volume, other than Russia, that was a part of the USSR.

Although there have been a number of changes of government since independence, there has been little wavering in the commitment to the reform process, whatever the parties in power. Imperfections in that process may reflect residual weaknesses in administrative capacity and in institutional restructuring rather than in political will. Land and residential privatization did not go smoothly initially, but markets are functioning now. Privatization of small and medium-sized firms is complete, and privatization of large state-owned enterprises is very nearly so. These have been accomplished primarily via sales to foreign businesses and secondarily with vouchers. Estonia's economy has a greater proportion of

* Teet Rajasalu and Vello Vensel deserve special thanks for their contributions to this chapter.

foreign ownership than any country in Europe. A very small country, Estonia has trade policies as liberal as any in the world. (That will change with accession to the European Union.)

After hyperinflation in 1992 Estonia adopted a currency board arrangement. The fiscal discipline with which Estonians have sought to restrain government budgets and inflation has been effective. Real GDP growth has been positive since 1994. When in 1996 the US government made Estonia the first of the emerging market economies to be cut off from American aid, the Estonian government threw a party. Although the European Commission put Estonia and the Czech Republic at the top of its list of the most successful emerging economies in tackling environmental problems, much remains to be done on environmental clean-up and protection.

There are some troubling questions that arise from Estonia's experiences since independence. Will the trade deficit continue to grow? Will reformers be able to resist demands for special treatment from the agricultural sector? Can politicians continue to be fiscally disciplined in controlling deficits? In particular, can spending on pensions and health care be controlled? Will Estonians continue to integrate their large Russian minority successfully? Can they rebuild stable and mutually satisfactory trade relationships with Russia? Can the Estonian economy stand up to international competitive pressures in the long run? Will Estonians be able to maintain and continue appropriate judicial and administrative improvements required by the European Union, now that they are in the first rank of accession candidates?

We examine Estonia's path to political independence and economic liberalization beginning with a description of the "golden era" of independence between the World Wars, moving in section 2 to the Soviet period, and finally to independence. Three topics take up the remainder of the chapter. We first review each of the five reforms discussed in Chapter 3 in terms of how they are contributing to growth via the channels discussed in Chapter 5. Next we examine the sustainability of reforms as a function of political and social considerations based on the model of Chapter 6, and finally we assess long-term growth prospects.

The first period of independence was important because it shaped Estonians' vision for the country's future; it provides the answer to the "transition to what?" question. Moreover, it reveals historical, social and economic influences that shape consumers' reactions to economic reforms. Those reactions determine the degree of resistance to reform and the likelihood of political sustainability of reforms. In terms of the growth models, historical influences determine two sorts of characteristics of consumers: how flexible they are between present versus future consumption, and whether they are good savers. Flexible consumers are willing to substitute consumption between periods in order to promote capital accumulation; patient consumers are farsighted with respect to saving. Inflexible individuals resist policies that inflict short-term costs and promise only long-term gains. Industrious, farsighted consumers are willing to sacrifice today for a better tomorrow. Estonia's first period of independence, 1918–1940, shaped the preferences of the consumer in our growth models.

ESTONIA BEFORE THE SOVIETS[2]

In assessing the likelihood of long-run political stability and economic progress in Estonia, it is important to look to the era considered by Estonians to be their political and economic norm, their first independence from 1918 to 1940. The inter-war years of independence meant that at the time of separation from the Soviets, Estonians were restoring their independent statehood, not establishing a new state. This fact strengthened their sense of legitimacy. Estonians claim to have occupied the same territory since 3000 BC (some recent studies indicate an even longer tenure) and trace their Finno-Ugric language back that far; it is a close relative of Finnish and a distant cousin to Hungarian. They have a powerful sense of permanence and identity based on language.

From the thirteenth century until 1918, Estonia was ruled from abroad. The strategic importance of the eastern Baltic Sea meant that Estonia has been at the heart of balance-of-power struggles or tensions throughout recorded history. Tallinn, the capital, became a member of the Hanseatic League under the Danes in 1280, who later sold much of the country to a German order of knights. Tartu, Viljandi and Parnu, main cities in Estonia, were also Hanseatic towns. Sweden took over in the sixteenth century, and Russia in the eighteenth, until independence was declared in 1918. Estonians made up about 90 percent of the population in 1918. Currently they number 1 million of a total of around 1.4 million; most of the others are Russian or near-Russians, such as Ukrainians and Belarussians.

While Estonians looked to Finland after the Second World War for their image of the Western world, their inspiration in seeking independence and transformation came also from memories of their first taste of independence. Because they had learned to take responsibility for self-governance and to accept the risks inherent in market systems, there was little paralyzing debate at the time of independence about what sort of system they would create.

The period just prior to the first independence was one involving balance-of-power machinations of two major powers of the day. After 1917 Estonia was caught in a tug-of-war between Germany and Russia. When German and Bolshevik talks collapsed in early 1918, the Germans almost immediately overran Estonia. The Bolshevik army offered only token resistance. A three-person committee empowered by an underground elected assembly declared Estonia independent on 24 February 1918, and Estonians celebrate this as their Independence Day. The Bolsheviks invaded Estonia late that year, when it was clear that Germany had lost the war. With some help from the British navy (for which Estonians remain grateful), the Estonians resisted, but the Germans and Bolsheviks continued to fight over the Baltics. The Estonian War of Independence went on during 1918 and 1919. With financial and manpower support from the Finns, the Estonians prevailed; and in 1920 they signed the Tartu Peace Treaty, the first treaty that the Soviets signed with any state.

An important characteristic of the Estonians that shapes their current social, political and economic goals is their identification with the Finns. This is a phenomenon of long historical and linguistic standing, reinforced in the decades before Soviet withdrawal by access to Finnish television in Tallinn (apparently the Soviets were unable to block all TV signals). This meant that many Estonians had a good idea of Western living standards. Today they see themselves, unequivocally, as Westerners. Their level of economic development before the Second World War was comparable to that of their Scandinavian cousins, so they have the feeling that the Soviet period was comparable to their having missed a departing train.[3] They see Western market-oriented economic organization as normal and the Soviet system as unnatural, even though they had been out of touch with market institutions for nearly five decades. They want the Finnish quality of life – including high material standards, democracy and nationhood – in the context of their own culture. Almost everyone is clear about the goals of the transition process, and there is no public argument against them.

It is notable that the Estonians saw themselves as a legitimate nation from 1918, in light of the fact that they had not experienced independence before. They identify themselves as Estonian first and Nordic second, in spite of centuries of outside domination. They achieved a moral victory in their War of Independence and enjoyed a period of peace until the Second World War. The other Baltic States, along with Finland, Hungary, Poland, Czechoslovakia and Austria, had also been parts of larger empires before the First World War and afterwards became modern nation states. During the inter-war period, Tartu University, the nation's oldest (founded 1632), began to use the Estonian language; Tallinn Technical University and the Estonian Academy of Sciences were founded. Writers flourished and cultural pride grew. The most important achievement of the first independence period was the firm establishment of a modern Estonian culture. The language was modernized and adopted throughout the entire educational system. Land reforms broke up the large German estates into family farms, which generated a remarkably equal distribution of farmland in the country. A cost of this land reform was poor economies of scale in agricultural production. Agricultural exports to the West were primarily high-quality meat and dairy products. Farming was considered among the most honorable of occupations, by both rural and city dwellers. A tendency to idealize rural life continues in Estonia today, even as the sector continues to shrink.

Estonia created its own currency and modeled it first after the Finnish marka. In 1928 the Estonian kroon was introduced. Its value remained fairly steady for a decade, trading at about four to the US dollar. This degree of stability allowed policy-makers to address some fundamental economic problems. The industrial base had, even in those days, been Moscow-designed to serve the Russian military, so industrial diversification was necessary, along with scaling down to meet domestic needs. Estonians were able to begin these processes in good times, and until the Great Depression the inter-war economy was prosperous, although the government continued to carry heavy debt from the independence war. The Depression caught up with the reformers before they had fully accomplished the planned changes, but they had a good start at establishing a market-based economy. By 1939 the Estonian standard of living was at approximately the same level as Finland and Denmark. By 1988 the Estonian per capita consumption level had fallen to about one-tenth that of Finland.

Politically, Estonia became a parliamentary democracy with too many parties. A party could win a seat with 1 percent of the vote, so 14 parties were elected initially. There were 100 seats to be won, with the whole country as one electoral district. (Election rules subsequently changed, but the problem persists. Governments are always coalition-based and the election system is complex.) But democracy did not last. As a result of a violent communist effort at a coup in 1924 with Soviet tanks standing on the border, and after a strong homegrown right-wing political attack in the early 1930s, Prime Minister Konstantin Pats became acting President. He consolidated and strengthened his power and ended democracy in 1934. Estonian authoritarianism in the 1930s was mild by Europe's standards: there were no political executions and political prisoners were freed in 1938. Although the rest of the decade was peaceful, non-violent and authoritarian, democratic elements were being reintroduced into the system in the later 1930s. The trend was interrupted by invasion. Estonians had achieved their national wish for independence, but it lasted less than twenty years.

HISTORY UNDER SOVIET RULE

The Second World War and the Soviet Takeover

During the Second World War the Estonians were overrun yet again by two contending powers, the Nazis and the Soviets. The Soviets occupied in 1940–1941 and again from 1944, the Germans from 1941 to 1944. The end of independence was a direct result of the secret Molotov–Ribbentrop pact of August 1939, a non-aggression agreement named after the Soviet and German Foreign Ministers who signed it. It designated spheres of influence in East-Central Europe between the two signatories and meant annexation for a number of countries. The Soviets got Estonia. The pact still represents to Estonians the essence of deviousness.

The Soviet occupation began in June 1940 and a puppet government was installed that proclaimed Estonia a Soviet Socialist Republic. Expropriation of industrial, financial and commercial property followed almost immediately. President Pats agreed to everything, including his own resignation in July, and he was deported a week later. The near-simultaneity of occupation and annexation meant that Baltic diplomatic facilities abroad were out of reach of the Soviets; some governments, including the United States, never recognized the legitimacy of the Soviet takeover.

In the first year shortages appeared. These shortages reflected in part the presence of the Soviet army and its demand for products. An artificially pegged ruble played a role. Finally, the Soviets expropriated banks, most commercial enterprises, factories with more than about a dozen employees, houses over about 2000 square feet, savings accounts over 1000 rubles and the contents of all safes. Leaving a job without the manager's permission or refusing to move to another plant meant two to four months in prison. Textbooks were altered, many books were banned and publishing was restricted. At Tartu University 70,000 theology books were burned; Estonian government leaders were arrested; critics of the regime and anyone deemed intellectually or politically dangerous disappeared. Arrests reached an average of ten per day. In one night in June 1941, 6640 people were deported with a few hours' warning. Families were separated, with men going to work sites and women and children sent to other Siberian villages. The Soviet army took 33,000 young men and most of them died in labor camps. Combined losses were perhaps 60,000 in one year, excluding 30,000 voluntary evacuees, but including 19,000 deportations and 2000 executions.

When the Germans attacked and subsequently occupied Estonia in 1941, these traditional enemies were supported by Estonian guerrillas; the Germans had become the lesser evil. The Nazis were no improvement over the Soviets except that they left cultural and religious life alone. Of the 5000 Estonian Jews, most escaped to Russia but 1000 stayed and died. Another 10,000 Estonians died in the German army, and 10,000 more left for the West after the war. Soviet troops attacked and occupied Estonia again in 1944; the Germans retreated. Over 60,000 Estonians fled to Sweden and Germany. By the end of the war, Estonia had lost 25 to

30 percent of its pre-1939 population through deportations, emigration, military deaths and deaths in camps.

Post-War Soviet Subjugation

Soviet domination can be divided into three periods between the end of the war and the 1980s, when dissent got under way: years of genocide from 1945 to 1953 (when Stalin died), years of hope until 1968, and years of suffocation to 1980.[4]

In a few days and nights in March 1949, as a part of the collectivization movement, Stalin deported at least 20,000 people. By 1950 the number of ethnic Estonians was at the level of 1880; the population has not yet recovered. Most 1949 deportees were farmers and their families; all were given ten minutes to two hours to pack belongings. They were taken to Siberian and Kazakh subsistence-level collectives; 80 percent of the farmers left behind had collectivized by the end of that year, and 90 percent by the end of the next. Soviet management was disastrous, and production dropped to half of pre-war levels by 1953. A bottle of vodka cost more than a bull. Daily pay on the collective was 3 kopecks and a pack of cigarettes cost 300 kopecks. Life was better in the cities. The last small service businesses were expropriated in the late 1940s and industrialization supported by extensive Russian colonization was promoted. To Soviet credit, reconstruction of war damage was finished by 1950, but housing was still in short supply because of migration off farms and Russian immigration. The Russians were eager to use Estonia's good human and physical capital stocks. A push for industrialization also provided a reason for bringing in more colonists, sometimes called the "civilian garrison" by Estonians. Between 1945 and 1953 the share of Estonians in the population fell from 94 to about 72 percent; arrests and deportations of natives numbered in the tens of thousands. Possibly half of Estonians with a college education fled to the West.

In 1950–1951 there was a great purge of culture and of the intelligentsia and also of the Communist Party leadership. This too extended to deportation and death in some cases. The Soviet terror eliminated German collaborators, anti-German Estonian patriots, many farmers, intellectuals and native communists. Fear and hopelessness became the norm for the people remaining. The decades just after Stalin's death in 1953 were different. The difference was stability; foreign occupation became foreign rule as people became less threatened by official repression and more accustomed to submission. A Soviet "thaw" lasted until 1956, when Hungary was invaded. In 1957 regional economic councils were set up throughout the USSR to provide some autonomy in managing local industry. Collective farms prospered and some became showplaces for foreign visitors. They all benefited from cheap energy, fertilizer and machine oil from Russia and from the huge Russian market for their products. Agricultural output was rising in Estonia, prices were set at non-confiscatory levels and compulsory product deliveries were abolished, so rural people were better off. They were still heavily dependent, however, on their small private plots. There was extensive destruction of forests and swamps, and damage from improper waste disposal. Official arbitrariness did not end: in 1958 a university student was sentenced to ten years in prison for sending abroad some unflattering photos of poor construction and of a radio jamming station.

On the other hand, many surviving deportees returned in the late 1950s. In the 1960s some Estonians were allowed to travel outside the country and some foreigners were allowed in. There was more housing available and it was less cramped, but it was still poor by Western standards. During this period Finnish television became available in northern Estonia, and Estonians still refer to it as their "window to the West." They could compare Helsinki to Moscow and it was no contest.

As the Soviets industrialized Estonia with relatively large factories for military production, output and consumption grew steadily. Estonia and Latvia became the wealthiest of the Soviet Republics and Estonia had the best overall living conditions of any republic, but it continued to fall ever farther behind the Scandinavian countries. The Russian immigrants that flowed into Estonia took jobs and scarce housing; sometimes they just moved into new apartments and officials did not dare challenge them. The colonists acted superior and were apparently uninterested in the local culture. Few learned Estonian.

The period of reasonably cooperative evolution ended with the Soviet crushing of the Prague Spring in 1968. After that and until about 1980, Estonians felt discouraged and even lower in political energy. The Soviet regime made more consumer goods available up to the middle of the 1970s and conspicuous consumption (at least relative to previous periods) took hold, but previous inadequate industrial investment meant that resources continued to be used inefficiently. Problems were made worse for a while by a series of crop failures, and economic conditions worsened in the later 1970s. Food shortages were more frequent after 1975, and about 60 percent of household income was devoted to food. Russian "tourists" raided Estonian stores, better stocked than their own. Moscow's management of the economy became less and less efficient; for example, Estonia's metallurgy and machine construction industries were subject to control by fifteen different agencies, most of them outside the country. Management might take place a thousand miles or more from the Estonian plant. City agencies were not consulted when new plants were established. One result of the centralized system was serious pollution.

In the late 1970s an intensive Russification campaign began, with an emphasis on making Russian the language of Estonia. Only 13 percent of Russians were fluent in Estonian. This and other evidence of Russian chauvinism fed the roots of dissent that surfaced early in the 1980s. The timing of this swing toward dissent is interesting, because Estonians had become accustomed to the socialism of the Soviet regime and to Soviet institutions that had by now shaped individual attitudes and behavior. Estonians somehow retained a sense of national culture, encouraged by their Western contacts, primarily with Finland and Sweden. Opposition to Soviet occupation existed throughout its tenure. Dissent and protests in Estonia peaked in the early 1980s, then waned during a time of serious economic stagnation from 1982 to 1986. During these years, important changes were occurring. The economic woes reflected the weaknesses in the central planning system, and the USSR was increasingly inefficient in meeting the economic needs of its constituent parts. Political repression of Estonian dissidents continued in the early 1980s; but after Mikhail Gorbachev assumed power, the situation began to change. Protest and dissident activity were never legalized, but the authorities were more likely to look the other way. This did not mollify the populace. They were unhappy about many things, such as the Estonian soldiers lost in the Soviet army in Afghanistan, and the effects of fallout from Chernobyl and requirements that Estonians work on the clean-up. Finally, during the no-growth mid-1980s, Estonians began to take over some of the top domestic administrative positions in Estonia. This may well have been a significant reason for the successfully non-violent transition to independence. It is noteworthy that administrators and those in authority were nearly all outsiders from the Soviet Union until the mid-1980s. From that time onward, Estonian leaders began to learn by experience.

POLITICAL TRANSITION AND THE BIRTH OF ESTONIAN REFORMS

In September 1988 at least a quarter of a million people – 300,000 by some estimates, 20 percent of the total population – gathered in one place to sing and listen to speeches. This Song of Estonia 1988 was organized by the Popular Front and was the centerpiece of what Estonians call their "singing revolution." It was a striking moment for nationalistic feelings, and powerful evidence and reassertion of cultural cohesion. Song festivals are popular all over Estonia, but none had ever been this large. Estonia's official restoration of independence on 20 August 1991 was less a sudden, spontaneous response to the collapse of the Soviet Union than was the case for satellite nations, because the Estonians had been preparing for this day for some time. Estonians had drafted plans for extensive economic reforms as early as the mid-1980s. These plans were for reform, not for independence from Moscow, and they referred to economic rather than to political issues. But they were an important part of the process of separation from the USSR.

The political environment changed significantly in 1987, more than it had during the previous thirty years. The Soviets had always been careless about the environmental impacts of industrial operations, and in 1987 they revealed plans to start up a new phosphate mine that threatened to contaminate water supplies throughout the country. This generated an environmental movement that virtually created Estonian public opinion as a force and stimulated action on a broad scale. This "Phosphate Spring" accomplished at least two things: it achieved some ecological success, and it taught people how to organize. The Estonian attitude changed from "it cannot be done" to "we will do it anyway." The phosphate dispute convinced the people that together they could in fact accomplish something. During that year a set of proposals for economic autonomy was published which instigated a great deal of debate about economic issues and stimulated the formation of dozens of task forces made up of economists and sociologists. The process focused the people's attention on economic issues and provided experience that would be particularly useful in structuring institutions in transition. During 1988 the specifics of Estonian economic autonomy, known by the acronym IME (*isemajandav Eesti*, or "self-managing Estonia") were formulated; the term *ime*, not coincidentally, means in Estonian "miracle." In 1989 supportive legislation was adopted in Estonia and in Moscow. Of course, an economically autonomous Estonia contradicted the rights and the needs of the Soviet Union as a sovereign state, and so in fact the reforms became a series of less than effective compromises. The bigger result, however, was that the independence movement gained momentum (as it was doing in the other Baltic States). While a wave of political reform moved throughout much of the Soviet Union and its satellites, Moscow began thinking in terms of market reforms within perestroika.

The spring and summer of 1988 were exciting times for Estonians. The Popular Front (Rahvarinne) was established, creating a political structure that was capable of reinforcing solidarity and promoting the cause of reform. Politically conscious organizations of all sorts were forming, but the Popular Front was the most cohesive and powerful, focusing the actions and feelings of the people. The blue, black and white national flag reappeared in spite of public prohibition, displayed prominently during the annual Old Town Days in Tallinn and at the Song Festival. The September "singing revolution" was a high point of communal feeling. Three important elements had come together to give power to the move toward independence: the phosphate dispute, the ideas of economic autonomy (IME) and foundation of the Popular Front. The first brought people together and demonstrated to them that they could effect change. The second, the IME, caused ideas of economic autonomy to be discussed widely and helped form an economic vision of the future. The Popular Front provided a political structure that attracted a large portion of the population and provided a framework that supported activism.

Throughout 1988 and 1989 negotiations went on with Moscow about issues such as trade relations, the banking system and payments into the federal budget. The activity and debates associated with IME had raised hopes for independence and set the stage for radical reforms. The solidarity of the Baltic States in their aspirations to freedom was illustrated dramatically when a human chain 600 kilometers long – people holding hands – was formed from Tallinn to Riga (Latvia) to Vilnius (Lithuania), organized by popular political movements in each capital. This event took place on 23 August 1989, the fiftieth anniversary of the hated Molotov–Ribbentrop pact, the secret deal whereby Hitler gave Stalin a free hand in the Baltics.

In late 1989 the ESSR (Estonian Soviet Socialist Republic) Supreme Soviet denounced the 1940 Soviet military occupation and annexation of Estonia and declared illegal the 1940 vote to join the USSR. The Soviet reaction was mild, and the Congress of People's Deputies went so far as to condemn the Molotov–Ribbentrop agreement. Moscow formally accepted economic autonomy for the Baltic States on 1 January 1990, and Estonia began instituting market reforms. However, the Soviets were unwilling to grant real autonomy and Estonians began to think about whether political independence would have to precede economic independence. The 1990 ESSR Supreme Soviet elections produced what became the Supreme Council, the ruling parliament of an occupied nation. There was considerable infighting within the Council, but it immediately determined the status of Estonia to be that of an occupied country and proclaimed Soviet authority unlawful, announcing that Estonia was in a state of transition toward a republic. In the next months, most Soviet symbolism was removed from the state. Gorbachev pronounced Estonia's decision (and a similar one in Latvia) null.

Throughout 1991 Estonia's economic situation steadily deteriorated. Shortages developed and trade with the West was nearly impossible. Industrial production was down. Economic reform efforts had produced few good effects and people were beginning to tire of domestic political battles. Some even began to question the merits of democracy. The national will and energy of a few years before was wearing thin. The Russian military occupation was still resented, as were most Russian colonists. Gorbachev refused to grant real independence, although Western governments increasingly recognized a legitimately elected non-communist parliament. In reaction to other Baltic independence movements, Soviet troops moved to take over buildings in Latvia and in Lithuania and killed people in both places. The Estonians erected tank barricades across roads leading up to Toompea, the hill in Tallinn on which the parliament building sits. At official levels, negotiations continued between the Estonian government and the Soviet Union. In August 1991 Gorbachev fell in a

Moscow coup. Soviet troops moved into Tallinn but there was no bloodshed. The Estonian Supreme Council adopted a resolution proclaiming independence two days after the Moscow coup. By the end of August some forty countries had officially recognized Estonia as an independent nation; the Swedish embassy opened in Tallinn on 29 August. The United States recognized the Baltic governments on 2 September and put pressure on the Soviets to do the same. A new Soviet State Council accepted Baltic independence on 6 September. The United Nations accepted the Baltic States as members on 17 September 1991. In telling the story of Estonian independence, one sees that interaction of Estonian aspirations to freedom and the economic and political collapse of the Soviet Union converged to provide an opportunity that the Estonians were able to exploit.

ATTITUDES TO REFORMS SINCE INDEPENDENCE

Since 1991 Estonians have been unified politically in their efforts to sustain reforms and reform has enjoyed broad public support. This is due in part to the fact that Estonians have a persistent image of themselves as an independent nation with a clearly defined culture; moreover, they look forward to a standard of living comparable to that of the Finns, their closest cousins. They define normality in terms of the two decades period of their first independence. They oppose anything reminiscent of the Soviet experience and so are willing to make sacrifices to achieve the benefits of a market economy. Another source of the support for reform measures among politicians and the general public is an ongoing fear of Russian efforts to reabsorb the Baltics.

How well do the people understand the political strategies that will achieve their economic goals? Some observers consider Estonians dangerously undereducated when it comes to political and public sector strategies that have been used to accomplish these broad objectives. This lack of understanding helps perpetuate political fighting between too many factions, a phenomenon that could slow or sidetrack reforms if the public loses faith in market processes. This is tied up with the public's willingness to sacrifice present for future consumption. It is important that those asked to make such sacrifices understand why they are doing so, and that they can evaluate the claims of politicians who argue for anti-reform policies, institutions or practices. Few Estonians identify strongly with any particular party; most distinguish only between political leaders. As in most democracies voters are swayed by personality, often at the cost of paying attention to issues.[5]

There are few staunch anti-reform elements in Estonia – no party or individual politician dare advocate a return to socialism. Of course, with Finland as a role model, the term "socialism" may require careful definition. The Estonians reject the authoritarian Soviet model, but the high level of government intervention in the lives of people common in North-Western Europe appeals to many Estonians. The government is from time to time under pressure to increase protection for the agricultural sector, to increase pensions for senior citizens and to increase special public support for other particular groups. All such pressures have constituencies and it is not easy to discredit their arguments. Finns, Swedes and Norwegians enjoy a good deal of government support and the "cowboy capitalism" of America is far removed from their experience. Anecdotal evidence can always be found to generate sympathy for various groups. Many pensioners are suffering, many farms are not viable and closing big state-owned enterprises has generated unemployment. Public servants (for example, police, judges and teachers) are underpaid. We review next the major elements of the liberalization process that is meant to generate prosperity.

ECONOMIC REFORMS: HOW COMPLETE, HOW SUCCESSFUL?[6]

After a severe contraction in 1990–1993, Estonia began to recover. GDP growth became positive from 1994 on (see Table 9.1). The collapse of trading arrangements, the impact of open competition and the necessity of acquiring and adjusting capital stock, plus an international recession, all contributed to the initial decline in real GDP. Real GDP was over 80 percent of the reported 1989 level by the late 1990s.[7]

Table 9.1 Real GDP growth rates, 1989–1999 (average annual percentage rates of change)

Year	% change	Year	% change
1989	8.1	1995	4.3
1990	–6.5	1996	3.9
1991	–13.6	1997	10.6
1992	–12.4	1998	4.0
1993	–8.5	1999	3.0
1994	2.0		

According to the Estonian Statistical Office, GDP growth fell to –1.1 percent in 1999, reflecting weak domestic demand and the Russian financial crisis of 1998, which occurred after the government defaulted on an issue of securities.[8] Although sales to Russia accounted for less than 15 percent of Estonia's exports, the crisis was in large part responsible for the slowdown in the rate of increase in Estonia's GDP. Growth resumed in late 1999 and GDP increased over 6 percent in 2000.

Price Liberalization

Price liberalization promotes economic growth via both demand-side and supply-side effects. On the demand side, it increases both the variety and the mix of products, which increases consumer utility as choices are broader and products better. However, it decreases utility for those individuals whose wages fall enough to cause real incomes to fall. Many consumer goods' prices rise, especially in early stages of transition, so that competitive markets can develop. On the supply side, price liberalization that leads to price increases allows product prices to reflect costs of production, and the production function will shift up. This raises real wages and real incomes.

When administrative pricing (centralized pricing) is done away with, prices regain their role as allocative instruments. The process of price liberalization began in Estonia in 1989,

Table 9.2 Inflation: consumer price index, 1989–1999 (average annual percentage rates of change)

Year	Inflation rate	Year	Inflation rate
1989	9.2	1995	28.8
1990	38.1	1996	23.1
1991	258.1	1997	11.2
1992	1076.5	1998	8.2
1993	89.8	1999	3.3
1994	47.7		

and by the end of 1991 free markets were determining many product prices. The government began removing rationing programs, and goods soon filled the markets. The change in the price level year on year peaked in 1992 at over 1000 percent when the ruble was replaced by the kroon. It fell to 89 percent the next year and less than 48 percent in 1994. The rate for 1995 fell another 20 percentage points; by 1998 the rate was in single digits. Table 9.2 reports inflation in the consumer price index from 1989 to 1999. No other transition country in Europe managed such steady progress up to 2000.

In 2000 some price controls still remained on goods produced or sold by state enterprises. These included prices for natural resources, electricity, natural gas and heating energy, some housing, postal fees, telecommunications services and public transportation (privatization of Estonia Railways and of oil-shale power stations began in 2000). The Estonian Central Bank authorities claim that this was to control possible pricing excesses where monopoly power exists. They nevertheless passed cost increases on to consumers, and may be responsible for a significant part of the inflation that persisted through 1997 by deliberately moving administered prices gradually upward in order to get them to world levels, especially for household energy. A good part of inflation since independence (according to the Bank, about two-thirds of inflation) was based on increases in regulated (administered) prices, especially for housing, transport, energy and communications services. Food prices sometimes contributed to inflation, as trade is completely open and Estonian food prices must reflect world prices in order to remain competitive. Services with regulated prices have a substantial influence on the consumer price index.[9]

Regulated prices still account for over 25 percent of the consumer price index basket. Authorities set the prices for only 0.9 percent of goods in the CPI basket, but they must give approval for nearly 17 percent of the goods, and taxes heavily impact upon another 8 percent of the basket. Decisions by central authorities still affect the rate of inflation as regulated prices are adjusted to ensure cost coverage.[10]

Privatization[11]

Privatization covers three sorts of properties: small businesses, medium-sized and larger enterprises, and residential units. The sell-off of small enterprises is complete, and larger ones are nearly all sold. The main privatization method has been direct sales through public auctions, public offering of shares, and auctions and international tender. Vouchers have been a secondary method, especially for housing. By 1999 companies from over one hundred countries had invested in Estonia; the US is the third-largest source of private sector investments. The Estonian Privatization Agency (EPA) was founded in 1993 and was patterned on the German Treuhandanstalt but differed in that it did not acquire ownership of properties to be privatized. As in the case of East Germany, the highest bid has not always won the right to buy. Plans to make new investments and to preserve employment have influenced EPA choices. A few medium-sized and large enterprises in Estonia remain in state hands; the intent initially was to keep the proportion to about 20 percent of all previously state-owned companies. This has been revised downward. The state still accounts for about 20 per cent of total output.

A number of problems common to most transition states plagued the privatization of large firms in Estonia, besides the basic facts that procedures were complex and big buyers scarce. (1) Claims for restitution slowed the process. (2) The splitting and sell-off of assets, sometimes called spontaneous restructuring, meant that the more valuable parts of enterprises were sold, with "leftovers" that are hard to sell remaining. This is one version of asset-stripping. (3) In some cases firms and their capital stocks were allowed to deteriorate in anticipation of privatization. (4) Landownership was an area of major uncertainty for years after independence. Legislation passed in December of 1995 extended ownership rights, previously confined to individuals, to legal entities. Before this, applications to purchase the land a company was sitting on were treated on a case-by-case basis. By 1996 legal entities could use vouchers for 50 percent of the price of land that they privatized. The EPA hopes to complete land privatization for private business activities before 2002.

Residential privatization exceeded 70 percent by 1996.[12] The processing of restitution claims by pre-war owners was slow and complicated at the local government level, and procedures for rehousing displaced residents were not clear. The Soviets had replaced with tower blocks one-third of the housing stock destroyed during the war. Nearly all construction was poorly done and maintenance was even worse. Some residents were hesitant to buy because of the low quality of their flats. (Low quality may refer to undesirable neighbors, decay, bad construction, small size or poor location.) Residents were also concerned about how buildings would be managed and maintained after privatization, especially as to what or who would replace the local authority. Some buildings were turned into cooperatives before 1991, in which case residents could buy their flats. Many small houses were never taken away from owners, although all land was declared the property of the people, which typically implied local government administrative control. Housing privatization began in 1993. According to the National Housing Board, by the end of 1995 nearly half of all state and municipal flats were privatized. Vouchers for housing were distributed among citizens based on how long they had worked and on age, adjusted for military service and time spent in labor camps; non-workers (children and senior citizens) also received vouchers. In April 1996 the land law was amended to make purchase of land easier, administratively and financially, for the owner of property built on that land.

Privatization of dwellings and of enterprises was complicated by the interest groups involved. These include insiders, usually management, employees or lessees and influential former owners and their descendants. New domestic entrepreneurs, often the *nouveau riche*, former privileged persons and *nomenklatura* who may have been managers, state employees or party officials have also muddied the process. Foreign investors, responsible for at least 40 percent (and probably more) of all large-scale privatization, and local governments (another strong pressure group that wanted possession of more properties and has controlled the administration of much of the privatization process itself) contributed to the difficulties. Privatization of assets controlled by local governments (ports, waste disposal companies, water and heating utilities) has accelerated. All businesses but a few large enterprises have been privatized. The service sector continues to grow and agriculture continues to shrink in importance.

Macroeconomic Stabilization

Macroeconomic stabilization refers primarily to fiscal and monetary measures that influence the inflation rate and exchange rate. (Exchange rate issues are covered in the section on trade liberalization.) Low inflation is crucially important if price liberalization is to have favorable effects on an economy and if economic agents are to have effective incentives to save. High inflation vitiates price signals, destroying the allocation function of the price system. Without price-level stability, other reform measures become moot.

Fiscal stabilization in the form of a balanced budget plays an important role in price-level stability, although judicious use of government spending may contribute to an improved allocation of resources in a transition economy. Estonian currency reform in 1992 was an important precondition for price stabilization and for trade liberalization. Carrying out independent macroeconomic policy from within the ruble zone proved to be impossible; the ruble simply did not fulfill the normal functions of money in those years, and certainly not in trade with the West.

Table 9.3 shows that until 1999 government sustained a near-balanced budget even when GDP was falling by double digits. The deficit relative to GDP shrank again in 2000. The record is remarkably good in the face of pressures upon politicians to spend in the interests of particular groups. Few doubt that various types of social spending could be higher, but a choice must be made between fiscal discipline and social spending that the economic system cannot afford. Potential problem areas at the beginning of the new century include local government spending and pensions and health-care outlays.

The tax system includes personal and limited corporate income taxes, a value added tax and excise duties. The personal income tax is a flat 26 percent, with sizable personal

Table 9.3 Central government fiscal balance 1991–1999 (deficit/surplus as a percentage of GDP)

Year	Deficit/surplus	Year	Deficit/surplus
1991	5.2	1996	–1.9
1992	–0.3	1997	2.2
1993	–0.7	1998	–0.3
1994	–1.3	1999	–3.0
1995	–1.2		

exemptions. The corporate income tax on all reinvested earnings was eliminated in 1999; otherwise it is also a flat tax of 26 percent. As in all transition countries, there is need of improvement in tax collection techniques and in educating taxpayers in order to improve compliance.

Monetary policy has been very restrained. When Estonians reformed the currency in 1992, they reintroduced the kroon and created a currency board, pegging the kroon to the Deutschmark at eight to one. (Banking and monetary reform already had a modest start with the founding of the first commercial bank in the USSR in Tartu in 1988; the Bank of Estonia was also established that year.) A currency board sets strict rules for central bank control of the money supply. The bank issues currency and commits itself to convert its notes into a specific foreign currency (here, the Deutschmark and therefore the euro) at a fixed exchange rate. The bank must hold reserves of foreign currencies and gold equal to at least 100 percent of the domestic currency issued at the fixed rate. Currency can be issued only when reserves are sufficient to back it.

The currency board system has three important implications. First, changes in the money supply are driven by changes in Bank of Estonia assets, which rules out the possibility of discretionary monetary policy as a stabilization tool. Reserves change as a function of the balance of payments. This arrangement works like a gold standard, but with foreign currency serving as the principal reserve asset. Second, the monetary authorities cannot print money to finance deficits. Finally, the central bank cannot act as lender of last resort to the commercial banking system because that would require creating additional currency.

The commercial banking sector included forty-two banks in 1992. Through bank failures and mergers, that number fell dramatically to seven in 2000. The sector is highly concentrated, and Swedish banking groups hold controlling interests in the two largest banks. Banks are healthy, with very little bad debt (about 3 percent of loans), possibly the lowest ratio in the former Eastern bloc.

Currency stabilization included removal of capital controls. The kroon is fully convertible. Corporate and private clients can open foreign exchange accounts in Estonian banks, and there are virtually no regulations on the import and export of foreign currency. The objectives of currency and banking reform were to create a reliable currency and a stable exchange rate and to increase the openness and self-regulation of the monetary system. Supporters credit the reform with helping break the dominance of trade with the East, with helping to bring inflation down, and with promoting foreign direct investment and growth of real income.

The supply side can pressure the price level on both internal and external fronts. Administered prices have risen faster than free-market prices. In 1997, for instance, prices in the sheltered sector rose nearly 16 percent and in the open sector 7.8 percent. Public sector goods and services were seriously underpriced during the Soviet years, and heavily subsidized. Gradual adjustment upward toward more normal price levels was undertaken by the state, according to Estonian economists, because international competition was not sufficient to control the monopoly pricing and because most large enterprises were slated for privatization.

State monopoly power has been a second source of supply-side pressure on prices. State enterprises were generally successful in passing on cost increases to consumers. Finally, the low exchange rate of the kroon, leading to higher-priced imports, generated supply pressures on the price level as well. Imports continue to grow more rapidly than exports; the fixed exchange rate is part of the explanation, as it reduces Estonian competitiveness. The situation is unlikely to change dramatically after accession to the EU because EU countries account for about two-thirds of Estonian trade.

Overall, macroeconomic stability has improved substantially since the 1999 slowdown. The government has kept its deficit and the rate of inflation under control. Foreign direct investment flows are strong and interest rates are down. The banking system is healthy and investment is up. Restructuring is a part of this strong economy, and that has led to high and rising unemployment. Real wages continue to rise.

Industrial Restructuring and Deregulation

In our growth models, deregulation of business acts like a decrease in the tax burden on capital, stimulating productive efficiency. This is an accurate characterization for Estonian enterprises. Efforts to provide a business-friendly environment have attracted one of the highest levels of foreign direct investment per capita in the transition states and have stimulated Estonian entrepreneurship.

Since adoption of the new Estonian Constitution in 1992, the country has created a set of civil laws compatible with the EU legal system. Even before adoption of the 1992 Constitution Estonia had a value added tax, a two-tier banking system and had begun making trade agreements. The currency board was established in 1992. Our sub-index for restructuring peaked in 1991–1992, much earlier than in other countries in our sample. In 1993 alone over 200 new laws were passed. Commercial codes based on German and Finnish models and tax legislation patterned after Anglo-American law were put in place. Bankruptcy laws have been applied since their inception in the early 1990s. Estonian lawmakers are justifiably proud of the country's competitive environment and its institutionalization of property rights.

The degree to which the spirit of the institutional framework is put into practice at government and at firm levels is another question. In the November 2000 EU assessment of progress toward meeting membership criteria, Estonia is criticized for neglecting to create a comprehensive strategy to modernize public administration. Government workers in most agencies need systematic training and upgrading. Estonia is urged to sustain its efforts to improve the judiciary and to pursue reforms in both civil and criminal law systems. Unfortunately the low salaries of judges, prosecutors and civil servants reinforce administrative and institutional weaknesses. This emphasizes again the importance of economic growth. EU standards are expensive but budget discipline is essential.

As recently as 1998, research at the firm level revealed that managers and entrepreneurs felt that the institutional environment was neither steady nor reliable, and that rules and policies changed without adequate notice and opportunity for feedback from businesses. Business people still do not always trust judicial procedures or judges to be objective and there remains some suspicion that money talks. Civil servants are seen as interfering and power-hungry.[13]

In spite of all this, business people are generally optimistic and continue to fight court decisions that they disagree with; they also continue to fight contrary civil servants through the court system. Managers and entrepreneurs do not feel that government regulations interfere to any serious degree with their operating, expansion or shutdown decisions. They do complain about the high cost of firing workers when trying to downsize and of the difficulty in arranging financing for expansion. There are predictable complaints about competitive imports.

The rules with respect to restructuring apparently look better on the books than they do in actual implementation and enforcement. The Estonian accomplishment of fast liberalization has not yet completely transformed the practices of administrative and regulatory agencies of the government. Old ways die hard.

Trade Liberalization

Trade affects growth through several channels. Free trade promotes increased specialization and an enriched mix of products available to consumers. Consumer utility grows also as a result of keener competition and therefore lower prices and higher-quality products. Finally, free trade enables technology transfer, which encourages modernization and the building of a more appropriate stock of capital. Estonia began reducing trade restrictions in 1991 and its trade policy is among the most liberal in all of Europe, although government in the late 1990s established some protection for agricultural interests. The aim has been integration into the global economy and redirection of trade away from dependence on Russia. The Estonians have been highly successful in finding Western trading partners. Until 1991, 95 percent of foreign trade was with the Soviet Union and the CMEA. By the mid-1990s this proportion had fallen to about one-third. The transition was not easy; the terms-of-trade shock in 1992 alone equaled a 20 percent fall in GDP and included a seventyfold increase in the price of gasoline.

The early adoption of a currency board helped the transition away from dependence on old trade ties. A credible peg to the Deutschmark meant that exchange rate risk was relatively low towards Western currencies and high relative to the ruble, which was depreciating at a variable rate. This increased the attraction of trade with the West. In the early 1990s, the undervalued kroon made exports relatively attractive, encouraging even stagnant enterprises and firms who were producing low-quality goods to seek new partners. Current account convertibility and relatively fast payments in hard currency eased the financing of trade with the West at a time when payments within the ruble zone took weeks or months. The currency board rule (the Bank of Estonia can issue no base money unless backed by foreign reserves) and the commitment to balanced budgets ensured convertibility at the fixed exchange rate. These policies also created a "demand barrier," a major impetus to trade reorientation. Initially, enterprises complained about weak domestic demand under the new macroeconomic and exchange rate policies. When they realized that no reinflation would be forthcoming and felt the pinch of tight financial policies, producers turned to the West in search of new markets. After independence, free trade agreements were signed with Sweden, Norway, Switzerland, Lithuania and Latvia, the European Union, and the European Free Trade Area. Agreements on trade and investment relations have been signed with at least ten other nations, including the Visegrad countries, some large CIS members and China. More agreements are in the works. Estonia joined the World Trade Organization in 1999 and is committed to membership in the European Union. Estonians hope for EU accession by 2004.

Trade flows have been growing since independence. Russia was the primary export market right after independence, with Finland quickly moving to a close second and Sweden third. Finland is now in first place, taking about one-third of exports; Sweden is second with over 20 percent. Germany is third with 8.5 percent, Russia is tenth with about 2.5 percent. Finland provides the bulk of imports, over 27 percent. Sweden and Germany account for less than 10 percent each; Russia is fourth with 8.5 percent.

After 1993 Estonia ran a deficit in its merchandise balance and a surplus in the services balance, generating a deficit in the current account; the capital and financial account has compensated with surpluses, and reserves increased (see Table 9.4). This implied increases in the money supply. Direct foreign investment in most years has outweighed the net outflow of capital in the form of portfolio investments.

Table 9.4 International trade and financial statistics (selected years)

Year	FDI* (% of GDP)	Imports (% of GDP)	Balance of trade (% of GDP)	Exchange rate (kroon/$)
1990	2.5	50.0	—	—
1995	5.6	69.4	–0.2	11.5
1997	5.7	91.5	–0.6	13.9
1998	11.0	90.6	–0.4	13.4
1999	5.6	87.0	—	12.0

Note: * Foreign direct investment.

Estonia, with Hungary and the Czech Republic, has the largest per capita foreign direct investment among the emerging market economies in Europe. The great inflow of foreign direct investment in 1994–1995 was in part related to privatization. There were several reasons for a serious drop in FDI in 1996. Since by 1996 the privatization of small and medium-sized enterprises was virtually complete, only a few new international tenders were submitted. Pending sales of large companies (power plants, for instance) subsequently boosted FDI from the end of 1996. Another reason for the decrease may have been the successful opening of the Tallinn Stock Exchange, which probably generated a switch into portfolio investment; also, Estonian companies began investing more outside the country. This latter phenomenon is new but will grow as prosperity increases. In addition, regulations were changed in 1996, raising the threshold share of a company defined as foreign direct investment from 10 percent to 20 percent. A purchase of 18 percent of a firm' s capital, for example, would have been defined as direct investment in 1995, but would have become portfolio investment after the rule change.

What products does Estonia trade? Estonia's high-volume exports are timber, paper products and furniture. Textiles and textile articles, foodstuffs, and machinery and electrical equipment are also important. The last category makes up the largest volume of imports; foodstuffs are second, and chemical industry products third. Table 9.5 shows the sources of Estonia's output by sector in 1997. The sector that has changed the most is agriculture. In 2001, agriculture accounted for less than 4 percent of GDP, having lost its dominant place

Table 9.5 Output by sector, 1997

Sector	% of GDP
Agriculture	7
Industry	28
Services	65

held between the World Wars, and many Estonians have difficulty adjusting to the fact. As elsewhere in the modern world small farmers find survival without government support increasingly difficult. The relative size of the agricultural sector inevitably continues to shrink.

The process of replacing collective and state farms with small plots and of reforming rural property laws has been difficult. There is not universal agreement about complete abolition of collective farms, and a few survive. There continue to be pressures from the agricultural sector for protection and for subsidies. Farmers are not particularly powerful in the parliament; at the turn of the twenty-first century, workers in agriculture make up less than 5 percent of the labor force and produce less than 4 percent of GDP. However, as government always consists of coalitions, farm interests may be able to exercise disproportionate power. Some leaders of rural-based parties are former managers of state and collective farms.

Since independence Estonia has been in the top three most liberal countries in the world (along with New Zealand and Australia) with respect to agricultural policies. By 1997 pressures were growing for agricultural subsidies and import tariffs, and an agricultural development commission recommended limited subsidies and tariffs on specific products. Some of these were implemented in 2000. The poor example of Western European agricultural support policies has been a disservice to reformers in transition economies by providing ammunition for agricultural lobbies. Estonia cannot afford wasteful subsidies, but accession to the EU will change agricultural trade policies again.

THE SUSTAINABILITY OF REFORMS AND THE FUTURE

Politics since Independence

Although every new government has proclaimed its allegiance to market reforms (there is no voice for the old system), voters have on occasion shown displeasure with the impacts of a decentralized economy. The reason for their growing tendency to avoid politics altogether is not clear. In 1991, 83 percent of eligible voters turned out for the independence referendum. In 1999, less than 57 percent of those eligible voted in the general election. This may reflect growing satisfaction with the *status quo* or it may reflect discouragement with a system that in 1999 involved 12 political parties and 1885 candidates (nearly 19 for each of the 101 seats in parliament).

Table 9.6 Elections, reforms and economic performance 1990–1999 (all variables cover election intervals)

Year	Votes for reformers (%)	Reform index (1995=100)	GDP % change		Inflation rate		Unemployment rate	
			After	Before	After	Before	After	Before
1990	61.0	120.1	–11.4	3.8	466.2	3.8	1.2	0.3
1992	54.7	107.2	–5.0	–11.4	165.5	466.2	7.4	1.2
1995	46.1	102.5	4.9	–5.0	23.8	165.5	9.9	7.4
1997	39.0	103.3	6.4	4.9	8.7	23.8	9.8	9.9

There is little grass-roots political activity in Estonia, and lobby groups exist only for certain business interests. Civil society in general – political activism, volunteer organizations, charitable causes – is weak but growing. It will take time, a degree of affluence and belief that individuals really can affect the system for that civil society to develop. In the meantime, politics languishes. People have yet to develop party allegiances and vote instead for personalities rather than platforms. Nevertheless, as Table 9.6 indicates, when Estonians vote for relatively more strong-willed reformers, reforms are more likely to occur. The highest reform index was for the early period 1990–1994. It was 120.1 in the 1990–1991 interval and 107.2 in the 1992–1995 interval. As votes left the more radical parties and moved to the moderate parties, the reform index fell as well.

Our political–economic interaction model represents accurately enough how the impacts of reform shape consumer perceptions and therefore voter reactions. In 1995 the first wave of strong liberal reformers was turned out of office; the trend moved across the newly independent European states, in spite of improving economic conditions. Expectations had apparently been too high, were not met by reality, and voters reacted. Although the parties brought to power made more populist noises, they continued Estonia's liberal policies, as did coalitions formed in later elections.

A general election in March 1999 returned the original set of market-oriented liberals to power, including Matt Laar, Prime Minister in 1992. His Pro Patria Party led a coalition with three other parties; on its own, Pro Patria laid claim to less than 10 percent of the electorate. The element of the population that speaks out for modification of reforms is the farmer element, represented primarily by the Country People's Party. The party represents 10 to 13 percent of voters and favors protection for agricultural products. The main left-wing party is the Center Party; it typically cooperates closely with the Country People's Party. Its supporters are drawn mainly from the less well-off, including pensioners, urban working-class people and Russian speakers. In a later national election an unprecedented coalition carried the day; it was led by the right-wing Reform Party and included the Center Party. The government's reform agenda remained unchanged.

Social Conditions

Estonia's human rights record has improved in the last few years as it has undertaken to treat the Russian minority better. Citizenship rules, residence permits and language laws have all been changed under EU pressure. The Citizenship and Migration Board has been upgraded. Ethnic Russians make up 28 percent of the population and the Estonians are finally accepting the idea that integration is good for everyone.

A newer source of social tension is an increasing degree of inequality in the distribution of income and of wealth. This naturally comes with a market system, but half a century of the egalitarian ethic has made Estonians sensitive to the issue. Russian non-citizens, pensioners and farmers are the most likely to be poor.[14] The EBRD reports a 40 percent poverty rate.[15] Support payments to pensioners, unemployment benefits and minimum wages are all very low.

By 1999 Estonians were nearing the reported level of per capita real income that they had just before independence. Of course current income does not reflect unreported income in the current period, and many people are working in the gray economy. An employed Estonian is likely to respond to the evidence of ten years of lower income by noting that, unlike Soviet times, there are now always goods and services available to buy, their variety is greater, their quality is infinitely better. "And – we are free."[16]

The Future

Estonians enjoy a remarkable degree of social consensus about democratic capitalism. After half a dozen changes of government, decision-makers persist in maintaining one of the most liberal economic systems in all of Europe, Eastern or not. The inflow of foreign investment is, on a per capita basis, in the top two or three among the newly independent countries of Europe. This reflects a degree of confidence by foreigners in political stability and long-range prospects for this small state. Estonia is in the first tier of applicants for accession to the EU and has worked diligently to attain that goal. In 1999 Estonia was accepted into the World Trade Organization. Joining NATO is another important objective.

Although Estonia is one of the success stories of Eastern Europe, population continues to decline even as infant mortality falls and life expectancy increases. Net emigration is positive. In 1999 the number of births increased for the first time in eleven years. Ethnic tensions still exist: Estonia has the largest population of Russians of any place outside of Russia – about half a million.

The Soviet system induced a feeling of powerlessness in citizens, coupled with a reliance on extensive centralized power and a dependence on social guarantees. Add to all that a deep mistrust (or at least suspicion) of nearly everyone beyond immediate family, and you have people ill suited to live in a capitalistic, democratic system. The Estonians have done a magnificent job of getting the framework right in transforming their system. They never lost sight of their Nordic kin; being small and homogeneous helped. Citizens are learning to create the society they want to live in, by learning how the system works and how to influence it, in both the private and the public sectors. This emphasizes the difference between the Soviet way, which required enormous effort to get around the system, and the Western way, which provides payoffs for learning to play the system, to use it to move ahead.

Estonia's history of an inter-war golden era of independence, coupled with a long period of mistreatment and occupation by the Soviets, has given the Estonian people both a goal and the determination to attain it. There is a broad and deep consensus about what is a desirable future, and the people are apparently willing to pay the costs of building that future. These are the basic reasons that Estonians have made the hard choices that support the institutionalization of economic reforms.

They have, furthermore, chosen to adopt appropriate economic reforms to promote long-term growth. Price liberalization, trade liberalization, privatization, macroeconomic stabilization and industrial restructuring have been undertaken with energy and with considerable success. The EU accession effort has been of great benefit by turning a spotlight on shortcomings in institutions and practices. This circumstance – of an emerging, formerly centrally planned economy undergoing the rigors of meeting the European Union's *acquis communautaire* – is comparable to the country being handed a game plan for institutionalization of Western standards.[17] We think Estonia will make it.

NOTES

1. See Tables B.1, Appendix B.
2. Taagepera (1993) provides an insightful political history culminating in independence in 1991. Raun (1991) is a wide-ranging history that begins with prehistory and ends in the spring of 1991. Van Arkadie and Karlsson (1992) offer an extensive survey of Baltic State economies in the early 1990s. See also the Library of Congress Country Study of Estonia.
3. This notion was expressed in 1995 by Tallinn Technical University economist Vello Vensel.
4. This classification is suggested by Taagepera (1993), Chapter 4.
5. Teet Rajasalu (then with the Estonian Academy of Science) made this observation in June 1995.
6. See European Bank for Reconstruction and Development, *Transition Report* series, for useful statistical indicators.
7. Well-known caveats about the use of data by communist regimes influence our interpretation of 1989 statistics.
8. Gelos and Sahay (2001).
9. *Eesti Pank Bulletin*, No. 2 (29), 1997, 1980.
10. European Union, *Estonia 2000*.
11. Frydman and Rapaczynski (1994) covers privatization in Russia, Ukraine and the Baltic States.
12. *Nordic Economic Outook*, No. 2, 1996, p. 23.
13. Vensel and Winlborg (2001) includes comprehensive treatment of restructuring issues and progress in Estonia, with emphasis on the institutional environment and the financial sector.
14. At the end of 1999 the minimum wage was about $100 a month, the average wage about $300 and a pension about $100.
15. See *Transition Report 2000*, p. 160.
16. Vello Vensel made this remark in September 1999 while visiting California.
17. The *acquis communautaire* is the 80,000 page EU document containing the obligations of membership. This includes the EU's aims of political, economic and monetary union as well as specific regulatory details.

10. A taste of Hungarian goulash*

Now the basic question is whether we can create a genuine socialist market economy based on the dominance of the market in the competitive sector and establish planning based on and harmonized with the wide-ranging impact of the market.

(Laszlo Antal, L. Bokros, I. Csillag, L. Lengyel and G. Matolcsy, 1987. In Bernard Chavance, 1994)

In some countries, England, Hong Kong and Wales for instance, people drive on the left side of the street. In other countries, the United States, Germany and France for instance, people drive on the right side of the street. Either side works as long as you choose one side and stick to it. In Hungary you are trying to drive on both sides of the street. This is not working too well ... Hungarians will have to choose between the left (socialism) and the right (capitalism). Until you choose one side or the other, you are going to continue to have lots of accidents.

(Paul Heyne speaking to Hungarian schoolteachers in Budapest, 1990)[1]

Hungary was the most successful of the Soviet satellite states. If there was a place that provided an ideological and economic bridge between the two Great Powers during the Cold War, Hungary was that place. More than any other country under Soviet control, it maintained some trade and tourism ties to the West. This can be explained in part by Hungary's particular relationship to the Soviet authorities.

Hungary's experience since the collapse of Soviet power supports our hypothesis about a country's history influencing the clarity of its goals and its determination in adopting and implementing market reforms. The Hungarians were unique in their dealings with the Soviets in that they negotiated a degree of economic independence in the 1960s. When political independence finally came, they were extremely proud of their market-based experience, unmatched anywhere in the Soviet empire. With a Hungarian penchant for complexity, they referred to their mixed economic model as the "Hungarian way," or "Hungarian goulash" (a stew made from whatever seems to work, with little reference to a recipe, and tastily spiced with paprika to hide any faults). In the early 1990s more than one Hungarian scholar told us that Hungary had a twenty-year head start in liberalizing the economy relative to the other former satellite states.

The economic independence that Hungarians exercised during the 1970s and 1980s undoubtedly paid off in terms of the country's ability to attract foreign investors in the 1990s. It has consistently led the league in foreign direct investment. The downside to the Hungarian adaptation to the Soviet occupation was that managers and policy-makers learned to be gradualists. They had to be in order to maintain their limited managerial control under the Soviets. Their economic accommodation reflected their political accommodation; they got the privilege of limited market activity in exchange for a pledge of political compliance.

* We thank Kalman Dezseri and Paul Gaspar for their help with this chapter.

In fact, most communist officials and politicians in Hungary were Hungarians; the party was homegrown. The system became their own system. The power was in Moscow but the day-to-day management of economic and political affairs was in Budapest.

During four decades of Soviet domination, the Hungarians learned to be successful gradualists. They carried that pattern into their early reform efforts after independence, and it slowed their progress. Our analysis will demonstrate that their early goals were unclear or at least not generally agreed upon. They continued to rely heavily on intervention and management by the state. Liberalization was uneven and slow. In the mid-1990s they took a deep collective breath, implemented an austerity program and became more focused in their reform efforts. The payoff in terms of economic performance has been impressive. They are at last putting their experience to good use. Budapest exuded its historical magic the first time we saw it, soon after independence. Now all of Hungary is beginning to sparkle.

History matters a great deal in Hungary. To appreciate the implications of the Soviet period and the country's direction since independence, one should begin in ancient Hungary. In this chapter we examine the history before, during and after the Soviets in order to appraise recent reform efforts in terms of our economic and political models, and in order to evaluate Hungary's future prospects for economic success.

HISTORY BEFORE COMMUNISM

Hungary, a crossroads between East and West on the plains west of the Carpathian Mountains, has suffered invasion with brutal devastation four times in 700 years. The Mongols invaded in 1241–1242. The Ottoman Turks occupied Hungary from 1526 to the 1680s. The Habsburgs ruled for about 250 years. In the twentieth century Nazi–Soviet battles battered the Hungarian lands, destroying cities, people and nearly everything else in their paths. Today much of the capital Budapest is largely modern because so much of the old was destroyed and had to be rebuilt.[2] From these traumatic experiences, Hungarians apparently learned to deal with invasion and foreign domination. Their courageous resistance to foreign cruelty led to revolt more than once and forced their rulers to tolerate local autonomy in domestic policy. Perhaps this history taught Hungarians the importance of rising above their local disagreements in order to rule themselves even while under foreign military occupation.

100–900: The Magyars

Little is actually known about the origins of Hungary before the 800s. The dominant strain of modern Hungarians is thought to have descended from an Asiatic tribe called Magyars. Between 100 and 600 the Magyar tribes migrated from the Ural Mountains to the Russian steppes and on into the Don and lower Dnepr rivers region. The Bulgarians and Turks, dominant forces in the region from the fifth to the seventh centuries, had a considerable influence on the Magyars, who were largely nomadic, wandering the plains to the east of the Carpathians. These Magyars migrated 300 years later into the region that is now Hungary. Some scholars argue that the word "Hungary," a Slavic form of the Turkish phrase "ten arrows," may represent the number of Magyar tribes that formed the nascent nation. Other scholars note that there were only seven tribes. Another view is that the label "Hungary" was a mistake born of confusing Huns with Magyar raiders. Although the origins of Hungarian are not known, the language is Finno-Ugric (not Indo-European) and has common antecedents with Estonian and Finnish. The Magyars continued their western migration over the Carpathians into the Danube–Tisza basin in 895 or 896 after successfully helping in the Byzantine wars against the Bulgars. Hungary, given its Central European location, is populated with many peoples, in addition to descendants of Magyars. These include Slavic groups, Slovaks, Croats, Serbs and Bulgarians; and non-Slavic peoples, Germans, Gypsies and Romanians. Nearly 98 percent of Hungarians are Magyars today.

900–1301: Hungary Becomes a Kingdom

Arpad, a Magyar chieftain, led the Hungarians into the Carpath basin. Though he died in 907, he began a royal dynasty that lasted until 1301. Legend has it that the clan chiefs swore allegiance to Arpad by sipping from a cup containing their comingled blood. The nomadic Magyars, resisting transformation to agrarian life, fought the Byzantine empire and other European powers. They were severely beaten by the Germans at Augsburg in 955. A Hungarian descendant of Arpad, Stephen I, ascended to power through a series of battles and agreements, and at his request was crowned King of Hungary by Pope Sylvester II. He ruled from 1001 to 1038. Stephen consolidated power and required the construction of Christian churches in many villages, thereby fostering Christianity in Hungary. Stephen I governed well and protected Hungary from direct governance by the Byzantine and Holy Roman empires, so that the Magyars came to enjoy a degree of domestic autonomy. He is revered today as the founder of Hungary as a Christian state.

During the late twelfth century under Bela III Hungary became a major power in Central Europe. Excessive spending forced Bela III and his successors to increase taxes on both nobles and their serfs. These taxes proved inadequate and the Kings began to sell off property to noblemen. Power eventually shifted toward the noblemen as less income was generated on royal land. The noblemen began to rankle under the imposition of heavy taxes and profligate royal spending.

In 1222 Magyar nobles forced King Andrew II to sign an agreement called the Golden Bull. Among other things, this Golden Bull limited the King's authority and restricted his taxing powers. This document, not unlike the Magna Carta, marked a significant step toward self-rule by the Magyars. The noblemen also acquired the right to petition the King about grievances and this was extended to all freemen. This opportunity to meet with and petition the King was the genesis of Hungary's first parliament, or Diet.

The first of three great invasions took place in 1241, when Mongols routed the Hungarian army and then ravaged a number of Hungarian cities, including Pest. They withdrew within a year, and the King ordered a fortress built on the mountainside of the Danube across from Pest, creating the city of Buda that would later become part of Budapest.

1301–1699: Renaissance and Agricultural Development

The period from 1301 until 1699 was one of renaissance, of warring armies and of religious and ethnic disputes throughout much of Europe. These forces battered Hungary and its neighbors in the region. Scholars nevertheless consider the first half of the fourteenth century to be a golden era for Hungary. Charles Robert of Anjou came to power in 1308. As Charles I, he brought peace and prosperity to the Magyars. In 1367 the first Hungarian university was founded, and Charles's son Louis I continued to abide by the Golden Bull when he ruled.

War between the Hungarians and the Ottoman Turks waxed and waned during the middle of the fifteenth century. In 1456 the Hungarians, led by Janos Hunyadi, defeated the Turks at Belgrade. The Hungarian nobles crowned Hunyadi's son, Matyas Corvinus, King. He enacted numerous social and political reforms. He limited maltreatment of serfs, introduced new legal rights, fostered Hungarian cultural activity, established a second university and supported a world-class library, named the Corvina. After Matyas died anarchy reigned, setting the stage for the second great foreign invasion of Hungary. In 1526 the Turks defeated the Hungarians, and the cities of Buda and Pest again were ravaged.

1700–1918: From the Habsburgs to the First World War

In 1541 the Turks and Habsburgs partitioned Hungary. This partition lasted until the Habsburgs defeated the Turks and all of Hungary became part of the Habsburg empire from 1700 to 1867. But Hungarians, bridling again under foreign oppression, revolted, eventually earning a good deal of autonomy in 1723 under the Pragmatic Sanction agreed to by the Habsburg monarchy. We see the Hungarian people once more able to force their foreign masters into concessions that would provide a degree of domestic self-rule, but the Austrian monarchy remained in control.

As Austria's Franz Josef became a weaker ruler, he lost battles to Sardinia and the French in 1851 and his army was defeated by the Prussians in 1866. Hungarians had revolted several times against the Habsburgs and been defeated, after which they suffered hard reprisals. But after losing to the Prussians, a weakened Franz Josef was forced into the Compromise of 1867, founding the Austro-Hungarian empire. The two nations were now near equals.

From 1875 to 1890, modernization and economic growth began, along with the rise of a middle class under Kalman Tisza as Prime Minister. Ruled from Vienna, the Hungarians were permitted to govern their domestic affairs. Another golden era for Hungary began, as its living standards approached those of Austria. (The condition of peasants was very bad, however, and an 1874 law allowed only 6 percent of the population to vote.) Their ability to reconcile with a dominant foreign power and achieve a good degree of local autonomy is yet another precursor to arrangements that would later be made with their twentieth-century rulers, the Soviets. The June 1914 assassination of Archduke Franz Ferdinand, who was to have ascended to the Austrian throne, precipitated the First World War. The dual monarchy continued to rule Hungary until war's end on 31 October 1918. Up until the era of the First World War Hungary was perhaps the most aristocratic country in Europe, controlled by landowners and the nobility.

As war ended, Hungary experienced a bourgeois–democratic revolt led by Mihaly Karolyi. A coalition of social democrats and communists lead by Bela Kun took over in March 1919 and a Soviet Republic was declared. Just as suddenly, authoritarian anti-communist military officers next seized control. A severe purge and terror ensued. The military government instituted the "white terror," during which communists, liberals, intellectuals and Jews were punished harshly. As many as 5000 Hungarians were executed outright.

1920–1945: Trianon Hungary

Hungarians, having chosen the losing side in the Great War, found their fortunes in the hands of foreign powers yet again. In the Treaty of Trianon in June 1920 Western powers placed Hungary under the rule of regent Admiral Miklos Horthy. Slovakia was separated from Hungary and put into Czechoslovakia, and some Hungarian land was taken over by Yugoslavia, Romania and Austria. Hungary lost 60 percent of its population and two-thirds of its land mass. Political turmoil in Hungary brought in extremist right-wing governments who forged ties with Italy and Germany. In the Second World War Hungary again chose the wrong side by assisting the Nazi invasion of the USSR. Hungary joined the Axis powers and declared war on the West in December 1941. In April 1943 Hitler's armies occupied Hungary in response to Hungary's efforts to withdraw from the war and protect its Jewish population. Hungary became a battleground when Stalin's troops drove the Nazis from Hungary in April 1945. Much of Budapest was again blasted into ruins.

HISTORY UNDER COMMUNISM

Stalinism

After the Soviets drove Hitler's army from Budapest, the imposition of communism by Soviet-supported puppets was not far off. However, in the national elections of 1945 the Communist Party got less than one-fifth of the votes. A republican constitution was adopted in 1946 and the government began much-needed land reforms. Early in 1948 the communists, through control of the Ministry of the Interior, arrested leading politicians, forced the Prime Minister to resign and took control of the state. In the next election there was a one-party slate and in August 1949 a Soviet-style constitution was ratified and the Hungarian People's Republic declared. From 1949 to 1953 a Stalinist command-and-control economic, social and political system was in place. Industry was nationalized and agriculture was collectivized. Hungarians chafed under the iron rule of Stalin. In 1953 Imre Nagy, Prime Minister and a reformer, tried but failed to counteract Soviet policies. Hungarians remained unhappy with the Soviet military occupation. Nagy lost power to the Stalinists in 1955 and the harsh Stalinist regime continued to stifle the populace, precipitating the revolt of 1956.

The Hungarian Freedom Fighters of 1956

A revolt broke out in Budapest in October 1956 following sympathetic student demonstrations for Polish independence. After firing on the parliament building as well as the radio and television stations, the revolutionaries demanded that reform-minded communist Imre Nagy lead the government. Nagy formed a coalition government demanding free elections and self-determination. Swift and at times deadly assaults on unpopular communist public officials and factory leaders ensued, causing some deep-seated and long-remembered hostilities among

Hungarians. On 3 November 1956, Khrushchev unleashed the Soviet war machine. Tanks and troops crushed the Hungarian freedom fighters, who were able to respond with only small-arms fire and handmade Molotov cocktails. The revolt was quickly crushed as the Western powers, distracted by the Suez Canal crisis and unprepared for revolt in Eastern Europe, looked on in horror. Perhaps the West took no action, fearing conflict with the Soviets, now a nuclear power. Hungarian communists helped the Soviets end the revolt. A young participant in this counter-revolution was a recent university graduate, Gyula Horn, later to play a major role in Hungary's political life.

The Soviets installed a communist puppet regime headed by rehabilitated national communist Janos Kadar. The Hungarian Workers' Party, renamed the Hungarian Socialist Workers' Party (HSWP), was a Soviet-controlled Communist Party. Some 190,000 people fled the country. Over 300 Hungarian freedom fighters, including Imre Nagy and some of his ministers, were secretly executed in 1958 despite Kadar's assurances of clemency. Many more who sided with the democratic movement were dismissed from their jobs and a period of severe repression and reprisals continued for five years or so. Hungary became an occupied police state with only nominal local control. Memories of the fierce and deadly revolt and its equally fierce and deadly response so frightened Hungarians of all political stripes that accommodation, compromise and reconciliation would mark the 1990s political transition, which would be even smoother than the Velvet Revolution of Czechoslovakia.

Kadarism

In 1962 Janos Kadar (who had been one of Nagy's ministers) purged the Stalinists who were held responsible for generating the revolutionary response of 1956. In 1963 Kadar, with evident approval of the Soviets, began to loosen the iron grip of the hard-line police state. He freed political prisoners and introduced some economic reforms and a degree of local independence, although quite incremental in nature. Small shareholders in agriculture and retail trade would come later, but the classical command economy was gradually decentralized around the edges and Kadar became popular with the people. During the early 1960s this loosening unleashed the pent-up economy, resulting in stronger growth than elsewhere in Central Europe. Table 10.1 shows the average annual growth rates in real GDP and domestic fixed investment for intervals beginning in 1961. The early 1960s saw average

Table 10.1 Growth of real GDP and fixed investment, 1961–1993 (average annual percentage change)

Period	Real GDP	Fixed investment
1961–1965	4.4	5.1
1966–1975	6.3	9.1
1976–1987	2.7	0.8
1988–1993	–2.6	–4.5

Source: Kornai (1996).

annual real GDP growth of 4.4 percent. With approximately 25 percent of GDP going to investment, fixed investment grew at an even faster rate of 5.1 percent. The second half of the 1960s was better yet.

The New Economic Mechanism

The period from 1966 to 1975 is often referred to as a "golden age" by socialist Hungarian observers. It was certainly not golden in terms of political, artistic or social freedom, but annual economic growth was, according to Hungarian sources, over 6 percent. Western analysts put growth at something over 3.5 percent per year. Reform socialism was born. It would later be dubbed "goulash communism" or hybrid socialism. It was formally named the New Economic Mechanism and introduced as such in January 1968. Subsequent economic success relative to other satellite countries in the Soviet constellation caused Western observers to call Hungary "the happiest barrack in the camp."

Meanwhile, the Soviets tolerated minor privatization of new small shops and retail stores and some rental arrangements of state-owned shops in Hungary. They also permitted the Hungarians to adopt American methods in large-scale agriculture. But these concessions came with a price. The Hungarians in exchange had to agree to support the glorious Soviet socialist state. Political stability between the Hungarian communists and the Soviets coincided with, and was perhaps caused by, the golden period of economic growth from 1966 to 1975.

This in turn freed the Soviets to concentrate their military might and imperial ambitions on East Germany, Poland and Czechoslovakia, buffer countries that were crucial to protecting the Soviet Union from the still-feared threat of German power. If Hungarian communists could guarantee no more uprisings by the troublesome Magyars, then modest concessions on small farm and retail shop privatization was a price worth paying. The Soviets protected and stabilized their buffer zone between East and West. Hungarian communists played their hand well, warding off Soviet interference so that Hungarians could make local decisions.

During the second half of the 1970s, economic growth associated with the New Economic Mechanism began to slow. Hungarian data suggest growth rates in real GDP fell from over 6 percent to an annual average of less than 3 percent. More ominously, gross fixed investment grew at less than 1 percent. This slow gross increment to productive capital formation meant a decline in capital per worker, which was undoubtedly inadequate to replace depreciating capital. Another troubling economic signal from 1975 to 1980 was the accumulation of a huge external debt.

How could Hungary pull itself out of this slowdown? One way out of the sluggish performance was to turn outward, which for Hungary meant westward. To do so required some accommodations to Western demands and thus more domestic economic reforms. In 1980 new incremental and modest reforms were initiated. These reforms included legalization of small private partnerships and encouragement of modest entrepreneurial behavior. Some prices were liberalized at this time as well. In 1982, to deal with its massive foreign debt problem, Hungary joined the International Monetary Fund (IMF) and the World Bank. Membership of the IMF and World Bank yielded unique access to Western loans and generated some economic credibility in the West that was not to be enjoyed by any other countries in our sample for a decade. Thus, when the impacts of the implosion of Soviet socialism hit Central Europe in 1989, Hungarians already had enjoyed some economic independence and had begun moving toward some private market activity. To Hungarians in the 1970s and 1980s, their economy was the pride of Central and Eastern Europe, performing better than that of their Soviet masters.

Despite the New Economic Mechanism, the inconsistencies and deficiencies of the socialist system became increasingly evident in the Hungarian economy throughout the 1980s. Gradualism continued to be the policy. More prices were liberalized in 1984. In 1987, the new communist regime, the Grosz government, loosened controls a bit more and an actual political opposition began to appear. A two-tier banking system introduced quasi-independent commercial banks which were not under direct control of the central bank. This fostered more private economic development, although tight bureaucratic networks continued to dominate financial decisions.

Trouble was brewing at least from 1960 in the mix of income sources in Hungary. Increasingly, less income was earned relative to transfer income from the state. Table 10.2 shows the share of earned income declining steadily relative to the share of transfer income. Transfer income steadily grew from 18.4 percent of the total in 1960 to over 40 percent by 1992. Hungary's reforms were evidently not increasing reliance on markets but instead increasing dependency on the state.

Table 10.2 Earned income versus transfer income (selected years 1960–1992)

Year	Earned income (%)	Transfer income (%)
1960	80.4	18.4
1970	76.1	22.6
1975	71.5	27.2
1980	68.0	32.0
1985	65.6	34.0
1990	58.1	39.2
1992	52.8	41.4

Source: Kornai (1996).

The data in Table 10.3 indicate that growth basically stalled in the last half of the 1980s. Some type of reform was sorely needed even before the collapse of COMECON, the trading system of the Soviet Union upon which Hungary largely depended in the 1980s. Real GDP growth ground to a halt and inflation hit double digits, and this was with a controlled non-convertible currency.

By 1988 inflation exceeded 15 percent per year and real GDP was falling. Stagflation was exacting its toll on support for the regime. Even the communist government recognized a need for reform. In 1988 some privatization of state-owned property was initiated. From November 1988 until May 1990 the Nemeth government, another communist reform regime, began to allow privatization of state property, more local and regional control and less centralization. Legislation to permit strikes was passed. In June 1989, formal negotiations

Table 10.3 Growth of output and inflation, 1980–1989

Year	Real GDP (%)	Inflation – CPI (%)
1980	2.7	9.1
1981	2.9	4.6
1982	2.8	6.9
1983	0.7	7.3
1984	2.7	8.3
1985	–0.3	7.0
1986	1.5	5.3
1987	4.1	8.6
1988	–0.1	15.5
1989	0.7	17.0

Source: Kornai (1996).

between the communist leadership and the incipient opposition began. The collapse of communism was close at hand.

October 1989 marked the beginning of the end of authoritarian domination by the Communist Party, the Hungarian Socialist Workers' Party (HSWP). The HSWP split and most former members joined the newly formed Hungarian Socialist Party (MSZP), hoping that the old-guard hardliners would drop out. It became clear that the communists no longer held monopoly political power. In October 1989 a constitutional amendment process began in which non-socialists could participate. Spontaneous privatization, quasi-legal and illegal partitioning of some large state enterprises (often by managers), was under way.

All the failures inherent in what Kornai (1992) calls "classical socialism" became increasingly evident to scholars in Hungary in the late 1970s and 1980s. Measured GDP growth fell from over 6 percent per year to under 3 percent. From 1988 to 1991 real GDP fell at an average annual rate of 4 percent. The economic system began to falter; chronic shortages became increasingly common. Lags in adopting technological innovation became increasingly obvious as access to information about living standards in the West became more widespread. The public expressed dissatisfaction with environmental decay, shoddy workmanship in state products, shortages and official insolence. Matters were dramatically aggravated by the Soviet leaders' loss of confidence in their own system. Within the Communist Party in Hungary splinter groups were forming; some reform communists were pushing for local glasnost and perestroika.

The final collapse of Hungary's political monopoly was realized when reform communist Gyula Horn received the Moscow go-ahead to allow Central Europeans on holiday to pass through the Iron Curtain to Austria. Droves of East Germans voted with their feet. The Iron Curtain border with Austria quickly became an open border. After it became clear that Mikhail Gorbachev would not in send Soviet tanks, local communists had little choice but to allow general elections; they began to share real power with non-communists. The extent to which this political sharing was internally driven by local reform communists and the extent to which sharing was forced by the opposition is not exactly clear. It is clear that this political stage in transition was essential for subsequent market reforms to be implemented.

THE POLITICAL TRANSITION

The most dramatic event marking the end of the communist monopoly of power took place in August 1989. Prime Minister Nemeth and Foreign Minister Gyula Horn met with Germany's Helmut Kohl before opening the border. Once East Germans realized exodus was possible, the trickle became a flood. It was evident to the socialists that they would have to concede broader participation in decision-making and would have to effect enough reforms to stabilize the situation.

Despite serious economic challenges and some political and social conflict, much economic reform in the forms of small-scale privatization in retail trade, more liberalized prices and some flexibility in regulation already had taken place before the first free elections in May 1990. Hungarian voters saw little need for radical economic reform once the transition began. Everyone seemed to favor economic reform, but exactly what reforms everyone favored was less clear. Relatively well off, the Hungarians had something to lose by moving too fast on restructuring, and in any case the freshness of political freedom at first distracted the polity from economic issues. Instead Hungarians focused their energies on things like political freedom, independence, restoration of religious values, Hungarian minority rights in neighboring countries and environmental clean-up.

This is not to say that serious problems with budget deficits, ineffectual state enterprises and non-performing financial assets of large banks went unrecognized; but to Hungarians, the preferred way of dealing with these issues was incremental. Political reform seemed highly likely, but like economic reform was to be slow and halting. To some, October 1989 marked the death of Hungarian communism.[3] The Hungarian Socialist Workers' Party, after forty years of monopoly rule, tried to reform, renaming itself the Hungarian Socialist Party. The new party, headed by Rezso Nyers and fourteen of the twenty-five members of the Presidium, was said to be one of "committed reformers." The socialists agreed to share power with the opposition. Ominously, though, the socialists retained the 60,000-strong "workers' guard," the private army that had crushed the 1956 rebellion. A referendum in May 1990 finally abolished the workers' guard. Thus, despite a general tone of support for reforms, the relative success under communism and the willingness of the party to try for internal reform contributed to the sluggish response to the opportunity to reform toward a free market economy.

Although a new constitutional system was devised by the new negotiating parties, we believe that the preconditions – relatively good economic performance, control by local communists and comparatively mild treatment by the Soviets in later days especially – all combined to sabotage radical departures from the old ways. History under communism slowed major economic reforms from the start. Cooperation and negotiation took place, rather than revolution. As a parliamentary system was devised, the socialists retained considerable power and influence.

No doubt some aspects of the new political design provided a stable political backdrop conducive to economic reforms. For example, the Hungarians designed a parliamentary system of chancellors. This created a range of power centers, since not all ministries served at the pleasure of the Prime Minister. Thus democratization was favored. To balance this, the Prime Minister was given considerable power. He could be ousted by a vote of no confidence, but only by a "constructive vote" of no confidence in which a replacement had to be chosen simultaneously with his removal. It is not adequate to be disenchanted with the leadership in power or current economic conditions; it is necessary to provide a preferable alternative. Thus, the executive branch was protected somewhat from immediate political pressures.

A second constructive measure was adopted: a 4 percent threshold and widespread representation via signature support in various districts was required for a party to be represented in the new parliament. The result of these two positive features of the political system, a strong executive and a 4 percent threshold, assured relative political stability in which compromise and cooperation dominated grandstanding and hard-edged attitudes.

One must balance against these positive political measures one significant negative feature that hamstrung parliament in passing effective reform legislation. Parliament was required to achieve a two-thirds vote to pass many laws. This enabled a minority to tie up reform proposals. Given the split in the country between those who favored socialism and those who favored markets, the parliament, rather than guiding the country forward, became known as the "Parliament of Professors," famous for chatter but not for action.

On 23 May 1990 the first democratically elected legislative body sat in the Hungarian parliament building. Six parties were represented; over 200 parties had run for office. The new government was a coalition of three non-communist parties: the Hungarian Democratic Forum (MDF) with 42.5 percent of the vote, the Smallholder Party (FKGP) with 11.4 percent and the Christian Democratic People's Party (KDNP) with 5.6 percent of the vote. The Hungarian Democratic Forum had won in part for its slogan "The Calm Force," implicitly promising stability. This would prove important later when a nasty strain of nationalism sprang from the right-wing branch of the MDF, precipitating a split.

The MSZP (former communists) garnered 8.6 percent of the vote. Radical dissidents, the Alliance of Free Democrats (SZDSZ), formed the main opposition party with 23.8 percent of the votes. These two parties combined with the Federation of Young Democrats (FIDESZ) to round out the opposition.

Even though virtually everyone outwardly favored reform, economic reformers who wanted a largely unfettered capitalist economy were weak in Hungary. This is partly because the debate between "shock therapy" and "gradualism" had not fully been resolved, and partly because most people did not know exactly what kind of economic system they wanted, socialist or capitalist. Nevertheless, the first non-communist government, the Antall government, introduced a series of reforms intended to move the Hungarian economy toward a freer market system. A number of important measures were passed in 1990. A state property agency was established and privatization began.

Over 75 percent of prices were liberalized quickly, and in a move toward stabilization, company subsidies were reduced. Monetary policy was placed in the hands of a marginally more independent central bank. As an important symbol, the Budapest Stock Exchange opened in 1990, although the only stock initially available for exchange was the only privatized state enterprise, Ibusz, the Hungarian trading company.[4]

Rather than making a political statement by replacing communist leaders (who were changing their spots to socialist ones), Hungarians in 1990 installed parties concerned with

Hungary's glory days as the centerpiece of the Austro-Hungarian empire. This nationalism took a nasty turn in 1992 when Istvan Csuraka, second-in-command in the ruling Democratic Forum, noting that 3 million Hungarians were living abroad in Romania, Slovakia and Serbia, called for policies to protect all these Hungarians. He even used the unfortunate word *Lebensraum*, intentionally evoking Adolph Hitler's expansionist sentiments. In June 1993 he was thrown out of the Hungarian Democratic Forum as the party split on philosophical grounds.

Opinion polls taken in 1992 indicate much stronger support for capitalism than for democracy. Over 78 percent of the population agreed that the "capitalist economy, based on free initiative, enables us to solve the problems of the country," and this consensus cut across social classes. At the same time, 40 percent of the population did not think democracy would help and 23 percent feared it would make matters worse.[5]

However, in light of the poor economic performance under the MDF it is perhaps not surprising that in the May 1994 general elections the reform socialists, led by the indefatigable Gyula Horn, returned to power in a landslide victory. The socialists increased their share of parliamentary seats from 33 to 209 as the Democratic Forum's share fell from 165 to 37. Horn at first promised to develop a "socialist market economy." This oxymoron surfaced fairly often in the transition economies of Europe in the 1990s. It was a topic of serious discussion among economists in the 1930s.[6] The notion appears to have captured the Hungarian public's hopes that the security and equity promised by socialism could be sustained while gradual and modest concessions to private markets evolved. They were, however, confronted by a great deal of evidence to the contrary. Hungarian gradualism was not serving the best interests of its citizens.

By 1994 it was evident that a number of state-owned enterprises were failing and suffered from insufficient capital while the banking system was already carrying a large volume of bad debt. The government's budget deficit peaked in 1994 (for the decade of the 1990s) at 8.4 percent of GDP and government spending was nearly 59 percent of GDP, a record high for all of the Central European transition countries for the 1990s. Hungary's deficit on current account also hit its 1990s high. Inflation had risen to 28 percent, approaching the levels suffered just after independence. Foreign direct investment was half of its 1993 levels. Foreign debt was rising toward a peak of 70 percent of GDP.[7]

Economic crisis was averted only by a drastic stabilization package engineered by the Finance Minister, Lajos Bokros.[8] Instead of introducing market socialism, Prime Minister Horn presided over an austerity package right out of Western economics textbooks that helped turn the Hungarian economy around. We observe in the macroeconomic stabilization portion of the next section that Gyula Horn tried in various ways to drag his feet with respect to liberalization of the economy, but the stabilization program was nevertheless the event that signaled a change in direction.

Government spending was cut and wages were reduced. The government's deficit and the rate of inflation began to move down. Manufacturers increased their share of GDP and exports improved dramatically. The first state bank was privatized in 1994 and a Securities and Exchange Commission was established in 1995. In 1995 Hungary became a member of the World Trade Organization and in 1996 won OECD membership. By 1997 Hungary was showing strong and steady growth in GDP and was by 2000 ranked as one of the stronger of the Central and Eastern European economies.

As our political economy model predicts, the Bokros austerity measures produced a backlash from voters; in 1998 they elected a coalition government headed by Victor Orban of the Hungarian Civic Party (FIDESZ). We discuss Hungary's progress on the five basic reforms next and in the process include the efforts of the Orban government.

A QUESTION OF POLITICAL WILL

In considering the implementation of basic economic reforms in Hungary, the interaction of ideology and politics is never far from the surface in the behavior of politicians. They are keenly aware of the voters' tendency to react strongly to the effects of economic policies.

Price Liberalization

Markets determined about 65 percent of prices in 1989. In 1990 this rose to 77 percent. However, Hungary seemed to move forward in fits and starts. In 1994 direct price controls still applied to transportation, rents, some food, telecommunications and pharmaceuticals. Deeply entrenched regulations on property, on wage policy and on other business practices remained, leaving less leeway for private owners than implied by the seemingly high level of price liberalization.

In addition to problems brought on by price controls and regulations, government's management of the money supply was uneven. The currency remained non-convertible until January 1996. Even after introducing a crawling peg exchange rate system in 1995, inflation reached nearly 30 percent. Even without direct price controls the signaling function of relative prices was obscured by poor macroeconomic stabilization measures. When the socialist government was replaced in 1998, monetary control improved and by 1999 supply and demand determined most consumer goods prices.

The government still administers prices for gas and electricity, telephone and mail services, water and sewers, radio and television broadcasting, and railway and bus transport. In 2000 the government capped prices on gas and electricity below levels that would cover energy costs. Suppliers had to absorb the losses. Pharmaceutical prices were also capped. Prime minister Orban, ostensibly a free-market advocate, claimed that he wanted to reduce inflation to protect low-income consumers. When the socialists began to look more popular in the polls in late 2000, Orban began to sound like a populist.

Property Privatization

The design of the enterprise privatization program contained the seeds of its early failure as well as contradictions inherent in Hungarian reform itself. The fact that government did not favor advocates of capitalism over socialism became evident in the privatization legal framework.[9] In 1990 the State Property Agency (SPA) was formed to initiate privatization of state property. The SPA was supposed to sell off state-owned enterprises, but at the same time the Law of Defense of State Property was passed. The Law of Defense of State Property implicitly contradicts the notion that capitalism is legally superior to monopoly socialism. This law was designed not to facilitate or accelerate privatization of SOEs, but instead to protect state property from being sold below a "good" price. A good price was determined in part by the very agencies up for privatization, as well as by the SPA.

The Hungarian Democratic Forum (MDF) was the first non-socialist regime to be elected in Hungary. In 1990 the MDF, in coalition with the Smallholders and the National Christian Democrats, passed the Transformation Act, the Accounting Act and the Banking Act, all intended to facilitate efficient privatization. The parliament later passed a New Labor Code and a Bankruptcy Act. In 1994 when the socialists were elected, some aspects of these measures were rescinded. The Transformation Act was repealed.

This was another demonstration of Hungarian ambivalence toward privatization, with its shift of ownership and control to private hands without bureaucratic involvement in decisions. Rather than seeing privatization as a means of forcing closure of failed enterprises and of reforming management conduct by subjecting it to competition, it was seen as a means of generating government revenues without relinquishing control. The view that government ownership of the means of production is legitimate was popular among socialists. Instead of a means to move society toward capitalism, privatization became a mechanism to finance the welfare state by carefully managed sale of state assets.

One natural difficulty this muddled policy encountered was in finding private buyers. Much state property, once the Soviet trading system disintegrated, was worthless. Semi-functional state enterprises were strapped with debt as a hangover from the collapsing regime in which financing arrangements involved inter-firm transfers of financial obligations. This arrangement continued to be supported by the central bank, and all these financial decisions were made by the same *nomenklatura* that had run the system down for decades. Confusion about the purpose of privatization, and deeply felt conflicts regarding goals of equity in a Marxist sense and efficiency in a capitalist sense, hamstrung privatization and reduced the flow of privatizing firms to a trickle.[10]

Some spontaneous privatization succeeded, but such extra-legal transfers undertaken directly by plant managers and other insiders were viewed by many as theft of public property. Other property was sold by the state in private deals with wealthy foreign enterprises. By June 1992 only about 15 percent of state enterprises had been privatized. Remaining enterprises were often poorly run, producing unwanted goods that used to go to the Soviet Union; they contained decrepit capital equipment and were unable to compete in international markets. In many cases outstanding debt exceeded the book value of assets.[11] According to a prominent Hungarian economist, some major SOEs, even if cannibalized and sold off in pieces, were worth less than 2 percent of their book value. Insider trading allowed asset cherry-picking, leaving the taxpayer with the residual failed enterprises. In short, the welfare state was perpetuated, but running on borrowed time.

The new Antall government in 1990 did facilitate sale of some property and did allow private firms with more than 500 employees to operate. Large-scale farming and heavy industry continued to be state run, and government regulations continued to hamper rental markets, employment and wage policies. Even though small firms were the easiest to privatize in every transition state, only 40 percent had been sold off by 1993 in Hungary.

The pace picked up in the next few years, and by 1997 nearly 90 percent of small firms had been privatized. Overall privatization, however, is still slow, and the state has retained a stake in many privatized companies. The State Property Agency will retain a permanent ownership share in ninety-three companies – for example, in energy, telecommunications and agribusiness. In 2000 the government claimed that 80 percent of GDP was produced by the private sector. Some economists question this statistic because the state continues to meddle in companies in which it holds a stake. Privatization is still a slow process and government intervention has slowed rather than promoted growth.[12]

Macroeconomic Stabilization

Between 1990 and 1994 reformers were unable to turn the economy around, not a surprise as long as the central authorities and *nomenklatura* continued to dominate decision-making and large-scale industry. Table 10.4 indicates that GDP growth continued to fall and inflation continued to rise. Economic conditions under the MDF were apparently worse than they had been under the communists. Many loss-making state firms continued to operate only because of government subsidies, and in spite of a law restricting central bank purchases of state deficit issues, the subsidies were funded by the bank printing money. Privatization also got a bad name as an illegitimate activity as a result of widespread insider theft of state assets. Monetary stabilization proved impossible and inflation accelerated from 17 percent in 1989 to 35 percent in 1991.

Table 10.4 Growth of output and inflation, 1989–1999

Year	Real GDP (%)	Inflation – CPI (%)
1989	0.7	17.0
1990	–3.5	28.9
1991	–11.9	35.0
1992	–3.1	23.0
1993	–0.6	22.5
1994	2.9	18.8
1995	1.5	28.2
1996	1.3	23.6
1997	4.6	18.3
1998	5.1	14.3
1999	4.0	10.0

Although they came to power early in 1994, reform socialists did not introduce a fiscal austerity program until March 1995. The forint was devalued 15 percent in 1994 but double-digit inflation continued and accelerated in 1995 to 28 percent. In March 1995 the government again devalued the forint, this time by 9 percent, imposed an 8 percent temporary additional import duty and introduced a crawling peg. The currency remained non-convertible as the government did not trust the marketplace to value its currency. Social benefits were curtailed. Child support became means-tested and some pension funds were privatized. Tuition fees were levied on students attending state universities.

Prime Minister Horn stalled reforms. He sacked the relatively successful and popular Privatization Commissioner, Ferenc Bartha, reversing plans to privatize state hotel chains.

The socialists continued to prop up the welfare state with deficit spending, currency mismanagement and halting sales of state property until Bokros's austerity program began to take effect in 1995. As fiscal discipline improved, the deficit fell in 1995 and 1996, then rose in 1997. After the socialists left office in 1998, the deficit began to move down again and continued to do so. Public expenditure is a problem in Hungary in part because a significant portion of it is precommitted. Pensions are about 8 percent of GDP and debt service is more than 5 percent (but falling).

From 1997 Hungary's economic performance has been strong and more consistent. Inflation continues to decline and unemployment is falling. Public debt, over 86 percent of GDP as late as 1995, was at 60 percent and falling in 1999. Growth in GDP is steady and was over 6 percent in 2000. In 1999 output levels reached those of 1989, according to the IMF. Hungary, named as one of the six countries in the first group to be considered for accession to the European Union, in 2001 was ranked the strongest candidate of the lot. This prosperity, however, may be tenuous and could be threatened yet again by political pressures. In an effort to shore up his image with voters, Prime Minister Orban was in late 2000 criticizing the "Bokros package," his term for the austerity program of 1995, saying that the selloff of state properties had been hard on the citizenry and that companies were sold for prices that were far too low. Worse yet, he announced his intention to raise pensions and other social spending.

Industry Restructuring and Deregulation

We have emphasized a behavioral characteristic of many Hungarian politicians and bureaucrats that seems virtually endemic. They meddle. It is difficult for them to let markets work without interference. It is difficult to tell the real extent to which the economy is privatized because the state retains some ownership in so many important companies. The right rules have been adopted, but it is likely that microrestructuring is the area in which reality may be farthest from appearances.

The government has done well in restructuring the banking system, which has become one of the strongest in Central and Eastern Europe. The financial sector is generally in good shape but authorities have some work yet to do on supervisory functions; the EU points in particular to financial supervision of pension funds.[13] The energy sector is another story: the government's involvement has extended to capping energy prices, causing utilities to lose money as their costs rise. The government decided to put a temporary (until after elections, perhaps) stop to price liberalization in this sector. In one instance Prime Minister Orban, in his populist mode, offered to renationalize the gas industry.

Foreign businesses seem to have a great deal of faith in Hungary's future and continue to put more direct investment dollars here than anywhere else in the former Eastern bloc. Foreign-owned companies are the driving force behind strong export growth and most are apparently happy with the business climate. There are exceptions in the energy sector, where complaints about the government have come from both domestic and foreign investors. In October 2000 one American company filed a suit against the government for allegedly breaking contracts. A Hungarian gas and oil company sued the government over price-cap losses. Both gas and electricity companies have become involved in expensive litigation since the nominally center-right Orban has been in place. He is not only holding energy prices down but has abandoned plans to privatize one big electricity wholesaler.

Another instance of governmental misbehavior with respect to foreign companies occurred in 2000 when a Japanese managing director was arrested in front of his employees for allegedly stealing from the company. The cash in question was found later in a company safe. The executive was released from jail without an apology. These stories serve to illustrate the point that Hungarian officials may not fully grasp the enormous importance of investor confidence and the extent to which unpredictable official behavior can damage it. Foreign direct investment has been perhaps the key stimulus to Hungary's economic transformation.

Small and medium-sized businesses employ 70 percent of the labor force and produce 45 percent of total output, mostly non-tradables. These businesses do not have adequate access to finance and financial services and this is a serious structural issue for Hungary's long-term success. The government has specifically undertaken to promote the well-being of local entrepreneurs, but in announcing the intention to build strong homegrown companies the Prime Minister used the opportunity to denounce the "cheap" sale of state assets to foreign investors. A Western diplomat referred to the Hungarian government's worrying tendency to bite the hand that feeds it.[14]

The EU reports some concern with labor mobility within Hungary, a problem not limited to the transition economies of Europe, and with health-care reform. Hungary's health-care sector is extremely inefficient. The Hungarians spend more on health care than similar countries and the care they get is of poorer quality. Restructuring the system is bound to have an effect on the government's budget, and fiscal discipline is particularly important to EU accession countries.

Trade Liberalization

Table 10.5 contains selected international trade statistics for Hungary from 1989 to 1999. The Hungarian governments, whether socialist or not, have made great strides in opening the economy to foreign trade. This has largely been accomplished by direct government deals with large foreign firms and in the face of a currency that was until recently only partially convertible. As the currency has been allowed to float and has become fully convertible, its value has steadily, though not dramatically, drifted down against the dollar. Nominally valued at 63.2 f/$ in 1990 (when the forint was not convertible and a thriving

Table 10.5 International trade and financial statistics (selected years)

Year	FDI* (% of GDP)	Imports (% of GDP)	Balance of trade (% of GDP)	Exchange rate (forint/$)
1990	0.9	26.0	0.3	63.2
1995	10.0	34.5	–2.5	125.7
1997	4.6	46.5	–0.9	186.8
1998	4.1	54.0	–2.3	214.3
1999	3.1	56.9	—	237.2

Note: * Foreign direct investment.

black market in currencies existed), the forint fell to 237.2 f/$ by 1999. Nevertheless, imports are over 50 percent of GDP compared to about 25 percent in 1990, and much of this growth in trade has been with the West. In fact, over 70 percent of Hungary's trade is with EU countries. The predominance of trade within the European Union demonstrates a considerable degree of integration that should help smooth the way to membership. In 2000 plans were under way to phase out the crawling peg regime gradually in preparation for joining the EU. The basket to which the currency is pegged was changed to being made up of only the euro. As soon as inflation falls to 5 percent and the inflation differential with major trading partners falls below 3 percent, the government will change to a fixed exchange rate target with wide intervention bands.[15] This will be the last step before moving eventually to the euro as Hungary's currency.

CONCLUSIONS AND OUTLOOK

Table 10.6 contains a glimpse of the history of national elections from 1990 to 1999. The first column of data is the percentage of the vote received by reformers as opposed to socialists, according to our allocation of the various parties (see Appendix B for details). Column 2 is the index of reform progress constructed from the information we collected in each of the five reform areas (most of the raw data for this compilation is in Table B.14). Next in the table is economic data. This information is presented by the period when a political regime was in power. The non-socialist Antall government was installed in 1990. In 1994 Hungary elected socialists headed by Gyula Horn. In 1998 the Hungarian Civic Party (FIDESZ) led by Victor Orban formed a coalition government and the MSZP (the socialists) led the opposition. It is worth noting that the reform index was lowest in the socialist years and highest after the recent period when non-socialists were elected. The earliest period was one of fervent nationalistic posturing. Control of inflation has been better since 1997 and economic growth is back on track.

Have Hungarians based their political and economic goals since independence on a "golden era" from the past? Strangely enough, that era may have been during the time of Soviet occupation. Hungary was the most prosperous state in the Second World, those countries behind the Iron Curtain, between 1966 and 1975. It was not only relatively rich,

Table 10.6 Elections, reforms and economic performance 1990–1999 (all variables cover election intervals)

Year	Votes for reformers (%)	Reform index (1995=100)	GDP % change		Inflation rate		Unemployment rate	
			After	Before	After	Before	After	Before
1990	42.7	110.2	–4.1	–0.4	26.4	3.5	9.9	0.8
1994	27.7	108.5	2.8	–4.1	21.8	26.4	10.7	9.9
1998	52.5	117.5	4.4	2.8	11.6	21.8	9.4	10.7

but it was growing. Hungarians had created the New Economic Mechanism and were enjoying a degree of economic independence and consequent wealth (however modest) unequaled elsewhere in the Soviet empire. They were able to maintain some small degree of familiarity with markets. They were also running the political system. Moscow ruled but the management responsibilities were in Hungarian hands. This period made management of the economy and the administration of the system somewhat easier after independence.

After the Soviet empire collapsed the Hungarians had the easiest time of all the affected states in establishing strong commercial contacts with the West. They felt the most sophisticated in the ways of the Western world of all the newly independent countries. They looked upon their experience as a great advantage. But their years exercising the New Economic Mechanism also convinced them that they could be capitalists and communists at the same time. They acquired a powerful ability to accommodate to both systems, to make their markets fit into socialist restrictions and to become comfortable with socialist guarantees and lack of economic risk.

They spent the earlier years of their transition taking a few steps forward and several back, thanks to the Soviet experience that had sharpened their taste for goulash. It looks as if they have in the last few years turned the corner. Their old ways continue to surface from time to time, but they have created a strong economy and a responsive democratic polity. They were accepted into NATO in 1999 and are at the front of the queue for membership of the EU. Accession to the European Union requires meeting 80,000 pages of regulations and standards. They are determined, and have improved their standing year by year through hard work and discipline. The EU reports that the Hungarians have a "broad political consensus on key aspects of economic policy."[16] The prospect of EU membership has provided the incentive to persist in their liberalization efforts. If they can maintain those efforts we believe they will be a long-term success story.

NOTES

1. A Conference on Teaching Economics, sponsored by The Foundation for Teaching Economics, Sacramento, California.
2. There was a settlement in the area in Neolithic times and from Roman times. The cities of Buda and Pest were destroyed more than once by foreign invaders, and were combined to become Hungary's capital in 1873. During the Second World War three-quarters of the flats in Budapest were damaged and every sixth flat destroyed.
3. See *The Economist*, 14 October 1989.
4. See *The Financial Times*, 6 June 1990.
5. Bruszt and Simon (1992).
6. For more on market socialism, see Bardhan and Roemer (1992), Easton and Walker (1997), Kornai (1990), Kovalik (1994), Lange (1938) and Stiglitz (1994).
7. European Bank for Reconstruction and Development, *Transition Report 2000*.
8. For an account by the architect of the austerity package, see Bokros and Dethier (1998).
9. Torok (1992) provides an excellent Hungarian appraisal of this situation.
10. See Vince (1993).
11. Torok (1992).
12. Professor Peter Milhayi is quoted in the *Financial Times*, 22 November 2000.
13. European Union, *Hungary 2000*.
14. *Financial Times*, 20 November 2000.
15. European Bank for Reconstruction and Development, *Transition Report 2000*.
16. European Union, *Hungary 2000*, p. 24.

11. Can Russia make it?*

We must kill more professors!
(Vladimir Ilyich Lenin[1])

They pretend to pay us and we pretend to work.
(Soviet humour of the 1980s)

The sternest test of our historical analysis of the politics of economic reforms is Russia.[2] As the motherland of the 1917 Bolshevik Revolution, Russia was taken over by homegrown communists who imposed the Soviet model under the guidance of Lenin. Unable to blame communism on someone else (as could the citizens of the satellite states)[3] and thus delegitimize communist ideas as foreign, reformers must overcome even greater political barriers to transform Russia from communism to market capitalism and democracy.[4]

Furthermore, history before communism provides no Russian example of a successful private market economy, much less of democratic capitalism. Nomadic, rural and agricultural for most of its history, Russia has during all of recorded history been dominated by authoritarian regimes. As Europe was industrializing from the middle of the eighteenth century to the early twentieth century, Czars empowered by history, by the aristocracy, by the Church and by the military paid little heed to the wishes of peasants or workers. This hierarchical class society, virtually feudal, was ill suited to the highly cooperative and integrated demands of the industrial state and thus Russia fell behind her modernizing Western European neighbors.

Nothing in Russia's past provides a model for reformers who want Russia to evolve into a pluralistic democratic system, supported by a rule of law and reliant upon a private market economy.[5] No sound model for the future can be gleaned from Russian history, and communism cannot be dismissed as associated with despised foreign domination.[6] These two facts mean that Russian reformers have higher hurdles to clear than the other countries we study in this book. Our historical analysis implies that Russia is less likely to transform successfully because the political preconditions make it difficult for reformers to justify on political grounds the structural economic reforms necessary to sustain growth.

Our analysis suggests it will be difficult for Russia to overcome the legacy that handicaps reformers. Unless reformers can capture the imagination of the Russian people, it seems unlikely that under new quasi-democratic rule they will accept the consequences of choices needed now to dismantle the old system before building a modern capitalist state. It is difficult to see how significant progress can be made without either moderating democracy or successfully educating the people about the inherent flaws in communism and the inability to transform directly their current state to a modern European welfare state. Clinging to

* We thank Igor Lukashin for contributing to this chapter.

the siren song of socialism in either its communist or its modern European guise may well inhibit economic growth and set the stage for another non-democratic regime to grasp power and turn Russia toward another historical dead end. Russia's current circumstances are easier to understand in light of the country's history before, during and since the Soviet period.

HISTORY BEFORE COMMUNISM[7]

Perhaps no period in history better reveals Russia's promise and curse than the reigns of Czar Peter the Great (1682–1725) and Czarina Catherine II (1762–1796). These two brilliant and powerful rulers brought Russia into major world power status and brought its aristocracy into contact with modern European culture. At the same time, both proved unable and unwilling to deal with the curses that would plague the Russian people through the end of the twentieth century. Russia was largely unified by the middle of the seventeenth century following consolidation under Ivan III from 1462 to 1505 of lands around Muscovy. This was the thriving portion of Russia that rose to influence after the Mongol invasions of 1223 to 1240 had devastated Kievan Rus'. Until sacked by the Mongols, the city of Kiev was the center of cultural life and of Christian life in Russia, one site of the St. Sofia cathedrals built by Prince Iaroslav the Wise in the eleventh century, and the center of a broad-based educational system. The liturgy was written in the native Cyrillic alphabet and the Duma was created in Kiev, providing a voice for leading warriors and officials.

In the eighteenth century, Peter the Great named himself Emperor as well as Czar, formed the formidable Russian navy and required all noblemen to serve either as military officers or as civil administrators. He created an Academy of Sciences, introduced the printing press and expanded state revenues 300 percent. Fascinated by Western culture, he required all male noblemen to get Western educations. The center of empire became St. Petersburg. As important as these advances were, Peter failed to prepare for modernization in three respects. These would plague Russia to the present time. First, Peter retained serfdom: all of his reforms dealt with the nobility. Feudalism doomed Russia to economic stagnation. With more independence and freedom, workers in the West were about to launch the industrial revolution. Russia's feudal structure inhibited its ability to exploit the individual initiative that drove the industrial revolution.

Second, while fascinated and impressed by Western culture, Peter failed to understand important aspects of the Enlightenment. His decision to educate the nobility but leave conditions of the peasants untouched deepened the divide between the elite and the masses, a condition that the Bolsheviks would exploit 200 years later. It was a problem that the Bolsheviks also would fail to correct. To this day, a gap in understanding separates Russian rulers from their people. This does not augur well for transition to democracy and capitalism. Failing to appreciate the growing desire for decentralized authority in the West, Peter did not imagine that the Enlightenment sounded the death knell of the legitimacy of authoritarian rule by divine right.

Third, Peter failed to solve the succession problem. Peter executed his own son and failed to specify a successor or a decision rule for selecting a successor. This problem would echo down the ages to plague communist Russia. Lenin, Stalin, Khrushchev, Brezhnev and the rest ascended to power amidst internal bickering and renewed problems of legitimacy. Each new leader had to repudiate his predecessors while trying to justify and solidify his own position. This persists in post-communist Russia. Unless and until Russians can agree to the legitimacy of a decision rule for selecting leaders, they will face uncertainty in every transition to new leadership.

After a period of unrest and war with the Ottoman Turks, in 1762 Catherine II dethroned her own husband, who had proven too pro-Prussia. Lacking hereditary rights, she assumed the mantle of Czarina. She made significant strides for Russia, expanding its territory to Odessa on the Black Sea, removing Poland from the map of Europe, stabilizing and homogenizing the empire and establishing a Charter of the Nobility which confirmed the liberation of the nobles.[8] Still, the problems of an alienated peasantry, an elite and detached nobility and no viable succession rule left Russia ill-prepared for the industrial revolution and the race to modernization.

By the middle of the nineteenth century Russia was a powerful nation, having dealt successfully with the Ottoman Turks, Austria and Prussia. It had an educated aristocracy, an advanced agrarian system, a modern education system and a uniquely Russian culture that could boast Pushkin, Gogol and Turgenev. Having defeated Napoleon in the war of 1812, Alexander I was known as the "Savior of Europe." Russia had become so powerful that by the mid-1800s Czar Nicholas I provided the major military force, suppressing uprisings throughout Europe. A disturbing harbinger of things to come was his establishment of the "Third Section," a system of spies and informers that would enforce government censorship and controls. Apparently Western culture, while interesting, was to be adopted on limited terms.

Another disturbing phenomenon became evident at this time. The ideas of democracy, equality, fraternity and law were associated with non-Russian sources. They were Western. As such, Slavophiles challenged these imports as foreign.[9] Only things Slavic were to be admired. A kind of Russian messianic fervor came to the fore.[10]

In the latter half of the nineteenth century, when 80 percent of Russian workers remained serfs and peasants, Alexander I introduced reforms. He emancipated 20 million privately held serfs. Courts were established to resolve criminal cases and domestic disputes. A broader-based but still powerless Duma was established. A Russian state bank was formed and the military through universal conscription began to educate both men and women. Nicholas II ascended to the throne in 1894 and began to modernize Russia economically. His Prime Minister, Sergei Witte, helped him to triple coal, iron and steel production between 1890 and 1900. He doubled the volume of rail track laid in the empire by constructing the Trans-Siberian railway, a marvel of modern economic development. Financed by the New York Stock Exchange, this was an indicator of Russia's great economic promise. The undereducated masses, however, were discontent with the remote aristocracy. This and excessive state spending led to Witte's downfall in 1905. These structural problems meant that Russia continued to fall behind Germany, France, England and the United States.

The period from 1850 to 1905 is known as the Age of Reason in Russian. Leo Tolstoy wrote *War and Peace* and *Anna Karenina*. Fyodor Dostoevsky wrote *Crime and Punishment* and *The Brothers Karamazov*. Anton Chekhov wrote plays that glorified the peasant class and lamented their treatment by the nobility. A young Russian radical, Aleksandr Ulyanov, was executed for trying to kill the repressive Alexander III (whose father, Alexander II, had been assassinated). This would-be assassin's death was to have a profound effect on the world through its influence on his younger brother, Vladimir Ilyich Lenin. Soon the First World War would thrust this ill-prepared society into a conflagration that set the stage for the October Revolution and the victorious Bolsheviks.

HISTORY UNDER COMMUNISM

From Lenin to Stalin[11]

Even with full access to the secret files of former communist regimes, one could not do justice to seventy years of communist rule in a single book, much less one chapter. Our modest goal here is to set the stage for the transition period by briefly analyzing both the political developments of the Soviet Union and the economic system that became nearly inoperable by the late 1980s (some of this material was covered in Chapter 1 on the collapse of the Soviet Union).

Many Westerners find the lure of socialism to Europeans of the late nineteenth and early twentieth centuries hard to understand. Soviet communism held that all comrades, without regard for self, should work for the good of the whole. A goal of Soviet communism was to eliminate personal differences to make way for pure Soviet man who would populate the socialist utopia. This idea has little appeal to Westerners weaned on the importance of the individual, on freedom of religion and on the value of differences and uniqueness.

The cavalier attitudes of Lenin and the Bolsehviks toward process and their absolutist conviction of the rightness of their position led to their determination to win total control. Allegedly control would be by the vanguard of the revolution; this set the stage for Josef Stalin's dictatorship. How does one balance Stalin's success in converting a primarily agrarian society into a modern industrial power against his maniacal reign of terror that gutted any residual honor communism might once have enjoyed?

From Khrushchev to Gorbachev[12]

It was left to Khrushchev to begin the disengagement of the Communist Party from the excesses of Stalin. Had he not denigrated Stalinism and the cult of personality, Khrushchev could not himself have captured the reins of power. His now famous "secret speech" in 1956, repudiating the excessive brutality under Stalin (in which Khrushchev played a part), had repercussions thoughout the USSR. It led directly to the Hungarian revolt. To crush the dissent that he had started, Khrushchev proved as willing as his predecessors to fall back on force, defeating the Hungarian freedom fighters with Soviet tank divisions.

The pace toward collapse of the USSR accelerated with Mikhail Gorbachev's secret speech, first tested in plenary session of the Central Committee in October 1987.[13] Like Khrushchev, Gorbachev intended to weaken the forces of stagnation in the bureaucracy and in the party. He had to establish an environment in which new ideas and approaches could be adopted and the economy could move forward. The obsession with secrecy and centralization had stifled initiative and inhibited sensible planning at local levels.

Successful at replication, continuation and well-defined engineering feats, the central planning model was not equipped for innovation nor capable of Schumpeter's creative destruction. Brilliant (and well-marketed) advances in space exploration and military production masked an increasingly stagnant economy. Change had become the constant of modern post-industrial society and the USSR had a system that stifled innovation and change. Like Karl Marx, Gorbachev had no clear notion of what could replace the failed system he saw crumbling around him. And once Gorbachev squeezed *glasnost* and *perestroika* out of the toothpaste tube, it was impossible to put them back in.

THE POLITICAL TRANSITION[14]

The end of the dictatorship of the proletariat came with the failure of the anti-Gorbachev coup in August 1991. Boris Yeltsin, standing on a tank and talking the troops out of crushing their own people, captured the imagination of Russians and Westerners alike. As important, though, was the inability of the coup leaders to rely on the loyalty of their followers. It seems they had no real notion of their goals, nor how they were going to attain them. When middle-level bureaucrats, mid-level soldiers and even senior military officers refused to crush the revolt, the *putsch* collapsed. The feared Soviet Union superpower imploded, revealing itself to have been yet another Potemkin village – a fake front propped up for show.

Unfortunately, it still remains unclear what will replace the old political and economic regime. Communists still run many parts of government and still control many levels of bureaucracy. Communists still control many cooperatives, factories and villages.[15] They have not gone away and have not been fully dismissed as illegitimate.[16] In fact, much of what Western businesses consider appropriate and normal activity is seen in Russia as illegitimate, because it was delegitimized by years of Marxist propaganda.

Judging from *The Federalist Papers* (Madison, 1987), the American revolution was followed by the design of a constitutional system based in part on skepticism of central power and on a recognition that men were flawed; it demonstrates some doubt about human nature, and creates a system to protect individuals from domination by the state. An extraordinary system of checks and balances and of constitutional separation of powers reflects the American founding fathers' fears of concentrated power. The Bolsheviks and Lenin, in contrast, suffered no such self-doubts. Theirs was the right way; history would inevitably lead to communism. No one would exploit the common man. Everyone would be equal. Marx was convinced that capitalism was inhumane and doomed to collapse. He viewed capitalism as a system built on greed in which the upper classes forced harsh working conditions on the masses in order to exploit their labor and reap profits.

Marx's followers were determined to build a perfect society in which no one exploited anyone else. Capitalists could not exploit workers because no one owned the capital. Landlords could not exploit peasants because private property would be outlawed. At first the Communist Party would need to destroy vestiges of the old ways, but eventually the state would wither away and everyone would pull together for a glorious future free of class distinctions. Unfortunately, Marx left out of his analysis just how society would actually transform itself into a system without private property, without class distinctions and without government. *Das Kapital*, Marx's famous book, was a fascinating and important social critique of the defects of capitalism. It was a persuasive (if incorrect) historical argument for the inevitable collapse of capitalism that would occur as opportunities for profits evaporated. The economics, while limited by some simplistic (by today's standards) models, was complex and rich and contained useful insights about capitalism. What *Das Kapital* lacked was a viable alternative model to capitalism.

This gap in the argument did not slow communists, nor weaken Marxist resolve to achieve the perfect state. It was this belief in achieving perfection (and this conviction that the party would be the vanguard of the proletariat) that led the masses to believe in the socialist society. The absolutism of the belief sowed the seeds of the cruelty and violence of Lenin and Stalin. If some individual landlords, capitalists, kulaks and ethnic groups needed to be shoved aside or even eliminated, this was a small price to pay to achieve the classless society in which the Soviet people would march forward arm in arm to an egalitarian future. Like Torquemada of the Spanish Inquisition, Lenin and his successors were so convinced of the correctness of their views that achieving their ends justified violent and brutal means.

Even when Khrushchev secretly was attacking the Stalin cult of personality, he held fast to the legitimacy of the Communist Party and its mission as the vanguard of the proletariat revolution. He knew he had to repudiate Stalinism and errors of the past if any progress was to be made out of the stultifying paralysis left by Stalin. Still he clung to the conviction that the march of communism toward the perfect Soviet society was valid, legitimate and inevitable. Khrushchev evidently saw nothing inconsistent in repudiating the cruelty of Stalin and then ordering his Soviet tank divisions into Hungary. Even Gorbachev in his 1988 secret speech held steadfastly to the virtues of socialism. Gorbachev saw *demokratizatsiya*, *glasnost* and *perestroika* as necessary elixirs to correct mistakes of the past and set the stage for the next forward advance toward the socialist workers' paradise.

Did communism have to lead inevitably to Stalinism? Since one cannot perform the counterfactual experiment, one cannot be certain. Similar periods of bloody purges have followed ascent to power by Marxists in China, Korea, Vietnam and Cambodia.[17] Lenin's Bolsheviks were successful in devastating all potential opposition power and in creating a totalitarian state. Once the crafty and paranoid Stalin had captured this regime nothing stood in his way. He was able to act out his madness.[18] It amazes Westerners that so many older Russians still admire him for the strength of his leadership.

ECONOMIC REFORMS

The Soviet Economy

The structure of Russia's industrial base could not have been worse for a transformation towards competitive markets.[19] Concentration of industrial activity was so great that after the empire collapsed entire industries were stranded in countries different from their suppliers and from their markets.[20] For example, in the entire Soviet Union synthetic rubber was produced in only three factories, one of which was in Russia. Russia had "five truck production complexes, each with production facilities concentrated primarily in a single city."[21] The central operating rule of the Politburo evidently was to concentrate economic activity in the fully integrated USSR to facilitate command and control. This partly reflected Stalin's ideal of "gigantism." Such excessive concentration of industry presented a serious problem for reformers who wanted to transform Russia into a competitive market economy.[22] What could they do with these massive state enterprises? Stabilizing the currency, balancing the budget, liberalizing prices and opening markets to foreign competition may contribute little to dismantling this centralization of enterprise. How much closer to competitive private markets would Russia be after privatizing its industrial dinosaurs?[23]

Collapse after seventy years of central planning left Russia in terrible trouble, unable to feed its people. Russia had not developed specialties for trade with neighbors to the west. Russia did not have a viable small-enterprise system. The Soviet Union boasted one-third of the world's forests. It was the world's largest producer of oil and natural gas, and it sported the world's largest ocean-going fishing fleet. Until the communists wiped out the kulaks when Stalin collectivized agriculture, Russia had always fed its own people and was a major grain exporter. Despite vast natural agricultural lands, the Soviet Union by the 1990s had become a major importer of grains and meats. Small private plots when and where permitted, though marginal in quantity and quality, were successful producers of meat, milk, eggs and vegetables.

Following Marx's recognition of the need for capital, the Soviet Union had stressed production of machinery, especially for metal working and production of military matériel. In terms of the sheer quantity of physical capital Russia had formidable productive capacity but stultifying bureaucracy offset the value of all of Russia's wealth. The system was characterized by overly detailed and centralized planning and counterproductive incentive systems. If that was not sad enough, Russia also suffered an intrusive, stubborn and cruel network of secret police.[24]

Other than the obvious desire for political control, why did the socialists organize their economy in such a centralized and controlled manner? This requires some understanding of methods of economic planning as well as the state of social science knowledge in early twentieth-century Europe.

In our view any economy built on the ideas of Marx is doomed to fail. Many scholars point out that the Soviet system was not really following Marx. We feel it is important to acknowledge that Marx left little to follow. Communists destroyed the price system, the monetary mechanism and the capital allocation system. They removed the wage and profit motives from production.[25] Lenin and his comrades added a venality that Marx and Engels had not envisioned.[26] Lenin and the Bolsheviks despised private initiative. People with entrepreneurial spirit were seen as "blood-sucking" exploiters who needed to be eliminated to make room for homogeneous Soviet man.[27]

Flexible relative market prices are the signals that induce constructive adaptation by suppliers and demanders to redress shortages and surpluses. In a healthy capitalist economy shortages and surpluses are transitory, as markets respond to price signals. To Marx prices were all part of the evil capitalists' and landlords' means of exploiting and controlling the masses. To Lenin and the Bolsheviks prices were political weapons with which to achieve political goals. Lowering prices of necessities like bread, energy and property rents was a means of satisfying the masses. High prices for television sets, radios, prestige cars and most Western products were a social statement by the party as to appropriateness.[28] Insiders like the party hierarchy arranged to get these bourgeois products, which were virtually unavailable to the masses. This was partly accomplished by restricting access to certain shops and stores that carried Western and luxury goods. Khrushchev himself is said to have boasted a considerable library of Western literature.[29]

Thus, the price mechanism was not allowed to work as it does in a market economy. Some other way of allocating goods and services had to emerge to replace the market-price system. The system that arose was one of queues, favoritism and, for most Russians, chronic shortages. Hedrick Smith (1990) tells of Russians carrying briefcases as they went about their daily tasks. He at first thought the Russian people were unusually studious to need briefcases, no matter their age or appearance. Later he learned that the briefcases were carried in the event one encountered a queue which meant something was available that other people wanted. So the Russian would get in the queue to buy the good, regardless of personal need. It could always be traded later for something useful.

Money, seen by Marxists as another tool used by exploiters to hold down the workers, had to be contained and its uses limited.[30] Among the heinous, the banker (moneylender or Jew – these terms were used interchangeably in Soviet propaganda) could not be allowed to issue credit and call debts. To Marx, bankers were useless leeches on society, providing no value to the economic system.[31] Thus, the monetary system was tightly controlled and organized so as to support the production plan only. Money did not serve as an incentive. Two types of money, both denominated in rubles as the unit of account, circulated simultaneously.[32] The central bank, Gosbank, printed ruble notes and coins which were issued by the planners to firms according to the wages to be disbursed by that firm to workers. These were not tied to output results, but rather to the rules of the plan. Workers were paid in rubles that they could use for consumption or savings. They purchased goods in rubles at administered prices. If they wished to save, they could deposit their rubles in the bank. Private bank accounts on which one could draw a check were not allowed, however, so one could withdraw only cash. Gosbank invested saved money according to the central production plan. Administered wages ordinarily provided no financial incentive to work hard. Firms could not fire workers, so that another lever that makes capitalism work was disabled.

A second medium of exchange (not cash) governed financial transactions within and between firms. When firms delivered intermediate products to other firms according to instructions in the plan, it was to receive credits issued by the Gosbank. However, these credits were issued according to the plan and firms generally did not know whether their credits and debits cancelled out. These credits were used by the central bank to see that it was supporting the plan. No attempt was made to see that firms were solvent. Money played no role in financially disciplining firms. If products were produced according to the plan, then the firm had done its job. Firms dealt in these ruble-denominated credits in their bank accounts, but only in cash when dealing with workers. Products bought and sold with credits tended to be intermediate goods exchanged between firms, whereas products purchased by consumers and workers were exchanged for cash rubles. The Soviet Union had two distinct systems of ruble exchange, rarely interacting with one another.

Capital played a unique role in Marx's thinking. The labor theory of value, which Marx believed correct, holds that all true value accrues from labor input.[33] This means that if any other input receives a return, it must be at the expense of paying the worker his true value. Thus, if capital receives a rate of return or if landowners receive rents, these payments must have been taken away from the workers, thus exploiting their labor. An unfortunate implication of this thinking is that capital assets cannot receive a return. This, in effect, outlaws market interest rates. Rental rates on property are administered as well, so rental returns cannot serve to allocate land.

We see the price system (in this instance, the interest price of capital assets and the rental return on land) stymied again in the Marxist world. If not by different market-driven prices and interest rates and market rents, how then are capital and land to be allocated? The answer is through the Gosplan.[34] The central authorities, the Politburo, would develop a five-year plan, the Gosplan, and everyone would follow it.

We begin analyzing the Gosplans with a useful tool for economic planning, the Leontief input–output (IO) table, designed by a Russian emigrant, Harvard Professor Wassily Leontief.[35] A generic Leontief input–output table is illustrated as Figure 11.1. The IO table lists every industry in the economy across the top row and also in the left column. Each cell represents an economic activity between the industries in that cell's column and in that cell's row. For example, reading across the row labelled "Construction" shows the uses of the output produced by the construction industry. The column labeled "Construction" contains all the inputs utilized by the construction industry in generating its outputs. In our hypothetical example, the construction industry requires 27 percent of mining output as input in its production process and the construction industry provides 39 percent of its output as input to the mining industry. The IO table helps to specify the framework of a central plan coherently. In creating the table, one fills out the plan for what each industry will need to achieve its output by using inputs from each other industry, and one fills out what output that industry will be able to produce and where it will go in the plan. Thus the Leontief input–output table allows one, in theory, to plan centrally the allocation of resources among industries in such a way as to be certain that the right amounts of inputs are available where the planners want them to go.

In order to devise an operational IO table, the planner needs to know the proportions of each input used in each production process. This is a considerable amount of information to expect a central planning committee to have. They must know the technical relations required in each industry to produce the output. This means they need to know both the ratios of all inputs and also the levels. Even in the unlikely event that the Politburo can get this information, how can members be motivated to use it appropriately? The public choice

		Output			
	Industry	Mining	Construction	Agriculture	Manufacturing
	Mining	24	27	34	15
Input	Construction	39	25	28	08
	Agriculture	20	33	22	25
	Manufacturing	17	15	16	52

Figure 11.1 Leontief input–output table illustrated (percentages)

aspects of decision-making in such a central body are complex. Bribes, threats, insider deals and coalition politics could all be expected. The idea that a central planner is an omniscient and benevolent dictator is appreciated only in certain planning models,[36] not in the real-world politics of the Politburo. Planning is a bit easier if the leader is a Stalin who states unambiguously that heavy industry and military matériel are to receive the bulk of resources. He also shows clearly that he will brook no opposition. Of course, even Stalinist methods cannot guarantee a sensible plan. The IO problem is far more complex than our table suggests. In principle one could devise a sub-table system for just the construction industry, detailing regions or sub-sectors within the construction aggregates. Thus the Politburo can, in theory, plan an entire economy down to the last detail.

Although it took seventy years for this to become obvious to communist planners, there are several details that render a central plan approach to practical economic organization worthless. Even if one could actually specify the exact input requirements and output coefficients for every industry, in practice one encounters problems. The choice of inputs and outputs is not strictly an engineering question. It is fundamentally an economics question that can be answered only by knowing relative scarcities as well as technical aspects of production. While this point may seem simple and obvious to an economist or manager, it still evades some planners. One economics professor in Hungary heralded the success of planning in large-scale Hungarian agriculture cooperatives as they had adopted advanced technological methods directly from American corporate farms. He did not realize that optimal factor proportions in Hungarian agriculture had to be different due to different relative scarcities. Nor had it occurred to him that copying the US was an admission that the US economic system was superior.

If one must take into account relative scarcities, then an engineering plan cannot simply be imposed from the top. Even if one could figure out the optimal mix taking relative scarcities into account by using a modern economic framework, one would have to redesign the entire table whenever any factor cost forced a change in the best mix of inputs for achieving a given output for a particular industry. In a dynamic world of changing technologies, resource supplies and labor skills, planners would constantly be revising the plan.[37]

An addition problem with central planning is the lack of adequate incentives. How does one solve the massive principal–agent problems of a central plan? How does one enforce the Politburo Gosplan on industrial ministries? How do the ministries impose their will on sectoral management? How does management impose its will on firms? How do firms impose their will on employees? This problem ripped apart the fabric of the economic system as certainly as dripping water can eventually shatter a rock. Most Soviet leaders, certainly Gorbachev and his aides, knew quite well by 1987 that the economy was grinding to a halt.

While it is difficult to build an economy from scratch, it is even more complex to build a modern economic system out of the mess left by decades of failed central planning.[38] Rebuilding Russia today is like trying to design and construct a new airplane from wreckage left by an earlier crash. Fixing a broken economic model is especially difficult when the old model, while unable to get off the ground, is not perceived to be total junk. Managers still run their factories. Cooperatives still work the land. Workers and farmers still go to work. Soldiers still march. Bureaucrats still enforce rules. The problem is that much of what gets produced is junk.

Table 11.1 Growth of real GDP (five-year intervals 1980–1999, average annual percentage change)

Period	Annual growth of GDP
1980–1984	4.0
1985–1989	3.3
1990–1994	–7.4
1995–1999	–1.9

Table 11.1 contains five-year averages of reported growth rates of GDP for Russia from 1980 to 1999. The figures for the first two intervals taken at face value make one wonder why the system collapsed. The economy was growing in real terms at rates over 3 percent during the decade prior to the collapse. Furthermore, judging from these data the so-called market economy has been an utter disaster.[39] A depression occupied the 1990–1994 interval with an average annual decline of almost 7.5 percent. The second five-year interval in the 1990s, 1995–1999, was better. The trough in growth rates was over and the economy was merely declining slowly at an average annual rate of about 2 percent.

To communists, data were just another tool of political propaganda.[40] One cannot take the growth rates from 1980 to 1989 very seriously. Even if the statistical agencies in the Soviet Union tried to produce accurate figures, output was not valued at market prices and thus the aggregates reflect weights determined by administered prices. In any case, the collapse did occur and measured output certainly fell.[41] Press reports suggest a collapse of the old system without any mechanism put in its place. The hope was that introducing reforms would be adequate to jump-start a private economy. The evidence suggests matters were much more difficult. The results to date are mixed. Some young and some well-connected entrepreneurs are very successful. Many people are not. Below we discuss some of the political difficulties of installing reforms in Russia and the prerequisite but missing formal and informal institutions. For Russia, the five reforms necessary for a viable market economy are insufficient in two respects. First, these economic reforms assume a level of supportive political and legal infrastructure that is lacking in Russia.[42] Second, the organization of the Soviet economy makes conversion into a network of competitive firms extremely difficult.

Price Liberalization

It was easy enough to stop announcing administered prices in many product areas as long as prices for essential goods like energy, foodstuffs and apartment rents did not rise. It proved more difficult to design an alternative price mechanism. Grigorii Iavlinskii, head of EPI Tsentr, the Center for Economic and Political Research, expressed misgivings about price liberalization in 1992. He pointed out that price liberalization meant in practice that instead of prices being set by a Gosplan administrator, they would be set by a private monopolist – the only enterprise producing the good. This is monopoly capitalism. The folly was especially obvious as long as firms were allowed to continue receiving state subsidies without ever going bankrupt.[43]

One may ask whether it was better to let firms, even monopolies, set prices rather than central planners. We would argue that under many conditions private firms would be better price-setters than the government. An economy in which every individual industry is run by a few large firms which are driven by the profit motive is healthier than one in which a bureaucrat sets prices. At least the motive to maximize profits will drive the monopolist to set prices so as to sell goods. Given the level and state of capital stock and the highly concentrated industrial organization, a monopoly price and output decision might be superior, on second-best grounds, to a competitive pricing rule.

It would seem to make more sense to privatize and price liberalize so that the market can start to work than to retain state ownership and control with price administered by government bureaucrats. The difference between an economy with fifty private monopolies and an economy with one government monopoly is that the former may have some incentive to compete with one another and thus to produce more efficiently. That is, private owners are residual claimants of their pricing decisions and this consequence forces a discipline on them that was obviously missing in the USSR. Unlike a bureaucrat, a monopolist can at least be driven by the profit motive. To the extent that the government promotes free trade, domestic monopoly producers will have to compete with foreign producers. Once the private sector is in place, even with a few very large former state-owned enterprises, the government may be able to begin antitrust efforts to promote competitive industries.[44] After monopoly firms start to operate, new services and new products may emerge.

This approach was not the strategy of choice. Instead, by fits and starts the post-communist governments tried to implement to various degrees the five generic reforms. In October 1990 the Russian parliament repudiated Soviet planning and approved the first radical economic reform package. This had the practical significance of the parliament standing up to the Soviet Union. In December of that year the Soviet budget was reduced to one-tenth of its previous level. Clearly Moscow was not able to support the Soviet Union financially. The next year saw a very unstable political system. In June, Yeltsin, in the first free presidential election, won the presidency. Hardliners tried to overthrow the elected government.[45] The coup attempt collapsed and Yeltsin held on to power. As the Soviet Union was disintegrating, Yeltsin withdrew financial support and the Soviet Union ceased to exist by the end of the year. In this process Yeltsin had been granted significant reform powers. He wasted little time in instituting price liberalization early in 1992.

Unfortunately reforms could not be effectively employed. Table 11.2 reports inflation in the consumer price index and growth of real GDP from 1989 to 1999; in 1992 the annual inflation rate exceeded 1500 percent. Barter and spontaneous monies substituted for the ruble as media of exchange in outlying regions.[46] Hyperinflation destroyed savings. Real output was falling at nearly 15 percent. Thus severe recession and hyperinflation accompanied price liberalization. What went awry?

It is essential to understand that hyperinflation cannot result from decontrolling prices. If economists know anything about monetary theory it is that hyperinflation results from oversupply of money. Egregious mismanagement of macroeconomic policies had to be occurring in 1992. Key to hyperinflation in Russia is that monetary policy remained under the control of communist anti-reformers. Monetary policy still was managed by the Supreme Soviet, a component of the Duma, and was heavily influenced by communists.[47]

Table 11.2 Growth and inflation, 1989–1999

Year	CPI (% rate of change)	Real GDP (% rate of change)
1989	9.2	1.5
1990	5.3	–3.0
1991	92.6	–5.0
1992	1526.0	–14.5
1993	873.5	–8.7
1994	307.6	–12.7
1995	197.5	–4.1
1996	47.6	–3.5
1997	14.6	0.8
1998	26.8	–4.6
1999	85.7	1.7

While the economy was failing around him, Yeltsin was looking for outside support. In June Russia joined the International Monetary Fund. In July Yeltsin attended a meeting of the G-7 nations. While he was evidently trying to achieve some political legitimacy for his regime, his countrymen remained unwilling to relinquish the old ways.

Property Privatization

Private property has always been controversial in Russia.[48] It was unpopular in the early 1990s partly because the economy was so slow to recover from the shock of the collapse of the empire. Rampant rent-seeking activity by former government officials and other insiders and the rise of a criminal element (often referred to as the Russian Mafia) discredited privatization.[49] Some scholars attribute the high crime rate to a failure of government credibility.[50] Yeltsin had started privatizing in 1992, but the Congress of People's Deputies was hostile to his plans and they clashed throughout the early years.[51]

Faced with a hostile Supreme Soviet, official corruption and rent-seeking "Red Directors" (company managers), Anatoly Chubais, the privatization czar from 1992 to 1996, agreed with President Yeltsin that the window for privatization would soon close. There was too little time to establish the institutional infrastructure that supports and protects private property. The overriding goal of the privatization process was to "depoliticize" the economy.[52] While managers may be corrupt, the Chubais team felt they would be easier to deal with than would politicians. They hoped that the new managers would at least operate in their economic self-interests.

Several different methods were used to privatize property,[53] but privatization faced trouble from the beginning. The parliament and the bureaucracy both remained hostile to private property. The tax system was punitive and incoherent, official corruption continued and the environment was ripe for organized crime.[54] Finally, the Red Directors proved all too willing to exploit the chaos by capturing ownership and control of firms. The inadequacy of the commercial code and legal system became evident, because former state enterprises, now private firms, were able to act as if the old "soft budget constraints" still prevailed. Creditors had little legal recourse for punishing debt-laden firms.[55]

In the case of oil production, privatization included plans to allow individual officials to transfer property ownership of wells directly to private parties. The incentive to dole out one property at a time and to capture some of the rents was evidently too much for most officials to resist. Still, in 1997 the government sold off six oil companies. The revenue paid $2.9 billion in long-overdue pension payments. Another method Chubais employed was vouchers. Every man, woman and child received privatization vouchers to invest in any enterprise they chose. The State Committee on the Management of State Property (GKI), the privatization agency, was created in 1991. Every method encountered difficulties. The levels of income and consumption were so low that few people could afford to bid in auctions, leaving the market to entrenched *nomenklatura* and criminal elements.[56] Few honest people could afford even to hold vouchers, so that they quickly fell under the control of insiders. Naturally this led to accusations of exploitation and concentration. The openly hostile Duma remained critical of privatization and sabotaged it when possible.

Under these difficult conditions, Chubais managed to privatize up to 77 percent of large firms and 85 percent of medium-sized enterprises. The private sector that had not existed in 1991 accounted for 70 percent of GDP by 1997. In 1995 and 1996 Chubais undertook a second wave of privatization in which the GKI auctioned off large state-owned enterprises. With foreigners staying away from Russia and most citizens too poor to participate, new integrated "financial industrial groups" (FIGs) emerged.[57] These organizations relied as much on political strength and insider dealing with regulators as they did on money. Still, Yeltsin had succeeded in removing a great deal of industry from the direct power of the state.

A frequent complaint of anti-reformers was the need to demonopolize. Widespread concern has been expressed about theft and Mafia control of industrial activities resulting in extortion, intimidation and even murder.[58] Boycko, Shleifer and Vishny (1993) argue that the point of early privatizing was not to create private property, but rather to insulate the military–industrial complex from losing its assets. A second purpose was to assign stock ownership rights to the government, not to private individuals. Another objective was to allow local government entities to sell off local property in order to generate income. The very notion of private property was apparently still a mystery to many in power. It is difficult to disentangle these complaints and confusions from resistance to the concept that private property is legitimate.[59]

Russian reformers did not give up trying to disentangle the government from property ownership. Yeltsin, although ill, announced in 1997 his "blueprint of the second phase of the economic revolution ..."[60] In May 1997 a new attempt was initiated to privatize housing. The natural gas, rail and electrical industries were also on the block. To jump-start the reforms, Yeltsin appointed Chubais as his First Deputy Prime Minister and brought in a new team of young liberal reformers. In September 1997 over 2000 enterprises were sold for a total of $2.5 billion.[61]

Many critics have concluded that the Russian privatization effort was a failure. We are not so certain of this. What might have been done instead? With parliament under the influence of the Communist Party, building a structure of institutions to protect and enforce Western-style property rights was not possible. Furthermore, any form of private property was going to be unpopular in Russia. Seventy years of egalitarian propaganda is hardly intellectual preparation for the distributive outcomes associated with capitalism. While one may object on moral grounds that the winners in the privatization sweepstakes were insiders, we believe that Russia is better off with many private owners than with continued control of the means of production by the state. Once the property is allocated, owners have an interest in establishing rights to protect it. Under capitalism, property owners, acting out of self-interest, will eventually respond to the wants of consumers. As our historical analysis showed, reformers were constrained in Russia. Chubais admitted that he had to give up a lot to entrenched powers in order to accomplish privatization at all. Did he give away too much to insiders and crooks? Perhaps, but what options did he have?[62]

Finally, as we have noted elsewhere, the data that purport to show continued economic decline are deeply flawed. A good deal of economic activity is extra-market and barter. The measurable sectors were producing unwanted or uncompetitive products anyway, so declines here are exaggerated. Certainly some people are getting richer than others, but that is the nature of market economics. While safety nets, worker safety laws, wage bargaining and redistributive taxes are not bad ideas, they are costly. Private property should provide the output to make such socially desirable measures affordable. The real test of privatization is whether or not enough has been done to protect property against arbitrary incursions of the state.

Macroeconomic Stabilization[63]

Russians were unable to agree about the basic cause of inflation, much less successfully manage a policy to stabilize the federal government's budget and stabilize growth of the money supply. Chronic large budget deficits, excessive monetary growth and high inflation were all symptoms of deeper social problems.

Severe fiscal and monetary instability forms an impenetrable barrier to progress toward private markets.[64] While the elected President of Russia strongly urged transition to markets, the Supreme Soviet retained control of the purse strings. The lower house of parliament, the Duma, remained under the control of communists in the early post-collapse years. Russia faced a fundamental problem: a lack of consensus on legitimacy. Consensus on core political issues was and is not evident. The collapse left Russia with no bedrock philosophy on which to anchor economic policy, but the Russian reformers struggled on. Chubais, charged in 1994 by Yeltsin to bring down the hyperinflation, did so. By 1995 the rate of inflation had fallen to less than 200 percent; it fell to less than 50 percent in 1996. The decline in output slowed considerably in 1995 and 1996 and even turned a little positive in 1997. Coincidentally the power of communists in the Duma (the lower house of parliament) was waning. Some semblance of budget restraint and monetary control began to emerge in 1996 and 1997, and in 1997 inflation fell to less than 15 percent.

Unfortunately, August 1998 saw the ruble collapse in the aftermath of the East Asian financial crisis and a decline in oil and non-ferrous metal prices. The Russian monetary system was not able to withstand the external shocks from Asia. The government devalued the ruble, defaulted on its debt and placed a moratorium on payments by Russian banks to foreign creditors.[65] Again conflict between communists and reformers dashed the fragile progress.

Before one can even begin to worry about stabilizing the budget and controlling currency growth, one must look to the deeper problem of inadequate social and political consensus on the appropriate roles of the public and private sectors. Put another way, macroeconomic instability (in Russia chronic large budget deficits and inflation rates that were imposing a tax of over 20 percent on financial capital) create serious economic problems. But solving them will not in itself lead to growth without first establishing some rudimentary political consensus on the appropriate role of the government and the private sector.

Despite these daunting problems, Russian reformers are trying to put in place an environment conducive to a decentralized, profit-driven market economy. In the area of fiscal policy, Yeltsin's first key economic advisor, Gaidar, tried from 1992 to 1993 to reduce the financial obligations to inefficient state enterprises, limit social payments obligations and reduce military and domestic spending in order to bring the budget closer to balance. Subsequently Anatoly Chubais and other reformers accelerated privatization and further tightened monetary control. Table 11.3 contains budget figures for Russia from 1989 to 1999. From 1994 to 1998 deficits were often nearly 10 percent of GDP. Perhaps these high budget deficits are not too bad when one recognizes the political weakness of reformers.

Table 11.3 Central government budget policy (deficit/surplus as a percentage of GDP)

Year	Deficit/surplus (%)	Year	Deficit/surplus (%)
1989	0.7	1995	–5.7
1990	1.3	1996	–7.7
1991	–2.7	1997	–9.2
1992	–4.1	1998	–9.1
1993	–7.4	1999	–1.9
1994	–9.0		

The conduct of monetary policy has been even less successful, as we have noted with the inflation figures of Table 11.2. Necessary structural revisions in the monetary system were enormous. Central banking and commercial banking needed to be disentangled. The system consisted of five highly centralized banks, each with its own function, and there was no competitive market for financial evaluation of business assets. The Gosbank was the central bank (like the Bank of England) and served as the fiscal arm of the government (like the US Treasury) for the Soviet Union. It undertook commercial banking activities as well. The Sberbank was the principal savings bank. The Vneshtorgbank handled foreign trade transactions and the Stroibank financed industrial construction. Each of the republics had branches of Gosbank and each of the other banks. But an entirely new structure for finance had to be created and assets and liabilities separated and allocated to each new nation.

Structurally the state of affairs in tax policy, in public sector allocation and in the severe split between the executive and legislative branches of government was dismal. Tax policy was in chaos. Tax rules were complex, overlapping, exculpatory and irrational. Voluntary compliance by both the business and personal sectors was minimal. Much of the growth in the monetary and banking sector from 1992 to 1995 reflected a flight of money from the tax collector – tax evasion and transfer of funds abroad. Partly this reflected incoherent and overlapping business tax rules and a lack of social consensus on the appropriateness of the tax rules. Tax revenue sources were inadequate and unreliable. Demands on state expenditures for the military, for government agencies and workers for state enterprise subsidies, and for social services exceeded revenue sources chronically by over 20 percent of the budget. Deficit finance and profligate monetary policy were substantial enough to warrant the conclusion that political consensus did not exist.

Communists dominated the Duma throughout most of the 1990s. The executive branch headed by Yeltsin swung from conservative to liberal. At times, former communists controlled important agencies and at other times reformers held the reins. When the reformers in the executive pushed for aggressive measures, the Duma reacted angrily, threatening votes of no confidence. The new constitution of 1992 gave the President tremendous power. He could disband the Duma but he could not control who would be elected once the current group had been removed. At the implementation level in many agencies, state-owned firms and local governments, the officials were the same bureaucrats who had thrived under communist regimes. To some this meant failure of the new democracy, but we argue that reform was beginning to take root.

Yeltsin had won at least three major political battles with KPRF (communist) hardliners: he defeated the 1991 coup attempt; he dissolved the parliament in 1993, establishing a presidential republic; and making the election of 1996 a referendum on communism, he beat back anti-reformers by winning re-election to a second term. He did this despite many economic difficulties. Although Yeltsin undertook vigorous periods of reform after each victory, reform was still tagged as anti-Russian.

Restructuring and Deregulation

The notorious level of social and economic crime in Russia is taken by many critics as *prima facie* evidence that the Russian government does not enjoy enough social credibility to protect property or people. If the government cannot guarantee basic safety and basic contracts and cannot control its own budget, then how can it establish a new economy? It is not clear that one can expect savings, investment and capital accumulation in a society in which theft and murder cannot be controlled. The low birth rate is an indicator that many Russians do not feel their society sufficiently well ordered to bring children into. The cost of child-rearing has shifted *de facto* from the state to the family.

Structural changes eventually have to be undertaken to demonopolize former state-owned enterprises.[66] Many bankrupt and inefficient plants and firms need to be shut down, and this has to be done while maintaining enough confidence in the government to continue basic operations like crime control. The Duma remains openly hostile to market reforms, with many members still firm believers in the ideology of Marx and Lenin.

Free Trade Liberalization

Table 11.4 reports international trade and financial statistics for Russia in selected years from 1990. The low percentage of foreign direct investment indicates the lack of confidence

Table 11.4 International trade and financial statistics (selected years)

Year	FDI* (% of GDP)	Imports (% of GDP)	Balance of trade** (% of GDP)	Exchange rate (ruble/$)
1990	0.1	26.9	—	—
1995	0.6	17.9	7.9	4.6
1997	1.4	15.9	2.9	5.8
1998	1.0	21.4	2.4	23.0
1999	1.2	23.0	—	24.6

Notes:
* Foreign direct investment.
** Balance on current account in US dollars.

foreign investors have in Russian reform and stability. Import figures are more impressive; the high figure in 1990 reflects primarily trade within the CMEA. The figures in the 1997–1999 period are in a more open trade environment. The early exchange rate figures are not altogether credible. Even after several significant monetary reforms the dollar exchange value of the ruble fell from 5.8 in 1997 to 23.0 in 1998.

ECONOMIC PERFORMANCE

Officially, real output in Russia fell every year from 1990 to 1996.[67] The worst period of negative output growth was from 1992 to 1994. Measured output fell 14.5 percent in 1992, 8.7 percent in 1993 and 12.6 percent in 1994. Official unemployment remained low, but this at best disguised underemployment because the fall in output was so substantial. In 1992 the money supply was out of control and inflation was 1526 percent, according to official statistics. While understandable in terms of the social and economic collapse and political struggles, this economic record is hardly one on which to build a new way of life. Inflation moderated somewhat in the next two years, but was still in triple digits: 875 percent in 1993 and 308 percent in 1994.

Enormous structural changes were taking place in this period on all fronts, including the dissolution of the USSR and creation of the Confederation of Independent States (CIS). Most former Soviet Union (FSU) republics were declaring independence of Moscow, trying to establish their own governments, banking systems and currencies. The Supreme Soviet retained control of the monetary mechanism, even when non-communists ran the government.[68] Even within Russia regional conflicts were emerging, with various local initiatives for independence.

Russia was struggling with its political constitution that involved core issues of the relative power of the executive and legislative branches and the transition rules. In 1990 the communists won a majority of seats in the Duma. Elections were held again in December 1993. Despite terrible economic performance in 1992 and only somewhat better performance in 1993, the communists received only 20.3 percent of the vote, and Yeltsin became

President with a modest mandate. Things got worse in terms of GDP in 1994, the decline again reaching double-digit levels at 12.6 percent.

The elections in December of 1995 saw a recovery of relative power by the socialists (former communists). They captured 32.7 percent of the parliamentary vote. The very authoritarian orientation of the new constitution allowed vast power to reside in the executive branch. If the Duma directly challenged Yeltsin he could disband it and call for new parliamentary elections. By 1996 inflation seemed to be coming under control at 48 percent, but unemployment reached 9 percent. This is a problem in a society where employment had been viewed as a right. Furthermore, the failure of the tax system to generate revenues along with *de facto* external convertibility of the ruble forced a battle over what budget items to withdraw. The financial collapse in August 1998 exposed structural weaknesses in the Russian economy and polity. Russia still suffered a crisis of identity. What role should the government play in industry? Price-setting? Social support? How big should the military be? How should the money to finance these activities be generated? These and other core questions are yet to be answered.[69]

CONCLUSIONS AND RECOMMENDATIONS

Table 11.5 reports the connections in Russia between votes for relatively reform-minded legislators and the reform index for Russia during the subsequent electoral interval. It also reports economic performance averaged over the period. Clearly the Russian politicians have been sensitive to voters' wishes. Yeltsin changed Prime Ministers like other men change ties. Reform progress followed these government changes as well. Start-up of reform measures produced a relatively high index of reform, 132.4 for the first free government of Russia. Coup attempts, votes of no confidence, fights with parliament and a hostile Duma all contributed to a low period of reform from 1993 to 1996. After 1996 and especially after the communists took heavy losses in the Duma in 1999, reforms kicked in again. Measured economic indicators look a little better after 1996.[70] The exception is the upward drift in unemployment.[71] This may reflect gradual improvement in reporting rather than a significant worsening of the situation.

Table 11.5 Elections, reforms and economic performance, 1990–1999 (reform indexes and economic variables are for election intervals annualized)

Year	Votes for reformers (%)	Reform index (1995=100)	GDP % change		Inflation rate		Unemployment rate	
			After	Before	After	Before	After	Before
1991	57.3	132.4	–10.3	–2.2	978.3	18.0	4.1	3.5
1993	27.9	104.5	–8.4	–10.3	459.5	978.3	7.7	4.1
1995	24.2	106.9	–3.5	–8.4	47.6	459.5	9.2	7.7
1996	57.4	124.1	–1.0	–3.5	43.0	47.6	11.3	9.3
1999	56.1	123.3	1.7	–1.0	85.7	43.0	12.0	11.3

Russians will continue to muddle through. Even former KGB agents such as President Putin openly support markets. The fact that he also espouses law and order while exploiting the power of the state to harass the press is troublesome. The absence of law and order makes effective economic reform difficult, so one need not assume that President Putin's pro-law and order stance is anti-market.[72] If by law and order he means obedience to a central Moscow authority, then Russia could be in for some backsliding.

One key to progress is the need to establish a consensus that communism and even socialism are a part of the past. A swift transition to a Western European-style welfare state is impossible. Private markets are necessary for a better life for the Russian people. An enormous educational task is needed to establish this point. It is sometimes hard to establish this point in the West, and harder yet in a world dominated for years by socialist propaganda.

Monetary control is a necessary precondition for growth. In Russia this means established laws that constrain budgets for large enterprises and enforce bankruptcy laws. It requires a transparent and sensible tax system. It requires independent private commercial banks.

Defining and protecting property rights through an independent judiciary would contribute a good deal to fostering markets. Laws must be transparent and reliably enforced to allow investors, both foreign and domestic, to protect their financial claims. Contracts must be enforceable.

The monopoly problem has been exaggerated. Private monopolies are easier to control than public ones. Oligarchs and bankers can be constrained; this problem is common to some extent to any form of democratic capitalism.

The sensitivity of reform efforts to parliamentary elections in post-collapse Russia suggests to us the importance of education of the electorate about economic issues. The electorate will support pro-market reforms if voters understand how markets can improve their lives.[73] Our model linking the voter's well-being as indicated by economic growth prospects to market reforms and then linking reform proposals to votes indicates how this nexus works. Reformers and international agencies interested in developing a healthy Russian market democracy would be well advised to put resources into economic education.

Despite their terrible difficulties, the Russians have made progress. Gorbachev ended the old regime. Yeltsin initiated many reforms, albeit with mixed success. He seems to have reformed enough practices and weakened enough central power to make regression to central planning impossible, although Putin displays centrist political preferences. It is now up to future leaders to promote the stability and credibility of the government. Two questions remain: will the leaders lead toward a market democracy, and will the Russian people stay the course?

NOTES

1. Remnick (1994).
2. Lipton and Sachs (1992), two important Western economic advisors to the Yeltsin administration, argue that the most serious challenge is not economic strategy but "political management of economic reforms." Nikolay Petrakov, Gorbachev's economic advisor, attributed Gorbachev's paralysis regarding "shock therapy" to the lack of consensus in Russia in comparison to Poland. See Aron (2000), p. 400.
3. Economist and presidential candidate Grigory Yavlinsky pointed out that the economy inherited by Russia

from the communists had been "created by central planning," as opposed to the economies of Central European states that were ruined by Stalin's forced central planning. Brady (1999), p. 236.
4. Vladimir Mau, advisor to the Prime Minister in the early 1990s, in his comment in Lipton and Sachs (1992), emphasized the difficulty of achieving political consensus in Russia. He attributed this to the homegrown nature of the communist revolution and the inability of reformers to blame foreign domination.
5. Aron (2000), pp. 401–4, notes that the Gorbachev program for reform in 1989 showed an "utter lack of market experience."
6. Lipton and Sachs (1992) identify three periods of liberalization: the reign of Alexander II in the 1860s, the efforts of Prime Minister Stolypn 1906–1911, and the New Economic Plan under Lenin in 1920. All were followed by periods of repression.
7. This sketch of Russian history draws on a number of sources. Gregory (1994) looks to economic history before 1991 as a guide to transition. Gatrell (1986) covers economic history before the October 1917 revolution under the Czars. Industrialization from 1860 to 1913 is the focus of Kahan (1989). Gregory and Stuart (1981) discuss economic history up to 1917 and the subsequent structure of the Soviet economy.
8. Russification of the empire under Catherine is reflected in Aleksandr Radishchev's 1790 *Journey from St Petersburg to Moscow*.
9. Yeltsin's plans encountered the same criticism from the Duma in 1992. Ruslan Khazbulatov, Chairman of the Supreme Soviet, attacked the Yeltsin–Gaidar reforms "as the 'Americanization' of the Russian economy" 'which, according to him,' 'presupposed a drastic reduction in the state's social functions" and the "privatization of all and everything." Aron (2000), p. 499. He opposed Gaidar's appointment as Prime Minister perhaps (Aron suggests) because Gaidar as editor of a pro-reform journal had rejected some of Khazbulatov's papers.
10. Gennadiy Zyuganov, Chairman of the Communist Party, was running against Yeltsin in 1996. In an attack of nationalistic fervor, he asked, "Where is the country's wealth?" His answer: it was being "stolen and taken abroad by 'insatiable carnivores",' Aron (2000), p. 598.
11. Salsbury (1997) provides a chronology of the period 1917–1967. The planned economy is discussed by Raymond (1978) and Von Rauch (1972). Remnick (1994) discusses Lenin's legacy, as does Brovkin (1998). Courtois et al. (1999) discusses the violent nature of the Soviet period leading up to Stalin's rule and including the post-Stalin era.
12. For a discussion of the continued violence under Khrushchev and the limited nature of his "secret speech," see Courtois, et al. (1999) and Library of Congress (1989). See also Volkogonov (1998) for a detailed analysis of the consequences of the Soviet leadership.
13. Filtzer (1994) discusses Gorbachev's goals and limitations. Brown (1988) contains papers on the perestroika period. Excellent coverage of Gorbachev's policies and the collapse are in Dallin (1995) and Bazer (1991). Hanson (1992) analyzes attempts to transform the economy during the Gorbachev period.
14. This section draws heavily on Aron (2000), Courtois et al. (1999), Voikogonov (1998), Remnick (1994) and Brady (1999).
15. In the December 1995 national legislative elections the Communist Party (KPRF) became the largest faction in the Duma. See Aron (2000), p. 563.
16. Aron (2000) notes that many observers viewed the 1996 presidential election as a public trial of Russian communism. The debate was over core issues, democratic capitalism versus communist rule; Aron (2000), pp. 623–5. The power of the Red Directors to resist and subvert reforms is discussed in Brady (1999), see for instance p. 141.
17. See Courtois, et al. (1999). One chapter deals with the Soviet Union. It illustrates the influence of Lenin on Stalin. Other chapters deal with harsh treatment of opponents by communists in other countries around the world.
18. Our emphasis on political violence may seem overdone to some readers, but the importance of the utter collapse of the USSR cannot be grasped without understanding the full extent of the totalitarian regimes and their consequences. It is the disintegration of the social structure that accompanied the collapse of the economy that makes reform so difficult in Russia. The lack of consensus on basic rules of law, on private property, on rules to govern commerce and on acceptable norms of social behavior greatly inhibits attempts to adopt market economics.
19. Aron (2000), p. 646, argues that "of all post-communist nations (with the exception of Albania) its economic legacy was the heaviest, its surplus population the largest both in absolute and relative terms, and its left the most radical."
20. "Stalinist industrialization had created thousands of 'company towns' where enterprises owned and operated kindergartens, hospitals, schools and the apartment buildings of their workers. Entire secret closed cities grew around missile and tank plants and nuclear research centers," Aron (2000), p. 646.
21. Joskow, Schmalensee and Tsukanova (1994), p. 312.
22. Leijonhufvud and Ruhl (1997) point out that such systems are only as strong as their weakest link.

23. According to Gustafson (1999), p. 8, "Russia remains 'hard-wired' to its Soviet past, by the layout of its pipelines and its power lines, the location and technologies of its industries, and the geographic distribution of its workforce."
24. Aron (2000), p. 738, sums up: "The attributes of the traditional Russian state – authoritarianism, imperialism, militarism, xenophobia – are far from extinguished." See also Brady (1999) on the mentality of Russians who after 70 years of socialism were unprepared for the self-reliance associated with private markets.
25. They relied on administered prices set by central planners. They limited the uses of money and mismanaged the ruble, a non-convertible currency. They did not let interest rates determine the allocation of capital among competing uses. Here too they relied on the central plan. Wages were based on "need" and profits were unacceptable.
26. Courtois et al. (1999), especially Chapter 3.
27. Courtois et al (1999). Lenin was also not fond of academics.
28. The ingenuity of humankind to deal effectively regardless of the incentive system is illustrated by a story reported by E.S. Savas, City University of New York. In Kiev, capital of Ukraine, in the late 1980s the price of a burned-out light bulb was five to six times the price of a working bulb. Prices of light bulbs were controlled; and since bulbs were thought to be necessary by the planners, the price was low. As a result of this low price, working bulbs were not available. What is a comrade to do when a bulb in his apartment burns out? Why not take one from the office? Not a bad idea, except you can get into trouble. What to do? The answer lies in the black market. Buy a burned-out bulb on the black market. Steal the working bulb from the office (or factory) and replace it with the burned-out bulb. This practice was widespread, so the black market accommodated the demand for burned-out light bulbs – but at a price!
29. See Smith (1990) for a fascinating discussion of life in Moscow in the decade prior to the collapse. He points to many of these distinctions in access to goods and services based on non-price allocation methods.
30. Woodruff (1999), pp. 62–3, argues that creation of a viable monetary regime is the essence of reform. He points out that the failure of money played a crucial role in the nature of exchange based on barter, the black market, bribes and *blat*, which refers to pull or influence. Brady (1999) also discusses the ruble overhang from the Soviet years.
31. The central bank of Russia remained under control of the Supreme Soviet until October 1993. In 1992 inflation exceeded 1500 percent and was 870 percent in 1993. Viktor Geraschenko, the former head of the state bank of the USSR, was made head of the central bank in July of 1992. Brady (1999).
32. Warren Coats (1993) has an excellent discussion of the ruptured monetary regime in Russia left over by the Soviets. Lipton and Sachs (1992) also discuss defects in the monetary regime inherited by Yeltsin.
33. See Karl Marx (1937).
34. Lipton and Sachs (1992).
35. See Leontief (1951), Dorfman, Samuelson and Solow (1958) and Joskow et al. (1994).
36. Academic economists use the central planning model as a device for analyzing optimal economic outcomes.
37. Business managers do this routinely. The difference is in the incentive system. In market economies the profit motive provides incentives for managers to adapt to the best (least costly) technology even if this means adopting technological changes. Managerial incentives in the central plan usually favor playing it safe with the old ways. It is also important to note that decentralized decision-making reduces the likelihood of long runs of big mistakes. The profit motive helps to eliminate capitalists who make bad decisions.
38. The Russians have come under criticism for not adopting the "Chinese variant," reforming economic sectors before trying political reform. Aron (2000), p. 182, points out that Gorbachev had tried to do this but failed. The leadership in Russia could not control its "political and economic elites," as could the Chinese leadership.
39. Data problems in Russia are legion. Aron (2000) says that from 1994 to 1997, between 35 and 45 per cent of the Russian economy was "missing" from annual reports filed by the state statistical agency, the Goskomstat. He and others speculate that the Russian economy was between 50 percent and 100 percent larger than the data indicate.
40. When in 1986 Mikhail Gorbachev asked Secretary Yuriy Andropov for access to budget figures, Andropov told him that the budget was off-limits to him. Gorbachev was *de facto* Deputy General Secretary at the time. See Aron (2000), pp. 177–8. Even the planners apparently did not know what was actually happening to the economy.
41. Ticktin (1992) focuses on the political and economic causes of disintegration. See also Chapter 1 of this book.
42. See Aron (2000), p. 400. Brady (1999), pp. 150–51, tells of the power of the Russian Mafia. For example, in 1995 shortly after Ivan Kivelidi, leader of Russia's Business Roundtable, criticized the state for failing to constrain the mob, he was poisoned in what was thought to be a mob hit.
43. Joskow et al. (1994), Table 9.
44. Joskow et al. (1994) discusses this debate.

45. In winter 1991 Yeltsin gave the Russians an opportunity for a Tiananmen Square option. The communists could arrest him, but according to Aron (2000), p. 423, "within hours millions of protesters would have been on the streets."
46. Woodruff (1999), pp. 150–51, tells of the creation of debt instruments by creditors, called *wechsels*. These were notes issued by firms that held desirable products. The *wechsel* was a promise to pay with these products. Brady (1999), pp. 176–8, tells of the industrial city of Magnitogorsk in the Urals that depended on local promissory notes and "long chains of complicated barter deals to get by."
47. Aron (2000), p. 497.
48. Murrell and Wang (1993) provides a cogent argument for delaying privatization in Russia based on legacies from the communist past.
49. Some of this may reflect criticism of entrepreneurs in the market by those who dislike capitalism. Private markets do generate concentrations of power and wealth. To those who are accustomed to all power residing in the state, this can be discomfiting.
50. Frye and Shleifer (1997) attributes crime both to lack of public sector credibility and to an ineffective legal apparatus. They characterize the government as a "grabbing hand."
51. G. Zyuganov, according to Aron (2000), p. 614, said, "'Land is Motherland … And one cannot sell the Motherland at an auction.'" This quote indicates the depths of disagreement between Yeltsin and Zyuganov, Chairman of the Communist Party.
52. Aron (2000), pp. 638–9.
53. Joskow, et al. (1994) and Boycko, et al. (1993) are two excellent sources for analysis of Russian privatization in the early years. Gustafson (1999) presents a measured appraisal of the situation toward the end of the 1990s. Josef C. Brada (1996) explains some of the difficulties in trying to privatize in Central Europe. Rapaczynski (1996) points to difficulties of forming viable legal systems that will protect property rights. He argues that legal property rights reflect rather than cause markets.
54. Black, Kraakman and Taarassova (1999) argue that the privatization effort has been a failure as a result of the failure to adopt appropriate institutions before privatizing. Their gauge of failure is that the Russian economy has shrunk since 1991.
55. See Gustafson (1999), pp. 48–9.
56. Some of these criminals were mainly black and gray market traders.
57. See Aron (2000) pp. 636–9.
58. Jean-Baptiste Naudet in *Le Monde* on 5 July 1996 reported that sex and pornography were thriving in the new Russia. Perhaps this reinforces the success of socially marginal enterprises.
59. Brady (1999) Chapter 3, points to the hostility of the Soviet media toward entrepreneurs. Pravda, for instance, "blasted entrepreneurs for being zhuliky and bandity – thieves and bandits," p. 54.
60. Aron (2000), p. 651. These involved tax, enterprise, housing and budget reforms.
61. Ibid., pp. 657, 662.
62. According to Brady (1999), 203–43, *Izvestia* editor Mikhail Berger felt the political influence of big business was "greatly exaggerated." In the autumn of 1997 Yegor Gaidar explained to Brady that "Russia never had liberal capitalism. It was a socialist dictatorship. We now have oligarchical capitalism." Later harassment by the Vladimir Putin regime of Vladimir A. Gusinsky (head of Media-Most that owns and operates NTV, the only independent national television station) seems to bear out the counter-argument that politicians hold the upper hand.
63. Lazear (1995) contains a number of excellent papers on stabilization and macroeconomic issues in Russia and other emerging nations. Fischer, Sahay and Vegh (1996) analyze stabilization and growth. Aslund, Boone and Johnson (1996) discuss stabilization issues in post-communist countries. See also Sachs and Woo (1994).
64. By severe, we mean budget deficits so large and chronic that debt growth exceeds growth in the tax base. By severe monetary instability we mean hyperinflation – growth in the price level at triple-digit levels that are accelerating.
65. Desai (2000) attributes this collapse directly to the divisions between the reform regime and the communist-dominated Duma. She notes that the trigger was the exogenous Asian financial crisis.
66. *The Economist* (12 July 1997) emphasized the inadequacy of privatizing without restructuring. Much of this reflected complaints of insider dealing.
67. Lipton and Sachs (1992) persuasively argue that measured output declines overstate the extent of deprivation in Russia. They report that actual consumption patterns based on consumer surveys indicate a much smaller decline than income figures (5 percent compared to 30 percent).
68. Aron (2000), p. 497.
69. Gaddy and Ickes (1998) distinguish between the measured economy of national statistics and the "virtual" economy that is almost a shadow economic system running on a parallel track with the nominal economic system. Gustafson (1999) argues that Russia has made it halfway toward markets and seems stuck in the

middle. He rejects the notion that a reactionary response to the collapse explains present Russia. He also rejects the rosier view of reforms. He argues that each view is correct, but that each captures only part of what is going on.

70. Many Russians felt the situation was precarious even as late as 1997. *The Economist* (12 July 1997) reports that one businessman had a picture of a ground-attack aircraft, a Sukhoi-27, on his desk. He had labeled it his "executive jet." He said, "You never know when you may have to leave in a hurry."
71. *The Economist* (12 July 1997) reported that 32 million Russians (22 percent of the population) live in poverty. Given a great deal of extra-market activity it is difficult to be certain of this.
72. The great Russian chess champion, Garry Kasparov, in the *Wall Street Journal* (20 January 1998), likened Russia to the Chicago of Al Capone. The same issue reported problems in agriculture caused by trying to stay in the middle ground between private markets and socialism in Russia.
73. Braguinsky and Yavlinsky (2000) make a similar point.

12. Will the Slovaks stay the course?*

> When I was eight years old, Fascism came to Slovakia. When I was eighteen we got communism. Democracy didn't come until I was already of retirement age. I never had the opportunity to be a democrat. Neither did most other Slovaks.
>
> (Lubomir Liptak, Historian, Slovak Academy of Sciences)[1]

> The figures still don't make their way down to people. People must feel the figures.
>
> (Mikulas Dzurinda, Slovak Prime Minister)[2]

During the Soviet period of domination of Central and Eastern Europe, Slovakia was an integral part of the multinational federation of Czechoslovakia. Its political history of the winning of independence from the Soviet Union is therefore substantially the same as that for the Czech Republic, from which it separated in 1993. For this reason we will not repeat the discussion (in Chapter 8) of the Velvet Revolution in 1989 and the 1993 Velvet Divorce. Slovakia has historic differences from the Czech Republic, both cultural and economic, and so the two countries have progressed in markedly different ways since the Divorce.

Slovakia's 5 million people live in an area of 50,000 square kilometers. In area, it exceeds Denmark, the Netherlands and Switzerland, and in population it is larger than Denmark, Finland and Ireland. It borders Austria, the Czech Republic, Hungary, Poland and Ukraine. About 84 percent of its people are Slovak. Their treatment of the Hungarian minority, around 11 percent of the population, has been a problem. It continues to improve, but slowly. As in most of Central Europe, discriminatory attitudes toward the Roma persist.[3]

Tales abound as to the fundamental ways in which Slovaks differ from their former countrymen; they are apparently more conservative in their attitudes to social change and to economic reforms than the Czechs. They are more prone to accept stronger state paternalism and more critical of the potentially corruptive elements of Western liberalism and materialism. They fared relatively well under communism. As a result they were slow to adopt market reforms after separation from the Czechs in 1993. While parliamentarians expressed a vague commitment to markets, they could not agree on how to pursue the goals of the nation, or even on what those goals were. A lingering reliance on the role of the state as manager and problem-solver remained. This statist tendency was confirmed by the popularity of nationalist Vladimir Meciar, who agreed with Czech leader Vaclav Klaus to the split. Meciar became Slovakia's first Prime Minister and held considerable influence from 1993 until his political demise in the general election of 1998. Many Slovaks preferred the old Soviet guarantees to the new market uncertainties, and Meciar fed their parochial proclivities and fears of foreign ways.

We believe that Meciar nearly single-handedly deserves credit for Slovakia's initial rejection for membership consideration by the European Union, NATO and OECD. Meciar's

* Ming Xie and Jarko Fidrmuc made extensive contributions to this chapter.

policies caused Slovakia to be diplomatically isolated. He expressed open contempt for and implemented hostile acts toward the domestic opposition. He ignored limitations on his behavior set by parliament, the President and the constitutional court. He was responsible for getting privatized property into the hands of his political supporters. He openly attacked various media, and he set up parallel organizations of trade unions and local government associations to establish central control. As a result of five years of Meciar, Slovakia lagged behind its transition peers in building democratic institutions, restructuring the economy and attracting foreign investment. Laws were passed in 1995 and 1997 that slowed privatization and renewed the soft budget constraints that protected inept state-owned enterprises.

Slovakia started the transition with particular economic disadvantages; the economy was built on heavy industrial production, primarily armaments and basic intermediate goods. Much of the production of these enterprises was obsolete once the Cold War ended. Few small or medium-sized businesses existed in the country, and most services were vertically integrated within large industrial conglomerates. The notion of market reforms was far from universally popular among citizens. The Soviets had improved the quality of life for many Slovaks by favoring them over the Czechs in order to equalize standards. In some ways, the Soviets left the country better than they found it. However, after separating from the Czechs, the Slovaks had to build a new state.

These drawbacks, combined with the leadership of Meciar, were very nearly fatal to the transition process. As Table 12.1 shows, however, the Slovak economy appeared to be a strong performer until the late 1990s. GDP growth rates were high, inflation was falling, many new businesses were started. Product quality was improved and productivity figures were up. Trade was reoriented toward the West. As a result of these successes, Slovakia was able to borrow significant amounts internationally between 1996 and 1998. These foreign loans helped sustain growth at the expense of building an enormous external debt.

Table 12.1 Real GDP growth rates (average annual percentage change)

Year	Percentage change
1993	–3.9
1994	5.0
1995	7.3
1996	6.6
1997	6.5
1998	4.4
1999	2.0

Policy-makers, reinforced by their constituents, lacked a clear commitment to reform. Meciar's leadership was arbitrary, to put it charitably. What then can explain the economic success that prevailed from 1994 to 1998? While the Slovak economy was in trouble by 1999, it had done well for some time. Initially, Slovakia had considerable export success, selling heavy industrial and intermediate products to the West. But the trade deficit grew as imports outpaced exports. The growing demand for consumer imports was based on rising incomes generated in large part by public sector spending. Large macroeconomic imbalances emerged in 1996. The government undertook huge construction projects and energy investment programs. Foreign direct investment was low and external debt was high. Before the general election in 1998, Slovakia lost its investment-grade currency exchange rating due to "fiscal indiscipline." The budget deficit rose as exports fell and the current account deficit ballooned. Monetary policy was tight and high interest rates led to severe crowding out of private investment. Banks, still not all privatized, found the number of bad loans growing, along with inter-firm debt and tax arrears. By the end of 1998, "the internal and external macroeconomic stance had become unsustainable, leading to periods of exchange rate tensions."[4]

In 1998 the Slovaks replaced Meciar's nationalists with the Slovak Democratic Coalition. The new government instituted an austerity program to combat fiscal and trade imbalances. This was received favorably by international investors and by international agencies such as the IMF, but it generated higher levels of unemployment and worker dissatisfaction. The government set about reforming bankruptcy law, accelerating the pace of privatization and tackling restructuring. In 1999 Slovakia returned to international capital markets to issue its first euro-denominated bond. The European Union declared that Slovakia had met the political criteria for accession and was close to being a functioning market economy, thanks to the courageous policy decisions and the impressive reform agenda of the new government.[5]

It was a late start, but apparently the Slovak Democratic Coalition leadership absorbed the lessons conveyed in the early chapters of this book. The policy-makers in power were, at last, looking to the future. Some familiarity with Slovakian history will help to explain the country's current situation and its future outlook.

SLOVAKIA BEFORE THE SOVIETS: YEARS OF FOREIGN DOMINATION

Between the eleventh century and 1918, Slovakia was a part of the Hungarian kingdom. During all of this period, Hungary was primarily agricultural and essentially feudal, fitting the traditional picture of Eastern rather than Central Europe, which was oriented more toward the West. Hungary was ruled by powerful landowners and had a financially weak bourgeoisie. The agricultural and industrial sectors of Slovakia's economy were more underdeveloped than were those of Hungary. The large estates were owned primarily by the Catholic Church and by the Hungarian nobility; poor peasants made up the bulk of the population.

The Slovaks generated their first nationalist movement in the middle of the nineteenth century.[6] This incorporated a general anti-feudal and democratic vision of Slovakia functioning within Hungary, along with a strain of anti-liberal thinking that admired Czarist Russia (the nationalist intelligentsia eventually became thoroughly disillusioned with Hungary) and viewed Western liberalism as corrupt and materialistic.[7] Although the initial movement codified Slovak literary language and prepared the way for a national literature, before 1918 there were no secondary or technical schools in Slovakia that taught in the national language, and no institutions of higher education at all.

Even when Hungary set out to industrialize in the latter part of the nineteenth century, plans were designed to benefit the large landowners, who were interested more in a food industry that would process the output of their estates than in broader-based industrialization. Some 15 percent of Hungary's food industry was in Slovakia, which had at least a fifth of Hungary's iron, timber, textile and leather production and over half its paper mill output. Slovakia was, however, still underdeveloped both culturally and economically.[8] Rural unemployment, coupled with a lack of industrial employment opportunities, stimulated emigration – to the Czech Lands, to North America and to Western Europe – that grew to half a million people in the two decades preceding the First World War.

By 1918, years of heavy-handed "Magyarization" had pushed the Slovaks to separate themselves from the kingdom they had been a part of for a thousand years; they chose to form one nation, the Czechoslovak Republic, with their Czech neighbors. The disparities between the new partners were great, creating new problems for both. Slovaks had far less political experience and a lower level of national consciousness than did the Czechs. And the union failed to solve Slovakia's economic problems. Czech industry was already powerful, more advanced and more efficient, and Czech competitive products soon wiped out much of Slovakian heavy industry.[9] Although the Slovaks were seriously short of skilled workers after nearly a century of Magyarization, they had initially expected to benefit greatly from cooperation with the Czechs.

Soon, however, the Slovakians grew tired of the superior attitudes of some immigrant Czech soldiers, administrators, teachers and other professionals. They were insulted by the disrespect for the Slovak religion that was embodied in certain anti-clerical measures taken by the government in Prague. There was resentment also when Czechs were appointed to positions for which Slovaks were qualified. As social discontent grew, de-industrialization continued throughout the 1920s, especially in heavy industry. However, some consumer products manufacturing appeared, such as footwear, textiles and synthetic fibers, all financed by private capital; and the government in Prague did create the arms manufacturing industry in Slovakia. Nevertheless, between 1918 and 1932 there was a net loss of jobs and a net shrinkage in the size of the industrial sector. Neither before 1918 nor during the inter-war period did Slovakia develop a solid agricultural or industrial foundation.

During the first Czechoslovak Republic (1918–1938) Slovakia did develop its own culture, a complete education system, its own intelligentsia, an entrepreneurial middle class, even the nucleus of a civic society, all from virtually nothing.[10] This was the first real law-abiding constitutional democracy in Slovakian history, and their last experience of it until 1989. A number of political parties emerged during this first period of parliamentary democracy. They developed along religious, social, political, ethnic and other lines, but they fell into certain broad camps. Several parties became strongly nationalistic, while the Social Democrats argued for closer cooperation with the Czechs and supported, along with the Agrarian, Christian and Socialist Parties, a republican ideal of maximizing individual liberties. The nationalists wanted autonomy, but within a common state with the Czechs. Others felt that the Slovaks still needed Czech capital and technical know-how, while the Social Democrats went so far as to argue that there were no fundamental differences between Czechs and Slovaks. The Communist Party was against both the republican and nationalistic views and sought to build a socialist society with domination of the proletariat. It was a period of lively political debate, and the subject of nationalism was a part of that debate throughout the inter-war years.

Slovakia became an autonomous state within the Czechoslovak federation in 1938, and then an independent state for a while under pressure from Hitler; this authoritarian regime generated a desire for a new partnership with the Czechs, expressed in a national uprising in 1944. The representatives of the major political views on the "Slovak question" spoke out and wrote a great deal over the years, some favoring autonomy in a cooperative framework with the Czechs but still critical of Czech politicians, others later opposing the repressive wartime government. The Slovak issue was at the forefront of debate for decades, from 1918 until after the Second World War. Political leaders were highly visible and their views were expressed and argued over a long period of time. This contrasts sharply with the circumstances of the Velvet Divorce in 1993, where debate was lacking.[11]

THE SOVIET YEARS

The first Czechoslovak parliament after the Second World War was democratically elected, with the ruling coalition, made up of two Slovak and four Czech parties, dominated by the communists.[12] The Prime Minister was a left-leaning Social Democrat, and one Deputy Prime Minister was a Slovak communist, the other a Czech communist. Key ministries were balanced between communists and other parties, although the civil service was professional and therefore supposedly not subject to political pressures. Slovakian communists were not in the majority, but the communists were the strongest political party in the Czechoslovak state. Had the non-communist parties maintained solidarity they could have outvoted the communists, but they did not. Nevertheless, the communists were initially pursuing socialism through democratic political means.

By mid-1947, Soviet pressure drove the Czechoslovak communists to give up their own path to socialism and the process of Stalinization got under way; one early move was to force Czechoslovak withdrawal from Marshall Plan negotiations. The Slovak communists in fact had made the first moves to intimidate all opposition parties and thereby provided the example for the communists in Prague to take power. A statement by the Prime Minister referring to counter-revolutionary reactionaries trying to overthrow the "people's democratic regime" amounted to the declaration of a nationwide purge. Eventually all non-communist ministers were forced to resign from government, and a party-organized demonstration was staged to get the President to accept their resignations and appoint a new communist national government.

All this was done according to constitutional rules, ostensibly through appropriate political channels and completely peacefully.[13] A Central Action Committee and local action committees were organized to purge the country of "reactionaries and traitors." Electoral laws were changed and by the 1948 general election, parliament existed in name only. It was in fact so intimidated by the communists that it gave an overwhelming vote of confidence to the government, knowing that this would be the end of the democratic system. Thereafter, single candidates were nominated by the National Front and much of the power of parliament was transferred to a Presidium, which looked strikingly like the Supreme Soviet. All non-communist political parties were abolished, and their leaders either escaped the country or were arrested. The judiciary was severely modified, with the constitutional and the supreme administrative courts abolished. In Slovakia, where the non-communist parties had been in the majority, the purge was more ruthless than in the Czech Lands. By 1950, all Slovak non-communist parties had ceased to exist.

Economic changes generated during the Soviet takeover were relatively advantageous to the Slovaks, because the Soviets pushed for Slovak development through industrialization. The Soviets actually imposed a kind of pro-Slovak, anti-Czech affirmative action program. It was also a pro-rural anti-urban program. The children of agrarian Slovaks received preferential treatment in educational advancement. These policies reduced the economic inequality with the Czech Lands, but turned out to be a mixed blessing at best. In 1945, over 60 percent of the total Czechoslovak industrial workforce was already employed in nationalized enterprises and another 15 percent was employed in "confiscates," enterprises taken away from German and Hungarian owners after the war.[14]

But about 25 percent of the labor force was employed in cooperatives and private enterprises, and markets were still working. Nationalized enterprises were committed to employee participation in management through factory committees. The economy had a large state element but was still mixed, and the ruling Communist Party plans allowed for considerable freedom and competition. In other words, the economy was not so deliberately centralized as the Soviet planning system. This changed with the Stalinization of Czechoslovak political and economic systems.

The communist plans to industrialize Slovakia involved transferring financial, equipment and technical resources from Czech industries; promoting industrial "integration processes" between the two areas, which amounted to concentration and specialization of industrial production; emphasis on development of Slovak power, mining, heavy engineering and defence industries; and communizing Slovak agriculture.[15] The last-mentioned operation generated surplus labor, which was absorbed into industry in Slovakia or transferred to the Czech Lands. By 1958, Slovakia's share in national industrial output had grown from 8 percent before the war to over 17 percent, and its share in national income had risen to over 20 percent.[16]

In the first half of the 1960s, the emphasis in Slovakia changed to metallurgical and chemical industries and then to developing some consumer industries such as food, textiles, footwear and housing construction. Slovakia's per capita income rose from around 60 percent of the Czech Lands in 1948 to nearly 80 percent in 1968. By 1970, Slovakia was at near parity. In the 1970s and early 1980s, investment was pumped into fuel, engineering, arms, metallurgy and petrochemical industries.[17] This pattern of development mirrored that of the Soviet Union, which was based in turn on Western industrialization in the late nineteenth century. It is for this reason that the industrialization was not so good for Slovakia as production and income figures imply. The economy was distorted in its dependence on armaments and engineering products and on markets in the Council for Mutual Economic Assistance (CMEA).[18] These characteristics have made the transition to a modern market economy much harder for the Slovaks than it was for the Czechs. The issue of inordinate emphasis on heavy industry in post-war Slovakia will be revisited when current economic reforms and current performance are discussed.

There is no doubt that the Soviets were responsible for forcing the pace of industrialization and urbanization of Slovakia and can be credited with improving physical infrastructure, human capital via an upgraded education system, and living standards. Socialist modernization also involved forced collectivization of agriculture, suppression of religion, dismantling of traditional lifestyles and an overall anomie. In creating the country's dependence on heavy industry, it suppressed entrepreneurship and encouraged an orientation to state paternalism, learned helplessness and social infantilism. This line of argument views Slovakia as underdeveloped not only economically but also politically and with respect to civic values, so that the Soviet version of modernization induced strong anti-liberal, statist attitudes in the populace. On the other hand, the people of Slovakia, isolated from most of the modern world, were not aware of the problematic characteristics of their society.[19]

All this accounts in part for the Slovaks' lesser antipathy toward socialism in comparison to the Czechs; more of the explanation can be found in the milder form of post-1968 "normalization" in Slovakia. The process of normalization started in 1969, and was the Soviet response to the reforms associated with the Prague Spring of 1968 (led by Alexander Dubcek, a Slovak) ended by Soviet military invasion in August 1968. Those reforms were equated with counter-revolution, which justified a move – called normalization – back to centralization. The normalized regime rested on three principal processes. The first was a purge of all major social and economic institutions, including the Communist Party itself, and of anyone associated with the pluralism initiated in 1967. The system was maintained thereafter with threats or applications of severe punishments for nonconformist behavior. The second was the strict control over the spread of unacceptable ideas and involved a purge of institutions engaged in the dissemination of knowledge and culture, especially the media. This helped the party leadership institutionalize and ritualize agreement and public acts of compliance in order to justify the process of normalization. The third was the centralization of the economy, which generated a tendency to overlook serious structural problems and deal instead with more manageable, short-term ones. These three processes established centralized control and institutionalized social conformity.[20]

Normalization was less severe in Slovakia than in the Czech Lands partly because counter-revolutionary activity was less in evidence. Slovak society was not as polarized as that of the Czechs, and opposition to the authorities was weaker, less visible and isolated from like-minded individuals, including the Czechs. Slovaks did not typically feel responsible for their country's situation, but rather tended to credit both good and bad developments to the central authorities in Prague.[21] This perception reinforced the historical tendency of Slovak society to adopt survival strategies, expressed during the normalization period in the "family model," called also "inner emigration," which dictated that confrontation with the omnipotent state be avoided by retreating into the private sphere, usually the family.[22] Particularly in Slovakia, the authorities offered intellectuals prone to cooperation some sort of voice within the system, which tended to keep them out of dissident groups. The policies of normalization were continued up to the time of the separation of Czechoslovakia from Soviet domination.

THE VELVET REVOLUTION AND DIVORCE, 1988–1993

Independence from domination by the Soviet Union was won by the Czechoslovakian state, and the evolution of the independence movement centers mostly on political activities in Prague. That movement is dealt with in Chapter 8 on the Czech Republic. The major events reviewed there involve dissident activities, open conflict with authorities, mass protests and a symbolic general strike that finally caused the regime to bow to the will of the people.

In December 1992 Klaus and Meciar agreed to split the country, and the independent Slovak Republic was born. The economic impacts of separation on the Slovak Republic were significant. A large portion of the Czech market for Slovak goods disappeared and federal fiscal transfers amounting to $1.5 billion, about 7 percent of GDP, stopped altogether. At the same time, the Slovak Republic had to incur expenditures for setting up embassies, issuing the new Slovak koruna (KS), building up customs administration facilities and so on. And the fundamental problem of an unbalanced industrial base remained. Political uncertainties and the structure of the economy have influenced the impact of market reforms and Slovakian economic performance.

The following section outlines basic reforms undertaken in the Slovak Republic since the collapse of Soviet domination, emphasizing the period since January 1993.[23] The costs imposed on Slovaks by the Meciar government's anti-reform stance illustrate our arguments in Chapters 2 to 5; the eventual response by voters illustrates the model in Chapter 6.

ECONOMIC REFORMS

Price Liberalization

This was the first of the reforms to be undertaken in Czechoslovakia. Although implemented rapidly, price liberalization did not generate undue inflation, as the federal government initially kept its deficit small and money tight. Retail food subsidies were the first to go, and then gasoline and diesel fuel prices were decontrolled. Some of the early rapid increases in food prices would have generated hardships, but the government provided a small monthly transfer payment to all citizens, financed by the savings on subsidies, with no budget effects. Public transport prices were raised initially by 30 percent for buses and 100 percent for trains.[24]

By January 1991 prices of goods and services representing about 85 percent of total sales were freed, at both retail and producer levels. In May subsidies on nearly all energy products were eliminated, but prices on other public utilities, transport and rents remained regulated, along with a few things considered of vital importance, such as medicines. By the end of the year the price of coal, for example, was about 832 percent higher than it had been in the 1980s, coke 358 percent and electricity 273 percent. Prior to 1989, when prices were strictly regulated, consumer price inflation was reported at 1 percent annually, but hidden inflation has been estimated at about 3.5 percent.[25] Increases in international oil prices and devaluation of the currency raised prices of tradable goods, and the 1991 inflation rate was around 60 percent.

Even though rents and various municipal service prices were liberalized in 1992, inflation dropped to about 10 percent. After the end of federation in 1993 and a devaluation, Slovakia's inflation rate rose to about 23 percent (see Table 12.2); this was a few points higher than that for the Czech Republic, about the same as Hungary's, and lower than Poland's and Estonia's rates. It dropped ten points the following year and continued to fall for a few more years. Inflation kicked in again in 1999 to double-digit levels, due in part to deliberate increases in administered prices. The prices of over 19 percent of items in the CPI are administered. These items include energy, rents and some public services.[26] Price liberalization proceeded rapidly and was accomplished quickly, and inflation was kept relatively low through man-

Table 12.2 Consumer price index 1993–1999 (average annual percentage change)

Year	Average percentage change
1993	23.2
1994	13.4
1995	9.9
1996	5.8
1997	6.7
1998	5.1
1999	10.1

agement of spending policies until the late 1990s (see the macroeconomic stabilization section below), with the exception of the first year of the Slovak Republic's separate existence. Inflation in 1999–2000 was based in large part on government decisions: energy prices were raised, indirect taxes were raised and an import surchage was implemented. The rate of inflation was falling by late 2000.[27]

Privatization

Czechoslovakia, unlike other centrally managed economies, had no private enterprises in domestic trade and distribution or in the service sector of either republic. Consequently trade and service sectors were first to be privatized. Over 70 percent of these businesses were hotels and restaurants. This "small" privatization was known as the "first wave" and it was completed before the end of 1992.[28] The process began in January 1991 and in the first wave, 80 percent of small shops in Slovakia became privately owned. This was accomplished through auctions and restitution procedures. About one-third of the small shops were returned to original owners or their descendants. Another one-third, typically built by state enterprises, were auctioned off, some with and some without the land they sat on. The remaining one-third were mainly service outlets on the ground floor of large apartment complexes, and they were leased for two or more years, "pending the privatization of the apartment block."[29] Most purchases were financed through loans from the savings banks, which were required by the government to extend the loans, typically with personal property as collateral. Special credits offered for privatization became depleted early on. Credit resources urgently needed for modernizing firms were very limited.

During the first two years of the program, about half of large and medium-sized firms were privatized under a coupon (voucher) scheme. This occurred before the Velvet Divorce. The voucher system, as discussed in the Czech Republic chapter, was somewhat less successful in Slovakia. Privatization evidently had a much lower priority for Merciar than it did for Klaus. This difference of opinion regarding the importance of private ownership may have contributed to the decision by Merciar and Klaus to dissolve the federation.

Once the federation was dissolved, political disputes about procedures slowed the privatization process significantly in the Slovak Republic. Meciar's government decided that the second wave would not rely solely on the coupon method because it was too closely associated with the Czech Republic; and suspended the second wave of privatization. Standard methods – public tender, "with investment and employment pledges given priority over prices"[30] – would be used for a majority of shares in large enterprises; coupon privatization could be used to transfer a minority share. This was supposed to allow large foreign or domestic investors to buy a controlling block of shares in large companies. There were problems with this. There was a serious lack of capital in the Slovak Republic, foreign direct investment was slow to appear, and there was no detailed implementation plan for using standard methods.

The Meciar approach to privatization embodied a different philosophy of property rights than the voucher privatization approach. Implicit in Meciar's policies was the notion that only the state is entitled to control the allocation of property. This philosophy produced privatization procedures that generated bureaucratic complexity and slowed the process down. The stagnation of privatization discredited the government's commitment to reform and this was one of the main reasons for the parliamentary no-confidence vote against Meciar's Cabinet in March 1994. Josef Moravcik's transition government (an election was scheduled for October) set about picking up the privatization pace. The National Property Fund (NPF) was the largest single owner of Slovakian enterprises. This state agency held companies in the privatization queue pending sale. The NPF began selling off companies through various direct methods – by selling shares on the Bratislava Options Market, the Bratislava Stock Market or through an over-the-counter system. Voucher booklets were brought back and went on sale in September 1994. Things were looking up.

But Meciar criticized Moravcik's government for giving in to Western demands, and won the October elections. He had promised a radical change in the privatization program, and within a day of taking office he suspended the Czech-style coupon plans. However, 3.5 million Slovaks had already subscribed to the coupon scheme in September, and many of the country's enterprises were extremely short of capital. The second wave of company shares sold for vouchers was scheduled to begin in mid-1995. No more than 46 percent of the shares in any one of the 200-odd companies going onto the market could be bought with coupons. The remaining assets would be sold through direct sales or tenders. A 1995 law prevented privatizing "strategic" firms, such as energy and armaments.[31]

A great deal of insider privatization went on during the Meciar years, often directed at maintaining access to financial institutions for ruling party cronies. Over half of Slovakia's sixty most profitable companies were sold to them at bargain prices. State-owned banks were financing many of these transactions, and at the same time these banks were keeping weak companies afloat. Banks of all sizes continued to accumulate bad debt. In 1997 parliament passed the Revitalization of Enterprises Act that assured continuation of government subsidies for unprofitable enterprises.

The troubled second wave of business privatization looks speedy when compared to residential privatization. A significant amount of commercial office space, urban housing and agricultural and vacant land remains in the hands of local authorities. Retail space in large blocks has already been mentioned. As these shops become privatized, new owners sign leases on the space "pending the resolution of the land title."[32] These leases are extended month by month, which discourages maintenance, investment and resale of the business. Residential and commercial occupants of urban buildings are also affected by the uncertainty of land title. Rents are low, often below maintenance costs, which hinders new development, repairs and renovations. The housing situation obstructs labor mobility and discourages intergenerational transfers. Local authorities have more influence than the state when it comes to residential markets. In 1993 legislation was passed that allowed buyers and sellers to negotiate price, subject to a specified price ceiling per square meter of usable space. "To deter speculation, windfall gains from resales when the owner is not an occupant will be subjected to near-confiscatory taxation for ten years."[33] This law was supposed to accelerate the privatization of housing.

In the October 1998 general election voters replaced Meciar's party with a four-party coalition led by Mikulas Dzurinda. Prime Minster Dzurinda was expected to repair the damage done during the Meciar years, and he seemed to understand the issues. Although state-owned banks in 1999 still held about 70 percent of all classified claims (bad loans), the government was prepared to privatize the system at a cost of perhaps 10 percent of GDP. The three leading banks (two of them held 40 percent of banking assets) were to be sold off in 2000, but they had to be recapitalized first. That was under way in 1999. The banks were virtually insolvent because they held bad loan instruments from state enterprises that had been propped up by the government.

The coalition government led by Dzurinda agreed in 1999 to retain a majority state ownership only in "natural monopolies" such as electricity, and gas and crude oil transport, but by 2000 privatization of public utilities was begun. The Strategic Companies Act was abolished. The year 2000 state plan was to retain some interest in the main retail bank, the dominant insurance company and Slovak Telecom.[34] We conclude that the Dzurinda regime's attitude toward private property appears promising, but will this attitude survive severe political winds?

Macroeconomic Stabilization

Fiscal policy

In 1993, Meciar's administration did not do as well in controlling expenditures as the Czechoslovakian regime had done. Meciar pressured the National Bank of Slovakia (NBS) to finance the deficits; inflation jumped to around 23 percent. New tax rates, including social and health insurance from earnings, were excessive, and tax compliance was a problem. The government prepared a balanced state budget but economists and even elements within the government questioned its viability from the beginning. Revenues had been seriously overestimated in the face of tax changes, a recession and the decline in trade with the Czechs. Expenditures were underestimated. The deficit was in fact larger than initially reported and Meciar's government was accused of having spent large amounts on "inappropriate items."

Sloppy fiscal policy, along with foot-dragging on the privatization program, generated a parliamentary vote of no confidence in the Meciar administration in March 1994 and Josef Moravcik became Prime Minister. The Moravcik administration tried to control the budget by holding down expenditures on social assistance, social benefits, health and education. The budget deficit fell from 7 percent in 1993 to less than 2 percent in 1994 (see Table 12.3). These austere fiscal measures went unappreciated and Meciar returned to power in late 1994.

Table 12.3 Central government budget policy (deficit/surplus as percentage of GDP)

Year	Deficit/surplus
1993	–7.0
1994	–1.3
1995	0.2
1996	–1.9
1997	–5.2
1998	–6.0
1999	–1.9

By 1996 heavy spending by the government was generating budget deficits and exacerbating the trade balance. According to the IMF and OECD, public investment spending was high in part because the government maintained support of and economic dependence on heavy industry like armaments and steel. The government took on the modernization of old state-owned enterprises. On the revenue side, incentives to buyers of privatized companies allowed them to deduct up to 60 percent from their purchase price for new investments. All these forces contributed to budget problems in 1997 and 1998.[35]

The EU Accession Report for 2000 lists the 1999 budget deficit as 3.4 percent of GDP. The Dzurinda government's 1999 austerity program reduced domestic demand, but the negative affects were modified by healthier net exports. The austerity program definitely reduced the government's deficit and set the stage for better economic performance. Transfer payments are still high and tax compliance, although improving, is not high enough.

Monetary policy

Monetary policy reform was largely hostage to poor fiscal policy decisions, lack of bank independence and Meciar's continued belief in central government control of the financial sector. When the federation split, the assets of the Czechoslovak central bank were divided up on a two-to-one basis, with the larger share going to the larger Czech Republic. The Slovak financial sector faced difficulties based on imbalances in regional development and capital concentration, and an inexperienced set of commercial bankers. The National Bank of Slovakia (NBS) supervised the banking system and adopted specific goals: to stabilize the exchange rate, maintain internal convertibility and control inflation. The bank initially provided credit auctions to get liquidity into the banking system and to establish market rates of interest, and rediscount facilities were offered to banks that loaned to agricultural enterprises and exporters. The bank soon found it necessary to impose credit ceilings to prevent imprudent risk-taking by banks with large non-performing loans. The admirable goals of the National Bank were undermined by pressure from the government to finance the budget deficit.

By May 1993 the credit auctions were suspended and the rediscounting facility became the main instrument for making liquidity available to banks. Banks tended to rely on the NBS for credit because it was less expensive than using deposits. As a consequence, loans to private enterprises began to dry up. The market for treasury bills was weak and so the NBS was forced to take on an increasing proportion of fiscal deficits. Domestic assets in the banking system were shrinking.

Pressures on the monetary authority to finance the government eased under Moravcik but this respite was brief. By 1996 both monetary and fiscal policy were being badly managed. Standard and Poor's lowered the rating of Slovak government securities to below investment grade, and Moody's did the same with respect to notes of the National Bank of Slovakia. In late 1997 the OECD and the IMF announced their inability to determine the status of financial matters in Slovakia and called for more financial transparency.

After the Meciar government fell in 1994 and the new four-party coalition government was installed, parliament passed the austerity program that included a measure to tighten fiscal policy. It began to take effect before the end of the year. Tighter fiscal policy meant lower interest rates; the improved government deficit outlook and the lower current account deficit led to a stronger exchange rate.

Slovakia illustrates the political economy of Chapters 1 to 5. Fiscal and monetary stability are necessary for healthy transition. Short-term gains from budget deficits can mask structural problems for a short while. Eventually, reforms that bite need to be undertaken. The crucial question of the early twenty-first century is whether voters of emerging economies will have the foresight to endure the effects of fiscal discipline, especially growing unemployment, in order to reap the long-term gains from sound macroeconomic stabilization policies and decentralization.

Industrial Restructuring and Deregulation

After separation in 1993 the Slovak government was not comfortable with market allocation of resources and failed to give up its supervisory role in the economy. This is still evident with respect to regulatory burdens on business. Efforts have been made to simplify the tax burden on enterprises, but it still includes a 50 percent payroll tax for social insurance programs. Of the 50 percent, 38 percent comes from the employer and 12 percent from the employee. A value added tax takes 6 percent from some services and 25 percent from many goods and other services. There is also a 45 percent corporate income tax. Foreign exchange restrictions have imposed other costs on businesses. All this has left little room in industry for private capital formation, reinvestment, enlargement and development. The Dzurinda regime promises to continue to lower tax burdens on business.[36]

Complex regulatory burdens have deterred establishment of new businesses. Getting a license to do business requires confirmation of qualifications (certification of lack of criminal record, number of years of specialized education and training and so on) and payment of substantial licensing fees. Several months typically elapse before approval of trade licenses by regulators. Inconsistent interpretation of registration requirements results in repeated filings and delays. Other regulations impose additional paperwork for environmental impact assessments, health and safety inspections, social security payments, customs duties and taxes. Government agencies penalize firms for mistakes with fines or by forcing them to start procedures all over again. These complexities have apparently discouraged both domestic and foreign business. Lack of information is another problem for foreign entrepreneurs.

Labor regulations are burdensome. There are heavy restrictions on dismissing employees. Employers are required to give months of advance notice of dismissal and to provide several months of severance pay. Collective bargaining agreements may extend these. Many managers consider job stability for employees to be an important management objective; such self-imposed behavior appears to affect management practices more than statutory restrictions and seems to be a hangover from the universal employment policies of the communist regime.

Slovakia's largest steel-maker, VSZ, illustrates a fundamental structural problem endemic to centralized economies. The essence of private property rights is that the owner is the residual claimant of benefits and also incurs the risks. This responsibility involves making difficult decisions. For instance, an entrepreneur may cut his losses by shutting down an enterprise. Close interconnections between government, banks and enterprises vitiate this power, because if the enterprise shuts down, banks may collapse and the government may fall. Thus, a collapse of one firm can reverberate throughout the entire society.

In the case of VSZ these relationships could translate the collapse of a major enterprise into problems for the internal and external financial communities. VSZ manufactures the highest-quality steel in Central and Eastern Europe and employs 25,000 people. It was a managerial and financial mess, loaded with debts it could not service, and closely tied up with unwise diversification ranging from newspapers and football to – significantly – insurance and banking. VSZ accounts for about 14 percent of Slovak exports. The health of this company is important to workers, to the banking system, to financiers and to the Slovak government. Even the international financial community is exposed if VSZ should fail. In fact, it is too important to fail. A Slovak-American banker, much trusted by the international financial community, was brought in to restructure the company. He persuaded US Steel, already a low-profile investor, to pay all back taxes and foreign debts and to invest $125 million. The point of this example is that the Slovak system of close public–private sector relationships, a hangover from Soviet times, can prevent failure. Any structure that prohibits enterprise failure inhibits long-range economic success.

Trade Liberalization

The Meciar government purported to welcome foreign investors, but wanted only those who "demonstrate a genuine interest in the long-term development of a factory" so that there will be no "exploitation" or "takeover of the domestic market" by outsiders.[37] Foreign investment has been extremely slow to move into Slovakia. As column 1 of Table 12.4 shows, foreign direct investment was less than 3 percent of GDP in its best year, 1998.

Slovakia tried to attract foreign investors with tax incentives, but this was ineffective. Low Slovakian wages and proximity to potential markets has not helped much. Wages are low relative to Western Europe but higher than in the Commonwealth of Independent States, including the border state of Ukraine, so some labor migrates in from the East and out to the West.

Some foreigners doing business in the Slovak Republic have found it mysterious that others hesitate to invest there. It has been suggested that foreign reticence is based on anti-Slovak propaganda generated in Budapest and Prague, where many foreigners base Central and Eastern European operations. "Hungary and the Czech Republic are passing Slovakia off as the country cousin ne'er-do-well."[38]

Table 12.4 International trade and financial statistics (selected years)

Year	FDI* (% of GDP)	Imports (% of GDP)	Balance of trade (% of GDP)	Exchange rate (Slovak Koruna/$)
1993	1.4	53.3	–0.6	30.8
1995	1.2	50.9	0.4	29.7
1997	0.9	53.1	–1.3	33.6
1998	2.8	63.7	–2.1	35.2
1999	1.1	60.8	—	41.4

Note: * Foreign direct investment.

The Slovaks would like more foreign direct investment; they have a liberal exchange control regime and no general restrictions on foreign investment. Foreigners have been reluctant to invest in Slovakia ever since independence in 1991. Foreign investors probably perceived Meciar's regime as too risky politically, and the Dzurinda regime has been more successful in attracting foreign capital. The government's 1999 structural reform program includes enhanced incentives for foreign direct investment.

If Dzurinda continues to demonstrate that Slovakia is a good place to do business, it can become a welcoming and safe haven for capitalism and foreign investment flows will grow. After all, its immediate neighbors, the Czech Republic and Hungary, despite higher costs than Slovakia, already attract more foreign direct investment than any other transition economies.

Slovakia has developed a "highly open economy."[39] It has free trade agreements with the EU, the European Free Trade Association (EFTA), the Central Europe Free Trade Association (CEFTA) and with Estonia, Israel and Lithuania, among others.[40] These agreements involve zero tariffs for specified non-agricultural products. Slovakia belongs to the WTO and is in the queue to join the EU. Slovakia's foreign sector is heavily dependent on the West; exports are over 60 percent of GDP and over 60 percent of exports go to the EU.[41] The current account balance has improved, thanks to the efforts of the post-Meciar government. Net exports rose, as did foreign direct investment, after it became clear that the government was serious about macroeconomic stability.

THE FUTURE LOOKS BETTER THAN THE PAST

Slovaks were altogether unused to liberty and to individual responsibility when independence from the Soviets was won in 1989. After the Velvet Divorce in 1993, Meciar fed the flames of nationalism that had been suppressed during the Soviet years. The people seemed to be distracted from the business of economic reform and preferred instead to concentrate on national identity and security issues. In addition they feared the loss of social guarantees and the exposure to competitive markets. Late in 1993 a survey found that 39 percent of the population believed that the pre-1989 economy did not require profound change; 49 percent thought that it did. A massive 89 percent believed the state should guarantee jobs for everyone, 80 percent wanted price regulation and 75 percent thought that the state should guarantee housing. A state-paternalistic attitude was very much in evidence. Only 20 percent supported liberal economic ideas.[42]

Slovaks have come a long way in adapting to economic and political independence. It was clear that things had changed by March 1997 when the Christian Democratic Movement opposition party collected over half a million signatures on a petition to support a referendum on direct presidential elections; the Slovak constitution requires the President to call a referendum if 350,000 signatures are collected.[43] The first direct presidential election took place in 1999 and Meciar, having lost the position of Prime Minister in the general elections of 1998, lost the presidential election as well.

Table 12.5 shows our summary election statistics for Slovakia. Unfortunately, there has not been enough variance in political outcomes for long enough periods of time to permit quantitative analysis of voting behavior, reforms and economic behavior. Meciar was out of office for less than a year in 1994 and was replaced in 1998, both times by a four-party opposition to his Movement for Democratic Slovakia (HZDS). Time will tell whether pro-market reforms will be sustained long enough to reverse the history of government domination of the economy. Statistics for 1999 were not encouraging, but 2000 looks better.

Table 12.5 Elections, reforms and economic performance, 1993–1999 (all variables cover election intervals)*

Year	Votes for reformers (%)	Reform index (1995=100)	GDP % change		Inflation rate		Unemployment rate	
			After	Before	After	Before	After	Before
1992	48.0	98.5	–4.5	–5.6	18.3	22.6	6.2	11.1
1994	45.2	97.7	6.3	–4.5	7.0	18.3	10.0	6.2
1998	57.2	88.8	2.0	6.3	10.1	7.0	19.2	10.0

Note: * The short interval in 1994 when the HZDS was ousted is too short to include and the data on post-1998 activity suggest early difficulties in economic performance.

Evidence of how far the public mind has moved since 1993 appeared in surveys in early 2000, showing 70 percent support among Slovaks for EU membership, higher than support in the Czech Republic.[44] After the 1998 elections, the government moved quickly to make up for lost time and past inertia in getting into the queue for membership. The accession process exposed the Slovakian economic and political systems to unprecedented scrutiny. The Slovaks have cleared major hurdles. The 1999 EU regular accession report states that the Slovaks have a functioning democracy and that "Slovakia can be regarded as a functioning market economy." The coalition, unlike its predecessors, was capable of expressing a clear consensus on its commitment to macroeconomic and structural economic reforms. It passed a new Banking Act in 1999, pledged to decrease government spending and undertake various fiscal reforms to promote macroeconomic stability, and adopted plans to restructure and to privatize state-owned enterprises and banks. It has so far kept its promises.

The economy itself was evolving. The share of heavy industry continued to decline and by 2000 accounted for less than 30 percent of GDP. Thanks in part to the creation of new businesses, services generated 46 percent of GDP. The government's restructuring program promotes foreign direct investment, which encourages technology transfer. The Slovaks hope that the movement of US Steel from a joint venture partner in the VSZ steel company to major investor has signaled to foreign entrepreneurs that the water is safe to dive into.

Everything optimistic about the future of Slovakia confirms our theoretical and heuristic arguments about the sources of economic growth. The government has at last a clear notion of its goals and what it takes to progress toward a functioning market system. The general public is apparently jumping onto the bandwagon. Slovaks are developing a stronger consensus about what they want the future to be, and the government is undertaking policies to move in the right directions. Policy-makers were slow to move away from a state-control mindset; the general public has evidently become more comfortable with the risks and rewards of capitalism. This is a work in progress. Macroeconomic stability was restored by 2000 but is endangered by spending proposals.

Much remains to be done. Crime and corruption are inadequately controlled. Little progress has been made on health and safety standards at work. Capital markets are illiquid and fragmented, and regulations (including banking supervision) are either weak or are in place but not being effectively applied. The civil service needs reform and regional development is still neglected. Regulatory bodies are not sufficiently independent, and commercial law enforcement is not strong enough.

CONCLUSIONS AND QUESTIONS

While optimistic about the Slovak Republic, we couch that optimism in great caution. The costs of the government's macroeconomic stability policies are high. In order to exercise fiscal discipline, Dzurinda's government instituted an austerity program. Unemployment in 1999 was over 16 percent and rising. How long will voters tolerate this pain? Workers have expressed great dissatisfaction by taking to the streets.

One big question is how long – or whether – Meciar-type politicians can be kept at bay. Reforms always carry the risk of reversal by unhappy voters who will then return anti-reformers to power. This could undermine Slovakia's resolute moves toward sustainable market capitalism. Can reformers consolidate and institutionalize their successes? In other words, can they convince voters to take the long view? Progress is encouraging but the situation is fragile.

NOTES

1. Murphy, Dean E. (1995), "Slovakia's Difficult Transition," *Los Angeles Times*, 24 November, p. A18.
2. Anderson, Robert (2001), "Slovakia's premier prepared to go the extra mile," *Financial Times*, 16 February.
3. Busik, et al. (1993), p. 7. See also European Union, *Slovak Republic 2000*.
4. European Union, *Slovak Republic, 2000* p. 25. By 1999 bad debts were 40 percent of total loans.
5. European Union, *Slovak Republic, 2000*.
6. Hrncir (1985).

7. Butora and Butorova (1993), pp. 705–36.
8. Selucky (1991).
9. Felak (1992), p. 139.
10. Butora and Butorova (1993), pp. 734–5.
11. This point is emphasized by Butora and Butorova (1993).
12. Post-war politics are thoroughly covered in Bradley (1991).
13. See Bradley (1991) for details of the communist takeover.
14. Selucky (1991), p. 161.
15. Krska and Susedka (1971), pp. 48–79.
16. Selucky (1991), p. 167.
17. World Bank (1994), p. 2.
18. World Bank (1994).
19. This argument about the effects of Soviet modernization is made by Butora and Butorova (1993), p. 715.
20. Wheaton and Kavan (1992), p. 6.
21. Butora and Butorova (1993), pp. 715–16.
22. Wheaton and Kavan (1992), p. 9.
23. As of 2000, Slovakia did not publish consolidated general government account data, so figures are estimates based on data from various government subsectors. See European Union, *1999 Regular Report.*
24. World Bank (1991), p. 56.
25. OECD (1991), p. 23.
26. See European Union, *Slovak Republic 2000*, p. 28. Price controls are also discussed in the US Library of Congress Slovakia country study.
27. European Union, *Slovak Republic 2000*, p. 26.
28. Busik et al. (1993), p. 31.
29. World Bank (1994), p. 50.
30. Ibid., p. 51.
31. Open Media Research Institute (1997).
32. World Bank (1994), p. 53.
33. Ibid., p. 54.
34. European Union, *1999 Regular Report.*
35. IMF (1998), p. 8; OECD (1999), pp. 37–8.
36. OECD (1999), pp. 45–6, contains a summary of the Dzurinda government program.
37. "Meciar, Capitalist Crawling Dog?", *The Economist*, 6 May 1995, p. 67.
38. Dana Milbank, "Independent Slovakia Defies Expectations," *Wall Street Journal*, 30 November 1994.
39. OECD (1999).
40. CEFTA includes Bulgaria, the Czech Republic, Hungary, Poland, Romania and Slovenia.
41. See OECD (1999) and European Union, *1999 Regular Report.*
42. Butora and Butorova (1993), pp. 724–5.
43. Open Media Research Institute (1997).
44. Wood (2000).

13. The long and winding road

Inevitably the Soviet Union disintegrated; fortunately it did so with little bloodshed. While its demise freed millions of people from intellectual and economic constraints, it at once made many of them poorer. Domestic economies collapsed, the trade regime shut down, political and social rules were shattered. It was a near-total collapse of a highly centralized and ossified system. We explain all this from the perspectives of growth theory and political economy before we address attempts at recovery.

Each newly independent country, born under difficult circumstances, has tried to modify or reform its economic system so that decentralized private markets can play a greater role in allocating resources. The difficulty and complexity of transforming an economic system and a political system while reconstructing new legal, financial and social structures has, over a period of ten years, become increasingly evident. Some countries have fared better than others. How does one measure economic success in this transition enterprise? Economic growth, calculated either as growth in GDP per capita, growth in personal income or growth in consumption per person, is the appropriate measure of the degree of success of economic reforms. Unless reforms lead to improvements in living standards in democratic regimes, reformers and their policies will be rejected.

Any reform is politically hazardous even under the best of circumstances, because it generates clearly identifiable and immediate losers even as it promises widespread winners in the long term. Under conditions of total societal collapse reform is even more problematic. The poor state of the Soviet-era capital stock, the restrictive nature of Eastern bloc trading arrangements that disappeared when the USSR did, the absence of viable banking and financial systems, and recession in the West all conspired to devastate the living conditions of the peoples of Central and Eastern Europe. Reformers often stepped into the breach. In retrospect quick success was not likely. Individuals oppose economic reforms because the costs are immediate and apparent and it is clear on whom the burdens will fall. It is unclear, however, who will enjoy the payoffs to reform and how far in the future those payoffs lie.

Paradoxically, reforms away from central planning and toward decentralized markets must be instituted by the very governments that are being supplanted as driving forces in the resource allocation process. This is because reforms are a public good that cannot be generated, at least quickly and adequately, by the private sector. The process is slow and halting because after decades of Soviet rule citizens were wary of central authorities of any sort and cynical about promises for long-term benefits.

Policy-makers, officials and bureaucrats resist reforms because most reforms are directed at closing down old agencies and firms owned by the state. In effect, reformers are expecting authorities to restructure themselves out of a job. A public agency is needed to move property and the means of production out of the hands of local and central government authorities and into the hands of private individuals. Often the latter may be foreigners or suspect former communists. New legal structures and new commercial, civil and criminal codes must be created and a reliable judiciary must be trained to protect the rights of the new private owners of property. At the same time the government has to adopt new and unfamiliar functions, some of which will be unpopular with the public; for instance, viable tax systems, private but regulated banks and financial markets. In some countries voters and politicians disagree about fundamental social, political and economic means and ends. The clearer and more universally accepted the goals of reform, the more successful countries are likely to be in liberalization efforts.

Five basic reforms are necessary steps toward successful private markets. Each is required to some degree for sensible growth of a market economy. Price liberalization means that private decentralized markets determine prices that will cover the social costs of production and therefore will help to allocate resources efficiently. The more efficient the allocation of resources, the greater will be the effective size of the economic pie. Property privatization creates individual owners who, as residual claimants, have incentives leading them to behave responsibly in both production and consumption decisions. This reform too promotes efficient use of scarce resources; products that people want are produced at least cost.

Macroeconomic stabilization, the implementation of sound fiscal and monetary policies, promotes price-level stability and militates against cyclical instability. Price-level instability vitiates price signals that the market system relies on to make proper allocation decisions. Deregulation gets politicians out of management of private sector resources. Restructuring promotes the formation of institutions such as courts, laws, central banks and financial markets that insure that the incentives that drive private decision-making work correctly. Trade liberalization allows any country to exploit comparative advantage and fosters the transfer of new technologies to the new private economies. Trade also disciplines local monopolies by forcing them to compete on international markets. Finally, trade reinforces fiscal and monetary policy discipline because a viable exchange rate regime signals a currency's viability.

In democracies politicians can sustain a reform program only if voters support them. Voters give their support to programs that will make them better off. To be sustainable, therefore, reforms must lead to rising living standards. This comes from higher worker productivity, and productivity improvement derives from increases in the quantity and quality of human and physical capital. We adapt growth models to integrate key reforms into growth prospects, thus linking reform policy actions directly to subsequent savings, investment and production decisions.

Resource prices and interest rates determined by private markets will respond to reform measures and then generate the optimal level of capital. In the case of the former Soviet Union, new and appropriate types of capital must replace poor-quality and inappropriate Soviet-era capital. Recently developed endogenous growth models with human capital have shown that human capital augmented by skill development and formal education has an additional payoff. It promotes technology transfer; highly skilled and well-educated workers are needed to make efficient use of new technologies. In order to increase productivity per worker, the growth in physical capital must exceed capital replacement requirements resulting from depreciation and the growth in the number of workers. A key insight of neoclassical growth models is that a growing capital stock requires growing savings. We show how a people's inclination to save and accumulate productive capital depends upon the national history that has shaped their attitudes, tastes and habits.

Exactly how do the five key reforms affect the growth process? Relative prices determined by decentralized markets instead of by central planners improve the consumer's well-being by improving the mix, variety and quality of consumer goods in response to the desires of the consumer. One must acknowledge that not everyone in the Eastern bloc will be made better off by market-determined prices, certainly not in the short run. Planners typically held prices of staples (for example, food, energy and housing) artificially low relative to a private market equilibrium. Some households, especially those that devote a large share of their budget to staples, will in the short run be worse off.

Privatization improves social welfare, defined as personal income, consumption and utility, through several different channels in growth models. Properly implemented privatizing will mean that inefficient and wasteful enterprises that had been propped up by state subsidies and soft budget constraints will not survive unless they improve. While business failures obviously generate short-term losses, closed factories and lost jobs, eventually resources are reallocated to better uses. New private property owners will be better off as they enjoy the fruits of wise management of their own assets. This in turn makes society better off as resources are used more efficiently in response to market demand rather than awkward and remote central orders unlinked to incentives. Private owners will have incentives to improve their human capital and to accumulate useful physical capital assets because they are the residual claimants of the fruits of their decisions.

Fiscal stabilization strengthens a market economy in a growth model because with disciplined management of public spending and taxes fewer resources go to waste. Though outside the models, fiscal discipline also leads to better monetary policy. The first purpose of monetary policy is to stabilize the price level. Judicious timing can also help to smooth cycles. Well-run central banks, not directly involved in the allocation of private sector loans, can enforce sound banking practices and foster appropriate (safe and constructive) financial flows that facilitate domestic investment spending. Sensible deregulation and microeconomic restructuring reduce the implicit burden imposed on the private cost of capital. Since capital is less costly when government gets out of the way, more will be accumulated, contributing to higher living standards. Removal of state subsidies and soft budget constraints allows the demise of poorly run state enterprises. A responsibly run public sector fosters a supportive environment for private entrepreneurial and profitable behavior. This leads directly to higher living standards.

Trade liberalization improves the mix, quality and variety of goods available to domestic consumers by exploiting comparative advantage. Trade improves resource allocation by weakening local monopolies, forcing them to compete on world markets. Open trade is a primary transmission mechanism for technology transfer from mature modern industrial economies to newly developing societies. Finally, trade, by requiring a workable exchange rate regime, disciplines monetary authorities. Exchange rate problems often reflect monetary instability. These exchange rate problems are price signals that can expose flaws in the conduct of monetary policy, forcing monetary reform.

We show that each reform creates losers in the short run, as well as winners. People who are active and productive workers may benefit much more than retired persons because pensions could evaporate as public revenues dry up. Applying the growth analysis to individuals at different stages of life and in different circumstances indicates that younger people are likely to benefit more from reforms that create new markets and new jobs than older people, who may find adaptation to new types of work difficult. An older worker laid off as a result of a collapsed state enterprise will have difficulty finding new work. Taxpayers will gain relative to those who are dependent upon transfers from the state when smaller governments and balanced budgets become priorities. Some new entrepreneurs will be major winners while employees of factories that make useless or low-quality products will be immediate losers. Ultimately, forward-looking people, those willing to save, improve their human capital and bank on a better future, will benefit much more than the relatively shortsighted and impatient. Those flexible enough to learn and adapt will benefit relative to those who are not able or inclined to do so.

Reform programs have no chance to work unless the politicians who support them can manage to stay in office. Reforms, new rules and institutions, reshape the economic regime. Politics can be viewed as the marketplace that establishes the rules of the economic game. There are demanders and suppliers in this political marketplace. The demand side is made up of voters and the supply side is made up of candidates and parties who propose and create new rules, programs and reforms.

Elections are the market-clearing devices that create new sets of rules. The performance of the economy influences the outcomes of elections because voters make decisions about how to vote based in part on how well they expect to do in the future if certain rules come into play. The supply of new rules (reforms) depends on candidates' analysis of polling information they have about voter preferences (created in the old regime) as well as on ideology. An election determines what the new regime (the new set of rules and reforms) will be, and thus politics shapes economic prospects.

These characterizations of the interaction of politics and economics, the lessons of growth models and the effects of reforms are common to all the newly independent countries in Central and Eastern Europe. They also share a particular set of problems to overcome. Their trade system, the Council for Mutual Economic Assistance, collapsed suddenly, depriving them of guaranteed inputs and guaranteed customers for their output. They had competed for neither during the Soviet period because the central planners had assured them they would have both. Independence revealed capital stocks that were generally outdated, worn out or inappropriate, devoted to the production of products that were uncompetitive or for which markets had disappeared.

Financial systems that could create money, credit and assets, match borrowers to lenders, ameliorate risk and promote the flow of investment to productive uses were non-existent. Banks had acted as depositories for savings or as conduits for subsidies to enterprises; early in the transition it became clear that they were loaded with debt that would never be paid off. State enterprises had routinely borrowed from each other, often in kind; and it was understood that such debt would never be repaid. The West, experiencing a sharp recession in the early 1990s, was not feeling generous about making loans to the East.

The likelihood of successful transformation and sustainable growth is not the same for each of our six country cases. Because of the common problems outlined above, they all continue to deal with some resistance to reforms. Some of the difference in their economic performance records and their long-term prospects can be related to the clarity and singularity of their goals. Social goals reflect in large part whether a country experienced a modern golden era, a historical period that provides the people with a vision of and a model for the future that political reformers can draw on. The difference in their prospects for success depend also on how much difficulty they will have in overcoming their legacy from the communist period.

Bulgaria's prospects are weak in terms of both goals and socialist legacy. Bulgaria's best economic period before independence was under Soviet rule. Reform has been slow and uneven and economic performance is worse than that of our other countries, with the exception of Russia. After a decade hopeful signs are appearing that Bulgaria may overcome its past, but there is much left to do with respect to both macroeconomic reforms and microeconomic restructuring. The people seem to be waking up to the importance of disciplined reform. Their desire to join the European Union is forcing them to go along with reform leaders. There is still, however, a strong socialist party that comes back to power when reforms begin to bite, and even the ostensibly market-oriented politicians display a woeful tendency to meddle in the private sector. Economic growth has been up and down, as has inflation. Unemployment remains high. Bulgarians are impatient for a better future but not decisive about how to get there. It is not clear whether economic performance is yet on an upward trend. The short-term situation is precarious and the long-term outlook fair – not hopeless by any means, but prosperity will be a long time coming.

The Czechs are boldly optimistic. They believe that they will eventually take their place among their equals in Western Europe. Before the Second World War they were much like Austria. Some claim that the Czechs were on a par with the Germans and are sure that they will be again. They suffered so severely under the Soviets that after independence they felt driven in their determination to escape the East and return to the Western fold. They were among the first of the transition countries to get their macroeconomic house in order: prices were quickly freed, trade was liberalized and macroeconomic stability was adopted – budget control and low inflation.

Although their voucher privatization program was universally admired and frequently emulated, it turned out to be a relatively weak link. The concept was noble and inventive but success was much harder to achieve. Vouchers did introduce Czechs to the risks and potential gains from asset ownership, but in designing the financial structure of the program policy-makers had not paid sufficient attention to the details. Fatally, the banks and funds were not properly restructured to support a private financial system. Most vouchers ended up in the hands of investment funds that were prevented by law from effecting better corporate governance in firms where they held shares. Even worse, these funds were themselves mostly owned by the few big banks so that firms, while nominally owned by private voucher-holders, were still in fact controlled and run by the same old state bureaucrats. To make matters worse, the banks had huge amounts of bad debt as they continued to subsidize weak firms.

Difficulties with the voucher program eventually revealed a fundamental flaw in the Czech transition process: whereas the Czechs got the macroeconomic reforms right, like stabilization and price and trade liberalization, they neglected careful institutional restructuring and deregulation. After eight years of a liberal government, the ruling party succumbed to political inertia and to allegations of illegal activities. Re-election became more important than reforms and progress stopped. The Czechs were the first of the transition states to experience a genuine post-reform homegrown recession. They have recovered and now have to decide how to face their difficulties. Long-term prospects look good, provided they do not get lazy about institutional reform, where old habits of bureaucratic meddling and corruption occasionally surface. They thought that transition would be easier than it has proved to be.

Estonians, who also saw themselves as Western, suffered mightily under the Soviets. Their reform model goal is absolutely clear: it is their linguistic first cousins, the Finns. Of our country cases, they have been the most consistent in their reform program and the most consistently disciplined fiscally. In early monetary reform they adopted a currency board, which removed any possibility of discretionary monetary policy; this in turn shaped fiscal policy.

Estonia was a Soviet republic and shares a long border with Russia. As a small country of 1.4 million people, Estonians fear the possibility of reabsorption by Russia. They are determined to tie themselves to the West in every way possible, including joining NATO and the EU at the earliest opportunity. Although it was the wealthiest of the Soviet republics, Estonia was and is poorer than some of the satellite states, the Czech Republic and Hungary in our set. Like other transition countries, about two-thirds of Estonia's trade is now with EU countries; Russia dominated trade before independence but is now far down the ranking of trade partners. Still, both Estonia and Hungary were strongly and adversely affected by the Russian financial crisis of the late 1990s. Estonia's long-term prospects are good, but per capita income is still only about 40 percent of the EU average.

Toward the end of the nineteenth century and until the First World War, Hungary produced a class of people who were well educated, well travelled and rich, sophisticated in the ways of the Western world. This might have been mistaken for a golden era, but it was not so for most Hungarians, largely peasants who were very poor. Hungary's turbulent history as the battleground and pawn of greater powers did not really allow it a period of self-governance and prosperity. Even though Hungary was far better off than Bulgaria or Slovakia when the Soviets took over, these countries share the characteristic of experiencing no pre-Soviet golden era in the sense we have defined it. Hungary had enough commercial interaction with the West to instill within the people a basic understanding of market systems.

Long historical experience with invaders played out with the Soviets, too: Hungarians had learned how to accommodate, to get along, to tolerate occupiers and still go their own way. Their pragmatic adaptability enabled them to strike a bargain with the Soviets after their own revolution of 1956 and the Prague Spring of 1968: they would behave like good Soviet citizens (rather than like Magyar street-fighters) in exchange for a degree of economic independence. They trace their liberalization from the late 1960s, and they might think of 1966 to 1975 as their golden era. They got a head start, but they also acquired a learned sense of gradualism, and this damaged their progress in implementing reforms during the first half of the 1990s.

More recently they brought reformers back into power and seem at last to grasp the importance of clear goals and disciplined change. By the early twenty-first century, Hungary was viewed as one of the more successful of the newly independent European states. The country squandered some of its twenty-year head start with its gradualist approach to transition in the years right after independence. However, our judgment is that in the long run the Hungarians will become much like Western European states. Still, their situation is precarious enough that they could delay that process for a generation by allowing old ways to dominate reforming zeal.

Russia is almost a world in itself. It was the seat of the Soviet empire, one of two great world powers, and adjusting to its reduced circumstances in the twenty-first century is difficult for policy-makers and for citizens. The fundamental circumstance that has militated against economic growth is that Russia in the late twentieth century had none of the characteristics of a society able to nurture and to adapt to markets. A market system cannot flourish in an environment lacking respect for property rights. Sufficient social infrastructure must be in place – civil, commercial and criminal legal codes, a reliable judiciary, clearly defined property rights, defensible contracts – for accumulation and unfettered competition to promote efficiency, for voluntary transactions to determine prices, for resources to move to their best uses, for the economic pie to grow.

Western states modernized through the Age of Reason, through the Enlightenment, through social experiences that the Russian people missed altogether. Russians had never known democracy in all of their history. Remarkably, they have made great strides in adopting it in the last decade. They knew nothing of markets as an organizing economic principle. Russia was not as rich as the West, but the state took formal responsibility for providing housing, jobs, health care and education. The citizenry had no experience of taking the risks inherent in a private market system. They relied on the government for everything, and they blamed the government whenever anything went wrong. They acquired a weakness and tolerance of mediocrity born of dependency. The world of competition, freedom and risk is a frightening one to those not accustomed to it.

We believe that Russia will eventually create some version of a market economy, but it could take a very long time and meanwhile political freedom is problematic. Central authorities still challenge freedom of the press to criticize the regime. Economic performance since the collapse of the USSR has been irregular, as has the official commitment to reforms. The government does not seem to have firm control of its spending or firm control of the money supply. Many production units are huge singular plants, virtually villages, which are difficult to convert. Some are transforming into full-service local social welfare centers that even manage local quasi-currencies.

Since Yeltsin, the government continues to concentrate more political power in the hands of the President. It would be a mistake, however, to lose patience with its halting progress. Reformers still need support and encouragement from the West. Of course Russians will have to sort out their own problems in their own way; young, well-educated Russians are up to the challenge, but neither the economic nor the political structure is well equipped to move such people into positions of influence. We suspect that flexible, farsighted individuals will find their way into positions of influence in the private sector and in the civil service. The old guard continues to hold on to power in the central government. We see hope for change in the very long run if, in the meantime, the leaders can control their authoritarian tendencies and can avoid disasters such as debilitating currency crises, expensive civil wars, social unrest and political disintegration.

The Slovaks experienced impressive economic development while still a part of Czechoslovakia and while under the control of the Soviets. That development was driven by the establishment of large plants producing mostly military hardware. The Soviets enforced a kind of pro-rural affirmative action program; as a result, the previously rural Slovaks caught up with the traditionally richer Czechs by most economic and social measures. If the Slovaks had a golden era, it was created by the Soviets. However, with the Velvet

Divorce, the Slovaks found themselves with few small and medium-sized enterprises or service firms. The anti-reformist leadership of Prime Minister Vladimir Meciar significantly slowed their transformation. His commitment to the idea of economic liberalization was weak and many foreign investors were repelled by the arbitrary nature of his governance. The Slovaks kept him on in part because he was seen as a tough leader, and older Slovaks were dependent on strong central authority in the same way as were older Russians. Meciar was also nationalistic, another popular characteristic, and was in fact more interested in establishing the Slovak Republic as a legitimate political entity than in transforming the economy.

When in 1998 the voters finally changed the government, Slovaks got a new Prime Minister with a genuine commitment to liberalization. Policy-makers became more clearly focused on the economy. They have achieved a degree of macroeconomic stability but potential spending demands endanger that stability. The austerity measures that helped reduce deficits also contributed to a high and rising level of unemployment. Unrest may well follow. Meciar is waiting in the wings for another shot at leadership. His successor, Mikulas Dzurinda, has done a great deal toward getting the country back on track. Experience tells us, however, that the costs of economic reform are often too high for voters to bear, and so effective reformers are soon out of office. Slovakia has improved the strength of its economy greatly in the last few years, but it will take little to reverse the gains. Slovakia's economic fate depends upon her voters. Meciar, or someone like him, could easily appeal to a population trying to deal with unemployment in excess of 16 percent.

Of these six countries, Russia is clearly the weakest and most troubled economically. Bulgaria is in better shape but still far weaker than the other four. Slovakia, while performing well now, is in a precarious position politically. Hungary is a front-runner in the race toward EU accession; perhaps its long head start at transformation is at last paying off. The Czech Republic and Estonia have recovered politically from Soviet domination and are progressing toward stable capitalist systems. The Czech Republic, Estonia and Hungary can count on strong inward flows of foreign direct investment.

Our most important point is that for all of the countries real investment in physical capital is crucial to long-term growth. Unfortunately domestic private sector investment is in short supply throughout Central and Eastern Europe. A part of the problem is weak financial systems. Stock exchanges are small and underdeveloped. Many banks still carry far too much bad debt. The reliability of public administration needs upgrading everywhere, as does the judiciary. Environmental degradation, a Soviet legacy, will be expensive to clean up and impedes economic transformation. Fiscally sound budgets mean hard times for pensioners and others heavily dependent upon transfer payments. We emphasize economic growth because successful growth will make all these problems easier to bear.

All our countries can eventually achieve Western standards of living, and they all are in the process of constructing economic systems meant to get them there. Some of them are in danger of slowing their progress and limiting their potential achievements by opting for an expensive form of welfare capitalism. Efforts to emulate Nordic social support systems will, we believe, mean slower growth and a smaller economic pie. The countries willing to resist populist pressures and to press on with market reforms will grow faster and become richer, allowing them the luxury of considering redistributive programs when they can afford to do so without seriously harming growth.

In our view, the Czech Republic and Estonia are most likely to be successful Western-style capitalists in the medium and the long term. Hungary clearly can be, but will have to stay focused on reforms and a more widely accepted objective of genuine market capitalism, with a strong and independent private sector that drives the economy. The Dzurinda government in Slovakia has demonstrated real determination to transform the economic system, but the political situation is fragile and reversals can be expected; commitment to capitalism is limited among voters. The economy has become stronger, and reformers have shown that they know what is required to establish a viable market system. Unfortunately, a lot of Slovaks still want to be taken care of by a strong, centralized welfare state.

Bulgarians are even less certain about their direction than are the Slovaks, and they are burdened with a weaker economy. A significant minority of older Bulgarians still prefers socialism to capitalism; the voting public wants a better standard of living and persistently throws out any government that does not deliver it. A vision of progress by means of economic liberalization is confined to a group of reformers who have not yet been able to educate the general public about either goals or what it takes to achieve them. The Bulgarian public is not sufficiently unified in its objectives, nor do the people appear patient enough to persist with reforms.

The prognosis for the Russians is the least optimistic. The necessary social infrastructure (rule of law, protection of property rights, trustworthy exchange) required to support a market economy is simply not in place. Russia's physical infrastructure is in terrible shape and the monopolized nature of Soviet production makes effective economic liberalization politically problematic. An aura of political instability, or at least of uncertainty with respect to how authorities behave, keeps foreign investors away. Financial capital is scarce for both private and public sectors. While elections seem to be free and fair, the President apparently still has unlimited power. Privatization and price liberalization have been reasonably successful, but macroeconomic stabilization and microeconomic restructuring less so. Russia can eventually establish a viable market-based economic system, but development of the requisite social and political institutions that must coexist with capitalism may take generations. Politicians and voters have not been clear about the direction of the economy nor have they been persistent in their implementation of reforms. The Duma fluctuates between a communist and a moderate agenda. Private sector allocation decisions reflect an uneasy blend of disinterested markets and Mafia enforcement.

We are cautiously optimistic about the outlook for our six countries, more optimistic about some and more cautious about others. They can all achieve Western standards of living, but they are traveling a long and winding road. We wish them Godspeed.

PART III

Appendices

Introduction to Part III

The appendices contain detailed analysis of reforms in the context of growth models and an econometric application of the political-economy model to data from ten years of experience in six countries. To the extent that this book contains assertions that are problematic or controversial, these appendices constitute our technical defense.

Appendix A develops the growth models explained in the text, but in greater mathematical and technical detail. We formally incorporate each of the five basic reforms into the growth framework to show specifically how each reform promotes economic growth. Each reform is shown to operate on economic outcomes through a specific set of behavior channels. The result is a model that can be used to anticipate responses to reforms by different social groups.

Appendix B presents the technical analysis that underlies Chapter 6 wherein politics and economics are shown to interact. Political candidates propose economic reforms and use campaigns to try to sell their programs to the public. The voters assess the potential effects of alternative reform proposals relative to current rules that govern the economy. They assess the consequences for their personal prospects of each proposal based on the behavioral channels through which reforms operate. Each person votes according to her personal analysis of the implications for her personal prospects of each candidate's proposed regime. Appendix B employs the model to test empirically the connections between reform proposals, election results and economic performance.

The results of various hypothesis tests are reported. We find, for example, that voting for politicians who favor liberalization does in fact lead to reforms being implemented, whereas voting for former communists or socialists tends to retard or even set back reform efforts. We also find that reforms have not greatly improved economic performance. This was especially true in the early 1990s. Some countries' voters have been more willing to support reform programs than others. In Russia under Yeltsin, for instance, reform progress was very sensitive to elections for members of the Duma.

Appendix A. Reforms in growth models

Western economists have identified five generic economic reforms that it is necessary for former socialist states to adopt in order to transform their economies into private market economic systems.[1] Table A.1 lists these reforms. Much of the research on transition economies has dealt with various aspects of these five reforms,[2] with most of the emphasis on fiscal and monetary policies, exchange rate regimes and other monetary and financial issues.[3] Researchers have also focused on privatization methods adopted in different countries that have had significantly varying degrees of success.[4] Industry deregulation is often referred to in transition research as "restructuring."[5] It means how the economies disentangle centralized organization and disengage central power from more microeconomic economic decision-making processes. Our focus here is on long-term consequences of reforms for the real economy rather than on financial issues.[6]

Table A.1 Five generic economic reforms

1	Price liberalization
2	Property privatization
3	Macroeconomic stabilization
4	International trade liberalization
5	Industry deregulation/restructuring

Part of the reason that different countries have adopted reforms in varying degrees is that there has been considerable variance in the virulence of political resistance. In some countries voters through democratic processes have at times ejected reform governments in favor of parties of former communists.[7] In others, resistance has taken the form of subversion by insiders and of corruption and violence.[8] But what can explain the variance in the pace of reform and economic performance among countries? More importantly, does reform imply better performance?

We pose some specific questions: (1) Can we explain why some countries adopt reforms faster and more completely than others? (2) Can we show why these reforms matter – what exactly do they accomplish? (3) Do reforms actually lead to higher living standards? (4) As these countries evolve simultaneously toward democracy and markets, how do political choices about reforms interact with voting behavior?

To answer these types of questions we develop a set of models that links improvements in consumer well-being to reforms. We then tie voting behavior to prospects for improved well-being. Next we establish dual-direction linkages between economic performance and the politics of reforms. Elections are central to the linkage. We begin the process by linking the five generic economic reforms to models of economic growth. We subsequently link the reform and growth framework to voting behavior. We then design an econometric model and test the models with evidence from six countries.

Here we begin with a simple corn economy that at each moment in time produces one homogeneous output (corn) Y_t with two inputs, labor N_t and capital (corn) K_t. Capital depreciates (corn rots) at constant rate δ.[9] Harrod-neutral technological change, A_t, falls to earth like manna from heaven[10] at the fixed exogenous rate γ. We assume formation of human capital occurs at a constant geometric rate that depends on two parameters: the proportion of time spent in education or skill development, φ, and on the "efficiency" of education, μ, as measured by its impact on labor productivity.[11] Output may either be consumed (eaten), C_t, or saved and invested (as seed corn) for additions to the stock of capital (corn plants), I_t.

We assume that private individuals acting in a competitive environment make all production and consumption decisions. In section 1, we develop this growth model in three stages. First, we develop a Solow production function with the above features and derive the solution system with exogenously determined savings at rate s. Second, we develop consumer behavior; and third, we develop producer behavior. We show how price liberalization and property privatization operate directly through parameters of this model.

In section 2 we introduce a government's budget, beginning with a balanced budget model. Revenues derive from head taxes X_t. Government expenditures contain two items: defense spending (corn given to potential enemies as bribes for good behavior), G_t, and transfer payments (corn simply reallocated among persons), Q_t. Net head taxes are $T_t \equiv X_t - Q_t$. We next allow a richer fiscal policy, taxes on capital income at rate z. We allude briefly to deficit spending. Government in the model provides new parameters through which macroeconomic stabilization and industry deregulation (restructuring) influence living standards.

In section 3, we introduce endogenous technological change.[12] This allows us to model the causes of technological change, A_t. Endogenous technological change models either assume that new capital spawns externalities or assume that scale economies characterize new technology. Assuming scale economies, a non-competitive (possibly patent-protected) sector uses labor input as researchers to produce new "ideas" or "designs" or, in the corn economy, genetically improved strains of corn. Thus, the rate of technological change will depend on three parameters: the rate of discovery, θ; the effect of existing knowledge A on the discovery rate, ϕ; and the elasticity of discoveries by researchers, ε.

In section 4 we open the economy so that trade can transfer technology from advanced societies, where it is most likely to occur, to transition economies. We assume technology is transferred through trade at rate κ to transition economies. This model provides a channel for free trade reform to influence living standards in transition.

1. THE CORN ECONOMY

From growth models one can determine paths over time for the flows of income, consumption expenditures, saving and the rate of capital accumulation. The steady-state conditions will be shown to depend upon the values of certain parameters: initial conditions, consumer tastes, the technology of production, savings rates, population growth, capital replacement rates and relative costs of capital and labor inputs.

Growth models traditionally are employed in cross-country studies in two ways. First, the models explain why different economies have different steady states. We show how reforms improve the steady state by altering specific steady-state conditions. Second, "transition dynamics" are used to explore the evolution of a transition economy toward a new reform-induced steady state. We suggest a third application of growth models, as inputs into the decision-making process of voters in elections.[13] We use the model to predict how people will vote when offered choices between various degrees of reform by different political parties or candidates in an election.

Specifically, we assume that each citizen views herself as the representative consumer in a growth model. She plugs the effects of each choice (implicitly or explicitly associated with each candidate or party) into her growth model, which is defined by the model that reflects her unique characteristics and tastes (which we develop more fully below). She then votes for the candidate whose policies regarding reforms make her better off in the calculus of her optimization problem. This integration of growth and political modeling formalizes the notion that voters act like economic agents: they are forward-looking, self-interested optimizers.

The steady state is determined and described first; then we will see how certain parameter changes cause the steady state to change, leading to a different path or outcome. This model informs how we integrate economic performance, reform measures and political outcome data for subsequent econometric analysis.

Production

Let Y_t, K_t and N_t, be the time t quantities of output, capital and labor respectively. We assume that the labor force grows at the constant rate η:

$$N_t = N_0 e^{\eta t}. \tag{A.1}$$

$N_0 > 0$ is the initial quantity of labor. The labor input is augmented by technological change and evolves over time as a result of the evolution of human capital. Consider technological change. Let A_t be the level of technological change at time t and define $E_t \equiv A_t N_t$. We have assumed the A_t grows at rate γ. Thus, $A_t = A_0 e^{\gamma t}$. Combining this with (A.1), $E_t = A_0 e^{\gamma t} N_0 e^{\eta t}$. E_t is the quantity of labor input at time t measured in efficiency units.[14] Now consider development of human capital. Let $H_t \equiv e^{\varphi\mu} E_t$, where φ is time spent in skill development and education and μ is the impact of this learning on labor productivity. Notice that human capital acquisition does not depend on time *per se*. Combining human capital and efficiency improvements from technology, we have

$$H_t = e^{\varphi\mu} A_0 e^{\gamma t} N_0 e^{\eta t}. \tag{A.2}$$

The Solow aggregate production function in Cobb–Douglas form is[15]

$$Y_t = K_t^{\alpha} H_t^{\beta}. \tag{A.3}$$

We assume that production is increasing in both arguments, and that marginal products are declining.[16] Both α and β are positive, constant and less than one. Taking natural logs and partial derivatives of (A.3) shows that α and β are the respective output elasticities of the inputs. In the corn economy Y_t is either consumed, C_t, or invested, I_t. Given δ, gross investment equals the sum of net new investment (growth in capital at time t) and replacement requirements, δK_t; thus, the growth path of capital obeys the differential equation

$$\dot{K}_t = I_t - \delta K_t \tag{A.4}$$

where $\dot{K}_t \equiv dK_t / dt$. If we assume constant returns to scale, then $\alpha + \beta = 1$, and if $y_{ht} \equiv Y_t / H_t$ and $k_{ht} \equiv K_t / H_t$, equation (A.3) may be rewritten as

$$y_{ht} = k_{ht}^{\alpha} \tag{A.3$'$}$$

Taking natural log derivatives of the definition of k_{ht} we have $\dot{k}_{ht} / k_{nt} = \dot{K}_t / K_t - \dot{H}_t / H_t$. Under constant returns to scale with constant growth of labor, the choice variable is the level of capital per H_t, k_{ht}. All the analysis is now done only in terms of equation (A.3′), that is, in units of output per worker measured in efficiency units of an effective human. Efficiency of an effective human allows both for technological change at rate γ and for evolution of human capital at rate $\varphi\mu$. Once the quantities of capital and output per efficiency unit of an effective human are determined, these same ratios will hold for all scale levels. Using the time path of capital, equation (A.4), we have

$$\dot{k}_{ht} = i_{ht} - (\gamma + \eta + \delta) k_{ht} \tag{A.5}$$

where $i_{ht} \equiv I_t / H_t$. If consumption is proportional to income (output) with marginal propensity to save of s,[17] then

$$\dot{k}_{ht} = s k_{ht}^{\alpha} - (\gamma + \eta + \delta) k_{ht}. \tag{A.5$'$}$$

Figure A.1 illustrates the situation. The top curve depicts equation (A.3′): output per efficiency unit of an effective human increases with capital per efficiency unit of an effective human at a declining rate (positive diminishing marginal product). The lower curve is the fraction of output per efficiency unit of an effective human not consumed, sy_{ht}, and thus invested, $sy_{ht} = i_{ht}$.

The ray from the origin is the sum of the growth rate of labor-augmenting technological change, labor growth rate and replacement requirements, $(\gamma + \eta + \delta)k_{ht}$. Consider points k_{h1} and k_{h2}. At k_{h1} investment exceeds the sum of the growth rate of technology, population and the rate of replacement requirements. At k_{h1}, then, K / H is increasing (the economy is in disequilibrium); it is moving toward k_h^* from the left. At k_{h2}, the rate of capital formation is less than capital replacement plus population growth plus technological change so that capital per efficiency unit of an effective human is falling – the economy is moving toward k_h^* from the right. Only at k_h^* does gross investment exactly offset the per-efficiency human capital requirements needed to accommodate growth in technology plus population plus capital depreciation, so that capital per efficiency unit of an effective human is constant. Thus, at k_{ht}^* the economy satisfies the steady-state condition that $\dot{k}_{ht} = 0$.

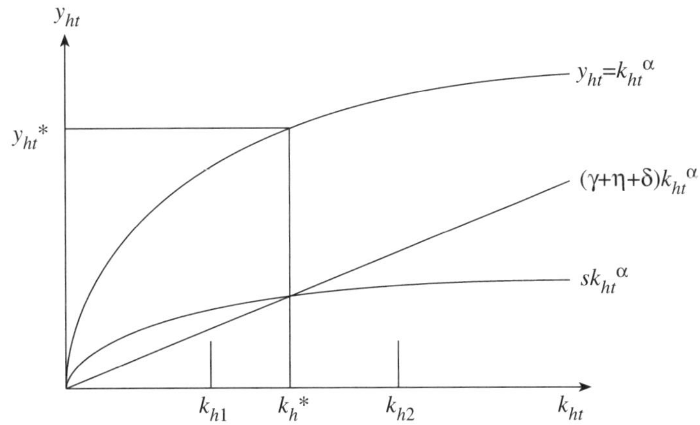

Figure A.1 *The corn economy*

Imposing the steady-state condition, $\dot{k}_{ht} = 0$, on equation (A.5′), the capital–output ratio is

$$k_{ht} / y_{ht} = s/(\gamma + \eta + \delta) \tag{A.6}$$

The capital–output ratio is a constant determined by the savings rate and the rates of technological change, population growth and replacement requirements. In the Cobb–Douglas case, steady-state k and y are

$$k_h^* = [s/(\gamma + \eta + \delta)]^{1/(1-\alpha)} \quad y_h^* = [s/(\gamma + \eta + \delta)]^{\alpha/(1-\alpha)}. \tag{A.6′}$$

This model with a constant savings rate reveals important economic forces that determine different living standards in different countries.[18] If the savings rate (in the sense of the proportion of output devoted to productive capital), s, is high, then living standards will be high. Low savings rates could reflect extreme poverty, or institutions, customs and policies that discourage acquisitiveness. *Ceteris paribus*, rapid population growth, η, or high replacement requirements, δ, imply lower living standards. Rapid population growth could reflect institutions, customs and policies that encourage large families or rapid reproduction rates and longer life spans, and high replacement requirements could reflect shoddy production methods. However, because (A.6′) indicates growth of capital and output per efficiency unit of labor, an increase in the rate of labor-augmenting technological change will cause growth in output per worker. Also, increases in the formation of human capital $e^{\varphi\mu}$ will raise output per worker. Finally, as α, the output elasticity of capital, converges on one, $\alpha \rightarrow 1$, living standards rise for each level of capital per worker.

The Consumer

We now drop the assumption of an exogenous savings rate, and model consumer behavior. Assume the representative consumer is forward-looking, self-interested and infinitely lived.[19]

Utility, u, at each moment in time depends only on consumption at that time, c_{ht}.[20] The present value of the consumer's future stream of utility is the continuous weighted sum of utility received at each moment in the future. Since she is evaluating future utility from today's perspective, she may choose to discount future consumption relative to current consumption. Let ρ be her subjective discount rate.[21] At time zero, utility U_0 is the present value of the discounted sum of the future stream of utility; each future moment's consumption is discounted by subjective rate ρ:

$$U_0 = \int_{t=0}^{t=\infty} u(c_{ht}) e^{-\rho t} dt. \tag{A.7}$$

If ρ is zero, then she does not prefer consumption now relative to consumption in the future.[22] The consumer receives income, y_{ht}, from two sources: labor (measured in efficiency units of effective humans) supplied inelastically earns wage w_t, and the capital stock, k_{ht}, which she owns, yields gross return v_t per unit.[23] The consumer selects the consumption–savings path that maximizes utility, subject to her income stream. She may either consume income or save it; thus income not consumed is saved and, therefore, available for investment, i_{ht}:

$$w_t = v_t k_{ht} = y_{ht} = c_{ht} + s_{ht} = c_{ht} + i_{ht}. \tag{A.8}$$

The sources of income, $w_t + v_t k_{ht}$, equal the uses of income, $c_{ht} + i_{ht}$.

To solve the consumer optimization problem, we augment the time t utility function to allow for the budget constraint. We introduce the budget constraint as imposed by the rate of growth of capital. The augmented optimization function, the Hamiltonian, is[24]

$$H_t = u(c_{ht}) e^{-\rho t} + \lambda_t \{ y_{ht} - [c_{ht} + (\gamma + \eta + \delta) k_{ht}] \}. \tag{A.9}$$

The variable λ_t, the costate variable, is the value at $t = 0$ of a time t increment to capital. The optimum requires that the Hamiltonian satisfy three conditions:[25]

(i) $\partial H / \partial c = 0$
(ii) $\dot{\lambda}_t = -\partial H / \partial k$
(iii) $\lim_{t \to \infty} k_t \lambda_t = 0$

Imposing (i) and (ii) for utility maximization yields the Euler condition:

$$[c_{ht} u'' / u'][\dot{c}_{ht} / c_{ht}] = \rho + \gamma + \delta + \eta - (\partial y_{ht} / \partial k_{ht}). \tag{A.10}$$

The first term in square brackets geometrically represents the degree of curvature of the utility function that reflects the degree of flexibility of consumer tastes in shifting consumption over time. As a consumer's tastes in terms of indifference between consumption over different periods become more rigid, $u'' \to \infty$. Right-angle Leontief indifference curves illustrate the extreme version of this case.[26] As a consumer's tastes become more flexible in terms of preferences for consumption among periods, $u'' \to 0$ and the indifference curves become flatter, approaching linearity.

If we assume the constant elasticity of substitution form for consumption between periods, then $[-u'/cu''] \equiv \sigma$; where σ is the elasticity of intertemporal substitution.[27] In this case, (A.10) becomes

$$\dot{c}_{ht} / c_{ht} = \sigma\{[\partial y_{ht} / \partial k_{ht} - (\eta + \delta)] - [\gamma + \rho]\}. \tag{A.10'}$$

The Euler condition for the steady state suggests an intuitive explanation of the forward-looking consumer's optimal policy behavior.

This rule governs the optimal time path of consumption and depends on four concepts: the intertemporal rate of substitution (flexibility of tastes), σ; the subjective discount rate (degree of patience), ρ; the rate of technological change, γ; and the term in the first set of square brackets on the right-hand side of (A.10′). As with any elasticity concept, σ ranges from zero to infinity. If $\sigma = 0$, then the consumer is unwilling to substitute consumption between periods and $\dot{c}_{ht} = 0$. If $0 < \sigma < 1$, then she has an inelastic rate of substitution between periods – she is reluctant to substitute one period's utility for another – she is comparatively inflexible. If $\sigma = 1$, her intertemporal elasticity is unitary and she will substitute between periods if conditions warrant it. As $u'' \to 0$, $\sigma \to \infty$ and she is becoming more flexible between consumption at different times.

The term in the first set of square brackets on the right-hand side of (A.10′) is the net marginal product of an increment of capital, that is, the net increment is the marginal product of capital minus replacement requirements for depreciation and population growth.[28] For $\sigma \neq 0$, consumption per efficiency unit of an effective human will grow over time when this net marginal product of capital exceeds the sum of ρ, the consumer's rate of time preference, and γ, the rate of technological change. If, however, the net marginal product of capital is less than the rate of time preference plus the rate of technological change, then consumption per efficiency unit of an effective human will be declining over time.

Thus, the savings–consumption choice that determines how much current output the consumer is willing to put aside for capital formation depends on σ, ρ, $\Delta y / \Delta k$, η, δ, and γ. *Ceteris paribus*, flexible consumers (easygoing people with high σ) will be more willing to substitute consumption between periods in order to accommodate capital acquisition. ρ reflects the consumer's degree of impatience; impatient crickets have a large ρ, so that *ceteris paribus* their savings rate is low. Farsighted ants have small ρ, so that *ceteris paribus* they will save more. A large value for η or δ discourages savings, because more of the gross marginal product of capital has to compensate for population growth or for more rapid depreciation. These forces can each reduce the net benefits from sacrificing consumption now.

Assuming that the parameters σ and ρ are fixed when the consumer is optimizing reflects the idea that historical, social, political and economic forces have already determined tastes. These historical forces influence behavior even of forward-looking consumers. This serves as a proof that initial conditions in transition economies will influence growth patterns. It furthermore indicates precisely how initial conditions enter the optimization calculus. This allows us to identify behavior of various different economic agents.

Older, inflexible and impatient consumers and myopic, carefree crickets will have a low value of σ and a high value for ρ. They will resist policies with short-run costs and long-range benefits. Young, flexible consumers and industrious ants with foresight will have large

σ and low ρ and will tolerate current sacrifice for future consumption.[29] Finally, if the marginal product of capital net of population growth and depreciation is large relative to the subjective discount rate, then the person will forgo current consumption for future gains from capital formation. This means that economic efficiency, population growth and the quality of capital goods will also influence the proportion of output devoted to savings and investment. The rate of technological change enhances the growth rate of per-person consumption growth, because $c_t = c_{ht}e^{(\varphi\mu + \gamma t)}$. Thus, c_t grows over time at rate γ faster than c_{ht}.

The Producer

The producer maximizes profits subject to input prices and the constraints of contemporary technology. Given exogenous labor growth η, exogenous evolution of human capital $e^{\varphi\mu}$ and exogenous technological change γ, the choice variable for the producer is the amount of capital per efficiency unit of an effective human, k_{ht}. Once this is determined for a steady state, the marginal product of capital, $\partial y_{ht}/\partial k_{ht}$, will be locked in and we can solve (A.10′) for consumption and saving.

The gross return on one unit of capital, v_t, is the sum of r_t, the net return on capital, and δ, the rate of depreciation.[30] The time path of capital can be derived by employing the fact that $s_{ht} = y_{ht} - c_{ht}$. The growth rate of capital per efficiency unit of an effective human equals income minus the sum of consumption expenditures and the amount of new investment goods needed to accommodate labor-force growth and improvements in worker efficiency (via technological change) and to replace depreciated capital:

$$\dot{k}_{ht} = s_{ht} - (\gamma + \eta + \delta)k_{ht} = y_{ht} - [c_{ht} + (\gamma + \eta + \delta)k_{ht}]. \qquad \text{(A.11)}$$

Equation (A.11) is the time path of capital condition. Consumer behavior is more complicated now so this equation is actually more complex than it may appear. Now consumption and therefore saving depends on utility maximization rather than being determined exogenously.

The producer maximizes the present value of his future profit stream. Profit at time t is output minus current labor and capital costs. Product price is normalized to one. In present value terms, profits are discounted from the future to the present at the net rate of return on capital, r:

$$\Pi_t = \int_{t=0}^{t=\infty} [k_{ht}^{\alpha} - (w_t + v_t k_{ht})]e^{-rt}dt. \qquad \text{(A.12)}$$

The producer selects the quantity of capital that maximizes profit, yielding

$$\partial y_{ht}/\partial k_{ht} = \alpha k_{ht}^{\alpha-1} = v_t = r_t + \delta. \qquad \text{(A.13)}$$

Thus, the producer's optimal decision rule is to set the marginal product of capital equal to the gross user-cost of capital at each moment in time.[31] This condition is called the marginal product of capital condition. Under constant returns to scale, the residual after payments to capital is equal to wage income. Recall that one unit of labor is measured by an efficiency unit of an effective human:

$$w_t = (1 - \alpha)k_{ht}^{\alpha}.$$

At the steady state, both inputs are paid the value of their marginal product; and under constant returns to scale, final product is exhausted by these payments.[32] The consumer's income is

$$y_{ht} = w_t + vk_{ht}.$$

This completes our derivation of the three steady-state conditions:[33] The Euler condition for optimal consumption (A.10), the time path of capital (A.11) and the marginal product of capital (A.13). The conditions depend upon the parameters σ, ρ, δ, η, γ, α, and on factor prices w and r.

The Modified Golden Rule

We can solve the steady state for the per-worker values of capital, output, consumption and utility. Let y^*, c^*, k^* and u^* be steady-state values for per-worker income, consumption, capital and utility. We begin with the Euler condition, (A.10′). At the steady state $\dot{c}_t = 0$, so that

$$y_k \equiv \partial y_{ht}/\partial k_{ht} = \alpha k_{ht}^{\alpha-1} = \alpha y_h^*/k_h^* = \rho + \gamma + \eta + \delta \quad \text{for } \sigma > 0. \qquad \text{(A.14)}$$

The steady-state marginal product of capital equals the sum of four terms: the subjective discount rate, the rate of technological change, the growth rate of labor and the rate of replacement. The capital–output ratio under constant returns Cobb–Douglas technology is the constant $\alpha/(\rho + \gamma + \eta + \delta)$. The firm hires capital up to the point at which the marginal product equals the gross cost of capital, v. Thus, from equation (A.14), $r + \delta = \rho + \gamma + \eta + \delta$. The net rate of return on capital, r, in the steady state is determined by the sum of the rate of time preference, ρ, the rate of technological change, γ, and the rate of labor-force growth, η.

The marginal product condition for capital (A.14) may be solved for the quantity of capital at the steady state, k_h^*.[34] The optimization problem brings ρ into the solution system. Higher discount rates usually lead to smaller steady-state capital stocks, because $\rho > 0$ indicates that consumers are less willing to sacrifice current consumption for accumulation and capital formation. In the Cobb–Douglas case,

$$\begin{aligned} k_h^* &= [\alpha/(\rho + \gamma + \eta + \delta)]^{1/1-\alpha} \\ y_h^* &= k_h^{*\alpha} \\ c_h^* &= y_h^* - (\gamma + \eta + \delta)k_h^* \\ u^* &= u(c_t^*). \end{aligned} \qquad \text{(A.15)}$$

Recall that $y_t = y_{ht}e^{\varphi\mu}A_0e^{\gamma t} = Y_te^{\varphi\mu}A_0e^{(\gamma+\eta)t}$, so that the growth rate of income exceeds the growth rate of income per effective unit of human capital by $\eta + \gamma$. Thus per capita income is growing at the steady state at rate γ. Furthermore, per capita income is increased at the steady state by higher human capital, $e^{\varphi\mu}$. Recall also that $c_t^* = c_{ht}^*e^{\varphi\mu}A_0e^{\gamma t}$ and that $u[c_{ht}^*]$, so that at the steady state when $\dot{c}_{ht} = 0$, consumption per person will be higher by the level of human capital and rising at the rate of technological change, γ. The second equation in (A.15) follows directly from the production function, $y_h = k_h^{\alpha}$. In general, the steady-state capital output ratio, k_h^*/y_h^*, will be constant. At the steady state, k_h^* is constant. Thus, from equation (A.11), $i_h^* = (\gamma + \eta + \delta)k_h^*$ and savings equals investment, and so the third equality in (A.15) follows; namely, consumption c_h^* is y_h^* minus $(\gamma + \eta + \delta)k_h^*$. Steady-state utility simply depends on c_{ht}^*, given the functional form of utility.

If we set the derivative of c_{ht}^* with respect to k_h^* to zero, we have the maximum steady-state value of consumption, c_{ht}^m. The consumer maximizes consumption when the marginal product of capital, y_k, equals $\gamma + \delta + \eta$. However, by equation (A.14), the steady-state marginal product of capital equals $\rho + \gamma + \delta + \eta$; thus, socially optimal consumption, c_g, will be less than c_m by ρ. Intuitively, this means that if consumers discount future utility then they will maximize utility at a lower c^*. Condition (A.14) modifies the golden rule, the famous rule for long-run maximization of consumption modified because the steady-state increment of output from capital must cover the subjective discounted rate ρ as well as $\gamma + \eta + \delta$. The marginal product of capital is larger at the modified golden rule if $\rho > 0$, so the modified golden rule levels of capital and income are also less than the maximum values: $(c_g, k_g, y_g) < (c_m, k_m, y_m)$ where mg represents the modified golden rule and m the maximum consumption levels.[35]

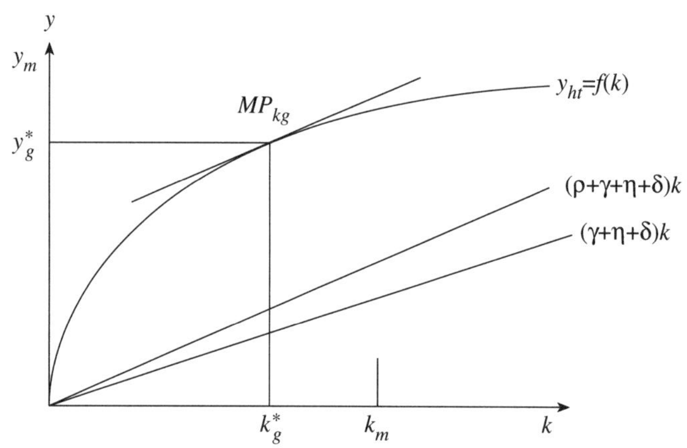

Figure A.2 The modified golden rule with $\rho > \gamma$

Figure A.2 illustrates the modified golden rule. The steady state occurs where the slope of the ray $\rho + \gamma + \eta + \delta$ is the same as the slope of the tangent to the production function. This point determines k^* and y^*. For $\rho > 0$, this ray is steeper than the replacement requirements for capital per efficiency unit of an effective human. This result in turn implies that k_g^* is lower than it would be in the case of the golden rule. Large discount rates mean that crickets are unwilling to sacrifice current consumption for capital accumulation and higher c_g^* at the steady state.

Reforms 1 and 2: Price Liberalization and Property Privatization

With this model we can show how three of the generic economic reforms influence the long-run growth path. First, price liberalization essentially replaces a system of administered prices with a system in which prices are market-determined. Thus prices now reflect consumer sovereignty. This means in turn that the mix of consumer goods will improve from the point of view of the consumer. Econometric interpretation of the formal model requires that the consumer good, c_t, be represented by an index of consumer goods. Thus, we model price liberalization as an increase in utility associated with each level of consumption:

$$U(c_t) > u(c_t) \quad \forall c_t$$

where U is the new, post-price liberalization utility function.[36] Price liberalization also applies to the prices of factor inputs so that the rate of return on capital, r, will rise too. One would also expect proper relative capital prices to lead to a lower depreciation rate δ in that those paying the appropriate price for capital would acquire less shoddy capital.

Second, property privatization also influences the steady state. The essence of property privatization is to foster improved production methods by creating private individuals as residual claimants of profits.[37] This reform has several important consequences for the steady state as represented by the solutions in equation (A.15). Private property owners are likely to develop better production methods. In our model this means an improvement in $f(k_{ht})$. This could be viewed as an upward shift in the production curve in Figure A.2. This is like a one-shot increase in Hicks-neutral technological change:

$$y_{ht} = a_t f(k_{ht})$$

where a_t is growing at an exponential rate and represents the shift that results from a Hicks-neutral technological change shock. Since the production process itself may improve, we represent the new, post-property privatization production technology as $\mathbf{f}$, assuming $\mathbf{f}(k_{ht}) > f(k_{ht})$ for all k_{ht}. In the model with Harrod-neutral technological change developed above, privatization has a sustained effect by increasing the rate of technological change, γ. Since property privatization improves production, it also reduces the rate of depreciation: $\boldsymbol{\delta} < \delta$, where $\boldsymbol{\delta}$ is the new depreciation rate. In terms of Figure A.2, slower depreciation means lower replacement requirements which rotates the rays from the origin downward, thus raising the steady-state capital–income pair.

Third, property privatization, by creating private residual claimants, will foster acquisitive behavior. More acquisitive people are *ceteris paribus* more thrifty. Thus, ρ should be reduced and steady-state savings s^* increased:

$$\boldsymbol{\rho} < \rho, \mathbf{s}^* > s^*.$$

The model with a specific functional form provides more insight into the growth consequences of property privatization. The utility function enters into the steady state in this model through two symbols, ρ and σ. As noted above, property privatization is likely to lower ρ because residual claimants have better foresight. Private property owners are likely to be more flexible and more involved in their economic choices as well, so we would expect σ to rise.

The human capital aspects of the models provide two new channels through which property privatization can raise the steady state. By fostering acquisitiveness, private property also encourages human capital acquisition via more education (φ rises) and via the transmission of this improved knowledge to production (μ rises). We turn now to vehicles through which macroeconomic stabilization reforms can enhance growth.

2. THE PUBLIC FISC AND PRIVATE BUDGETS

Assume the government spends amount G_t on goods and services. The government also spends Q_t on transfer payments such as retirement benefits, welfare payments, veterans' benefits and other social spending. These outlays are financed in part by either direct taxes on the consumer, X_t, or taxes on capital income, v_tK_t, at rate z. We can simplify the derivations by defining all government budget magnitudes in the same units as output, capital and consumption; namely, amounts per efficiency unit of effective human capital. Defining $g_t \equiv G_t / N_t$ and $g_{ht} \equiv G_t / H_t$, recall the definition of H as

$$H_t \equiv e^{\varphi\mu} A_t N_t \tag{A.16}$$

Therefore, $g^t = g_{ht} e^{\varphi\mu} A_t$ and $\dot{g}_t / g_t = \dot{g}_{ht} / g_{ht} + \gamma$.

These results show that growth of government spending per capita will exceed growth of government spending per efficiency unit of effective human capital by the rate of technological change γ. These formulations illustrate the point that once we solve the system in H units, we can employ (A.16) to solve for per capita values.

Defining net taxes to be head taxes net of transfers, $\tau_{ht} \equiv x_{ht} - q_{ht}$, then a balanced budget policy implies that $g_{ht} = \tau_{ht} + zv_tk_{ht}$. If $g_{ht} > \tau_{ht} + zvk_{ht}$, then the government issues bonds, $\dot{b}_{ht}$. The public, indifferent between holding bonds and capital, purchases the bonds. The government must pay the competitive bond rate r the same net rate of return as capital. Table A.2 summarizes the growth model with human capital, exogenous technological change and a government budget.

Consequences of Fiscal Policy

Fiscal policies affect the private sector through the consumer's budget constraint and the producer's cost of capital. The after-tax cost of capital becomes $(1 - z)v_t = r + \delta$. This means that the productivity of the private capital stock must not only cover a return to the owner of capital, but also the proportion of tax revenues paid out of capital income.

Recall that the consumer's income derives from her ownership of the means of production as well as from her wage income. Her budget constraint is changed in two ways by taxes. First, she must pay τ_{ht} taxes net of transfers (she will be a net recipient if transfers exceed head taxes). Second, her income (say, in the form of dividend income) from capital is based on the after-tax cost of capital.

Table A.2 Growth model assumptions

1. Technology: Labor growth rate η
Production linear homogeneous $\alpha + \beta = 1$
Capital depreciation rate δ
Diminishing marginal product
$\partial y / \partial k = (\alpha - 1)\alpha k_{ht}^{\alpha-2} < 0$
Harrod-neutral technological change rate γ
Human capital from education $e^{\varphi\mu}$
$\Rightarrow$ growth rate rule of capital per human efficiency unit or
$\dot{k}_{ht} = i_{ht} - (\gamma + \eta + \delta)k_{ht}$

2. Producer: rational, self-interested, forward-looking
price taker w, r
pays capital tax rate z
labor (H) supply elasticity = 0
$H_t = e^{\varphi\mu} A_0 e^{\gamma t} N_0 e^{\eta t}$
chooses quantity of capital k_{ht}
maximizes profit
$\Rightarrow$ max PDV of output minus costs or
$\text{Max} \int [k_{ht}^{\alpha} - \{w_t + [(r + \delta)/(1 - z)]k_{ht}\}]e^{-rt}dt$

3. Consumer: rational, self-interested, forward-looking
utility additive over time $U_0 = {}_t\!\int u_t dt$
utility depends on consumption per human $u(c_{ht})$
(efficiency unit of an effective human)
maximizes PDV of utility
owns capital stock k_{ht}

$c_{ht} \equiv C_t / H_t = C_t / e^{\varphi\mu} E_t = c_t / e^{\varphi\mu} A_t e^{\gamma t}$

$\Rightarrow$ max PDV of future utility stream (subject to the budget constraint) or
max $\int U(c_{ht})e^{-\rho t}dt$ subject to $y_{ht} - \tau_{ht} = w_t + (1 - z)v_t k_{ht}$

4. Government: spends on goods and services g_{ht}
transfers payments q_{ht}
collects head taxes x_{ht}
net head taxes are τ_{ht}
taxes capital income rate z
finances deficits by issuing bonds b_t
$\Rightarrow$ sources and uses of GDP
$y_{ht} = c_{ht} + i_{ht} + g_{ht} = c_{ht} + s_{ht} + \tau_{ht} + zvk_{ht}$

Balanced Budget

If the government balances its budget, then $g_{ht} = \tau_{ht} + zv_t k_{ht}$; and $\dot{b}_{ht} = 0$, then $s_{ht} = i_{ht}$, private uses of income (consumption plus investment) equal private sources of income (wage income plus after-tax capital income minus taxes net of transfers):

$$c_{ht} + i_{ht} = w_{ht} + (1 - z)v_t k_{ht} - \tau_{ht}. \tag{A.17}$$

The new time path of capital is

$$\dot{k}_{ht} = y_{ht} - g_{ht} - [c_{ht} + (\gamma + \delta + \eta)k_{ht}]. \tag{A.18}$$

We assume that government expenditures do not alter marginal utility, so the consumer maximizes the same subjectively discounted future utility stream subject to the new budget constraint.[38] The new Hamiltonian is

$$H_t = u(c_t)e^{-\rho t} + \lambda_t\{y_{ht} - g_{ht} - [c_{ht} + (\gamma + \eta + \delta)k_{ht}]\}. \tag{A.19}$$

The tax on capital income alters private market performance. The gross cost of capital, v, now equals $(r + \delta) / (1 - z)$; that is, v is deflated by one minus the marginal tax rate on capital income. Thus, the cost of capital is higher since it has to yield taxes before the producer can earn capital income. Given diminishing marginal product, this implies a smaller equilibrium capital stock. Wage income is the residual from total earnings minus gross income earned by capital. As above, this result follows from constant returns to scale technology. Recall that if each factor is paid the value of its marginal product, then all income is exhausted.[39]

More demands are placed on aggregate income now that the government uses a portion of output. Income, y_{ht}, must now accommodate government spending, g_{ht}, as well as private consumption and investment for replacement, labor-force growth and Harrod-neutral technological change. All of these uses must be accommodated before income can contribute to growth in capital per worker and thus improvements in living standards.

Although we caution interpretation of government in this model,[40] two fiscal policies reduce the steady-state values of consumption and capital, (c^*_{ht}, k^*_{ht}). First, the marginal product of capital is higher because it equals $(\rho + \delta + \eta)/(1 - z\alpha)$. As long as tax rate z is positive, the gross marginal product must be greater and consequently the steady-state quantity of capital, k^*, lower. That is, capital taxes distort the private economy away from capital formation.

Steady-state consumption is

$$c^*_{ht} = y^*_{ht} - [g^*_{ht} + (\gamma + \eta + \delta)k^*_{ht}]. \tag{A.20}$$

Second, the level c^* at each k^* is lower by the size of government – namely its spending level in the sense of its use of GDP. Since k^* itself is lower, output is lower, thus c^* is even smaller. We re-emphasize here that this does not imply that all government spending is bad. In fact from an econometric viewpoint it makes sense to think of infrastructure investment as part of the investment term and of government consumption goods as part of consumption.

Table A.3 Steady-state conditions

1.	The Euler condition $\dot{c}_{ht}/c_{ht} = \sigma[(\rho + \gamma + \delta + \eta) - (1 - z\alpha)y_k]$
2.	The modified golden rule $\partial y_{ht}/\partial k_{ht} \equiv y_k = (\rho + \gamma + \eta + \delta)/(1 - z\alpha)$
3.	The dynamic path of capital $\dot{k}_{ht} = y_{ht} - [g_{ht} + c_{ht} + (\gamma + \eta + \delta)k_{ht}]$
4.	Steady-state consumption $c_h^* = y_h^* - [g_{ht} + (\gamma + \delta + \eta)k_{ht}^*]$

Government in our model consists of expenditures that are no longer necessary in a private market economy. This would include Warsaw Pact military expenditures and subsidies to prop up inefficient state-owned enterprises and so forth. The main point is that government spending has a social cost that must be balanced against potential gains from its expenditures. Table A.3 summarizes the steady-state conditions.

Budget Deficits

In the analysis so far we have only modeled balanced budget policy. The effects of deficit spending in growth models on private sector decisions vary with the specification. In some cases deficits have no effects beyond those associated with the level of government activity itself. This is because in order to guarantee stability, constraints must be imposed on borrowing over the long term. This means that deficits are eventually cancelled out by surpluses – which means that the choice of taxing in the current period or running deficits has no effect on output – a case of Ricardian Equivalence.[41]

If arbitrary constraints were not imposed on long-term government borrowing, then governments would be able to postpone taxing to finance past deficits indefinitely, creating a Ponzi scheme outcome. Clearly such Ponzi schemes may well explain the behavior of state enterprise and financial officers in the endgame preceding the collapse of the Soviet system.

Reforms 3 and 4: Macroeconomic Stabilization and Industrial Restructuring

We can now link two additional reforms to growth. First, consider macroeconomic stabilization. If reform consists of shrinking wasteful government spending, then we model this by a reduction in g. A lower value for g implies more private consumption at each steady-state level of income. In the context of Central Europe, this reform reflects reductions in two types of government spending: Warsaw Pact spending on the military, and inefficient subsidies for state-owned enterprises that could be better run by private owners.

Centralized governments had also established enormous systems of transfers creating various classes of wards of the state such as veterans, retired workers, ill citizens and so on. Recall that transfers in the model are just negative head taxes, $q = -x$. From a modeling perspective, reducing q has the effect of reducing taxes on some people and reducing benefits for others. While harmless in the aggregate model, this is an important result for each individual, because it suggests why some persons would endorse such a reform and some would not. This ambiguity reflects the ubiquitous welfare state debate over entitlements.

The government model includes a tax on capital income at rate z that distorts the economy away from capital formation and growth. In the model, this means that the after-tax earnings by the private sector fall and less capital is accumulated. We use this parameter as the one through which industry restructuring (deregulation) operates on the steady state. In many transition economies, nominal privatization has been easier than reducing burdensome government regulations on industry. Wage controls, restrictive hiring and firing practices, and confusing tax rules may combine with inadequate enforcement institutions for private property rights to impede effective privatization. Thus, reducing inefficient government regulations on private enterprise acts like an increase in the after-tax rate of return on capital. Less regulation lowers z, the effective "tax and regulatory" burden imposed by government.

3. ENDOGENOUS TECHNOLOGICAL CHANGE AND TECHNOLOGY TRANSFER

The endogenous technological change model builds on the Harrod-neutral technological change with human capital model developed in section 1. Endogenous models are based on several key insights. The first is that new technologies, rather than falling like manna from heaven, may be costly to produce; that is, the development of new technology requires inputs that cannot be used to produce corn. Suppose a share of the labor force produces new " ideas," so that

$$N_t = N_{yt} + N_{At} \text{ and } s_A \equiv N_A / N_, \tag{A.21}$$

where N_{yt} is labor-producing final product (corn), and where N_{At} is labor that is producing research (or ideas). The second insight is that ideas have unique characteristics that force us to treat them as public goods – they are non-rivalrous and non-excludable. Once a new idea is discovered additional people can consume it without cost, and these additional users cannot be easily excluded from consumption of the idea once it is discovered. Put together this means that we assume that new ideas have initial setup costs in discovery, but are then free to reproduce and easy to disseminate. These features mean that technology of production in the ideas-producing sector is characterized by increasing returns to scale.[42] Increasing returns requires a non-competitive sector in order to achieve efficient allocation of new ideas. We will assume that government issues patents to researchers who discover new varieties of seed corn.

Assume that new varieties add to the supply of capital available for production. Suppose the stock of capital is the sum of A types of seed corn, so that

$$K = \sum_{j=1}^{j=A} x_j \tag{A.22}$$

This formulation is awkward because the quantity of capital simply grows as new technology is brought on line.[43] Because research is non-competitive, we need to model the demand side for new varieties of corn. Suppose we let the demand for each variety be the same, then $K = xA$. Under these assumptions the derivation of the steady state can be easily produced.

If we start with the human capital production function, then

$$Y_t = F(K_t, H_t) = K_t^{\alpha}(e^{\varphi\mu}A_tN_t)^{1-\alpha} = A_t(K_t / A_t)^{\alpha}(e^{\varphi\mu}N_t)^{1-\alpha} = A_t x^{\alpha}(e^{\varphi\mu}N_t)^{1-\alpha}. \quad \text{(A.23)}$$

The human capital model is the same form as this model, because

$$Ax^{a} = \sum_{j=1}^{j=A} x_j^{\alpha}$$

The advantage of endogenous over exogenous models is that one can model the causes of A_t. Recall that $H_t \equiv e^{\varphi\mu}A_tN_t$; human capital is the number of effective units of human capital measured in efficiency units. We maintain the assumption that $e^{\varphi\mu}$ reflects additions to effective human capital from education and training, and we maintain the assumption of constant geometric growth of labor η.

Before we model A_t we show that the solution system for final product is of the same form as the Solow model with exogenous technological change and human capital. Now, however, we require a fraction of the labor force to be tied up in research. Only a fraction of workers are engaged in production of final product, corn; and thus, we define the proportion of workers in the competitive final output sector in efficiency units of effective human capital:

$$H_{yt} \equiv e^{\varphi\mu}A_tN_t = e^{\varphi\mu}A_t(1 - s_A)N_t. \quad \text{(A.24)}$$

From the point of view of modeling production in the final goods sector, the setup is exactly the same as the previous model, except that we will measure output and capital in efficiency units of effective human capital working in the final product sector. Defining $y_{\tau t} \equiv Y_t / H_{yt}$ and $k_{\tau t} \equiv K_t / H_{\tau t}$, the new solution system with constant savings rate is

$$k_{\tau t}^{*} = [s / (\gamma + \eta + \delta)]^{1/(1-a)} \text{ and } y_{\tau t}^{*} = k_{\tau t}^{*\alpha} \quad \text{(A.25)}$$
$$y_t^{*} = y_{\tau t}^{*}e^{\varphi\mu}(1 - s_A)A_t.$$

We now model technological change. This research originates with Romer (1986). Much of this modeling has been controversial, because some of these models suggest some rapid growth of output at the steady state resulting from increments of the labor force doing research. Jones develops a model that includes Romer's insights but avoids some of the problematic conclusions. The rate of change of new technology depends on two variables: the number of workers in the research sector, N_A, and the existing stock of technology (that is, the number of ideas already discovered or simply the state of knowledge), A_t:

$$\dot{A}_t = \theta A^{\phi}N^{\varepsilon} \quad \text{(A.26)}$$

θA^{ϕ} is the rate of discovery with ϕ representing the effect on the rate of discovery of the state of knowledge; ε is the researcher elasticity of discoveries. Jones discusses these parameters for advanced societies in which new research and development is taking place. He argues that $0 < \varepsilon < 1$, where values less than one mean that researchers are less productive at the margin.

Values of ϕ depend upon one's view of the implications for research of existing knowledge. Romer had implicitly assumed $\phi = 1$. A case can be made for $\phi < 0$ – the early researcher fishes out the biggest ideas first and only smaller ones remain to be discovered later. If $\phi > 0$, then the idea is that today's researchers "stand on the shoulders of giants." Today's researchers produce more varieties per unit of labor input than their predecessors did, because their predecessors did the groundwork. If $\phi < 1$, we can divide (A.26) by A_t, so that the left-hand side is the growth rate of discoveries. If discoveries occur at the constant geometric rate γ, then the left-hand side of (A.26) over A is the constant rate γ, and we have

$$\dot{A}_t / A_t = \theta A^{\phi-1} N^{\varepsilon} = \gamma. \tag{A.26$'$}$$

Taking natural log derivatives of (A.26′), we have

$$0 = \varepsilon(\dot{N}_t / N_t) - (1 - \phi)\, (\dot{A}_t / A_t) = \varepsilon\eta - (1 - \phi)\gamma.$$

The rate of technological change, should it reach a constant rate, is

$$\gamma = \varepsilon\eta / (1 - \phi). \tag{A.27}$$

Thus, the rate of technical change, in this model, depends on the growth of the labor force, η (assuming a fixed proportion do research), the effect on the discovery rate of new researchers, ε, and the effect on discoveries of the state of knowledge, ϕ.

We can also solve (A.26′) for A_t:

$$A_t = \theta [s_A N_t]^{\varepsilon} A_t^{\phi} / \gamma. \tag{A.28}$$

Replacing A_t in the (A.25) solution for the steady-state income per person (living standards) with (A.28) yields

$$y_t^* = y_{\tau t}^* [e^{\varphi\mu}(1 - s_A)] \{\theta [s_A N_t]^{\varepsilon} A_t^{\phi} / \gamma\}. \tag{A.25$'$}$$

Equation (A.25′) tells us that steady-state per capita growth (which is, in effect, living standards) reflects three types of forces. First, $y_{\tau t}^*$, from equation (A.25), says that higher savings rates will mean a higher level of income, but rapid population growth and shoddy construction will vitiate this effect. We have been developing these forces throughout the modeling process; a high rate of accumulation of quality capital relative to population growth implies higher living standards. The development of consumer behavior in equation (A.10′) introduced ρ and σ, two parameters through which reforms that benefit consumers are channeled.

The second set of forces in equation (A.25′) involves the level of human capital in the society that is working in the final product sector, $e^{\varphi\mu}(1 - S_A)$. This includes education and skill development and the implementation of that education on producing output. The third set of forces, $\theta[s_A N_t]^\varepsilon A_t^\phi / \gamma$, reflects the underlying causes of technological change. In this model, the level of technology depends on the proportion of workers involved in research, $[s_A N_t]^\varepsilon$, and the extent to which incremental researchers influence the discovery rate. The growth rate of technology rises with both N and A; however, their effects depend upon unknown parameters, θ and φ. These parameters reflect the nature of thc research process, the evolution of discovery, and its effective impact on output.

In order to illustrate the model's contribution to understanding growth in transition economies, we now model how technology may be transferred to transition economies from the advanced countries like Germany, the US and Japan.

4. TECHNOLOGY TRANSFER

We attribute pure technological change to advanced societies only and treat the growth rate of technology in these advanced countries as exogenous to emerging economies. We begin with the model in which magnitudes were measured in efficiency units of labor, but we replace A_t with L_t, which represents the learning level of workers in transition economies in adopting new technologies. Thus, we define $E_t = L_t N_t$, so the production function is

$$Y_t = F(K_t, E_t) = K_t^\alpha (E_t)^{1-\alpha} = L_t (K_t / L_t)^\alpha (N_t)^{1-\alpha}. \tag{A.29}$$

We now define the stock of capital for a transition economy as the sum of the number of strains of technologically different corn that can be used in production by the workers in this economy. The equation for the stock of capital will be similar to (A.22). The number of strains will depend upon how much the workers have learned, L, up to the level of the most advanced world technology from industrial countries, A:

$$K = \sum_{j=1}^{j=L} x_j = Lx \tag{A.30}$$

The second equality follows from the same reasoning as in the endogenous technology models. It also follows that $y_t^* = y_t^* E_t$. Now we define the learning process in the transition economy, just as we had defined the evolution of technological change in advanced economies in earlier models:

$$\dot{L}_t = \kappa e^{\phi\mu} A_t^\gamma L_t^{-\gamma}. \tag{A.31}$$

Directly from the earlier models, we now have

$$y_t^* = y_{et}^* H_t^* = y_{et}^* \kappa e^{\phi\mu} (A_t / L_t)^\gamma N_t. \tag{A.32}$$

Equation (A.32) differs from equation (A.25′). For a transition economy, we have integrated domestic learning (skill and education development) and the accumulation of new capital as a result of technological change. The idea behind this model is that as a transition economy's workforce learns more about new technologies, workers can employ more advanced technologies via capital. However, because L enters in the denominator of the right-hand side of (A.32), as $L \rightarrow A$ increments to L become less able to advance income per capita. This means that it is simply harder to accumulate knowledge as one gets closer to the frontier of knowledge. Recall that L is the level of knowledge in the developing (emerging) economy and A is the level at the world frontier.

Reform 5: Trade Liberalization

The key new parameter in equation (A.32) is κ. This is the parameter through which advanced world technology is transferred from developed economies to emerging economies. One can think of κ as the elasticity of human capital in an emerging society as a result of adoption of new technologies from advanced societies. Income is increased because domestic human capital in the emerging society rises. Since these new technologies are transferred from developed economies, we assume they do so through the degree of free trade between the emerging economy in question and advanced economies of the world.

We see this new parameter κ as the vehicle through which the free trade reform influences the steady state. The argument is that a consequence of free trade is that domestic industries are forced to compete on open markets. Another consequence is that multinational corporations with new technologies enter the emerging economy. These new firms bring with them new ideas. The domestic firms, in order to compete in international markets, also adopt new (cost-saving) technologies. These advances in technology in emerging markets occur only if free trade is allowed between the emerging and advanced economies. Thus, free trade increases κ. We would expect free trade to alter other aspects of the steady state as well. For instance, free trade lowers costs and improves the mix of consumer goods. It also improves, via comparative advantage, the quality of capital and thus lowers depreciation.[44]

NOTES

1. Blanchard et al. (1992) and Lazear (1995) are two good examples.
2. The burgeoning literature on this subject cannot be done justice here, but see Chavance (1994), Prust et al. (1990), Wijnbergon (1992b), Frydman and Rapaczynski (1994), Gotting (1993), Portes (1994), Hall and Koparanova (1995), Roemer (2000), Svejnar (1993) and Willett et al. (1995).
3. See, for some examples, Oesterreichische Bank (1996, 1997, 1998, 1999, 2000), Bonin and Székely (1994), Willett et al. (1995), Hochreiter (2000), Kutan and Brada (2000), Lainela and Sutela (1995), Miller and Petranov (1993) and Nuti (1992).
4. See Brady (1999), Boyco, Shleifer and Vishny (1995), Kotrba (1993), Rondinelli (1994), Torok (1992), Vince (1993), Murrell and Wang (1993), Yamada and Braguinsky (1999).
5. Hrncir (1992).
6. See Brown and Earle (2000), Gustafson (1999) and Gylfason (1994).
7. Bulgaria elected socialists (former communists) in July 1990 and in December 1994. Hungary elected former communists (MSZP) in June 1994. In May 1998 communists received 32 percent of the vote in Hungary. In the Russian Duma (the lower house of parliament that to some extent reflected popular sentiment), communists held pluralities in the elections of March 1993 and December 1995 with over 20 percent of the vote. Slovakia split from the Czechs and was largely under the control of former communist leader Meciar from December 1994 until October 1998.
8. Russia is of course the most prominent case of criminal conduct in economic affairs, but other transition

economies were not immune. See Black, Kraakman and Tarassova (1999), Brady (1999), Gaddy and Ickes (1998), Gustafson (1999) and Frye and Shleifer (1997). See also Wissels (1996), Winiecki (1989, 1990), Murrell and Wang (1993), Brainerd (1998) and Yamada and Braguinsky (1999).

9. This model follows the famous Solow (1956, 1970) model, which has formed the basis of growth analysis for over forty years.
10. If new technology augments the labor input, it is called Harrod-neutral technological change. We discuss below alternative models of technological change which include Hicks-neutral, capital-augmenting and labor and capital embodied.
11. Jones (1998) suggests that development of human capital may be the transmission mechanism through which free trade assists in the transfer of technology from advanced to developing economies. The idea of human capital is used extensively by Becker (1964, 1993).
12. This material is based on Jones (1998) as well as on earlier sources.
13. Hall and Jones (1997), Jones (1998), Gylfason (1994), and Easterly and Levine (1997) all suggest that institutions are key to explaining why some economies are less successful than others. We take this one step farther by linking specific economic reforms to voting behavior, which is in turn linked to growth. This helps to bridge the gap between growth theory and public choice analysis.
14. Suppose, for instance, we start with 100 efficiency units of labor at time t. Let the number of workers increase by 1 percent and technology augment the efficiency of all workers (not just the new ones) at a 0.05 percent rate. Then E at time $t + 1$ is 101.05.
15. We begin here the practice of presenting only the Cobb–Douglas version of the models. In general all results that we exploit hold for the general case in which production satisfies constant returns to scale and diminishing marginal product of inputs.
16. This means that $\partial Y/\partial K>0$, $\partial Y/\partial N>0$, $\partial^2 Y/\partial K^2<0$, and $\partial^2 Y/\partial N^2<0$. In the Cobb–Douglas case $0 < \alpha < 1$ and $0 < \beta < 1$. Below we add the assumption that $\alpha + \beta = 1$, constant returns to scale.
17. We allow the consumer to choose s later; for now it is not necessary.
18. We use the phrase "living standards" loosely here to refer to output per worker. In growth models, population and labor force growth are assumed to be the same.
19. Since N is growing over time at rate η, we can think of the representative consumer as a family.
20. We maintain the assumption of constant returns to scale and measure all quantity variables in units per efficiency unit of an effective human: $c_h \equiv C/H$. The consumer maximizes c_h. Recall that $H \equiv e^{\varphi\mu}EN$ where E represents Harrod-neutral technological change and $e^{\varphi\mu}$ is human capital. One could assume that the consumer maximizes utility from consumption per family member, not per efficiency unit of an effective human; however, this yields an unreasonable result: consumption does not grow as a result of new technology, because the consumer discounts utility to offset future gains from technological change. This may be the case, but it suggests current generations can anticipate the rate of technological change.
21. In Aesop's fable the cricket played all summer while the ant worked. Crickets have high values for ρ and ants have low values, perhaps even zero, for ρ.
22. As with the production function, we will consider special cases of utility functions. At this time, though, this detail is not elucidating. An obvious candidate is the Cobb–Douglas function with constant returns to scale: $u(c_{ht}) = c_{ht}^{\xi}$. Unfortunately, with only one argument in the utility function, constant returns to scale restricts $\xi=1$. The Cobb–Douglas form forces the elasticity of substitution parameter to one. A more general form is the constant elasticity of substitution form:

$$u(c_{ht}) = \begin{cases} (c_{tht}^{1-\xi} - 1)/1 - \xi & \text{for } \xi > 0 \text{ and } \xi \neq 1 \\ \text{In } c_{ht}, & \text{for } \xi = 1 \end{cases}$$

Here, the elasticity of substitution, $\sigma = -\xi^{-1}$, is constant. Other specific functional forms have been employed in growth modeling, including quadratic and log linear. In general, σ is not constant and depends on c_{ht}. With technological change the parameters of the utility function will enter into the steady-state condition.

23. The consumer is taking input prices as given. The steady-state values for these terms will only be known after optimizing by the producer and the consumer.
24. Here we follow Blanchard and Fischer (1989). See also Intriligator (1971).
25. Condition (i) yields $\lambda_t = u'(c)e^{-\rho t}$, where $u' \equiv du(c_{ht})/dc_{ht}$. Solving this expression for $\lambda\bullet_t$, the left-hand side of condition (ii) is

$$\dot{\lambda}_t = [u''(c_{ht})\dot{c}_{ht} - \rho u'(c_{ht})]e^{-\rho t}.$$

If we assume the simple Cobb–Douglas technology then the right-hand side of condition (ii) is

$$-H_k = \lambda_t[(\gamma + \eta + \delta) - \alpha k_{ht}^{(\alpha-1)})].$$

Equating the two sides of condition (ii) yields

$$[u''(c_{ht})\dot{c}_{ht} - \rho u'(c_{ht})]e^{-\rho t} = \lambda_t[(\gamma + \eta + \delta) - \alpha k_{ht}^{(\alpha-1)})].$$

Using (i) to remove λ_t, we have equation (A.10).

26. A Leontief utility function illustrates the extreme case: $u(c_1 + c_2) = \text{Min } [c_1, c_2]$.
27. See note 22 for a detailed discussion of the CES form. The CES function satisfies this condition.
28. Since the consumer is optimizing consumption per efficiency unit of human capital the rate of technological change enters into the Euler condition.
29. This is not to say that all young consumers are flexible and all old consumers are inflexible. These are illustrative extreme examples.
30. The relationship between capital prices, say q_t, and the service prices v_t, rate of return r and depreciation δ may be derived from the dual to the producer optimization problem; see Hulten (1992).
31. The last equality is for the constant returns Cobb–Douglas case.
32. In the Cobb-Douglas case with constant returns, $w + vk = (1 - \alpha)k^{\alpha} + \alpha k^{\alpha-1}k = 1$.
33. Blanchard and Fischer (1989) show that an additional condition in this type of problem, called the transversality condition, must also be satisfied to prevent a solution that explodes and in which consumers could always accumulate capital without lack of benefits. This condition is satisfied by our system:

$$\lim_{t\to\infty} k_t u'(c_{ht})]e^{-\rho t} = 0.$$

This condition rules out Ponzi scheme financing.

34. This solution follows from the assumption of diminishing marginal product, because in this case f' is a monotonically decreasing function of k. Since y is increasing in k, we can also solve for y.
35. Blanchard and Fischer (1989) show that such a steady state is stable. All points in (c, k) space are characterized by pressures moving the economy toward a saddle path that leads to the modified golden rule steady state.
36. Since utility here is ordinal, this is simply a rescaling, but the fact is that a better mix of consumer goods implies a happier consumer.
37. Intertemporal optimization implies that accumulated capital lasts over time. To induce private agents to acquire such capital requires some degree of certainty that ownership rights will not be eradicated by nationalization. The wide political swings from pro-market reform regimes to socialist (former communist) regimes certainly causes concern for potential investors, especially foreign investors.
38. It is important to note that g may enter the utility function, and consumers may be willing to accept lower consumption and growth if the government spending is worth the costs. In the case of European transition economies, we now expect little utility from Warsaw Pact military spending and continued soft budget constraints that prop up failing state-owned enterprises. Productive infrastructure investment is in the investment term. This implies it has to meet the same rate of return requirement as private investment expenditures.
39. Inserting the producer decision rules for hiring capital and labor into the budget constraint yields a new expression for the growth path of capital:

$$\dot{k}_t = y_{ht} - \{[z(r + \delta)/(1 - z)k_{ht} + \tau_{ht} + c_{ht} + (\gamma + \eta + \delta)k_{ht}\} = y_{ht} - [g_{ht} + c_{ht} + (\gamma + \eta + \delta)k_{ht}].$$

40. See note 38 and the next paragraph of the text.
41. See Blanchard and Fischer (1989) for derivations of the deficit case and an excellent discussion of the results.
42. The research sector in the corn economy uses genetics to produce new types of corn stalks that produce more corn per seed unit.
43. Jones (1998) provides a lucid analysis of this model.
44. This conclusion does not contradict the notion that the mix of capital may eventually transform into faster-depreciating assets, like computers instead of abacuses. But for a given asset type, comparative advantage indicates that broader trading zones allow more specialization, and improved product quality should be a by-product.

Appendix B. Political influence, economic performance and reform efforts: an econometric analysis of six newly independent countries, 1989–1999

Here we develop an econometric model linking voting decisions, economic reforms and economic performance. In this model politics influences economics and economics influences politics. We briefly review the integration of five generic economic reforms (price liberalization, property privatization, macroeconomic stabilization, trade liberalization and industry restructuring and deregulation) into the growth model framework.[1]

In section 2 we link analysis of growth and reforms to voting behavior. Next we model the relationship between decisions by voters, proposals by reformers and election outcomes.[2] Finally, we model an intertemporal sequence linking historical economic performance and proposed reforms to decisions by voters in elections. We also argue that reform regimes carry the effects of the past on to contemporary economic performance. Reform regimes follow from election outcomes and votes for reformers depend on prospective reforms. Thus we encounter possible simultaneous equation bias. We model this in section 3.

Before dealing with data we analyze in section 4 the concern that votes do not reflect pocketbook issues. Some people choose not to vote at all and others vote for non-economic reasons. We model this problem employing analysis from the labor market supply literature.

In section 5 we explain construction of the variables for reform and voting to be used in subsequent analysis.[3] We begin the empirical analysis in section 6 with a model using simple (crude) binomial (0 – 1) dummy variables for voting and reforms. Section 7 reports on increasingly sophisticated estimation techniques using indexes of reform and percentages of votes and seats as variables. This section contains ordinary least squares and two-stage least squares models. We sum up with conclusions about voting, reforms and economic performance that we derive from the empirical research.

1. REFORMS AND THE GROWTH MODEL

We summarize here the influence reforms will have on the representative consumer in a growth model. Six sets of forces which express behavior of consumers, producers, and government and the constraints they each face carry reform measures into the computation of economic prospects. We summarize these functions, the profit function, the utility function, the consumer budget constraint, the producer production and technology constraint and the government spending policies and its budget constraint, in illustration 1.[4]

Illustration 1. Behavioral and constraint functions

Profit function:

$$\Pi_0 = \int_{t=0}^{t=\infty} [f(k_{ht}) - (w_t + v_t k_{ht})]e^{-rt}dt \tag{A.12}$$

Production function:

$$Y_t = K_t^{\alpha}(H_t)^{1-\alpha} \tag{A.3}$$

Utility function (case of constant elasticity of substitution):

$$U_0 = \int_{t=0}^{t=\infty} u(c_{ht})e^{-\rho t}dt, \text{ where } \sigma \equiv [-u'/cu''] \tag{A.7}$$

Consumer's budget constraint:

$$y_{ht} = w_t + (1 - z)v_t k_{ht} - \tau_{ht}$$

Government budget constraint (balanced budget policy):

$$g_{ht} = \tau_{ht} + z v_t k_{ht}$$

We summarize in illustration 2 below the nature of the steady-state equations. Some reforms operate on these conditions and do not appear in the behavioral and constraint equations.

Illustration 2. Steady-state conditions

Euler condition:

$$\dot{c}_{ht} / c_{ht} = \sigma[(\rho + \delta + \eta + \gamma) - (1 - zv)\alpha]$$

The modified golden rule:

$$\partial y_{ht} / \partial k_{ht} = (\rho + \gamma + \eta + \delta) / (1 - z\alpha)$$

The dynamic path of capital:

$$\dot{k}_{ht} = y_{ht} - [g_{ht} + c_{ht} + (\gamma + \delta + \eta)]k_{ht}$$

Steady-state output:

$$y_t^* = y_{et}^* H_t^* = y_{et}^* \kappa e^{\varphi\mu}(A_t / L_t)^{\gamma} N_t$$

Steady-state consumption:

$$c_h^* = y_h^* - [g_h + (\gamma + \delta + \eta)k_h^*]$$

Each reform has specific effects on the steady state, either by altering the path of steady-state values of certain variables (changes in growth rates) or by altering the level of variables on the steady-state paths (level effects). Since all of this is discussed in Appendix A, we merely summarize these effects here with the help of the equations in illustrations 1 and 2.

Price liberalization raises the steady-state level of utility associated with each level of consumption. This increase in utility reflects the improved mix of consumption goods resulting from a market-driven price set that reflects consumer preferences rather than prices administered by a central agency.[5]

Property privatization, operating on the incentives of producers and savers, alters many aspects of the behavioral relations and the steady-state conditions. Individual producers, after privatization, are the residual claimants of the profit function. This alone has many consequences for production, employment, capital acquisition and the path of capital at the steady state. Thus, we expect privatization to improve productive efficiency through many channels. Private property also influences the behavior of consumers, because they become the residual claimants of savings. We identify, therefore, three distinct effects of property privatization on production. (1) It jolts output upward for each mix of inputs. (This effect acts like a one-time positive Hicks-neutral technological shock.) (2) It also alters the nature of the production function itself by causing a more efficient production process. These two effects are a direct result of creating a private residual claimant. Both operate directly on $af(kh)$, where a is the rate of Hicks-neutral technological change.[6] (3) Private investors will purchase or produce higher-quality capital. Thus, we would expect lower depreciation rates for every type of fixed capital (structures, machinery and equipment).[7] The depreciation rate δ enters the Euler condition, the modified golden rule and the dynamic path of capital at the steady state.

Private market economies tend to be more dynamic than administered systems. Thus, we believe privatization will increase the rate of technological change. This effect alters the growth rate at the steady state through the Harrod-neutral parameter γ.[8] The behavior of private individuals will also change when they become residual claimants of private property. Knowing that one's savings will result in high rates of return implies savings rates will rise. The subjective rate of time discount, ρ, will fall as well since people will have more confidence in gains from sacrifice of contemporary consumption for saving; that is, saving has a higher rate of return. This parameter enters the Euler condition. Finally, if privatizing encourages savings, then it will also increase the rate of accumulation of effective education and skill development. Two parameters of steady-state output, under a human capital model, φ and μ, will rise. Recall that φ represents the level of education and μ is the effect on productivity of education.

Stabilization policy, while operating primarily on the financial side of the economic system via low inflation, also has real effects. Stabilization operates in our modeling through government budget policy. A lower level of government spending allows for higher consumption at each steady state; that is, if g^* falls, then c^* rises for each y^*. We emphasize here that this analysis refers to government spending on Warsaw Pact military activity and on inefficient state-owned enterprises. We do not intend the model to apply to government spending on education and infrastructure investment. These would more properly enter the model as part of the development of human capital, $e^{\varphi\mu}$, and acquisition of physical capital k.

Large shares of satellite states and former Soviet government budgets consisted of transfer payments. Balancing the budget and reducing the size of government can mean lowering transfers. In our model this term, τ, influences the consumer budget constraint. Obviously net transfer recipients lose income whereas net taxpayers gain income.

Restructuring and deregulation, while targeted toward specific firms and industries, amounts to reducing government interference in private decisions to employ capital. Thus, the tax on capital income term, z, is the parameter through which deregulation influences the steady state. This z term also reflects actual taxes on capital, so that both stabilization reform and deregulatory reform act on z, the implicit tax on income from capital.

The fifth reform, free international trade flows, operates in several ways in the analysis. The Ricardian view, that trade exploits comparative advantage and thus benefits both trading partners, is central to economists' well-known advocacy of free trade. This means that free trade improves the mix and quality of consumer goods, which in turn increases utility derived from each level of consumption. For the same reason free trade will lower economic depreciation by improving the mix and quality of capital goods. The endogenous growth model that allows technology transfer from advanced economies to emerging ones introduced the κ-term. This term is the parameter through with technology is transferred from advanced to emerging economies. Thus, the free trade reform raises the rate of transfer of technology. This mechanism reflects two different effects. First, domestic producers, forced to compete on international markets, adopt more efficient methods. Second, foreign firms producing domestically use new technologies.

2. VOTING BEHAVIOR AND THE GROWTH MODEL

In principle, an economic agent could compute the gains or losses that she expects to accrue from a reform or a package of reforms. Consider an economic and political agent (possible voter) who confronts the choice of voting for a reform (or reform package). If the reformer wins, the reforms will be installed and this will alter her economic environment. If the reformers lose, then reforms will not be installed. According to our growth model, the outcome of the election will influence her calculation of the present discounted value of her future utility stream, based on her optimal plan. How will she vote?

Suppose she exploits the model in the previous section to compute her expected income and well-being under the reform(s) and compares this to her economic well-being in the previous period without the reforms. Let U_t^* be the utility expected from implementation of the reforms given information available to the economic agent at time t of the election:

$$U_{i,t}^* = \Im_i[U_{i,t} : R_t^*, E_{t-1}, C_i] \tag{B.1}$$

where $\Im$ is an expectation operator contingent on the information about R_t given E_{t-1} and C_i. R_t^* is the package of economic reforms proposed by reformers in the election at time t. C_i is the relevant characteristic set of individual i that enters into her calculation of U_t^*. Utility at t–1 is determined from known economic conditions at that time:

$$U_{i,t-1} = U[E_{t-1}, C_i] \tag{B.2}$$

where E_{t-1} is the state of the economy prior to the election. The economic agent computes her utility from her knowledge of economic conditions before the election.

Let the difference for person i in the time t election be

$$D_{i,t} \equiv U_{i,t}^* - U_{i,t-1}. \tag{B.3}$$

Her voting decision is straightforward. Let $v_{i,t}$ be a variable that takes on the value 1 if she votes yes and 0 if she votes no. Then we have

$$v_{i,t} = \begin{cases} 1 & \text{iff } D_{i,t} > 0 \\ 0 & \text{iff } D_{i,t} \leq 0 \end{cases} \tag{B.4}$$

If $i = 1, 2, \ldots, n$, then

$$V_t \equiv \sum_{i=1}^{i=N} v_{i,t} > n/2 \quad \Rightarrow \quad \text{reformers win the election.}^{9} \tag{B.5}$$

If our model were strictly accurate and if we had certain data, we could forecast the vote of each person. We would need data on the pertinent characteristics of each individual voter (or subset of voters). We would need data on each proposed reform as well as on economic conditions each period before the election. With this information, we could compute D_{it} and predict how each person will vote in the election. In theory such information is available before each election. That is, nothing we assume to know in our calculations is unobservable in principle. Of course, the world is not so well behaved, our model is not strictly accurate and such detailed data are unavailable for transition economies.

Nonetheless, we focus on two econometric problems. First, we deal with the simultaneous and interactive nature of economic events, reforms and elections. Second, our model applies to people who vote according to their own immediate economic self-interest and assume that their votes count. There are people who do not do this. After all, some people do not vote. Some people vote for reasons unrelated to their own self-interest – perhaps ideology, for example. We develop a conceptual model for this problem in section 4.

3. SIMULTANEOUS EQUATION SYSTEM

Our model implies that the vote in an election for reformers will depend on specific factors. Existing economic conditions, $E_{i,t-1}$, determine $U_{i,t-1}$ in equation (B.3) for each individual i. The proposed set of reforms, R_t^*, will determine $U_{i,t}^*$, the potential future gains for voters of reforms. This is seen in equation (B.1). The characteristics of the voting population, C_i, will influence how each $D_{i,t}$ is determined and translated into an actual vote. Recalling that V represents the number of votes for reform parties, we have

$$V_t = V_t[C_i, R_t^*, E_{t-1}, Y_{t-1}] \quad \forall\, i = 1, \ldots, n. \tag{B.6}$$

The variable Y_{t-1} represents non-economic factors that influence elections. The model formalizes the result that the outcome of a political event, the votes in an election, depends on the proposed reform package and on economic conditions before the election. Thus, politics depends on economics as well as on the proposals by candidates during the election.

As we argued in Chapter 6 of the text, economic performance at time t depends on previous elections through the rules set by the party in power during previous periods, R_{t-1}. Thus,

$$E_t = E_t[R_{t-1}, E_{t-1}, H_j] \tag{B.7}$$

where H_j represents forces other than prior economic performance and the reform (or non-reform) regime of the previous election and the subscript j indexes countries. E_{t-1} represents inertia in the economic system. H_j will be used empirically to distinguish attitudes toward capitalism that have resulted from historical experiences or lack thereof with capitalism and with relative well-being under communism.

In addition to economics influencing voting and voting influencing economics through reforms, reforms undoubtedly reflect votes for reformers as well as historical experiences. This gives us:

$$R_t = R_t[V_t, H_j]. \tag{B.8}$$

Equations (B.6)–(B.8) comprise a three-equation system. We think of C_i as a country-specific dummy variable so that some countries, voting may be influenced by different non-economic factors. H_j is a possible dummy variable for differences in historical experience before and during communist control.

We linearize the system as follows:

$$\begin{aligned} E_t &= \alpha_0 + \alpha_{31}R_{t-1} + \alpha_{41}E_{t-1} + \alpha_{61}H_j + \varepsilon_t^E \\ V_t &= \alpha_{02} + \alpha_{22}R_t^* + \alpha_{42}E_{t-1} + \alpha_{52}C_i + \varepsilon_t^V \\ R_t &= \alpha_{03} + \alpha_{13}V_t + \alpha_{63}H_j + \varepsilon^R. \end{aligned} \tag{B.9}$$

Since we have no independent data on expected and realized reform regimes, we represent them empirically by the same variable R. Therefore (expected) reforms, measured as realized reforms, influence votes and votes influence subsequent reforms. This creates simultaneous equation bias. To correct for this bias we will employ two-stage least squares methods. In model equation-system (B.9) the coefficient of V in the reform equation, α_{13}, is over-identified.

We ran Hausman tests for simultaneous equation bias and, as will be shown later, these tests confirmed the bias of the ordinary least squares estimator of α_{13}. To illustrate the theory of the two-stage least squares estimation procedure in this case, we rearrange terms in equation system (B.9) for matrix notation:

$$\begin{aligned} E_t \qquad\qquad\qquad & - \alpha_{01} - \alpha_{31}R_{t-1} - \alpha_{41}E_{t-1} \qquad - \alpha_{61}H_j = \varepsilon_t^E \\ V_t - \alpha_{22}R_t - \alpha_{02} \qquad & \qquad\qquad - \alpha_{42}E_{t-1} - \alpha_{52}C_i \qquad = \varepsilon_t^V \\ - \alpha_{13}V_t + \quad R_t - \alpha_{03} \qquad & \qquad\qquad\qquad\qquad\qquad - \alpha_{63}H_j = \varepsilon^R \end{aligned} \tag{B.9′}$$

Using matrix notation, we define variables as follows:

$$y \equiv [E_t, V_t, R_t] \quad \Gamma \equiv \begin{bmatrix} 1 & 0 & 0 \\ 0 & 1 & -\alpha_{13} \\ 0 & -\alpha_{22} & 1 \end{bmatrix}$$

$$X \equiv [1 \quad R_{t-1} \quad E_{t-1} \quad C \quad H]$$

$$B \equiv \begin{bmatrix} -\alpha_{01} & -\alpha_{02} & -\alpha_{03} \\ -\alpha_{31} & 0 & 0 \\ -\alpha_{41} & -\alpha_{42} & 0 \\ 0 & -\alpha_{52} & 0 \\ -\alpha_{61} & 0 & -\alpha_{63} \end{bmatrix} \quad \varepsilon \equiv [\varepsilon^E \quad \varepsilon^V \quad \varepsilon^R]$$

The matrix y is the matrix of endogenous variables, X is the matrix of exogenous and predetermined variables, and ε is the matrix of stochastic terms. The model is

$$y\Gamma - XB = \varepsilon.$$

Solving for y we have

$$y = XB\Gamma^{-1} + \varepsilon\Gamma^{-1}.$$

Finally, defining

$$\Pi \equiv B\Gamma^{-1} \quad \text{and} \quad \mu \equiv \varepsilon\Gamma^{-1}$$

we have

$$y = X\Pi + \mu. \tag{B.10}$$

Equation (B.10) is a system of three equations that can be used to estimate the unknown parameter set Π. The structural parameters in B and Γ depend on Π. As we noted earlier the coefficient for the vote variable in the reform equation, α_{13}, is over-identified. We determine α_{13} from Π using two-stage least squares. Before turning to estimation, we consider problems resulting from the fact that some eligible voters choose not to vote and some who do vote do not base their choice on their own personal self-interest (pocketbook issues). With the right kind of data, this problem can be dealt with by modifying the second equation in the equation system (B.9).

4. ALLOWING FOR NOT VOTING POCKETBOOK ISSUES

The model above applies to individuals who vote in their own economic self-interest, that is, they "vote their pocketbooks." People may vote for reformers because they think the reforms will improve their long-range economic prospects. Other people vote against reformers because they expect reforms to result in personal losses. In either case, we modeled above the conduct only of agents who vote their pocketbooks. Voting behavior is of course far more complex. Many people do not vote their pocketbooks and some people do not vote at all. Some people vote for ideological, social or other reasons without regard to pocketbook issues. Furthermore, a sensible voting model needs to allow for two people with the same economic prospects to vote differently, or to allow for one person to vote while another does not.

It would also be interesting to model the intensity of interest in political events. Some people devote enormous energies to electoral politics and some pay little attention. We turn now to a model that allows some of these distinctions in voter behavior.

The model exploits the notion that voting takes time and that time is valuable. This allows us to adapt a model from labor market theory.[10] Suppose utility, W, derives from goods, G, and from leisure, L:

$$W = W(G, L) = G^{\alpha}L^{\beta}.$$

Solving for the marginal rate of substitution between goods and leisure in the Cobb–Douglas case yields

$$MRS_{L,G} = (\beta / \alpha)G / L.$$

Recall that D was the gain (or loss) expected to accrue from the election. If we let T be the time needed to vote, then the gain from the election is $D \times T$. If leisure time is lost for voting, then the time to vote costs lost leisure. If we normalize on leisure time, then $L = 1 - T$. If income from sources uninfluenced by the reform package is Θ, then $G = D \times T + \Theta$. Since different people have different tastes regarding goods versus leisure, we introduce a stochastic term η so that

$$W = [D \times (T + \eta) + \Theta]^{\alpha} [1 - (T + \eta)]^{\beta}.$$

The marginal rate of substitution is:

$$MRS_{L,G} = (\beta / \alpha) [D \times (T + \eta) + \Theta] / [1 - (T + \eta)].$$

Some people will not vote at all and others will vote for reasons other than their own economic self-interest. Consider a person for whom $T = 0$ because, based on the economic implications for his own utility, he does not find it "worth his time to vote." At what level do benefits from voting rise just enough to persuade this person to vote? The answer is the point at which benefits exactly equal the time cost of voting. We call this level of benefits the "reservation benefit." (This is analogous to the concept of a reservation wage.) Letting D_r be the reservation benefit, we have

$$D_r = (\beta / \alpha) [(D \times \eta) + \Theta] / [1 - \eta].$$

For any give value of η, people will find it worth their time to vote their pocketbook if and only if

$$D > D_r \text{ or } D > (\beta / \alpha) [(D \times \eta) + \Theta] / [1 - \eta].$$

Following Berndt, define $\varepsilon \equiv -\eta$; $b \equiv \beta / (\alpha + \beta)$ and define $J \equiv (1 - b) - b(\Theta / D)$. The following decision rule determines who will vote their pocketbooks and who will not:

$$T > 0 \quad \text{iff} \quad \varepsilon > -J \quad \Rightarrow \quad \text{Vote your pocketbook.} \tag{B.12}$$

$$T = 0 \quad \text{iff} \quad \varepsilon \leq -J \quad \Rightarrow \quad \text{Do not vote your pocketbook.} \tag{B.13}$$

For $T > 0$, then $D = MRS_{L,G}$ and we can solve for T:

$$T = (1 - b) - b(\Theta / D) + \varepsilon \quad \text{for } T > 0. \tag{B.14}$$

This model may now be used to explain the decision process by which people decide how to vote. The model may be interpreted in one of two ways. One approach is to assume that T is zero, in which case the personal economic implications of an election are not relevant to the potential voter. He either fails to vote or votes for reasons unrelated to reforms. If T is not zero, we assume the person chooses to vote. He must then decide whether to vote for or against reforms. Notice that the decision to vote for reformers involves two decisions. One is a decision to vote and the second is a decision to vote yes or no on the reform proposal (or candidate).

Suppose we consider data only on voters. We are implicitly ignoring the first stage of the decision and censoring our sample. One implication of the model is that the variables that determine how one would vote are the same variables that determine whether or not to vote. This means that if we fail to allow for non-voters, then the disturbance term in our voting equation will be correlated with the variables in the voting equation, causing biased estimators. To generate unbiased estimators of an equation explaining votes, we need to account for non-voters. To do this, we recognize that the decision to vote yes on reform is determined by a system of equations, equations (B.13), if $T = 0$, and equations (B.12) and (B.14) if $T \neq 0$. With data on Θ, D and T one can build an econometric model based on (B.12)–(B.14).

A second interpretation of the above model is that it explains the amount of time one spends in voting one's pocketbook. That is, it could explain variations in the value of T when $T > 0$. Equation (B.14) comes into play when $T > 0$. This equation explains how much time a person will spend on voting. It depends on α, β, Θ, and D and ε. Put another way, this model tells us how much effort one may put into electoral politics. The amount of time depends on specific variables described next.

The coefficients α and β represent the elasticity of substitution between tastes for goods and for leisure. The term Θ is income unrelated to the election. If the person has many resources available unrelated to the election, she will be less likely to vote. However, given Θ if D is large, then a lot is at stake in the election and she is likely to spend a lot of time in electoral politics. Perhaps this helps to explain why some elections bring out many union voters or special-interest voters or senior citizens. In our context, it helps to explain why employees of state-owned enterprises may be politically very active and why young, low-income voters with long-range prospects may be very active. Older people who feel their pensions are threatened are also likely to vote their pocketbooks and spend some time involved in the political process.

The model has another nice feature. The term ε can be thought of as the person's "taste for voting." This means two people with the same Θ and D, the same non-political sources of income and same stakes, may behave differently. One may vote and devote energies to politics and one may not.

We turn now to estimation considerations of this model. Let ε_i be person i's taste for voting. This could be his ideological belief in voting or his enjoyment of the process. Let J_i be the value of J given (α, β), Θ_i and D_i. We assume a normal distribution for ε and a variance of σ^2:

$$\varepsilon_i \sim N(0, \sigma^2).$$

It follows that $\varepsilon_i / \sigma \sim N(0, 1)$. Thus the probability that person i votes is

$$P(i-votes)=P[(\varepsilon_i>-J_i \Leftrightarrow (\varepsilon_i/\sigma_i)>(-J_i/\sigma_i)]$$
$$=\int_{z=-J_i/\sigma}^{z=\infty} f(z)dz = 1-F(-J_i/\sigma_i)$$

where

$$f(z)=(1/\sqrt{2\pi\sigma^2})e^{-\{T-[\gamma_1\gamma_2 b(\theta/D)]\}^2/\sigma^2}$$

where $\gamma_1 = (1-b)$ and $\gamma_2 = b$ and where we let $\gamma = [\gamma_1\ \gamma_2]$.

The likelihood function is

$$\Gamma=\prod_{i\in\Omega}[1-F(-J_i/\sigma)]\prod_{i\in\Omega}F(-J_i/\sigma)$$

where Ω is the set of voters. Maximizing the log of the likelihood function with respect to γ_1, γ_2 and σ yields three normal equations from which we can estimate the three unknowns γ_1, γ_2 and σ. Empirical implementation of this model requires information on the unknown parameter set α, β, Θ, and D for specific individual voters (or groups of voters.) We do not have such data for transition economies. We next employ the data that we do have for six transition economies.

5. ECONOMETRIC RESULTS AND THE DATA

In the econometrics we focus on three questions drawn from the theoretical models in Chapters 3 to 5. First, does it make sense for us to talk about reformers versus non-reformers? In some countries such a distinction may seem inappropriate. Unless reformers can be distinguished from non-reformers, then we have no way of assessing the relationship between politics, reform and economic outcomes. If everyone is an equivalent reformer, then the voters' choices are not relevant to whether reforms occur or not. We thus explore this question before we look at the interactions between election outcomes, reform policies and economic performance. We believe that in most countries some political parties are more inclined toward strong reform policies than other parties. In Europe, liberals are typically strong advocates of market-based reforms and socialists may resist such reforms.[11] In some countries, however, such distinctions are blurred.

The second question (contingent on answers to the first) deals with votes for reformers. Under what economic conditions and with what reform proposals do reformers get elected? We consider several measures of economic performance, several indicators of reform, and several measures of election outcomes. Third, how have transition economies performed during and after political regimes strongly inclined toward reform and away from socialism? Even partial answers to this last question may indicate problems that reform supporters will have to confront in moving economies toward markets.

The data used in the regression analysis had to be converted from the detailed election outcome results and reform indicators compiled by the authors. Economic data, was converted from an annual basis to an election interval basis for some tests. We report on constructed reform indexes for each country and each year. Table B.1 contains reform indexes that we constructed, when possible, for each country in each year from 1989 to 1999. Each country's reform index in Table B.1 is compiled from annual indexes for each of the five reform areas, when adequate data are available. Thus, these indexes represent reform progress in each country, across all five reform areas, with a common base, 1995 = 100. We first constructed sub-indexes for price liberalization, property privatization, macroeconomic stabilization, trade liberalization, and restructuring and deregulation. The country annual index number is an average of the five sub-indexes. Where feasible, each sub-index received the same weight.

Table B.1 Reform progress indexes by country, 1989–1999

Year	Bulgaria	Czech Rep.	Estonia	Hungary	Russia	Slovakia
1989	76.9	94.0	131.6	102.3	110.9	—
1990	84.9	106.8	112.3	128.9	116.6	—
1991	96.0	101.7	119.3	109.7	109.6	—
1992	108.9	96.5	129.1	115.0	141.1	—
1993	105.5	96.0	97.4	105.4	134.2	91.9
1994	98.1	102.5	111.0	81.0	108.9	105.0
1995	100.0	100.0	100.0	100.0	100.0	100.0
1996	96.0	87.2	104.8	115.5	106.9	98.2
1997	119.0	84.9	101.6	122.8	141.4	82.0
1998	121.6	100.4	106.0	117.5	114.6	114.8
1999	—	—	96.0	—	123.3	86.5

We illustrate the procedure in Table B.2, which has the five sub-indexes for Bulgaria. The underlying data for the sub-indexes comes from reform data compiled by the authors. Data for each reform policy were quite different so that each index in Table B.2 had to be compiled in a different manner. In the cases of price liberalization and property privatization, we had only general and occasional pieces of information; see, for example, Table B.14. We know when key laws or agencies were created and when the reform process was announced and initiated. We also have occasional information on the percentages of prices liberalized or of certain types of property privatized. One cannot always be certain of the quality of government data. The data on restructuring and deregulation consist of binomial data signifying only when major changes were made in the organization of the finance sector, bankruptcy laws, wage controls, major international trade agreements, fiscal reforms and so forth. These are intended to reflect the disentanglement of the government from normal private market activity. Price liberalization, property privatization and restructuring indexes are thus rough indicators of reform progress built from non-cardinal data sources.

The reform indexes for stabilization and trade policies contain some data that are more traditional and typically cardinal. In the case of stabilization, we have data on budget deficits by year and on changes in exchange rates per year. We have some data on money growth.

Table B.2 Reform sub-indexes for Bulgaria, 1989–1998 (1995=100)

Year	Prices	Privatize	Stabilize	Trade	Restructure	General
1989	57.5	79.0	77.0	71.0	100.0	76.9
1990	57.5	79.0	85.0	84.0	118.7	84.9
1991	125.4	81.5	76.0	78.2	118.7	96.0
1992	125.4	99.3	98.0	102.9	118.7	108.9
1993	125.4	101.9	84.0	97.5	118.7	105.5
1994	100.0	104.5	93.0	92.8	100.0	98.1
1995	100.0	100.0	100.0	100.0	100.0	100.0
1996	100.0	98.6	76.0	105.2	100.0	96.0
1997	100.0	130.5	88.0	128.0	148.7	119.0
1998	100.0	130.5	121.0	107.8	148.7	121.6

Each of these sources contributed to our stabilization index. In the case of the trade liberalization index, we used data on foreign debt and imports as percentages of GDP. We used balance on current account figures and the ratio of foreign direct investment to GDP.

To form indexes of each area of reform, we had to find a way to integrate information from disparate sources. We wanted to compute averages from each data source in order to use all the data and minimize the importance of any individual source of error. The relative importance of each element of an average depends on its variance. Thus, we wanted to deal with the problem that one source of data with a large variance could dominate and distort the average. This is undesirable, because one source may contain errors and because while progress may have been unusually good or bad for any one indicator, reform overall might have been different. To achieve our goal from the "raw data," we compiled the Table B.2 sub-indexes as follows. For each data source, say the budget deficit, we took the observations over the period and converted them into a variable that centered on 100 with a variance of 25. This resulted in giving each data source the same influence on variance. We normalized each series by setting 1995 to 100, and then averaged the several raw data series for that reform area to obtain the sub-index for that reform.

Table B.3 contains the values per election interval of the country-specific reform indexes. It also contains the percentage of votes for reform parties in each election, derived from actual election outcomes and from our best judgment regarding composition of reform and non-reform parties and coalitions. The first column contains a binomial 0–1 variable for whether pro-reform parties were elected or not. Column 2 is the percentage of the vote for reformers in each election. There were a total of 25 national elections in the six countries from 1989 to 1999. We determined these percentages from the figures reported both for elections and for parliamentary seats actually acquired. We had to delete three elections due to data limitations on some variables. The reform indexes, column 3 in Table B.3, are averages of the annual reform indexes for the intervals between elections.

Reform indexes are calculated for the relevant election intervals on an annualized basis. That is, reform variables are weighted averages of underlying annual data. The weights reflect the number of months of each year during the election interval. In other words, if an

Table B.3 Election regimes and a reform index by country, 1989–1999

Month/year	Regime 1⇒ reform	% vote-reformers	Reform index
		Bulgaria	
6/1990	0	43.0	91.0
1/1992	1	49.5	104.0
1/1995	0	45.4	98.0
4/1997	1	59.7	120.6
		Czech Republic (Czechoslovakia until 1993)	
6/1990	1	51.5	101.7
6/1992	1	36.7	96.4
12/1996	0	33.3	90.1
6/1998	1	49.0	100.4
		Estonia	
5/1990	1	61.0	120.0
9/1992	1	54.7	107.2
3/1995	0	46.1	102.5
3/1997	0	39.0	103.3
3/1999	1	76.7	(96.0)
		Hungary	
4/1990	1	42.7	110.2
5/1994	0	27.7	108.5
5/1998	1	52.5	117.5
		Russia (Duma)	
3/1989 (Yeltsin)	1	(89.4)	113.1
6/1991 – Pres.	1	57.3	132.4
12/1993 – Duma	0	27.9	104.5
12/1995 – Duma	0	24.2	106.9
7/1996 – Pres.	1	57.4	124.1
12/1999 – Duma	1	56.1	123.3
		Slovak Republic	
12/1992	0	48.0	98.5
3/1994	1		
12/1994	0	45.2	97.7
10/1998	1	57.2	(88.8)

Table B.4 Elections, reforms, and economic performance (six countries, 1990–1999, all variables cover election intervals)

Year	Votes for reformers (%)	Reform index (1995=100)	GDP % change		Inflation rate		Unemployment rate	
			After	Before	After	Before	After	Before
				Bulgaria				
1990	43.0	91.0	–10.8	–4.3	233.6	14.1	8.0	0.8
1992	49.5	104.0	–2.3	–10.8	86.7	233.6	14.8	8.0
1995	45.4	98.0	–4.8	–2.3	233.9	86.7	12.1	14.8
1997	59.7	120.6	–0.5	–4.8	11.3	233.9	14.0	12.1
				Czech Republic				
1990	51.5	101.7	–9.0	2.6	33.5	4.2	2.9	0.5
1992	36.7	96.4	1.6	–9.0	12.1	33.5	3.2	2.9
1996	33.3	90.1	–0.2	1.6	9.1	12.1	5.0	3.2
1998	49.0	100.4	–1.3	–0.2	5.0	9.1	8.8	5.0
				Estonia				
1990	61.0	120.1	–11.4	3.8	466.2	3.8	1.2	0.3
1992	54.7	107.2	–5.0	–11.4	165.5	466.2	7.4	1.2
1995	46.1	102.5	4.9	–5.0	23.8	165.5	9.9	7.4
1997	39.0	103.3	6.4	4.9	8.7	23.8	9.8	9.9
				Hungary				
1990	42.7	110.2	–4.1	–0.4	26.4	3.5	9.9	0.8
1994	27.7	108.5	2.8	–4.1	21.8	26.4	10.7	9.9
1998	52.5	117.5	4.4	2.8	11.6	21.8	9.4	10.7
				Russia				
1991	57.3	132.4	–10.3	–2.2	978.3	18.0	4.1	3.5
1993	27.9	104.5	–8.4	–10.3	459.5	978.3	7.7	4.1
1995	24.2	106.9	–3.5	–8.4	47.6	459.5	9.2	7.7
1996	57.4	124.1	–1.0	–3.5	43.0	47.6	11.3	9.3
1999	56.1	123.3	1.7	–1.0	85.7	43.0	12.0	11.3
				Slovak Republic				
1992	48.0	98.5	–4.5	–5.6	18.3	22.6	6.2	11.1
1994	45.2	97.7	6.3	–4.5	7.0	18.3	10.0	6.2

election occurs in May, the fifth month of the year, then seven months of that year are attributed to the new regime. We do not have monthly data, so we assign a weight of $7/12$ to that year's reform index.

Table B.4 combines the voting and reform data from Table B.3 with corresponding economic variables, after deleting unusable observations. We actually used two sets of economic data. We used the percentage changes in GDP, the inflation rates and the unemployment rates for the specific year after the election and the year before the election. Like the reform index, economic variables were also calculated for election intervals. These figures are in Table B.4. All regressions were run using both annual economic data and election-interval economic data.

6. VOTES, REFORMS AND PERFORMANCE: DUMMY VARIABLE MODELS

Before we can begin to analyze the relationships between economics and politics, we first need to establish whether votes for parties that we refer to as "reformers" actually lead to reforms. Thus, our first set of results concerns the influence votes for reformers have on subsequent reforms.

Binomial Dummy Variables

The econometric analysis begins with a simple model using binomial dummy variables to represent votes for reformers or socialists and dummy variables for reforms. These data are constructed as follows. All the countries and elections are pooled, though specific country dummy variables are used to explore certain country-specific hypotheses. Each election is treated as a discrete event in which the winners can be identified as either pro-reform or anti-reform. Dummy variables identify the outcome. The variable Vote is 1 when a reform government won an election, and Vote is 0 when reformers lost. The socialist (non-reform-oriented) variable, Votsoc, is simply 1 when socialists win and 0 otherwise. As noted above, in many cases, the interpretation of pro-reform versus anti-reform is open to argument. In Hungary, for instance, many communists lay claim to favoring reforms. As explained earlier, we regard these claims as problematic. While changes in how business is undertaken had to occur and new legislation had to be proposed and passed, this is not the same as reform aimed at establishing a viable climate for private markets. The types of reforms needed to make capitalist economies work are not likely to be endorsed by communists, whether reform-minded or not.

The dummy variable Reform indicates whether an actual major reform period occurred or not. This simplification of real-world events assigns a distinctly non-continuous variable to a qualitative set of activities. The dummy variable Reform is set to 1 when significant economic reforms were installed (the reform index exceeds the average for the country) and 0 when not. There are two incumbency dummy variables: one for incumbent, for an election in which voters retain the (dominant) incumbent parties, and one for elections in which reform incumbents are retained. The continuous economic performance variables include the rate of real GDP growth, the rate of inflation in the consumer price index and the unemployment rate. We also add the inflation and unemployment rates to create a misery index. Economic data are from official international and governmental agency sources.[12]

Why Reform?

Votes for reformers are consistently correlated with subsequent reforms. The coefficients indicating the effect on reform of votes for reformers (the variable Vote) are positive in every reform equation in Table B.5. All vote coefficients are significantly different from zero – we can reject the null hypothesis that voting for reformers has no effect on reforms taking place. The coefficient of the lagged reform variable is negative and significant in two of four equations. This result indicates that reforms can lead to the removal of reformers. This observation would be consistent with our view that reforms are going to be unpopular in the short run, so that undertaking reforms is a risky political business. Reform progress toward capitalist markets in former socialist states is likely to be a stop–go process, since unpopular reform results in removal of reform parties. Socialists then replace reformers until a new economic crisis induces re-election of reformers.

The only country variable that was significant in the reform dummy equations was the Slovakian dummy that was positive, which suggests that reform occurred in Slovakia even though reformers were not elected.

It seems evident from the raw data that the reformers enter office during extremely poor economic conditions, usually depression or hyperinflation or both. While this point may seem obvious, socialists are unlikely to relinquish power unless forced to by crisis. Perhaps more importantly, official statistics of economic conditions, while probably flawed, imply that economic conditions deteriorate more after reformers are in office. These facts have important implications for the political dimensions to economic reform. Every reform regime has to make a case for people tolerating hard times before reforms are going to bring about a turn of events. This is a major problem for economic reforms in any democracy. How does one get the electorate to accept the down time before reforms can kick in? It is especially difficult in former communist regimes in which promises of a better future were a well-worn mantra.

Indeed, positive economic performance slightly favors socialists. Voters may not risk losing the security of the welfare state and the siren song of socialism unless under severe economic distress. The hard reforms needed to achieve Western-style market economies are unlikely to be popular. Incumbency, as in the West, tends to help both parties. It strongly favors the socialists, who apparently have to mess the economy up pretty badly to be unseated. Reformers have had a more difficult time sustaining power. This may reflect the fact that economic performance is poor under their leadership. Unfortunately for reformers, successful economic performance can lag significantly behind political actions that set the stage for such performance. This creates a serious political challenge for supporters of reform.

Should They Vote for Reformers?

The next set of dummy variable regressions, Table B.6, attempts to explain voting behavior as a function of reforms, economic forces and country dummy variables. While reforms

Table B.5 Dummy regression results on reforms (Reform = R[Votes, Economics, Country])*

	Reform dummy – dependent variable						
Constant			–.1018	–.0333	.1049		
			(.6791)	(.1629)	(.8668)		
Vote	.6944	.6919	.7271	.7317	.9418	.7947	.8198
	(6.794)	(7.9972)	(4.8150)	(4.324)	(6.4241)	(6.7322)	(6.8624)
Reform –	–.4434	–.5100	–.2847	–.3215			
lagged	(2.8950)	(3.6059)	(1.6798)	(1.6880)			
Income					.0380		.0166[L]
					(2.6936)		(1.1088)
Misery					.0006	.0004	.0005
					(2.6936)	(1.2975)	(1.4404)
Gov. deficit	–.0389	–.0252	–.0229	–.0321			
	(2.0480)	(1.2895)	(.8770)	(1.1277)			
Slovakia	1.0165	1.0029	.5727	.5168	.8390	.6632	.7242
	(4.2877)	(4.4252)	(2.5256)	(2.0247)	(3.2979)	(2.6079)	(2.8003)
Hungary	–.3675	–.3187		–.3229	–.4731		
	(2.1058)	(1.9257)		(1.2148)	(2.3073)		
Bulgaria				.1219			
				(0.4763)			
Incumbent	.2033[R]	.2192	.3356	.1646	–.4737	–.3436	–.3006
	(1.0464)	(1.9819)	(2.5256)	(.8695)	(3.2918)	(2.1976)	(1.8770)
	Equation statistics						
R^2	.7804	.8190	.6791	.6783	.7642	.6120	.6381
DF	16	15	16	14	15	18	17
F-statistic	11.3739	11.3141	6.7723	4.2176	8.1012	9.4625	7.4947
R-bar^2	.5946	.5850	.5172	.4522	.5458	.5245	.5166
N	22	22	22	22	22	22	22

Notes:
* The t-statistics are in parentheses beneath coefficients.
L: Variable lagged one period.
R: Incumbent reformers only.

mildly tend to support better economic performance, the presence of reform governments indicates poorer economic performance. This latter effect probably reflects the poor conditions inherited by reformers and their inability in many instances, especially in Bulgaria, Russia and Hungary, to obtain decisive majorities that would have allowed them to institute robust and meaningful reforms.

Table B.6 *Dummy regression results on vote variables (Vote = R[Reform, Economics, Country]**

	Dependent variable						
	Vote for reformers			Reform incumbent		Vote for socialists	
Constant	.1332	.2131	.5677	.1356	.0880	.4012	.4630
	(1.0362)	(1.8010)	(4.7545)	(1.5371)	(1.1767)	(2.8037)	(3.9682)
Reform	.6003	.5984	–.536[L]	.5078[L]	.5048[L]	–.6484[L]	.5103[L]
	(3.5221)	(3.4233)	(1.6809)	(3.8261)	(4.1924)	(3.2592)	(1.7340)
Income			.0034[L]	.0040[L]			.0274
			(0.2081)	(0.4419)			(1.5006)
Inflation	.0004			–.0001[L]			
	(1.4077)			(.5478)			
Gov. deficit				.0453[L]	.0398[L]	–.0408[L]	
				(2.2885)	(2.1720)	(1.3458)	
Bulgaria						.3587	
						(1.5752)	
Slovakia							.4396
							(1.2453)
Incumbent	.2854	.2213	1.0059			.1967	–.8169[R]
	(1.4566)	(1.1235)	(2.6300)			(1.5752)	(2.1457)
	Equation statistics						
R^2	.5127	.4590	.2799	.5713	.5362	.4789	.3945
DF	18	19	18	17	19	17	17
F-statistic	6.3120	8.0606	2.3317	5.6627	10.9834	3.8998	2.7689
R-bar^2	.4394	.4153	.2399	.4624	.4851	.3874	.3193
N	22	22	22	22	22	22	22

Notes:
* The t-statistics are in parentheses beneath coefficients.
L: Variable lagged one period.
R: Incumbent reformers only.

Measured Economic Performance

Table B.7 contains regressions to explain economic variables with lagged economic variables and other economic variables as well as dummy variables for votes and for reforms. The first four equations are attempts to explain income. The lagged reforms variable tends to be negatively correlated with income. This result suggests that reforms do not quickly lead to increases in growth rates. Income has some trend in it, judging from the positive coefficient on lagged income. Inflation lagged has a negative effect on income growth. This is certainly consistent with traditional analysis of inflation's negative effects on market per-

Table B.7 Economic variables on dummy variables for reform and votes (Economics = D[Vote, Reform, Economics, Country])*

	Dependent variable						
	Income						
	Per year		Per election interval		Inflation		
Constant	.7357	1.6978			–270.654		–213.969
	(.3417)	(0.8003)			(2.1675)		(1.6215)
Vote	–3.1601	–3.3644	–2.7644	–1.2727			
	(1.3418)	(1.0336)	(1.5290)	(0.7496)			
Reform	–3.2777	–3.3262	–4.5994	–4.3858	131.014	–151.526^L	–110.457^L
	(1.5916)	(1.6902)	(2.3035)	(2.1018)	(1.2345)	(1.4996)	(1.153)
Income	.5404^L	.5403^L		–.0229^L	–22.525	–20.695	–24.5902
	(3.2081)	(3.3640)		(0.1463))	(2.2366)	(2.0276)	(2.4699)
Inflation	–.0053^L	–.0056^L	–.0092^L	–.0091^L	.7088^L	.5728^L	.5837^L
	(1.4622)	(1.6239)	(2.6450)	(2.2035)	(3.7156)	(3.0019)	(3.2780)
Unemploy.					52.348	34.258	54.813
					(3.3577)	(3.9673)	(3.5779)
Gov. deficit	–.9015^L	–.8446^L	–.9392^L	–.8165^L	70.578^L	56.723^L	59.102^L
	(2.5042)	(2.3843)	(2.2755)	(1.9497)	(3.2782)	(2.6058)	(2.9390)
Czech R.		–3.2697	.9317	–2.7944		–35.692	
		(1.5059)	(1.7452)	(1.6126)		(1.3775)	
Bulgaria		–3.6747	–4.3941	–5.1616	–377.340	–280.692	–334.775
		(1.4693)	(1.5503)	(1.7467)	(3.0014)	(1.9378)	(2.6147)
	Equation statistics						
R^2	.5860	.6722	.4927	.4876	.7632	.7282	.7603
DF	16	14	16	15	15	15	15
F-statistic	4.5298	4.1021	3.1081	2.3795	8.0555	6.6981	7.9311
R-bar^2	.4465	.4482	.3754	.3483	.5451	.5201	.5431
N	22	22	22	22	22	22	22

Notes:
* The t-statistics are in parentheses beneath coefficients.
L: Variable lagged one period.

formance. Lagged government budget deficits have persistent negative effects on income growth, again a result consistent with our expectations.

The inflation variable seems to us to be one of the more reliable economic indicators. In Table B.7, columns 5 to 7 are attempts to explain this economic variable. Inflation follows lagged inflation and corresponds to lower income and lower unemployment. Government budget deficits, lagged, raise the inflation rate. The negative significant coefficient on the Bulgarian variable implies, *ceteris paribus*, lower inflation than elsewhere. We now turn to more precise measures of voting behavior and reform regimes.

7. VOTES, REFORMS AND PERFORMANCE: PERCENTAGE OF VOTES AND REFORM INDEXES

Does the percentage of votes cast for reform parties (as we identify them) lead to more reform in the subsequent election interval? We ask a corollary question. Are any countries different in terms of the influence of elections on reforms? Some observers have claimed that "everyone is a reformer." This is most certainly not true in some countries. Bulgaria, for instance, has two sets of parties or coalitions that have distinct differences of opinion regarding markets. Socialist and agrarian parties have tended to resist reforms, whereas the UDF has been very strongly pro-reform. The socialists have also proven unwilling to correct fiscal imbalances and have been slow to accept central bank independence. The relative power of the communists in the Russian Duma also seemed to have an important impact on Yeltsin's willingness and ability to adopt strong reforms.

However, in some countries identifying reformers is much more problematic. In countries like Estonia and Hungary the issue is much less obvious and differences are blurred. Still, we tried to distinguish parties likely to have stronger pro-market orientation from those who may resist the more difficult pro-market policies. In Hungary, for instance, the socialist parties have a lot of former communists who may feel lukewarm about privatization, stock markets and restructuring. In Czechoslovakia the Velvet Divorce reflected strong differences of opinion between the Czech leader Vaclav Klaus and the Slovak leader Vladimir Meciar. The former was, at least in the early years, a staunch pro-market advocate, whereas the latter held to the old ways. Later in the Czech Republic, under a weakened ODS (Civic Democratic Party) led by Klaus, reform stalled. In fact, the opposition parties ran against the ODS on the ground that more restructuring was needed. Indeed, it became evident that the highly visible voucher privatization had in fact led to less "private" and more "government" influence than had been advertised. The central bank retained significant influence through ownership of financial assets of many companies, especially in the financial sector; and the government controlled banks that in turn controlled investment funds that held most vouchers.

Many local analysts felt the slump in the Czech economy in the late 1990s reflected the failure of the Czech government to adopt stronger restructuring efforts. Not only was central control of the financial sector sustained, but also many state-owned enterprises with large numbers of workers stayed on the government payroll. It was these delays and the position of Klaus's opposition that caused us to identify him as a "relative non-reformer" and them as "relatively pro-reform" prior to the 1996 and 1998 elections.

Estonia is an interesting case, because everyone purports to favor reforms. This is as we had expected, given the antagonism toward external domination and the subsuming of all Estonia into the centrally planned economy of the Soviet Union. Estonians are in a hurry to return to the Western fold. Still, even here the socialist ways are hard to give up and the pace of reforms has not been even over election cycles.

Country-Specific Analysis

Table B.8 reports country-specific regressions of the following equation:

$$\text{Reform} = \alpha + \beta \text{ Vote} + \varepsilon$$

Table B.8 Country-specific and pooled regressions on reform (Reform = α + β Vote + ε)*

Variable	Country equations					Pooled data	
	Bulgaria	Czech Rep.	Estonia	Hungary	Russia		
Constant	19.1237	75.7583	72.0684	98.0517	88.2783	79.8486	67.2115
	(3.2520)	(12.2291)	(4.6526)	(13.5202)	(14.3782)	(8.6831)	(13.228)
Vote	1.7060	.4952	.7207	.3421	.6716	.5975	.7409
	(14.4502)	(3.5187)	(2.3679)	(1.9874)	(5.1518)	(3.0527)	(6.1464)
History under communism							16.6763
							(7.4078)
Equation statistics							
R^2	.9905	.8755	.7371	.7986	.8984	.3178	.8245
DF	2	2	2	1	3	20	19
F-statistic	208.809	14.0637	5.6071	3.9661	26.5406	9.3187	44.6218
R-bar^2	.6603	.5837	.4914	.3993	.6738	.3027	.7459
N	4	4	4	3	5	22	22

Notes:
* The t-statistics are in parentheses beneath the coefficients.
History under communism is 1 for Russia and Hungary. 0 otherwise.

where α and β are the unknown intercept and slope coefficients to be estimated and ε is the unknown disturbance term. For most countries we have few observations because they have not held many national elections. These regressions do indicate the degree of correlation between votes for reformers and subsequent reforms.

The slope coefficients in the country-specific regressions are positive and range from 0.34 for Hungary to 1.71 for Bulgaria. Evidently votes for reformers as we measure them are correlated with the index for reform as we measure it. We have few events, so statistics do not tell us much, but these results fail to rule out a connection between votes for reformers and subsequent reforms. The last two regression columns in Table B.8 are pooled data for all six countries. The last regression includes a dummy variable equal to 1 for Russia and Hungary. This variable, History, represents the idea that strong local support for communist philosophy is retained in these two countries. We elaborate on this idea below.

Analyzing Reform with Pooled Data

To look in more detail at whether one can distinguish reformers from non-reformers, we ran a number of regressions on pooled data. Table B.9 contains reports on eight regressions. The reform index for each election interval, the dependent variable, depends on the percentage of

Table B.9 Do votes for reformers result in reforms? (Reform = R[Vote, Economics, History])*

Variable	Linear forms				Natural log-linear forms			
Constant	67.212	68.405	65.417	68.81	3.20	3.62	3.52	3.52
	(13.23)*	(13.57)	(11.677)	(14.34)	(20.79)	(20.20)	(18.91)	(19.12)
Vote	.741	.701	.770	.699	.2614	.2592	.2767	.2772
	(7.15)	(6.65)	(6.94)	(6.99)	(5.79)	(5.49)	(6.02)	(6.06)
Misery		.0068	$.0041^{L}$			.0021	$.0098^{L}$	
		(1.374)	(0.80)			(.242)	(1.29)	
Income %chg real				.4238				
				(1.73)				
Inflation				.0137				$.0098^{L}$
				(2.22)				(1.36)
History under communism	16.68	15.72	16.36	15.91	.1605	.1581	.1588	.1591
	(7.41)	(6.82)	(7.09)	(6.73)	(6.67)	(5.96)	(6.71)	(6.75)
				Equation statistics				
R^2	.8245	.8411	.8305	.8647	.7672	.7680	.7869	.7888
DF	19	18	18	17	19	18	18	18
F-statistic	44.62	31.77	29.39	27.16	31.31	19.86	22.16	22.41
R-bar^2	.7459	.7210	.7118	.7000	.6942	.6583	.6745	.6761
Best	Russ – 93	Bulg – 92	Bulg – 92	Esto – 92	Russ – 93	Bulg – 92	Esto – 95	Esto – 95
Worst	Bulg – 97	Bulg – 97	Bulg – 97	Bulg – 97	Bulg – 97	Bulg – 97	Esto – 90	Esto – 97

Notes:
* The t-statistics are in parentheses beneath the coefficients. All variables cover election intervals.
L ≡ lagged one period. We included 22 elections, so n = 22.
Best ≡ observation with the smallest error term.
Worst ≡ largest error.

votes garnered by reformers, on an economic variable (or set of variables) and on a history variable. The history variable is a dummy variable – 1 for countries (Russia and Hungary) that had strong homegrown communist parties and relative success while under communist control. Of course, considerable additional experimentation was done and Table B.9 is illustrative. We tested for history before communism – Estonia, the Czechs and Hungary all had golden eras of success in recent periods prior to the ascent of communism. We tested another history under communism variable; some countries had relatively good relations with communists (Bulgaria and Slovakia). Only the history under communism representing the strong version of well-being under communism mattered. We can reject the null hypothesis that history under communism does not matter to subsequent reform efforts.

The effect on reform actions, given voting behavior, is clearly different for Russia and Hungary than for other countries in the sample. (Equations with the one history variable outperformed two separate dummies, one for Russia and one for Hungary.) It appears that reformers are even more sensitive to voters in Russia and Hungary. These two countries still have politically strong communist influences. The Russian Communist Party control of the

Duma is historic. The socialist parties populated by many former communists continue to dominate Hungarian politics. These countries also seem to be ambivalent about adopting reforms. We expected this. Both Hungary and Russia had relatively good relations with the communist leadership. In the case of Russia, of course, this was the seat of power for the entire Soviet Union and the satellite countries and, with the exception of Lenin's train ride to Russia from Germany, communism was homegrown. Despite the collapse of the Soviet Union, Russians are conflicted about abandoning the old ways. This evidently has made reformers quite sensitive to votes for members of the Duma. Yeltsin was criticized for not stabilizing the economy and legal system, but he may have had little choice given the post-Soviet power of Russian communists.

Many in Hungary harbor affection for communism for a different reason. After the Hungarian revolt in 1956, even though Russian tanks destroyed the resistance, Hungary eventually was allowed a good deal of independence. As long as Hungarians maintained outward support for socialism and participated fully in the Warsaw Pact, they were allowed to develop small-scale markets. Hungary was referred to as "the happiest barracks in the camp" precisely because their economy was the strongest in Central Europe. This relative success of socialism blended with small-scale market economics and the authority of local communists gave Hungarians less reason to despise communist rule. This in turn meant that Hungarians felt less eager to overthrow the old regime.

It is evident from Table B.9 that votes for reformers are positive and statistically significant. We reject the null hypothesis that votes for reformers do not lead to reforms. Put another way, our reform index is positively correlated with the percentage of votes for reform parties. This result holds up in both linear and log-linear forms and regardless of the economic variables included in the equation. The vote variable was also positive and significant in similar equations (explaining reform) using annual economic data rather than economic data per election interval. We also experimented with dropping observations where we felt the data might be less reliable. We deleted the first election in every country to see if poor early data had a significant impact on results. They did not.

What Explains Votes for Reformers?

Suppose through campaigns that voters know what to expect from the more reform-oriented parties. Will these reforms and contemporary or lagged economic variables lead to votes for reformers? Does history under communism make a difference – do some countries' voters act differently? Table B.10 contains results of eight regressions intended to shed light on these questions. Regressions in Table B.10 explain about 65 to 75 percent of the variation in votes for reformers. Reforms are invariably a significant variable and values are positive. A 10 percent increase in a reform index is associated with a 10 percent increase in votes for reformers.

Economic variables do not seem to have substantial effects on votes. Economic variables were rarely significant. We tested the percentage change in GDP, the inflation rate, the unemployment rate and a misery index (inflation plus unemployment). Lagged values of all economic variables were also examined.

While insignificant, the economic variables tended to work against reformers. These empirical results may reflect several factors. One is that some of the data, especially unem-

Table B.10 Why do people vote for reformers? (Vote = V[Reform, Economics, History])*

Variable	Linear forms				Natural log-linear forms			
Constant	–53.30	–56.06	–48.57	–48.41	–7.44	–7.37	–7.18	–7.23
	(3.76)	(3.63)	(3.44)	(3.16)	(3.82)	(3.66)	(3.86)	(3.90)
Reform	.984	1.014	.945	.9433	2.44	2.42	2.41	2.42
	(7.146)	(6.65)	(6.94)	(6.41)	(5.79)	(5.49)	(6.02)	(6.06)
Misery		– .0031	–.008 L			.0078	–.0379^{L}	
		(0.509)	(1.47)			(.301)	(1.75)	
Inflation				–.0081^{L}				–.037^{L}
				(1.295)				(1.79)
History under	–17.51	–17.55	–16.14	–16.04	–.440	–.445	–.4221	–.424
communism	(5.53)	(5.43)	(5.02)	(3.77)	(4.96)	(4.82)	(4.97)	(5.02)
				Equation statistics				
R^2	.7384	.7421	.7664	.7663	.6607	.6623	.7098	.7119
DF	19	18	18	17	19	18	18	18
F-statistic	26.81	17.26	19.68	13.93	18.50	11.77	14.68	14.83
R-bar^2	.6680	.6361	.6569	.6203	.5977	.5677	.6084	.6102
Best	Bulg – 92	Russ – 91	Esto – 95	Esto – 95	Russ – 91	Bulg – 92	Czec – 90	Czec – 90
Worst	Russ – 95	Russ – 95	Hung – 94	Esto – 97	Russ – 95	Russ – 95	Russ – 95	Hung – 94

Notes:
* The t-statistics are in parentheses beneath the coefficients. All variables cover election intervals.
L ≡ lagged one period. 22 elections, so n = 22.
Best ≡ observation with smallest error term.

ployment and GDP figures for early years, are suspect. Second, all of the countries in our sample went through deep slumps with double-digit declines in income. These occurred early in the period, right after the country swept away the communist government. The ways of doing business had to change in all countries since the trading regime had collapsed. This first government after communism also had the first opportunity to institute reforms. Thus, just as the economies and in fact the entire social structures were collapsing around them, reformers tried to institute new reforms; price liberalization and property privatization initiatives were common. These initiatives contributed to our index of reforms. Thus, reforms are correlated in early years with the collapsed economies.

Regardless of how one stands on the issue of shock therapy or on the quality of the data, one must accept the reality that reform is correlated, at least early on, with poor economic outcomes. As we have noted, this correlation is part of the reason reforms are difficult to adopt. Benefits accrue only after a long lag. Furthermore, the intent of reforms is to set the stage for long-run economic growth, not for instant gratification. The fact that the economic variables are not significantly and negatively correlated with votes for reformers is itself an indicator that people have been willing to give reform a chance.

The dummy variable for relatively positive performance under communism, the History variable, has a negative and significant coefficient. Voters in Russia and Hungary, two countries with strong domestic communist parties, relatively happy under communism, are less likely to respond positively to reforms than are voters in the other four sample countries.

Can Economic Performance Variables Be Explained?

Table B.11 contains results of six equations intended to explain variations in two economic variables, inflation and income. Economic data seem to be much poorer than the voting data. Measured GDP leaves out work at home and on small farms, which blossomed during the early stages of transition, and in some countries it may have been difficult to capture growth in small retail firms. Failing large-scale former government enterprises cause severe decline in measured output, but this may exaggerate the decline in real underlying income since

Table B.11 Can economic performance be explained? (Economics = E[Reform, Vote, $Economics_{t-1}$, History])*

Variable	Inflation – dependent variable (% rate of change in CPI)			Income – dependent variable (% rate of change in GDP)		
Constant	–1502.	–1499.	–1503.	–24.96		
	(2.22)	(2.22)	(2.35)	(1.71)		
Vote				–.241	–.076	–.205
				(1.42)	(1.79)	(1.95)
Reform	15.80	15.82	15.47	.352	.076	.080
	(2.42)	(2.42)	(2.50)	(1.73)	(1.61)	(1.71)
Income			–15.24^L		.436^L	–.514^L
			(1.75)		(2.82)	(4.02)
Inflation		.764^L	.579^L	–.019	–.0029	
		(3.00)	(2.76)	(4.22)	(0.905)	
Misery	.7641^L					
	(3.99)					
History under communism	–368.1	–367.8	–339.2	–3.80		
	(2.34)	(2.35)	(2.27)	(1.01)		
			Equation statistics			
R^2	.4992	.5002	.5767	.5283	.5005	.4778
DF	18	18	17	17	18	19
F-statistic	5.980	6.005	5.789	4.760	6.012	8.691
R-bar²	.4279	.4288	.4668	.4277	.4290	.4323
Best	Hung – 98	Hung – 98	Russ – 93	Czec – 98	Russ – 96	Hung – 94
Worst	Esto – 92	Esto – 92	Esto – 92	Slov – 94	Esto – 97	Esto – 97

Notes:
* The t-statistics are beneath coefficients. All variables cover election intervals.
L ≡ lagged variable. 22 elections, so n = 22.
Best ≡ observation with smallest error term.

some gray market and extra-market activity began to take place in these plants and factories during early phases of transition. Also, loss of production from some state-owned enterprises may have involved loss of product that was unwanted in the first place.

We focus on two issues raised in our theory work. First, are reforms related positively to economic performance? If not, then the political work by reform-oriented political parties is more difficult. Unless growth follows reforms pretty quickly, people may tire of promises. After all, the communists always promised a better tomorrow. A task of political leaders is to educate the public about the benefits of new programs that will improve welfare, even if there are short-run costs. This task is hard if reforms deliver benefits only after a lengthy delay.

Second, do differences in historical experiences among countries play a role in economic performance? We had two historical hypotheses. One, the existence of a golden era, in which capitalism and democracy were successful before the communist period, gives a practical "goal" for reform to achieve. This suggests that countries like Estonia, the Czech Republic and Hungary should fare better than Russia, Slovakia and Bulgaria. The latter three countries have almost no experience with democracy or successful capitalist industrialization. Estonia, the Czech Republic and Hungary were relatively well off and Westernized before the advent of communism.

The second historical hypothesis is that the experience under communism will influence the pace of adopting reforms. Relatively good times under communism could make it more difficult to repudiate communism. It is easier to discredit communist ways if they were imposed from outside and if your people were maltreated. Russia and Hungary came to be governed by willing local leaders. Despite, or some say because of, the 1956 Hungarian revolt, local communists were given a good deal of freedom in adopting a mixed economy. The Soviets gave Hungarians some control over their economic fortunes as long as they remained loyal to socialism. Communism, while unpopular with many Russians, was largely a homegrown product. Repudiating communism's ways is harder when they resulted from decisions made by Russians. The Estonians and Czechs disliked the Soviet imposition of communism. The Slovakians and Bulgarians were better off in some respects under communism, and never really had a golden era of industrialization under capitalism and democracy. Thus, history under communism should influence the adoption of reforms, votes for reform parties and economic performance.

We attempt to explain variations in two economic outcome variables, income and inflation. Income, measured as the growth rate of GDP, is closest to the growth variable our theoretical work focuses on, but the quality of data is suspect. Inflation may be a more reliable statistic, at least for most countries after the fall of communism. Even this statistic is subject to serious criticism related to inadequate correction for quality improvements. Early price liberalization resulted in nominal price increases that indicated an increase in inflation. However this index increase merely reflected adoption of a market-price system, a very different process from inflation. Nonetheless, these are the data available. We report six equations in Table B.11. Inflation is the dependent variable in equations of columns 1 to 3 and income, measured as the percentage rate of change in real GDP, is the dependent variable in equations of columns 4 to 6.

The explanatory power of the economic variable equations is lower than that of reform and vote equations. The R-bar^2 (coefficient of determination adjusted for degrees of freedom) ranges from 43 to 47. The R^2 values are around .5, so that almost half the variation in economic variables can be explained by the equations. Inflation is positively correlated with the reform index. This may suggest that reformers liberalized prices. Lagged inflation influences inflation, suggesting inertia. The history variable (1 for Russia and Hungary and 0 for the other countries) is negative and significant. Evidently, inflation is worse for countries that performed relatively well or had homegrown communist leadership.

Variations in the growth rate of GDP are harder to explain. The model explains nearly half the variation in real GDP; the political variables have little influence on measured economic variables. Neither reforms nor history seem to matter much in explaining variations in measured GDP growth. Though reforms have a modest positive effect on income, votes for reform have a modest negative effect. Neither vote nor reform is statistically significant. Only lagged growth in real GDP has a positive and significant correlation with the growth rate of real GDP. This suggests inertia in the income figures. Contemporary inflation is negatively correlated with growth in real GDP, a sensible result. Recall our belief that economic variables are probably rather unreliable. Also, they are being reported for highly unstable periods. This project suggests the importance of serious revisions of economic data from new market economies. Still, even if the economic data do not reflect actual performance, these figures can influence policy. A disconnect between adoption of painful reforms and measured economic success can deflate reform efforts.

Two-Stage Least Squares Results

Table B.12 contains results from two-stage least squares estimation models to determine the effect on reforms of votes for reformers. Equation system (B.9) is the model we are estimating. We estimated several different versions of the model to check for robustness of the results.

There are two sets of results presented in Table B.12. The first row equation estimates the coefficient of Vote from predetermined and exogenous variables of the system: Reform_{t-1}, Bulgaria, Inflation_{t-1}. We estimated several different versions of this equation. For instance, the second set of results in Table B.12 excludes Bulgaria from the first equation. We also replaced Inflation_{t-1} with Income_{t-1} and tested for serial correlation with Inflation_{t-2} and Income_{t-2}. These variables added nothing to the equation. We repeat that the income data again seem to contain severe measurement error. However, the results for the second-stage estimator of the over-identified coefficient in the reform equation were the same for all variants of the model.

Recall that in the second stage, the stage I estimators of Vote (or Vote*) replace the variable Vote in the reform equation. The coefficient of Vote* indicates that an increase in the vote received by reform parties tends to lead to a nearly proportional increase in the rate of reforms.

The Hausman tests indicate that simultaneous equation bias was present for the vote variable. Hausman test 1 involves testing whether the coefficients on Vote* and Error* are the same. We cannot reject the null that they are the same indicating bias. Hausman test 2 amounts to the null hypothesis that with bias the coefficient on Error* is zero. We cannot reject this null. These tests hold for all variations in the model specification. These coefficient estimates are .93 to .95 for the effect of votes on reform. (These are the last two equations of each set in Table B.12.)

Table B.12 Two-stage least squares estimation (model Vote = V[Reform$_{t-1}$, Bulgaria, Economics$_{t-1}$] Economics = E[Reform$_{t-1}$, History, Economics$_{t-1}$] Reform = R[Vote, History])*

Stage I

Vote = –.1300 + .445 Reform$_{t-1}$ + 11.257 Bulgaria – .020 Inflation$_{t-1}$
(.006) (2.240) (1.870) (2.781)
n=22 DF = 18 R^2 = .3450 F-statistic = 2.161 *R*-bar^2 = .2957

Inflation = –1499 + 15.82 Reform – 367.8 History + .764 Inflation$_{t-1}$
(2.219) (2.422) (2.435) (3.997)
n=22 DF = 18 R^2 = .5002 F-statistic = 6.005 R-bar^2 = .4288

Stage II

Reform = 58.925 + .9330 Vote* + 15.255 History
(4.836) (3.603) (4.619)
n=22 DF = 18 R^2 = .6154 F-statistic = 15.203 R-bar^2 = .5568

Hausman test 1

Reform = 57.641 + .9490 Vote* + 16.776 History + .6326 Error*
(7.240) (5.611) (7.705) (5.152)
n=22 DF = 18 R^2 = .8446 F-statistic = 32.612 R-bar2 = .7239

Hausman test 2

Reform = 57.641 + .9490 Vote + 16.776 History – .3164 Error*
(7.240) (5.611) (7.705) (1.527)
n=22 DF = 18 R^2 = .8446 F-statistic = 32.612 R-bar^2 = .7239

Model without Bulgaria

Stage I

Vote = 21.483 + .254 Reform$_{t-1}$ – .017 Inflation$_{t-1}$
(1.146) (1.403) (2.250) 0
n=22 DF = 19 R^2 = .2177 F-statistic = 2.644 R-bar^2 = .1970

Stage II

Reform = 59.608 + .9298 Vote* + 13.783 History
(3.571) (2.577) (3.770)
n=22 DF = 19 R^2 = .5203 F-statistic = 10.305 R-bar^2 = .4708

Hausman test 1

Reform = 58.471 + .9332 Vote* + 16.482 History + .6852 Error*
(5.790) (4.276) (7.295) (5.825)
n=22 DF = 18 R^2 = .8337 F-statistic = 30.087 R-bar^2 = .7146

Hausman test 2

Reform = 58.471 + .9332 Vote + 16.482 History – .2480 Error*
(5.790) (4.276) (7.295) (1.002)
n=22 DF = 18 R^2 = .8337 F-statistic = 30.087 R-bar^2 = .7146

Notes:
Vote* is the estimated vote from the stage I vote equation.
Error* is the error from the stage I vote equation.
*The t-statistics are in parentheses beneath the coefficients.

The second stage of the two-stage process provides an estimate of about .93 for the coefficient capturing the effect on reform of votes for reformers. Table B.9 indicated coefficients for this variable between .7 and .8. All of these estimators of the unknown α_{13} in the third equation of system (B.9) are all close to but less than 1. We conclude that reform policy response is nearly proportional to votes for reformers. This result indicates that the political system is quite effective in determining the pace of reforms.

Logit Results

The dependent variable in the vote equation in stage I is the percentage of the vote received by reformers. As a percentage it cannot be distributed as normal. Even though most observations are far from the likely tails of the distribution, we transformed Vote using a logit model. These results are presented in Table B.13. They confirm results from Table B.12. The logit model Hausman tests confirm simultaneous equation bias of the vote coefficient in the reform equation. The effect on reform of votes for reformers is still close to but less than one, around .94.

Table B.13 Logit analysis with two-stage least squares (Model [ln (Vote/1–Vote)] = V[Reform$_{t-1}$, Bulgaria, Economics$_{t-1}$] Economics = E[Reform$_{t-1}$, History, Economics$_{t-1}$] Reform = R[Vote, History])*

Stage I

$$\text{Logit-Vote} = \underset{(2.312)}{-2.0650} + \underset{(2.171)}{.018}\ \text{Reform}_{t-1} + \underset{(1.857)}{.474}\ \text{Bulgaria} - \underset{(2.793)}{.001}\ \text{Inflation}_{t-1}$$

n=22 DF = 18 R^2 = .3437 F-statistic = 3.143 R-bar^2 = .2946

Stage II

$$\text{Reform} = \underset{(5.006)}{59.912} + \underset{(3.587)}{.9155}\ \text{Vote}^{**} + \underset{(4.618)}{15.287}\ \text{History}$$

n=22 DF = 18 R^2 = .6140 F-statistic = 15.113 R-bar^2 = .5555

Hausman test 1

$$\text{Reform} = \underset{(7.420)}{58.003} + \underset{(5.656)}{.9424}\ \text{Vote}^{**} + \underset{(7.703)}{16.788}\ \text{History} + \underset{(5.160)}{.6336}\ \text{Error}^{**}$$

n=22 DF = 18 R^2 = .8443 F-statistic = 32.540 R-bar^2 = .7237

Hausman test 2

$$\text{Reform} = \underset{(7.240)}{58.003} + \underset{(5.656)}{.9424}\ \text{Vote} + \underset{(7.703)}{16.788}\ \text{History} - \underset{(1.515)}{.3088}\ \text{Error}^{**}$$

n=22 DF = 18 R^2 = .8443 F-statistic = 32.540 R-bar^2 = .7237

Notes:
Vote** is the predicted vote computed from the anti-log of the stage I vote equation.
Error** is the error from the stage I vote equation transformed to be comparable to Vote**.
*The t-statistics are in parentheses beneath the coefficients.

Table B.14 Some key reform dates

	Bulgaria	Czech R.	Estonia	Hungary	Russia	Slovak R.
			Price liberalization			
Initial effort	1991	1991	1990	1968	1/1992	1991
Progress				41% – 87 62% – 89 77% – 90 85% – 99	Not staples	1999
			Market Privatization			
Initial Effort	1992 18% – '97	1991	1991	1982	11/1992	1991
Major Progress	12/1998 70%	1992	1992	10/1989	1/3rd 93 6/1994	1998
Vouchers	1997–98	1992 W-I	10/1994		10.1992	1992
Setback (Law)	1995–96	1995 W-II	3/1995	7/1994 1/1996	Stop-94/5	9/1995
			Stabilization			
Two-tier banking		1/1990	1991	1987		1/1990
Tax Reform	1997/98		1991 VAT		1990 VAT	1/1996 VAT
Fiscal Reform	1998		1992	12/1995		9/1990
Pensions				1997–98		
Currency reform	1991	9/1990	1992	1995	7/1993	1995
Currency board	7/1997		6/1992			
Serious setback	1994–96 Ponzi	5/1997 1995–97	11/1992		10/1994 1/1996	1996–97
Tightened Budget	1998					1998
Stock Exchange	10/1997		5/1996	5/1990		
			International trade			
EU – first tranche		1999	1999	1999		
EU associate	Mar 1993					
Liberalize effort		1991	12/1991	1982		
Setback	1996–97				1995–97	7/1994
IMF	3/1997	1990	5/1992	1982	6/1992	3/1994
Setback	1996	5/1997			On/off	1996–97
WTO	1996					1/1995
OECD		12/1995		5/1996		
FDI	1998			2xCzech		
			Deregulation – restructuring			
Soft credits and no big failures	1991–96 ZUNK					
Dump SU plans					10/1990	
Cut $ off Ministries					11/1991	
Bankruptcy Laws	1999			1/1992		

Note:
This table was compiled by the authors from a wide variety of sources, all of which are in the references. The compilation involved the equivalent of an entire appendix. The authors can make this available on request. The most important sources of the raw data for this table were Federal Research Division, Library of Congress; US Army, Country Study, Area Reports; OECD Economic Surveys of countries, specific country statistical agencies and central banks, the OECD, IMF, World Bank and UN Statistical sources.
W-I and W-II: waves 1 and 2 of voucher issues. VAT: value added tax. ZUNK: junk bonds.

8. CONCLUSIONS AND RECOMMENDATIONS

We conclude with the key points we draw from the empirical analysis.

- Voting for reform parties does result in reforms. Votes for reform parties tend to lead to nearly proportional increases in the reform indexes. This result holds up for a variety of functional forms, for nearly all countries and for a variety of specifications and data measures. Socialist and agrarian parties are slower to adopt reforms than are European liberals.
- History matters. Voters are less likely to endorse reformers in both Russia and Hungary. This is consistent with our hypothesis that countries that had enjoyed relatively good economic performance under homegrown communist leaders have a more difficult time adopting capitalist rules through reform. We found no empirical evidence that history before communism made a significant difference in voting behavior, adoption of reforms or measured economic performance. We conclude from these observations that countries without past experience with capitalism can achieve reform. However, to the extent they are unwilling to abandon the old ways or unable to constrain socialist impulses, transition to capitalism will be difficult, contentious and slow.
- Economic variables for misery, inflation and income are negatively correlated with reforms. The economic data do not support the view that reform quickly improves economic performance. While one may suspect this result, it does not augur well for reform. This increases political pressure on reform advocates.
- With the possible exception of inflation figures, economic performance variables are poor quality. International and national statistical agencies should shore up these data so analysts can get a more accurate picture of the transition process.

The problems with economic data are severe and important. Errors in the data may reflect obfuscation on the part of national statistical agencies, practices that were common under communist rule. Such practices may still take place. But even in countries with conscientious and honest statistical agencies, meaningful measures of economic performance are not available. These can be attributed to several well-known measurement problems in compiling statistical aggregates. But, while well known among Western measurement specialists, these problems are more severe in transition economies and can lead to serious distortions of the transformation process. These distortions can work against attempts to reform these economies.

Specific measurement problems that require attention are an overemphasis on the costs of the decline in state-owned enterprises. This reflects the relative ease of obtaining nominal output data from these sources and the failure to measure adequately the usually poor quality of the output these firms had been producing. The quality of output was poor both in terms of physical characteristics of the goods themselves and in terms of the market values of these goods in the post-Cold War environment. Many big state-owned enterprises were producing shoddy goods for markets that were not there.

A second problem, the flip side of the first, is inattention to the importance in early transition of do-it-yourself, trade-out and small-scale gray market production. Many small entrepreneurial enterprises in the transition stage are extra-market. People take on second jobs, work for one another without formal compensation, build additions to their homes for rentals and undertake numerous other activities that are inadequately captured by statistical agencies. There may well be a buzz of economic activity that is replacing the failing and wasteful production of the dinosaurs, the large-scale state-owned enterprises.

International statistical agencies could serve a constructive role for transition economies by sending in measurement teams to produce viable data for economic performance. Data collection and analysis may serve a more important role than traditional research efforts when major shocks to the social system accompany economic transformation.

NOTES

1. The five reforms come from Blanchard et al. (1992), and are discussed in detail in Chapter 3. Appendix A contains the growth model analytics. Growth modeling is explained heuristically in Chapter 4. The relation between reforms and growth is developed in Appendix A and discussed intuitively in Chapter 5.
2. Modeling voting, reform and economics is explained in Chapter 6.
3. The authors can provide details about the raw data on request.
4. These equations are taken from Appendix A in which we develop the growth models. The symbols are defined in Appendix A.
5. In growth models the only good is consumption. No distinction is made between different goods in the consumption bundle. The only choice consumers have is between consumption and saving (that leads to capital formation and future consumption). Empirically, consumption must be represented by some aggregate index of consumer goods. It is in altering the mix of the goods that comprise the underlying index toward those chosen by consumers that will increase utility from any given quantity of aggregate consumption.
6. Hicks-neutral technological change is not used in Appendix A. Harrod-neutral is used. We reference Hicks-neutral here only because it is a simple one-off shot to output given the nature of technology imbedded in the production function.
7. The mix of capital may change. For instance, private producers may decide to use more computers and fewer structures. This could raise the aggregate depreciation rate. However, we are talking about improvements in the efficiency that should result from the private profit motive, of every type of capital.
8. The parameter γ is the growth rate of technological change. See Appendix A. This parameter enters into the Euler condition, the modified golden rule and the steady-state output equation.
9. We abstract here from tie votes and other anomalies.
10. This model is from Berndt (1991), pp. 617–29.
11. See Chapter 2 illustrating different possible targets for reforms. Capitalism is clearly not the only option.
12. Authors can provide details on request.

Bibliography

Abrams, Burton A. and Kenneth A. Lewis (1995), "Cultural and Institutional Determinants of Economic Growth: A Cross-Section Analysis," *Public Choice*, **83**, 273–89.

Aganbegian, Abel Gezevich (1988), *The Economic Challenge of Perestroika*, translated by Pauline M. Tiffen, edited by Michael Barratt Brown, Bloomington, IN: University of Indiana Press.

Aghion, Philippe and Olivier Jean Blanchard (1994), "On the Speed of Transition in Central Europe," NBER Working Paper no. 4736, Cambridge, MA: National Buereau of Economic Research.

Alexeev, Michael (1991), "If Market-Clearing Prices Are So Good, Why Doesn't (Almost) Anybody Want Them?," *Journal of Comparative Economics*, **15** (2), 380–90.

Angelov, Ivan, et al. (1994), *Economic Outlook for Bulgaria, 1995–1997*, Institute of Economics, Bulgarian Academy of Science, Sofia.

Aron, Leon (2000), *Yeltsin: A Revolutionary Life*, New York: St. Martin's Press.

Aslund, Anders, Peter Boone and Simon Johnson (1996), "How to Stabilize: Lessons from Post-Communist Countries," *Brookings Papers on Economic Activity*, **26** (1), 217–313.

Avramov, R. and K. Guenov (1999), "The Rebirth of Capitalism in Bulgaria," National Bank of Bulgaria *Bank Review*, 4, 3–24.

The Baltic Times (1996–2001), Baltic News, Riga. www.baltictimes.com

Balzer, Harley (ed.) (1991), *Five Years that Shrank the World: Gorbachev's Unfinished Revolution*, Boulder, CO: Westview Press.

Bardhan, Pranab and John E. Roemer (1992), "Market Socialism: A Case for Rejuvenation," *Journal of Economic Perspectives*, **6** (3), 101–16.

Barr, Nicolas (ed.) (1994), *Labor Markets and Social Policy in Central and Eastern Europe: The Transition and Beyond*, Oxford: Oxford University Press.

Barro, Robert J. (1989), "A Cross-Country Study of Growth, Saving, and Government," NBER Working Paper No. 2855, Cambridge, MA: National Bureau of Economic Research.

Barro, Robert J. (1994), "Democracy and Growth", NBER Working Paper no. 4909, Cambridge, MA: National Bureau of Economic Research.

Barro, Robert J. (1996a), "Democracy and Growth," *Journal of Economic Growth*, **1** (1), 1–27.

Barro, Robert J. (1996b), *Getting It Right, Markets and Choices in a Free Society*, Cambridge, MA: MIT Press.

Barro, Robert J. (1997), *Determinants of Economic Growth, A Cross-Country Empirical Study*, Cambridge, MA: MIT Press.

Barro, Robert J. and Xavier Sala-i-Martin (1995), *Economic Growth*, New York: McGraw-Hill.

Bates, Robert H. and Anne O. Krueger (1993), *Political and Economic Interactions in Economic Policy Reform*, Oxford: Blackwell.
Beaumont, C., P. Doyle, K. Hviding and J. Ligthart (1999), "Hungary: Selected Issues," IMF Staff Country Report No. 99/27, Washington, DC: International Monetary Fund.
Becker, Gary (1950), "Pressure Groups and Political Behavior," in R.D. Coe and C.K. Wilber (eds), *Capitalism and Democracy: Schumpeter Revisited*, Notre Dame, IN: University of Notre Dame Press, 120–46.
Becker, Gary (1964), *Human Capital*, 3rd edition, 1993, New York: Columbia University Press.
Becker, Gary (1985a), "Public Policies, Pressure Groups and Dead-Weight Costs," *Journal of Public Economics*, **28** (3), 329–47.
Becker, Gary (1985b), "Special Interests and Public Policies," Acceptance Paper, Frank E. Seidman Distinguished Award in Political Economy, 26 September, Rhodes College, Memphis, TN.
Becker, Gary (1993), "Government, Human Capital, and Economic Growth," Presidential Address to the Mont Pelerin Society, *Industry of Free China*, **79** (6), 47–56.
Bergson, Abram (1984), "Income Inequality under Soviet Socialism," *Journal of Economic Literature*, **22** (3), 1052–100.
Berndt, Ernst (1991), *The Practice of Econometrics: Classical and Contemporary*, Reading, MA: Addison-Wesley.
Black, Bernard, Reinier Kraakman and Anna Tarassova (1999), "Russian Privatization and Corporate Governance: What Went Wrong?," Working Paper No. 178, John M. Olin Program in Law and Economics, Stanford Law School, Stanford, CA.
Blanchard, Olivier, Rudiger Dornbusch, Paul Krugman, Richard Layard and Lawrence Summers (1992), *Reform in Eastern Europe*, Cambridge, MA: MIT Press.
Blanchard, Olivier and Stanley Fischer (1989), *Lectures on Macroeconomics*, Cambridge, MA: MIT Press.
Blanchard, Olivier Jean, Kenneth A. Froot and Jeffrey D. Sachs (eds) (1994), *The Transition in Eastern Europe: Country Studies*, Vol. 1, Chicago: University of Chicago Press.
Boeri, Tito and Michael C. Burda (1995), "Active Labor Market Policies, Job Matching and the Czech Miracle," CEPR Research Paper No. 1302, London: Centre for Economic Policy Research.
Bokros, Lajos and Jean-Jacques Dethier (eds) (1998), *Public Finance Reforms during the Transition: The Experience of Hungary*, Washington, DC: World Bank.
Bonin, John P. and Istvan Székely (eds) (1994), *The Development and Reform of Financial Systems in Central and Eastern Europe*, Aldershot, UK and Brookfield, VT: Edward Elgar.
Boycko, Maxim, Andrei Schleifer, and Robert W. Vishny (1993), "Privatizing Russia," *Brookings Papers on Economic Activity*, 2, Washington, DC: Brookings Institution.
Boycko, Maxim, Andrei Schleifer and Robert W. Vishny (1995), *Privatizing Russia*, Cambridge, MA: MIT Press.
Boyer, George R. (1998), "The Historical Background of the Communist Manifesto," *Journal of Economic Perspectives*, **12** (4), 151–74.
Brada, Josef C. (1996), "Privatization Is Transition – Or Is It?" *Journal of Economic Perspectives*, **10** (2), 67–86.

Brada, Josef, Inderjit Singh and Adam Torok (1994), *Firms Afloat and Firms Adrift: Hungarian Industry and the Economic Transition*, Armonk, NY: M.E. Sharpe.
Bradley, John F. M. (1991), *Politics in Czechoslovakia, 1934–1990*, New York: Columbia University Press.
Brady, Rose (1999), *Kapitalizm: Russia's Struggle to Free Its Economy*, New Haven, CT: Yale University Press.
Braguinsky, Serguey and Grigory Yavlinsky (2000), "Incentives and Institutions: The Transition to a Market Economy in Russia," excerpt from book of same title, *Milken Institute Review*, **2** (2), 57–80.
Brainerd, Elizabeth (1998), "Winners and Losers in Russia's Economic Transition," *American Economic Review*, **88** (5), 1094–116.
Brovkin, Vladimir (1998), *Russia after Lenin: Politics, Culture and Society*, London and New York: Routledge.
Brown, J. David and John S. Earle (2000), "Competition and Firm Performance: Lessons from Russia," SITE Working Paper No. 154, Stockholm School of Economics, Stockholm.
Bruszt, Laszlo and Janos Simon (1992), "The Great Transformation in Hungary and Eastern Europe," Working Paper, University of Southern California workshop on Political and Economic Liberalization, 7 December, Los Angeles.
Bulgarian National Bank (1991–1999), *Monthly Bulletin*, Sofia.
Bulgarian National Bank (1995), *The Bulgarian Banking System*, Sofia.
Bulgarian National Statistical Institute (1995), *Socialno-Ikonomichesko Razviti na Republica Bulgaria prez Perioda 1990–1994 Godina*, Sofia.
Bulgarian National Statistical Institute (1991–2000), *Statisticheski Godishnik* [*Statistical Yearbook*], Sofia.
Bulgarian Statistical Publishing and Printing House (1995), *1995 Main Macroeconomic Indicators*, Sofia.
Burant, Stephen R. (ed.) (1989), *Hungary: A Country Study*, Federal Research Division, Library of Congress, sponsored by US Army Intelligence, Washington, DC.
Busik, Jozef, Jarko Fidrmuc, Jan Foltin, Igor Kosir, Pavol Ochotnicky and Andreas Worgotter (1993), "The Slovak Republic," *Country Report*, Bank of Austria, Vienna.
Butora, Martin and Zora Butorova (1993), "Slovakia: The Identity Challenges of the Newly Born State," *Social Research*, **60** (4), 705–36.
Campbell, Robert W. (1991), *The Socialist Economies in Transition: A Primer on Semi-Reformed Systems*, Bloomington, IN: Indiana University Press.
Center for Co-operation with the Economies in Transition and Bulgarian National Institute (1996), *National Accounts for Bulgaria, Sources, Methods and Estimates*, Paris: Organization for Economic Cooperation and Development.
Center for Economic Research and Graduate Education and Economics Institute (1998), *Czech Republic 1997: The Year of Crises*, Prague: CERGE-EI, Charles University and the Academy of Sciences. www.cerge.cuni.cz
Center for Economic Research and Graduate Education and Economics Institute (1999), *Czech Republic 1998: Facing Reality*, Prague: CERGE-EI, Charles University and the Academy of Sciences. www.cerge.cuni.cz
Center for Economic Research and Graduate Education and Economics Institute (2000),

Czech Republic 1999: Back to the Drawing Board, Prague: CERGE-EI, Charles University and the Academy of Sciences. www.cerge.cuni.cz

Central Intelligence Agency, *World Fact Book, 1998*. www.odci.gov/cia/publications/factbook/country.html/

Chatelot, Christophe (1997), "Bulgaria Learns to Live with Its Turks," *Le Monde* in *Guardian Weekly*, 11 May.

Chavance, Bernard (1994), *The Transformation of Communist Systems: Economic Reform since the 1950s*, Boulder, CO: Westview Press.

Coats, Warren (1993), "Understanding Money in New Institutional Settings: The Case of the Former Soviet Union," International Monetary Fund Photocopy, Washington, DC: IMF.

Corbo, Vittorio and Stanley Fischer (1995), "Structural Adjustment, Stabilization and Policy Reform: Domestic and International Finance," in J.R. Behrman and T.N. Srinivasan (eds), *Handbook of Development Economics*, Vol. III, Amsterdam: North-Holland Press.

Courtois, Stephane, Nicolas Werth, Jean-Louis Panne, Andrzej Paczkowski, Karel Bartosek and Jean-Louis Margolin (1999), *The Black Book of Communism: Crimes, Terror, Repression*, translated by Johathan Murphy and Mark Kramer, Cambridge, MA: Harvard University Press.

Crampton, R.J. (1994), *Eastern Europe in the Twentieth Century*, London and New York: Routledge.

Crisp, Olga (1976), *Studies in Russian Economy before 1914*, New York: Harper and Row.

Czech Republic Central Bank, Prague. www.cnb.cz/

Dawson, John W. (1998), "Institutions, Investment and Growth: New Cross-Country and Panel Data Evidence," *Economic Inquiry*, **36** (3), 603–19.

Denison, Edward (1962), *Sources of Economic Growth in the United States and the Alternative before Us*, New York and Washington, DC: Committee for Economic Development.

Denison, Edward (1967), *Why Growth Rates Differ*, Washington, DC: Brookings Institution.

Desai, Padma (1989), *Perestroika in Perspective: The Design and Dilemmas of Soviet Reform*, Princeton, NJ: Princeton University Press.

Desai, Padma (2000), "Why Did the Ruble Collapse in August 1998?" *American Economic Review*, **90** (2), 48–52.

Desai, Raj M. and Itzhak Goldberg (2000), "The Vicious Circles of Control: Regional Governments and Insiders in Privatized Russian Enterprises," Georgetown University Working Paper, Washington, DC.

Dewatripont, Mathias and Gerard Roland (1995), "The Design of Reform Packages under Uncertainty," *American Economic Review*, **85** (5), 1207–23.

Diamond, Peter (ed.) (1990), *Growth/Productivity/Unemployment: Essays to Celebrate Robert Solow's Birthday*, Cambridge, MA: MIT Press.

Dietz, Raimund (1997), "Bulgaria in Financial Disarray," *Institute for Market Economics Newsletter*, United Democratic Forces, Sofia.

Dobrinsky, Rumen (1997a), "The Fiscal Implications of Enterprise Restructuring in the Transition from Plan to Market," Workshop on Enterprise and Bank Restructuring in Central and Eastern Europe, February, Athens.

Dobrinsky, Rumen (1997b), "Transition Failures: Anatomy of the Bulgarian Crisis," Vienna Institute for Comparative Economic Studies Research Report No. 236, Vienna.

Domar, Evsey (1946), "Capital Expansion, Rate of Growth, and Employment," *Econometrica*, **14** (2), 137–47.

Dorfman, Robert, Paul A. Samuelson and Robert M. Solow (1958), *Linear Programming and Economic Analysis*, New York: McGraw-Hill.

Duke University, Country Risk Studies. www.duke.edu/~charvey/county-risk/conindex.htm/

Dyba, Karel and Jan Svejnar (1991), "Czechoslovakia: Recent Economic Developments and Prospects," *American Economic Review*, **81** (2), 185–90.

Earle, John S., Roman Frydman and Andrzej Rapaczynski (eds) (1993), *Privatization in the Transition to a Market Economy*, New York: St. Martin's Press.

Earle, John S., Roman Frydman, Andrzej Rapaczynski and Joel Turkewitz (1994), *Small Privatization, the Transformation of Retail Trade and Consumer Services in the Czech Republic, Hungary and Poland*, CEU Privatization Reports, Vol. 3, Budapest, London and New York: Central European University Press.

Easterly, William and Stanley Fischer (1994), "The Soviet Economic Decline," NBER Working Paper No. 4735, Cambridge, MA: National Bureau of Economic Research.

Easterly, William and Ross Levine (1997), "Africa's Growth Tragedy: Policies and Ethnic Divisions," *Quarterly Journal of Economics*, **112** (4), 1203–50.

Easton, Stephen T. and Michael A. Walker (1997), "Income, Growth and Economic Freedom," *American Economic Review*, **87** (2), 328–32.

The Economist (1997a), "Kingmaking Time," 25 January, 48.

The Economist (1997b), Russia Survey, 12 July, 3–18.

Eesti Pank (Bank of Estonia), *Annual Report* and *Bulletin*, Tallinn. www.ee/epbe

Estonian Economy 1995–1996, Ministry of Economic Affairs, Tallinn, 1996.

Estrin, Saul (ed.) (1994), *Privatization in Central and Eastern Europe*, London: Longman.

European Bank for Reconstruction and Development (1999), *Transition Report 1999*, London: EBRD.

European Bank for Reconstruction and Development (2000), *Transition Report 2000*. London: EBRD.

European Union (1999), *1999 Regular Report from the Commission on Bulgaria's Progress toward Accession*, 13 October 1999. http://europa.eu.int/comm/enlargement/bulgaria/index.htm (A 1999 progress report is available for each accession country.)

European Union (2000), *Bulgaria 2000, Regular Report from the Commission on Bulgaria's Progress toward Accession*, 8 November 2000. http://europa.eu.int/comm/enlargement/bulgaria/index.htm.

European Union (2000), *Czech Republic 2000, Regular Report from the Commission on Czech Republic's Progress toward Accession*, 8 November 2000. http://europa.eu.int/comm/enlargement/czech/index.htm.

European Union (2000), *Estonia 2000, Regular Report from the Commission on Estonia's Progress toward Accession*, 8 November 2000. http://europa.eu.int/comm/enlargement/estonia/index.htm.

European Union (2000), *Hungary 2000, Regular Report from the Commission on Hungary's Progress toward Accession*, 8 November 2000. http://europa.eu.int/comm/enlargement/hungary/index.htm.

European Union (2000), *Slovak Republic 2000, Regular Report from the Commission on*

Slovak Republic's Progress toward Accession, 8 November 2000. http://europa.eu.int/comm/enlargement/slovakia/index.htm.

Felak, James (1992), "Slovak Considerations of the Slovak Question: The Ludac, Agrarian, Socialist and Communist Views in Interwar Czechoslovakia," in John Morison (ed.), *The Czech and Slovak Experience*, New York: St. Martin's Press, 136–63.

Feng, Yi and Paul J. Zak (1999), "Determinants of Democratic Transitions: Theory and Empirical Evidence," *Journal of Conflict Resolution*, **42** (2), 162–77.

Fernandez, Raquel and Dani Rodrik (1991), "Resistance to Reform: Status Quo Bias in the Presence of Individual-Specific Uncertainty," *American Economic Review*, **81** (5), 1146–55.

Fidrmuc, Jarko, Anreas Worgotten and Julia Worz (1999), "East–West Trade: 10 Years After," *East–West Report*, Oesterreichische Nationalbank.

Filtzer, Donald (1994), *Soviet Workers and the Collapse of Perestroika: The Soviet Labor Process and Gorbachev's Reforms, 1985–1991*, Cambridge: Cambridge University Press.

Financial Times (1997), "Czechs Find Transition Harder Than They Thought," by Vincent Boland, 3 April.

Financial Times (2000), "Strong Signs of Progress," by Kester Eddy, 22 November, p. 2.

Fischer, Stanley (1991), "Growth, Macroeconomics and Development," in Olivier Jean Blanchard and Stanley Fischer (eds), *National Bureau of Economic Research, Macroeconomics Annual 1991*, Cambridge, MA: MIT Press, 329–63.

Fischer, Stanley and Alan Gelb (1991), "The Process of Economic Transformation," *Journal of Economic Perspectives*, **5** (4), 91–105.

Fischer, Stanley, Ratna Sahay and Carlos A. Vegh (1996), "Stabilization and Growth in Transition Economies: The Early Experience," *Journal of Economic Perspectives*, **10** (2), 45–66.

Fogel, Robert William and Stanley L. Engerman (1974), *Time on the Cross: The Economics of American Negro Slavery*, Boston: Little, Brown.

Friedman, Milton (1982), *Capitalism and Freedom*, Chicago: University of Chicago Press.

Frydman, Roman and Andrzej Rapaczynski (1994), *Privatization in Eastern Europe: Is the State Withering Away?*, Budapest, London, New York: Central European University Press.

Frydman, Roman, Cheryl Gray, Marek Hessel and Andrzej Rapaczynski (1999), "When Does Privatization Work? The Impact of Private Ownership on Corporate Performance in the Transition Economies," *Quarterly Journal of Economics*, **114** (4), 1153–92.

Frydman, Roman, Andrzej Rapaczynski, John S. Earle et al. (1993a), *The Privatization Process in Central Europe*, CEU Privatization Reports Vol. 1, Budapest, London, New York: Central European University Press.

Frydman, Roman, Andrzej Rapaczynski, John S. Earle et al. (1993b), *The Privatization Process in Russia, Ukraine and the Baltic States*, CEU Privatization Reports Vol. 2, Budapest, London, New York: Central European University Press.

Frye, Timothy and Andrei Shleifer (1997), "The Invisible Hand and the Grabbing Hand," *American Economic Review*, **87** (2), 354–58

Fukuyama, Francis (1992), *The End of History and the Last Man*, New York: Macmillan.

Fukuyama, Francis (1995), *Trust: Social Virtues and the Creation of Prosperity*, New York: Free Press.

Fukuyama, Francis (2000), "Social Capital and Civil Society," IMF Working Paper 00/74, Washington, DC: International Monetary Fund.

Gaddy, Clifford G. and Barry W. Ickes (1998), "Russia's Virtual Economy," *Foreign Affairs*, **77** (5), 53–67.

Gaidar, Yegor (1997), "The IMF and Russia," *American Economic Review*, **87** (2), 13–16.

Galbraith, John Kenneth (1967), *The New Industrial State*, Boston: Houghton Mifflin.

Gatrell, Peter (1986), *Tsarist Economy 1850–1917*, New York: St. Martin's Press.

Gelb, Alan H. and Cheryl W. Gray (1991), "The Transformation of Economies in Central and Eastern Europe: Issues, Progress and Prospects," Policy and Research Series, Paper No. 17. Washington, DC: World Bank.

Gelos, R. Gaston and Ratna Sahay (2001), "Financial Market Spillovers in Transition Economies," *Economics of Transition*, **9** (1), 53–86.

Ghez, Gilbert and Gary S. Becher (1975), *The Allocation of Time and Goods over the Life Cycle*, New York: Columbia University Press for the National Bureau of Economic Research.

Glenny, Misha (1993), *The Rebirth of History: Eastern Europe in the Age of Democracy*, New York: Penguin Books.

Gordon, Robert A. and Lawrence Klein (1966), *Readings in Business Cycles*, London: George Allen and Unwin.

Gotting, Ulrike (1993), *Welfare State Development in Post-Communist Bulgaria, Czechoslovakia, and Hungary, A Review of Problems and Responses (1989–1992)*, Centre for Social Policy Research, University of Bremen, Bremen, Germany.

Greenwood, Jeremy, Zvi Hercowitz and Per Krusell (1997), "Long-Run Implications of Investment-Specific Technological Change," *American Economic Review*, **87** (3), 342–62.

Gregory, Paul R. (1994), *Before Command: An Economic History of Russia from Emancipation to the First Five-Year Plan*, Princeton, NJ: Princeton University Press.

Gregory, Paul R. and Robert C. Stuart (1981), *Soviet Economic Structure and Performance*, 2nd edition, New York: Harper and Row.

Gustafson, Thane (1999), *Capitalism Russian-Style*, Cambridge: Cambridge University Press.

Gylfason, Thorvaldur (1994), "Structural Adjustment, Efficiency, and Economic Growth," Centre for Economic Policy Research, Paper No. 91, London: CEPR.

Haggard, Stephan and Robert K. Kaufman (1995), *The Political Economy of Democratic Transitions*, Princeton, NJ: Princeton University Press.

Haggard, Stephan and Steven Webb (eds) (1994), *Voting for Reform: Democracy, Political Liberalization and Economic Adjustment*, New York: Oxford University Press.

Hall, Robert E. and Charles I. Jones (1997), "Levels of Economic Activity across Countries," *American Economic Review*, **87** (2), 173–77.

Hall, Stephen G. and Malinka S. Koparanova (1995), *Modelling and Forecasting Structural Change in Transition: The Case of Bulgaria*, Centre for Economic Forecasting, London Business School, London.

Ham, John C., Jan Svejnar and Katherine Terrell (1998), "Unemployment and the Social Safety Net during Transitions to a Market Economy: Evidence from the Czech and Slovak Republics," *American Economic Review*, **88** (5), 1117–42.

Hanson, Philip (1992), *From Stagnation to Catistroika: Commentaries on the Soviet Economy, 1983–1991*, New York: Praeger.

Hansson, Ardo H. (1992), "Transforming an Economy While Building a Nation: The Case of Estonia," Stockholm Institute of East European Economies Working Paper No. 62, Stockholm.
Hanousek, Jan and E. Ǩocenda (1998a), "Effects of the Czech Voucher Scheme on the Corporate Governance," in P. Tchipev (ed.), *Mass Privatization Schemes in Central and East European Countries, Implications on Corporate Governance*, Sofia: Gorex Press, 117–33.
Hanousek, Jan and E. Ǩocenda (1998b), "Monetárni vazby na českem mezibankovnim trhu (The Czech Money Market: Emerging Links among Interest Rates)," *Finance a ú vét*, **48** (2), 99–109.
Hare, Paul G (1991), "The Assessment: Microeconomics of Transition in Eastern Europe," *Oxford Review of Economic Policy*, **7** (4), 1–15.
Harrison, Lawrence E. and Samuel P. Huntington (eds) (2000), *Culture Matters: How Values Shape Human Progress*, New York: Basic Books.
Harrod, Roy (1939), "An Essay in Dynamic Theory," *Economic Journal*, **49** (193), 14–33.
Hayek, Friedrich A. (ed.) (1935), *Collectivist Economic Planning*, London: G. Routledge and Sons, Ltd.
Hayek, Friedrich A. (1944), *The Road to Serfdom*, Chicago: University of Chicago Press (1972).
Held, Joseph (ed.) (1992), *The Columbia History of Eastern Europe in the Twentieth Century*, New York: Columbia University Press.
Helliwell, John F. (1994), "Empirical Linkages between Democracy and Economic Growth," *British Journal of Political Science*, **24**, 225–48.
Hicks, John R. (1946), *Value and Capital*, 2nd edition, Oxford: Oxford University Press.
Hiden, John and Patrick Solmon (1994), *The Baltic Nations and Europe: Estonia, Latvia and Lithuania in the Twentieth Century*, London and New York: Longman.
Hillman, Arye L. (1991), "Liberalization Dilemmas," in Arye L. Hillman (ed.), *Markets and Politicians*, Dordrecht: Kluwer Academic Publishers, 189–207.
Hingley, Ronald (1991), *Russia, A Concise History*, London: Thames and Hudson.
Hochreiter, Eduard (1995), "Central Banking in Economies in Transition," in Thomas D. Willett, Richard C.K. Burdekin, Richard J. Sweeney and Clas Wihlborg (eds), *Establishing Monetary Stability in Emerging Market Economies*, Boulder, CO: Westview Press, 127–44.
Hochreiter, Eduard (2000), "Exchange Rate Regimes and Capital Mobility: Issues and Some Lessons from Central and Eastern European Applicant Countries," *North American Journal of Economics and Finance*, **11** (2), 155–71.
Hochreiter, Edward and Tadeusz Kowalski (2000), "Central Banks in European Emerging Market Economies in the 1990s," Oesterrerchische National Bank Working Paper no. 40, Vienna: Oesterreichische National Bank (Austrian National Bank).
Hosking, Geoffrey A. (1990), *The First Socialist Society: A History of the Soviet Union from Within*, Cambridge, MA: Harvard University Press.
Hosking, Geoffrey A. (1994), *The First Socialist Society*, Cambridge, MA: Harvard University Press.
Hrncir, Miroslav (1985), *The Social Preconditions of National Revival in Europe*, Cambridge: Cambridge University Press.

Hrncir, Miroslav (1992), "The Transition to a Market Economy: Lessons from the Experience of the CSFR," in Michael Keren and Gur Ofer (eds), *Trials of Transition, Economic Reform in the Former Communist Bloc*, Boulder, CO: Westview Press, 151–72.

Hulten, Charles R. (ed.) (1990), *Productivity Growth in Japan and the United States*, National Bureau of Economic Research, Studies in Income and Wealth, 53. Chicago: University of Chicago Press.

Hulten, Charles R. (1992), "Growth Accounting When Technical Change Is Embodied in Capital," *American Economic Review*, **82** (4), 964–80.

Hulten, Charles R. and Robert M. Schwab (1993), "Infrastructure Spending: Where Do We Go From Here?" *National Tax Journal*, **46** (3), 261–75.

Humpage, Owen F. and Jean M. McIntire (1995), "An Introduction to Currency Boards," *Economic Review*, Federal Reserve Bank of Cleveland, **31** (2), 2–11.

Hungarian National Bank. www.mnb.hu/index-a.htm/

Huntington, Samuel P. (1993), "What Cost Freedom?" *Harvard International Review*, **15** (2), 8–13.

Husain, Aasim M. (1994), "Private Sector Development in Economies in Transition," *Journal of Comparative Economics*, **19** (2), 260–71.

Iavlinskii, Grigorii (1992), "On the Brink, A Two-Part Interview with Grigorii Iavlinskii," *Russian Politics and Law*, March–April, 1994, from *Literaturnaia gazeta*, 28 October and 4 November 1992.

International Finance Corporation, World Bank Group, Washington, DC, www.ifc.org/economics/

International Monetary Fund (1994), *Estonia*, IMF Economic Reviews, 7, Washington, DC: IMF.

International Monetary Fund (1998), *Slovak Republic: Recent Economic Developments*, IMF Staff Country Report No. 98/60, Washington, DC: IMF. www.imf.org/external/pubs/CAT/scr.cfm/

International Monetary Fund (1999), *Czech Republic: Selected Issues*, IMF Staff Country Report No. 99/90, Washington, DC: IMF.

International Monetary Fund (1999), *Hungary: Selected Issues*. IMF Staff Country Report No. 99/27, Washington, DC: IMF.

Intriligator, Michael (1971), *Mathematical Optimization and Economic Theory*, Englewood Cliffs, NJ: Prentice Hall.

Intriligator, Michael (1971), *Econometric Models, Techniques, and Applications*, Englewood Cliffs, NJ: Prentice Hall.

Johnson, David B. (1991), *Public Choice*, Mountain View, CA: Mayfield.

Jones, Charles I. (1995a), "R & D-Based Models of Economic Growth," *Journal of Political Economy*, **103** (4), 759–84.

Jones, Charles I. (1995b), "Time Series Tests of Endogenous Growth Models," *Quarterly Journal of Economics*, **110** (2), 495–525.

Jones, Charles I. (1998), *Introduction to Economic Growth*, New York: Norton Press.

Jorgenson, Dale W. (1995), *Productivity, Volume 2: International Comparisons of Economic Growth*, Cambridge, MA: MIT Press.

Jorgenson, Dale W. and Zvi Griliches (1967), "The Explanation of Productivity Change," *Review of Economic Studies*, **34** (99), 249–83.

Jorgenson, Dale W., Frank M. Gollop and Barbara M. Fraumeni (1987), *Productivity and US Economic Growth*, Amsterdam: North-Holland Press.

Joskow, Paul L., Richard Schmalensee and Natalia Tsukanova (1994), "Competition Policy in Russia during and after Privatization," *The Brookings Papers on Economic Activity*, Microeconomics, 301–74.

Kahan, Arcadius (1989), *Russian Economic History: The Nineteenth Century*, edited by Roger Weiss, Chicago: University of Chicago Press.

Kahler, Miles (1990), "Orthodoxy and Its Alternatives," in Joan M. Nelson (ed.), *Economic Crisis and Policy Choice*, Princeton, NJ: Princeton University Press, 33–62.

Kamien, Morton I. and Nancy L. Schwartz (1981), *Dynamic Optimization: The Calculus of Variations and Optimal Control in Economics and Management*, New York: North-Holland Press.

Kaplan, Robert D. (1994), *Balkan Ghosts: A Journal through History*, New York: St. Martin's Press.

Kaser, M. C. (ed.) (1996), *The Economic History of Eastern Europe*, Vols I–III, Oxford: Clarendon Press.

Kenningham, Andrew (1997), "Bulgaria: Leveraging Off the Deutsche Mark," Merrill Lynch "Economic Outlook and Fixed Income Investment" series (unpublished), Los Angeles.

Keynes, John Maynard (1933), *Essays in Persuasion*, London: Macmillan.

Koen, Vincent (1994), "A User's View on National Accounts in Russia," IMF Working Paper 94/6, Washington, DC: International Monetary Fund.

Kornai, Janos (1990), *The Road to a Free Economy, Shifting from a Socialist System: The Example of Hungary*, New York: W.W. Norton.

Kornai, Janos (1992), *The Socialist System: The Political Economy of Communism*, Princeton, NJ: Princeton University Press.

Kornai, Janos (1996), "Paying the Bill for Goulash Communism: Hungarian Development and Macro Stabilization in a Political Economy Perspective," Political Economy Seminar Working Paper, University of Western Ontario, London, Ontario.

Kornai, Janos (2000), "What the Change of System from Socialism to Capitalism Does and Does Not Mean," *Journal of Economic Perspectives*, **14** (1), 27–42.

Korosenyi, Andras (1994), "Demobilization and Gradualism: The Political Economy of the Hungarian Transition, 1987–1992," in Joan M. Nelson (ed.), *A Precarious Balance: Democracy and Economic Reforms in Eastern Europe*, San Francisco: International Center for Economic Growth and Overseas Development Council, Institute for Contemporary Studies, 71–124.

Kotrba, Josef (1993), "Privatization Process in the Czech Republic: An Overview," Economic Institute of the Academy of Science, Czech Republic, and University of Pittsburgh, Working Paper.

Kotrba, Josef (1994), "Czech Privatization: Players and Winners," CERGE-EI Working Paper No. 58, Prague: Center for Economic Research and Graduate Education-Economics Institute, Charles University and Academy of Sciences.

Kowalik, Tadeusz (ed.) (1994), *Economic Theory and Market Socialism: Selected Essays of Oskar Lange*, Aldershot, UK and Brookfield, VT: Edward Elgar.

Kozera, Nicole (1996), "Voucher Privatization in the Czech Republic," Working Paper, Pomona College, Claremont, CA.

Krska, Eugen and Pavol Susedka (1971), "Industrialization of Slovakia: Program and Its Implementation," *Czechoslovak Economic Digest*, **6**, 48–79.

Krueger, Anne O. (1993), *Political Economy of Policy Reform in Developing Countries*, Cambridge, MA: MIT Press.

Kutan, Ali M. and Josef C. Brada (2000), "The Evolution of Monetary Policy in Transition Economies," *Federal Reserve Bank of St Louis Review*, **82** (2), 31–40.

Lainela, Seija and Pekka Sutela (1994), *The Baltic Economies in Transition*, Helsinki: Bank of Finland.

Lampe, John R. and Marvin R. Jackson (1982), *Balkan Economic History: 1550–1950*, Bloomington, IN: Indiana University Press.

Lange, Oskar (1938), *On the Economic Theory of Socialism*, Minneapolis, MN: University of Minnesota Press.

Lazear, Edward P. (ed.) (1995), *Economic Transition in Eastern Europe and Russia: Realities of Reform*, Stanford, CA: Hoover Institute Press, Stanford University.

LeGrand, Julius and Saul Estrin (eds) (1989), *Market Socialism*, Oxford: Clarendon Press.

Leijonhufvud, Axel and Christof Ruhl (1997), "Russian Dilemmas," *American Economic Review*, **87** (2), 344–8.

Leontief, Wassily (1951), *The Structure of American Economy, 1919–1939*, 2nd edition, New York: Oxford University Press.

Leontief, Wassily (1966), *Input-Output Economics*, New York: Oxford University Press.

Library of Congress, *Country Studies*, Washington, DC, http://lcweb2.loc.gov/frd/cs/cshome.html/

Lipton, David and Jeffrey D. Sachs (1992), "Prospects for Russia's Economic Reforms," *Brookings Papers on Economic Activity*, 2, 213–65.

Lugus, Olev and George A. Hachey, Jr. (eds) (1995), *Transforming the Estonian Economy*, Estonian Academy of Sciences, Institute of Economics, Tallinn.

Maddison, Angus (1982a), *Phases of Capitalist Development*, Oxford: Oxford University Press.

Maddison, Angus (1982b), *The World Economy in the Twentieth Century*, Development Centre of the OECD, Paris: Organization for Economic Cooperation and Development.

Maddison, Angus (1987), "Growth and Slowdown in Advanced Capitalist Economies: Techniques of Quantitative Assessment," *Journal of Economic Literature*, **25** (2), 649–98.

Madison, James, Alexander Hamilton and John Jay (1987), *The Federalist Papers*, Isaac Kramnik (ed.), Middlesex, UK: Penguin Books. (First published 1788.)

Manchester, William (1978), *American Caesar: Douglas MacArthur, 1880–1964*, Boston, MA: Little, Brown.

Mankiw, N. Gregory, David Romer and David N. Weil (1992), "A Contribution to the Empirics of Economic Growth," *Quarterly Journal of Economics*, **107** (2), 407–37.

Martinez-Vasquez, Jorge and Robert M. McNab (2000), "Tax Reform Experiment in Transitional Countries," *National Tax Journal*, **53** (2), 273–98.

Marx, Karl (1867), *Das Kapital*, New York: Modern Library (1936).

Marx, Karl and Friedrich Engels (1848), *Manifesto of the Communist Party*, Chicago: Encyclopedia Britannica (1955).

Mason, David S. (1994), *Revolution in East-Central Europe: The Rise and Fall of Communism and the Cold War*, Boulder, CO: Westview Press.

McAuley, Mary (1992), *Soviet Politics, 1917–1991*, Oxford: Oxford University Press.
McKinnon, Ronald I. (1991), "Financial Control in the Transition from Classical Socialism to a Market Economy," *Journal of Economic Perspectives*, **5** (4), 107–22.
Mejstrik, Michal and James Burger (1994), "Privatization in Practice: Czechoslovakia's Experience from 1989 to Mid-1992," in Dennis A. Rondinelli (ed.), *Privatization and Economic Reform in Central Europe, The Changing Business Climate*, Westport, CT: Quorum Books.
Melitz, Jacques and Claire Waysand (1996), "The Role of Government Aid to Firms during the Transition to a Market Economy: Russia 1992–1994," *Journal of Policy Reform*, **1** (3), 299–334.
Milanovic, Branko (1993), "Social Costs of the Transition to Capitalism," World Bank PRE Working Paper Series, No. 1165, Washington, DC: World Bank.
Miller, Jeffrey and Stefan Petranov (1993), *The Bulgarian Banking System*, Sofia: Bulgarian National Bank.
Minasian, Garabed, et al. (1994), *Ikonomikata na Bulgaria Dnes I Utre* [*The Bulgarian Economy Today and Tomorrow*], Sofia: Institute of Economics, Bulgarian Academy of Science.
Mosse, W. E. (1996), *An Economic History of Russia 1856–1914*, New York: I.B. Tauris.
Munnell, Alicia H. (ed.) (1991), *Is There a The Shortfall in Public Capital Investment*? Series No. 34, Boston: Federal Reserve Bank of Boston.
Murphy, Kevin M., Andrei Shleifer and Robert W. Vishny (1992), "Transition to a Market Economy: Pitfalls of Partial Reform," *Quarterly Journal of Economics*, **107** (3), 889–906.
Murrell, Peter (1995), "The Transition According to Cambridge, Mass.," *Journal of Economic Literature*, **33** (1), 164–78.
Murrell, Peter (1996), "How Far Has the Transition Progressed?," *Journal of Economic Perspectives*, **10** (2), 24–44.
Murrell, Peter and Yijiang Wang (1993), "When Privatization Should Be Delayed: The Effect of Communist Legacies on Organizational and Institutional Reforms," *Journal of Comparative Economics*, **17** (2), 385–406.
Nordic Economic Outlook (1996), No. 2, 25 July, Federation of Swedish Industries.
North, Douglass C. (1990), *Institutions, Institutional Change and Economic Performance*, Cambridge: Cambridge University Press.
North, Douglass C. (1999), "Understanding the Process of Economic Change," Wincott Memorial Lecture (October 1998), Washington, DC: Institute of Economic Affairs.
North, Douglass C. and Robert Paul Thomas (1973), *The Rise of the Western World, A New Economic History*, Cambridge: Cambridge University Press.
Nuti, Domenico Mario (1992), "Privatization in Hungary," in Michael Keren and Gur Ofer (eds), *Trials of Transition: Economic Reform in the Former Communist Bloc*, Boulder, CO: Westview Press, 193–202.
Oesterreichische Nationalbank (1996–2000), *Focus on Transition*, Vienna.
Olson, Mancur (1965), *The Logic of Collective Action*, Cambridge, MA: Harvard University Press.
Olson, Mancur (1982), *The Rise and Decline of Nations: Economic Growth, Stagflation, and Social Rigidities*, New Haven, CT: Yale University Press.

Olson, Mancur (1991), "Autocracy, Democracy and Prosperity," in Richard J. Zeckhauser (ed.), *Strategy and Choice*, Cambridge, MA: MIT Press, 131–57.

Olson, Mancur (1993), "Dictatorship, Democracy and Development," *American Political Science Review*, **87** (3), 567–76.

Olson, Mancur (2000), *Power and Prosperity: Outgrowing Communist and Capitalist Dictatorships*, New York: Basic Books.

Open Media Research Institute (1997), *Daily Digest*, OMRI Net, 4 March. www.hri.org/news/agencies/omri/

Organization for Economic Cooperation and Development (1991), *OECD Economic Surveys 1990–1991, Czech and Slovak Federal Republic*, Paris: OECD.

Organization for Economic Cooperation and Development (1998), "Czech Republic 1997–1998," *OECD Economic Surveys 1997–1998, Czech Republic*, Paris: OECD.

Organization for Economic Cooperation and Development (1998), *OECD Economic Surveys 1997–1998, The Russian Federation*, Paris: OECD.

Organization for Economic Cooperation and Development (1999), *OECD Economic Surveys 1998–1999, Bulgaria*, Paris: OECD.

Organization for Economic Cooperation and Development (1999), *OECD Economic Surveys 1998–1999, Hungary*, Paris: OECD.

Organization for Economic Cooperation and Development (1999), *OECD Economic Surveys 1998–1999, Slovak Republic*, Paris: OECD.

Organization for Economic Cooperation and Development (2000), *OECD Economic Surveys 1999–2000, Czech Republic*, Paris: OECD.

Organization for Economic Cooperation and Development (2000), *OECD Economic Surveys 1999–2000, Baltic States, A Regional Economic Assessment*, Paris: OECD.

Organization for Economic Cooperation and Development (2000), *OECD Economic Surveys 1999–2000, Russian Federation*, Paris: OECD.

Owen, Thomas C. (1995), *Russian Corporate Capitalism from Peter the Great to Perestroika*, New York: Oxford University Press.

Pehe, Jiri (1992a), "Czechs and Slovaks Define Postdivorce Relations," *RFE/RL Research Report*, **1** (45). (Radio Free Europe/Radio Liberty.)

Pehe, Jiri (1992b), "Czechoslovak Parliament Votes to Dissolve Federation," *RFE/RL Research Report*, **1** (48). (Radio Free Europe/Radio Liberty.)

Penev, Victor (1996), *Privatization Success in Transition, Lessons from the Czech Republic and Bulgaria*, Senior Thesis, Pomona College, Claremont, CA.

Pindyck, Robert S. and Daniel L. Rubinfeld (1991), *Econometric Models & Economic Analysis*, 3rd edition, New York: McGraw-Hill.

Pipes, Richard (1999), *Property and Freedom*, New York: Alfred Knopf.

Portes, Richard (1993), *Economic Transformation in Central Europe: A Progress Report*, London: Centre for Economic Policy Research.

Prust, Jim, Jeremy Carter, Adrienne Cheasty, Benedicte Vibe Christensen, Leif Hansen, Nadeem U. Haque and Tessa van der Willigen (1990), *The Czech and Slovak Federal Republic: An Economy in Transition*, Washington, DC: International Monetary Fund.

Przeworski, Adam (1991), *Democracy and the Market: Political and Economic Reforms in Eastern Europe and Latin America*, Cambridge: Cambridge University Press.

Przeworski, Adam and Fernando Limongi (1993), "Political Regimes and Economic Growth," *Journal of Economic Perspectives*, **7** (3), 51–69.
Radishchev, Aleksandr N. (1790), *A Journey from St. Petersburg to Moscow, 1958*, Cambridge, MA: Harvard University Press.
Rajasalu, Teet (1995), "Macroeconomic Stabilization and Development," in Olev Lugus and George A. Hachey, Jr (eds) *Transforming the Estonian Economy*, Tallinn: Estonian Academy of Sciences, Institute of Economics, 16–51.
Ramsey, Frank P. (1928), "A Mathematical Model of Saving," *Economic Journal*, **38** (152), 543–59.
Rapaczynski, Andrzej (1996), "The Roles of the State and the Market in Establishing Property Rights," *Journal of Economic Perspectives*, **10** (2), 87–103.
Raun, Toivo (1991), *Estonia and the Estonians* 2nd edn., Stanford, CA: Hoover Institution Press.
Rautava, Jouko (1994), "Interdependence of Politics and Economic Development: Financial Stabilization in Russia," Working Paper 18, Oesterreichische Nationalbank, Vienna.
Raymond, Ellsworth (1978), *The Soviet State*, New York: New York University Press.
Rebelo, Sergio (1991), "Long-Run Policy and Long-Run Growth," *Journal of Political Economy*, **99** (3), 500–521.
Remnick, David (1994), *Lenin's Tomb: The Last Days of the Soviet Empire*, New York: Random House.
Riecke, Werner and Laszlo Antal, (1993), "Hungary: Sound Money, Fiscal Problems," in Richard Portes (ed.), *Economic Transformation in Central Europe: A Progress Report*, London: Centre for Economic Policy Research, 107–29.
Roberts, Paul Craig (1990), *Alienation and the Soviet Economy*, New York: The Independent Institute.
Rodrik, Dani (1995a), "The Dynamics of Political Support for Reform in Economies in Transition," *Journal of the Japanese and International Economies*, **9** (4), 403–25.
Rodrik, Dani (1995b), "Trade and Industrial Policy Reform," in J.R. Behrman and T.N. Srinivasan (eds), *Handbook of Development Economics*, Vol. III, Amsterdam: North-Holland Press.
Roemer, John E. (2000), "Democracy, Egalitarian Redistributions, and the Level of Public Bads," in Eric Maskin and Andras Simonovits (eds), *Planning, Shortage and Transformation: Essays in Honor of Janos Kornai*, Cambridge, MA: MIT Press.
Romer, Paul M. (1990), "Endogenous Technological Change," *Journal of Political Economy*, **98** (5) Pt 2, S71–S102.
Rondinelli, Dennis A. (ed.) (1994), "Privatization and Economic Reform in Central Europe", *The Changing Business Climate*, Westport, CT: Quorum Books.
Rosen, Harvey S. (1999), *Public Finance*, 5th edition. Chicago: Irwin/McGraw-Hill.
Russian European Centre for Economic Policy (1996), *Russian Economic Trends 1995*, **4** (4), European Union's Tacis Programme, Moscow: Government of the Russian Federation.
Russian European Centre for Economic Policy (2000), *Russian Economic Trends 2000*, **9** (4), Moscow: Working Centre for Economic Reform, Government of the Russian Federation.
Sachs, Jeffrey D. and Wing Thye Woo (1994), "Structural Factors in the Economic Reforms

of China, Eastern Europe and the Former Soviet Union," *Economic Policy*, **9** (18), 101–45.

Saffran, Bernard (1998), "Recommendations for Further Reading," *Journal of Economic Perspectives*, **12** (2), 235–42.

Salisbury, Harrison E. (ed.) (1967), *The Soviet Union, The Fifty Years*, New York: Harcourt, Brace and World.

Schankerman, Mark (1997), Book review of *Privatizing Russia* by Maxim Boycko, Andrei Shleifer and Robert Vishny, *Journal of Economic Literature*, **35** (2), 817–20.

Schroder, Philipp J. H. (2000), "A Formalisation of the Stakeholder/Shareholder Conflict in the Mass Privatisations of Transition Economies," paper presented at the 49th International Atlantic Economic Association conference, March, Munich.

Scully, Gerald W. (1988), "The Institutional Framework and Economic Development," *Journal of Political Economy*, **96** (3), 652–62.

Selucky, Radoslav (1991), "From Capitalism to Socialism," in Gordon Skilling (ed.), *Czechoslovakia, 1918–1988*, New York: St. Martin's Press, 154–73.

Sepp, Urmas (1994), "Inflation in Estonia: The Cost of Development," Bank of Estonia Working Paper for conference on Restructuring Financial Institutions in Emerging Market Economies, October, Tallinn.

Shleifer, Andrei and Daniel Treisman (2000), *Political Tactics and Economic Reform in Russia*, Cambridge, MA: MIT Press.

Shleifer, Andrei and Daniel Treisman (1998), *The Economics and Politics of Transition to an Open Market Economy: Russia*, OECD Development Centre Studies, Paris: Organization for Economic Cooperation and Development.

Sirowy, Larry and Alex Inkeles (1990), "The Effects of Democracy on Economic Growth and Inequality," *Studies in Comparative International Development*, **25** (1), 126–57.

Siskova, Anna (1997), "Slovakia's Western Integration in Danger," Open Media Research Institute, OMRI Net, **1** (552), 14 February.

Smith, Adam (1759), *The Theory of Moral Sentiments*, D.D. Raphael and A.L. Macfie (eds), New York: Oxford University Press (1976).

Smith, Adam (1776), *An Inquiry into the Nature and Causes of the Wealth of Nations*, New York: Random House (1937).

Smith, Adam (1976), *The Russians*, New York: New York Times Book Co.

Smith, Hedrick (1990), *The New Russians*, New York: Random House.

Smith, Vernon (1992), "Economic Principles in the Emergence of Humankind," Western Economic Association International Presidential Address, 30 June 1991, *Economic Inquiry*, **30** (1), 1–13.

Solow, Robert A. (1956), "Contribution to the Theory of Economic Growth," *Quarterly Journal of Economics*, **70** (1), 65–94.

Solow, Robert A. (1970), *Growth Theory: An Exposition*, Oxford and New York: Oxford University Press.

Spulber, Nicolas (1997), *Redefining the State*, Cambridge: Cambridge University Press.

Stiglitz, Joseph E. (1994), *Whither Socialism*?, Wicksell Lectures, Cambridge, MA: MIT Press.

Sujan, Ivan and Milota Sujanova (1994), "The Macroeconomic Situation in the Czech

Republic," CERGE-EI Working Paper No. 46, Prague: Center for Economic Research and Graduate Education-Economics Institute.

Svejnar, Jan (1993), "Czech and Slovak Federal Republic: A Solid Foundation," in Richard Portes (ed.), *Economic Transformation in Central Europe*, Centre for Economic Policy Research, 21–57.

Svejnar, Jan (ed.) (1995), *The Czech Republic and Economic Transition in Eastern Europe,* San Diego, CA: Academic Press.

Taagepera, Rein (1993), *Estonia – Return to Independence*, Boulder, CO: Westview Press.

Temple, Jonathan and Paul A. Johnson (1998), "Social Capability and Economic Growth," *Quarterly Journal of Economics*, **113** (3), 965–90.

Thorne, Alfredo (1993), "Eastern Europe's Experience with Banking Reform," *Journal of Banking and Finance*, **17** (5), 959–1000.

Ticktin, Hillel (1992), *Origins of the Crises in the USSR: Essays on the Political Economy of a Disintegrating System*, Armonk, NY: M.E. Sharpe.

Torok, Adam (1992), "Reflections on the Transition to a Free market Economy in Hungary," Working Paper, Institute of Industrial and Business Economics, Budapest: Hungarian Academy of Sciences.

Trade Links (1993), "The Czech Republic in a Nutshell," Prague: IPS.

Trade Links (1993), "Privatization in the Czech and Slovak Republics," Prague: IPS.

United Nations, *Monthly Bulletin of Statistics*, New York: UN.

United States Information Agency (1992), *Research Memorandum*, 3 February, Washington, DC: USIA.

Van Arkadie, Brian and Mats Karlsson (1992), *Economic Survey of the Baltic States*, New York: New York University Press.

Vensel, Vello (1996), "The Political Economy of Macroeconomic Developments, Central Bank and Tax System Reform in Estonia," Center for Economic Reform and Transformation Discussion Paper No. 96/6, Heriot-Watt University, Edinburgh.

Vensel, Vello and Clas Wihlborg (eds) (2001), *Estonia on the Threshold of the European Union: Financial Sector and Enterprise Restructuring in the Changing Economic Environment*, Tallinn: Department of Economics at Tallinn Technical University.

Vince, Peter (1993), "Stages of State Involvement: Dilemmas and Turning Points for Privatization in Hungary," KOPINT-DATORG Discussion Paper No. 19, Budapest.

Volkogonov, Dmitri (1998), *Autopsy for an Empire: The Seven Leaders Who Built the Soviet Regime*, translated by Harold Shukman, New York: Free Press.

Von Rauch, Georg (1972), *A History of Soviet Russia*, 6th edition, translated by Peter and Annette Jacobsohn, New York: Praeger.

The Wall Street Journal (1994), "Independent Slovakia Defies Expectations," by Dana Milbank, 30 November, A14.

Weitzman (1998), "Recombinant Growth," *Quarterly Journal of Economics*, **113** (2), 331–60.

Wheaton, Bernard and Zdenek Kavan (1992), *The Velvet Revolution, Czechoslovakia 1988–1991*, Boulder, CO: Westview Press.

Wijnbergen, Sweder van (1992a), "Intertemporal Speculation, Shortages, and the Political Economy of Price Reform," *Economic Journal*, **102** (415), 1395–406.

Wijnbergen, Sweder van (1992b), *Economic Aspects of Enterprise Reform in Eastern Europe*, Washington, DC: World Bank.
Willett, Thomas D., Richard C. K. Burdekin, Richard J. Sweeney and Clas Wihlborg (eds) (1995), *Establishing Monetary Stability in Emerging Market Economies*, Boulder, CO: Westview Press.
Winieki, Jan (1989), "Large Industrial Enterprises in Soviet Type Economies: The Ruling Stratum's Main Rent-Seeking Area," *Communist Economics*, 1, 363–83.
Winieki, Jan (1990), "Why Economic Reforms Fail in the Soviet System – A Property Rights-Based Approach," *Economic Inquiry*, **28** (2), 195–221.
Wissels, Rutger (1996), "Pessimism Confounded? Economic Recovery in Eastern Europe," Oesterreichische Nationalbank Working Paper No. 22, Vienna.
Wolf, Holger C. (1999), *Transition Strategies: Choices and Outcomes*, Princeton Studies in International Finance, No. 85, Princeton University, International Finance Section, Department of Economics.
Wood, Barry D. (2000), "Slovakia Heads West," *European Affairs*, May, 28–29.
Woodruff, David (1999), *Money Unmade: Barter and the Fate of Russian Capitalism*, Ithaca: Cornell University Press.
World Bank (1991), *Czechoslovakia: Transition to a Market Economy*, Washington, DC: World Bank.
World Bank (1993), *The Transition to a Market Economy*, Washington, DC: World Bank.
World Bank (1994), *Slovakia: Restructuring for Recovery*, Washington, DC: World Bank.
World Bank (1996), *From Plan to Market, World Development Report 1996*, Oxford: Oxford University Press.
World Bank (2000), *Transition: The Newsletter about Reforming Economies*, Selected issues. www.worldbank.org/html/prddr/trans/WEB/trans.htm/
The World Competitiveness Yearbook, http://itpress.de/wcy/99.htm
Wyzan, Michael (ed.) (1995), *First Steps toward Economic Independence: New States of the Post-Communist World*, Westport, CT: Praeger.
Yamada, Akira and Serguey Braguinsky (1999), "Implications of Corruption and Rent Protection for Efficiency in Privatization: A Second-Best Solution through Institutional Comparative Advantage," Working paper, Yokohama City University, Yokohama.
Yeager, Timothy J. (1999), *Institutions, Transition Economies and Economic Development*, Boulder, CO: Westview Press.
Young, Alwyn (1998), "Growth without Scale Effects," *Journal of Political Economy*, **106** (1), February, 41–63.
Zak, Paul J. and Stephen Knack (1999), *Trust and Growth*, Claremont Graduate University Working Paper.
Zickel, Raymond E. (ed.) (1989), *Soviet Union: A Country Study*, Library of Congress Federal Research Division, US Army Area Report, Washington, DC: US Defense Department, Army. http://lcweb2.loc.gov/frd/cs/cshome.html
Zloch-Christy, Illiana (ed.) (1996), *Bulgaria in a Time of Change: Economic and Political Dimensions*, Aldershot, UK and Brookfield, VT: Avebury.
Zloch-Christy, Iliana (1994), *Eastern Europe in a Time of Change: Economic and Political Dimensions*, Westport, CT: Praeger.

Index